An Exploration of Writing

An Exploration of Writing

Peter T. Daniels

With a foreword by
David L. Share

SHEFFIELD UK   BRISTOL CT

Published by Equinox Publishing Ltd.

UK: Office 415, The Workstation, 15 Paternoster Row, Sheffield, South Yorkshire S1 2BX
USA: ISD, 70 Enterprise Drive, Bristol, CT 06010

www.equinoxpub.com

First published 2018

British Library Cataloguing-in-Publication Data

A catalogue record for this book is available from the British Library.

ISBN-13   978 1 78179 528 6   (hardback)
          978 1 78179 529 3   (paperback)

Library of Congress Cataloging-in-Publication Data

Names: Daniels, Peter T., author.
Title: An exploration of writing / Peter T. Daniels.
Description: Sheffield, UK Bristol, CT : Equinox Publishing Ltd, [2017] |
   Includes bibliographical references and index.
Identifiers: LCCN 2017003855 (print) | LCCN 2017031946 (ebook) | ISBN
   9781781796092 (ePDF) | ISBN 9781781795286 (hb) | ISBN 9781781795293 (pb)
Subjects: LCSH: Writing--History. | Alphabet--History. | Graphemics--History.
   | Graphology--History.
Classification: LCC P211.5 (ebook) | LCC P211.5 .D26 2017 (print) | DDC
   411--dc23
LC record available at https://lccn.loc.gov/ 2017003855

Typeset by JS Typesetting Ltd, Porthcawl, Mid Glamorgan
Printed and bound in Great Britain by CPI Antony Rowe, Chippenham

for
Bernard and Sandra
Woody and Kathy
James and Scott
always there for me

my teacher
I. J. Gelb

Richard Venezky
"I wish I knew."

Contents

Illustrations

Maps

Foreword

Verba volant scripta manent

"Humankind is defined by language; but civilization is defined by writing" is how Peter Daniels opened *The World's Writing Systems* some twenty years ago. Modern civilization has been *re*defined by the advent of the printing press and the wide availability of cheap paper. And today, technology is again transforming our world as the digital revolution turns David Olson's *World on Paper* into a paperless world. Yet the key to the world of writing, whether on computer screen, paper, clay, or stone, remains unchanged: rapid access to the meanings locked in the symbol strings of the written text. For many, this key is beyond their grasp. The illiterate and semi-literate are excluded. The literacy divide continues to separate cultures, communities, and even individual family members, empowering the literate while disempowering the illiterate and semi-literate. As a vehicle for emancipation, learning to read and write, even possession of a book, was once outlawed among slaves and women, often on pain of death. Even today, global literacy remains an elusive goal, with an estimated 800 million adults functionally illiterate. And in most parts of the world, rich and poor alike, illiteracy goes hand in hand with poverty, crime, and human misery.

Why is literacy such a challenge? A major factor lies in fundamental differences between spoken and written language, differences with profound human consequences.

Emerging from the depths of human prehistory, spoken communication conferred immense evolutionary advantages and so became universal across all human cultures. Evolving over tens of thousands of years, dedicated neurobiological mechanisms now ensure that spoken language develops very rapidly and very early. In contrast, writing, and the literacy it affords, is very new—a cultural-technological invention that appeared a mere 5000 years ago, well beyond the reach of evolution. With no dedicated brain basis forged by evolution, literacy is forced to become a neural hitchhiker exploiting the brain's remarkable neuroplasticity by recycling brain regions designed for other purposes. As a consequence, neither writing nor literacy is universal or early-emerging. A majority of the world's languages have no written form, and many others have deficient writing systems that were once better adapted to earlier speech forms, or to the language from which they were borrowed, but are now poorly adapted to the current needs of their users. Even in today's most literate societies, formal instruction in foundational reading and writing skills typically begins only around ages five to seven, at a time when spoken language is already fluent. And massive public investment is still required to establish and maintain the institutions charged with inculcating literacy. Even half a century after the appearance of the educationist Jeanne Chall's ground-breaking monograph *Learning to Read: The Great Debate*, heated and frequently vitriolic debate continues unabated over the best method for teaching reading.

Will the technological fruits of our digital age eventually produce a literacy "quick fix," allowing us to circumvent the long, arduous, and lamentably inequitable process of literacy learning? As Daniels explains in this volume, pure non-linguistic meaning-based communicative technologies ("semasiographies") can never replace the myriad expressive capabilities of written language. Indeed, most literate societies are becoming ever more "print-rich" and hence "literacy-demanding." As the new digital media continue to reduce the effort and cost of producing and transmitting the written word, young people today seem to be spending *more* rather than less time processing print. Certainly, media such as videos, stills, animations, and emojis are now integral to the digital landscape, but the infrastructure remains the same: the printed word, whether comprising letters, *aksharas*, or characters. Paradoxically, at a time when printed matter is disappearing, communication by means of written language appears to be expanding, even encroaching on face-to-face spoken communication as the new generation of rapid-fire texters spend increasing amounts of time communicating via digital technology, each clutching their beloved devices, riveted to a screen intently interacting with both text and non-text media. It is *written* text, nonetheless, that remains the immovable bedrock of digital communication. (A note of caution, however, must be sounded. Quantity notwithstanding, some, like the psychologist Maryanne Wolf, warn of the loss of sustained "quality" reading in the new digital world of hypertext and hypermedia.)

So the technologies for producing and reproducing written text may change, but writing itself remains indispensable because it not only affords faster information transfer (typical reading speeds among skilled readers far exceed typical speaking speeds), but also engenders new forms of thought and communication that have transformed and will continue to transform the fabric of human existence. Writing and literacy alone are not sufficient for social and economic progress but, if coupled with the right sociopolitical conditions, make possible new cultural, social, and economic modes; the world of today is simply unimaginable without writing.

It is puzzling, therefore, why many of the luminaries of twentieth-century linguistics, including Saussure and Bloomfield, regarded written language as unworthy of the attention of linguists. Writing is the chief lens through which linguists view language, yet they seem curiously blind to the presence of the lens itself. As Florian Coulmas observed in the first of his textbooks, every writing system is a linguistic analysis of spoken language. Many of the central concepts in linguistics are clearly artifacts of written language, including "sentence," "word," and "phoneme." Even the analysis of natural language today—"corpus linguistics"—is typically undertaken by means of highly script-specific transcription schemes that convert spoken language into a form of written language. Not only is linguistic inquiry inescapably influenced by the architecture of our writing systems, but becoming literate has repeatedly been shown to alter the ways we hear, produce, and recall speech. Brain imaging reveals that learning to read and write alters our brain's language circuits anatomically as well as functionally, as summarized by Stanislas Dehaene and colleagues. Furthermore, already a decade ago it was becoming increasingly evident in the neuroimaging literature that different writing systems configure the brain in ways that are partly shared yet partly distinct, as described by Donald Bolger and colleagues.

The pervasive influence of writing extends well beyond language *per se*, literally shaping the way we look at, comprehend, and organize the world around us, as brought out by José Morais and Régine Kolinsky and by David Olson. As a tool for molding a collective *Weltanschauung*, writing has proven to be a powerful means for uniting peoples speaking diverse languages and dialects, as in the case of Chinese in East Asia, Latin in Western Europe, Old Church Slavonic in Eastern Europe, literary Arabic in the Muslim world, and, perhaps now, English in the digital hi-tech world. Understandably, the translation of the Bible into the spoken vernacular—notably, German or English—was once considered heretical. The choice of a written standard represents one of the potent statements of cultural identity, typically elevating one speech form to a privileged status as the "correct" form, other dialects maligned as "incorrect," "corrupt," or "inferior."

Writing, first and foremost, records language. It is a linguist, therefore, to whom we must turn for a first introduction to the topic of writing. Daniels is today the world's leading authority on the linguistics of writing systems. Daniels was the first to uncover the syllabic origins of the world's first writing systems—in China, in Mesopotamia, in Mesoamerica—a discovery that dovetails with the now well-established body of psycholinguistic research into speech perception showing the ready psychological accessibility of the syllable (as opposed to the phoneme) among non-literates and pre-literates alike—a parallel discovery that revolutionized the psychology of reading. As a student of the legendary I. J. Gelb, the founding father of the modern study of writing systems, Daniels was among the first to appreciate the pioneering genius of his teacher, but he also recognized the shortcomings of Gelb's unidirectional logographic-to-syllabic-to-alphabetic theory. Daniels moved on to develop a more nuanced five-way taxonomy of writing systems, now the most widely accepted in the field, coining the terms "abjad" and "abugida" to describe Semitic consonantal writing and Brahmi-derived Indic *akshara*-based scripts respectively. Together with William Bright, Daniels went on to compile the world's most comprehensive and authoritative exposition of *The World's Writing Systems*, a work that is surprisingly un-encyclopedic in the way it weaves a coherent narrative throughout its 900 pages. Daniels brings his narrative talent and unsurpassed scholarship to the present volume, offering many new insights into both well-studied and little-known writing systems, dispelling many of the popular misconceptions about writing and writing systems, yet never letting the reader lose sight of the big picture even as he unravels the intricacies of specific systems.

No student of linguistics, or educator, psychologist, or social scientist concerned with literacy, can afford to remain ignorant of the fundamentals of writing systems. It is a great honor to commend to the reader a work of such exceptional scholarship.

October 9, 2016

David L. Share
Professor and Chair, Department of Learning Disabilities
Faculty of Education, University of Haifa, Israel

and

Edmond J. Safra Brain Research Center for the Study of
Learning Disabilities, University of Haifa, Israel

Acknowledgments

My first thanks go to John Davey of another publisher, who asked me to write this book—and to try to make him laugh. He promptly retired, bequeathing me to his successor, who (steering me away from nested, parenthesized clauses) guided its development but ultimately decided that it did not fit the format of the series it was prepared for. Janet Joyce promptly accepted the project for Equinox, and her guidance has been invaluable. Valerie Hall has ably dealt with technical matters, and Sarah Lee coordinated the production. Jill Sweet coped valiantly with the obstacles thrown in the way of typesetters by software merchants ignorant of non-Roman scripts, and Mark Lee designed the cover. The copyeditor, Gina Mance, asked just the right questions. Equinox had the good sense to commission Don Shewan to craft the maps that I have been wanting to see for several decades. I thank Equinox's two readers, Geoffrey Sampson for his immediate approval and Mark Aronoff for his detailed critique of the discussion of *grapheme*.

Several people provided scarce materials that figure in the discussions, even if not all are explicitly cited; in the order they appear in the book: Ben Zimmer, accounts of the history of *ghoti*, and discussion; Abby Cohn (Cornell University), Richard Venezky's master's thesis; Josef Fioretta (Hofstra University), Venezky's Ph.D. dissertation; Eleanor Yadi (New York Public Library, Dorot Jewish Division), details on Babylonian Jewish Aramaic orthography; Jack Sasson (Vanderbilt University), excerpts from his commentary on the book of Judges; Mahnaz Moazami (Columbia University) and Susann Rabuske (Berlin), scarce Iranistic material; and Christopher Ray Miller (Montreal), the Working Papers of the Tokyo conference on scripts of island Southeast Asia. The Brooklyn Public Library permitted me to scan the entire contents of the similar volume assembled by Eleanor Gibson and Harry Levin in 1963, its copy being one of very few registered in any library (though I omitted from my scanning the items that were subsequently published).

An enterprise like this would not have been possible without a plethora of "exotic" fonts. Scripts that are in use somewhere in the world today were supplied, for the most part, as components of Microsoft Windows 7 or Microsoft Office 2007 (which is almost fully adapted to non-Roman script-handling). A number of others were found by online searches, and I'd like to express my appreciation to the many designers who created their fonts for nothing more than love of their ancestral cultures or of philological scholarship. But several typographers must be acknowledged by name: Juan-José Marcos, who customized for me his AlphabetumUnicode font, which provides for hundreds of lettershapes used in Classical studies and beyond; George Douros, whose font Aegean does the same for "ancient scripts in the greater Aegean vicinity"; Paul Hardy, who in his Unifont fonts is providing specifically for all

Unicode code points that no one else has yet covered—who altered his plans in order to create glyphs for two ranges that I needed to display in Table 3.3; Emily Blanchard West, who recoded her Avestan alphabets (available at avesta.org) to fit Unicode, so that the aberrant forms found in the Unicode documentation could be avoided; Behdad Esfahbod (to whom I was directed by Richard Sproat), who is working on the development of Google's Noto Sans family of fonts, which is also intended to cover all of Unicode, who was able to clarify why some fonts simply did not yet work in Office or Windows; and Andrew Glass (Microsoft), who sent me his fonts for portions of Brahmi script that were omitted from Unicode, and for Kharoṣṭhi, his academic specialty—and who is working to enable all Unicode-compliant fonts to cooperate with Microsoft products. Invaluable is Andrew West's BabelMap character map application, which I use almost daily: http://www.babelstone.co.uk/Software/BabelMap.html.

Assistance on specific points was provided by a number of friends and colleagues: John Huehnergard (University of Texas), the postulated vocalization of Byblos Phoenician; Chris Miller, who read an early version of Chapter 5, and has remained an unquenchable source of bibliography and insight in all Indic topics; Jim Unger (Ohio State) and David Prager Branner, who never hesitate to reply to queries about East Asian script matters and read an early version of Chapter 6; Tim Vance (Tokyo), who not only provided the example at the heart of §7.1, but also read what became §§ 4.1 and 7.1; Christopher Woods (Chicago) and Philip Jones (University of Pennsylvania Museum) advised on cuneiform; John Baines (Oxford) helped with Egyptian; H. Craig Melchert (UCLA), who has been answering my questions about all things Anatolian for, it seems, decades, with unflagging generosity, assisted here as well; Mikael Thompson (Indiana University and Ulan Bator) does and did the same for Inner Asia; and Nicholas Sims-Williams (SOAS) and Prods Oktor Skjærvø (Harvard) advised on Iranian matters. Michael Carrasco (Florida State University), Scott A. J. Johnson, and Joshua D. Englehardt (El Colegio de Michoacán) provided valuable information on Mesoamerican scripts. Part of the formulation of §11.2 is taken from a chapter commissioned by the Museo de Cultures del Món (Museum of World Cultures), Barcelona, for a 2015 exhibition catalogue whose publication seems to have been suspended. Invaluable help with the maps has been provided by M. C. A. Macdonald (Oxford), Craig Melchert, Chris Miller, and Keren Rice and Chris Harvey (Toronto).

I'm grateful to prof. em. Alan Millard (Liverpool) for the drawing of the Fekheriyeh inscription, and permission to reproduce it, in the *editio princeps* of which he participated in 1982; and to Scott A. J. Johnson for arranging for the gratis use of his glyph illustrations. The other illustrative material was either found in apparent public domain on line, or else scanned from sources no longer in copyright. I'd like to acknowledge the offer of Aline and Ross Caldwell to create maps for the chapters as a gift, though they weren't permitted by the previous publisher; and Paul Newman, Professor of Linguistics, Anthropology, and Law at Indiana University, for legal advice.

* * *

In recent years, David Share, who invited me out of the blue, with the mediation of David Olson (Toronto), to a symposium at Haifa University in 2012, has become a valued friend and has had considerable influence on my work on writing systems, especially during his two-year sabbatical at the Graduate Center of the City University of New York, turning my attention to psychological research into reading. He's read the entire text most attentively and been with me every step of the way and was kind enough to contribute the Foreword. Nicholas Ostler (Foundation for Endangered Languages), too, read the entire manuscript and it has benefited greatly from his cogent comments.

I'd like to take this opportunity to thank my teachers (in chronological order) at Cornell University who shared their passion for the study of language with a then-rare undergraduate linguistics major: John U. Wolff, and the late Jim Gair, Fred Agard, Robert A. Hall, Jr., and Chas Hockett. They sent me on to the University of Chicago, where I fell under the spell of (not in chronological order) I. J. Gelb, Erica Reiner, Gene Gragg, Howard Aronson, Eric Hamp, and Jim McCawley.

And the catalyst for my academic study of writing systems may have been Irving Finkel (British Museum), who, for three of my years as Manuscript Editor of the Chicago Assyrian Dictionary, was Research Associate at the allied Materials for the Sumerian Lexicon project. In 1977 or so, he noticed that University of Chicago staff members could sign up for University Extension classes at half price and suggested we take Calligraphy. He dropped out after a few weeks, but I kept at it with the teacher R. Williams, a noted calligrapher who was a book designer at the University of Chicago Press. I didn't become a calligrapher, but one outcome was my first journal article, "A Calligraphic Approach to Aramaic Paleography" (1984). And it was also Irving who whispered into my ear, when I was looking into little-known decipherments, "Edward Hincks," at the time all but forgotten—which led in 1992 to my first invitation to speak abroad, "Edward Hincks's Decipherment of Mesopotamian Cuneiform" (1994).

All these people set me on my unique voyage through the nearly uncharted waters of graphonomy. I'm profoundly grateful.

Introduction

Decisive grammar given unto queens,—

Other explorations of aspects of language or linguistics can draw on a century or more of investigation or speculation. It's different, however, for writing. Until somewhat more than a century ago, the only languages thought worthy of investigation by philologists were the classical written languages. With the discovery of languages beyond the familiar European ones, initially in Africa and North America, and the realization that "primitive" languages (meaning languages of "primitive" peoples) exhibited every bit as much complexity as the familiar Latin, Greek, and Hebrew (and Sanskrit)—and often more—, the attention of linguists was diverted. It was realized that unwritten languages were as worthy of study as written ones, and the dogma became established that writing was secondary to speech and need not be investigated beyond the steps that had been taken before the introduction of modern

Details

The recommended readings are confined as much as possible to English-language materials. In one respect this is unfortunate, because the only comprehensive, compact collections of the facts about writing systems are James-Germain Février, *Histoire de l'écriture* (1959), and Johannes Friedrich, *Geschichte der Schrift* (1966). Sadly, neither was translated in its day, and after half a century, a mere translation would fail to incorporate a considerable number of new discoveries. Dating from the same era are the only two comprehensive surveys of writing, David Diringer, *The Alphabet* (1968), and Hans Jensen, *Sign, Symbol and Script* (1969); as well as Marcel Cohen, *La grande invention de l'écriture* (1958), supremely disorganized but brilliantly insightful. Akira Nakanishi, *Writing Systems of the World* (1980), illustrates each script in general use with the front page of a newspaper and a one-page description, and also includes a picture and brief description of many obsolete scripts. My own brief summaries of the history of writing may be found in Peter T. Daniels, "Grammatology" (2009a) and "Writing Systems" (2001) and its thorough revision "Writing Systems" (2017b). An entertaining miscellany is Florian Coulmas, *The Blackwell Encyclopedia of Writing Systems* (1996). A great deal of information is included, but every topic appears in alphabetical order with little attention to connections and relations among topics, and the reader wonders why some things are covered and some are not; Janet S. (Shibamoto) Smith, review of *The Blackwell Encyclopedia of Writing Systems* by F. Coulmas (1999), identifies the most important contributions to graphonomic theory.

Peter T. Daniels and William Bright, eds., *The World's Writing Systems* (1996), is intended to provide information on how each script of the modern world represents its language, as well as some material on historical development and ancient scripts. Amalia E. Gnanadesikan, *The Writing Revolution* (2009), is a highly readable narrativization of *The World's Writing Systems*, but for the most part does not incorporate discoveries of the intervening period. A useful linguistic methods. As the most important figure in the history of American linguistics put it in 1933, "Writing is not language, but merely a way of recording language by means of visible marks. ... For the linguist, writing is, except for certain matters of detail, merely an external device, like the use of the phonograph." For most of the past century and a half, the study of writing has been mostly limited to its external history—decipherment of newly discovered scripts, and establishing the historical relationships among writing systems.

But during the same century and a half, practical attention to writing was proceeding—in a way that it had for many centuries: in Late Antiquity, Eastern Christianity had, on the basis of Greek writing, developed new alphabets for much of Eastern Europe; Arabic writing had come to Persia: proselytizers for various religions brought literacy to their converts or would-be converts. In most cases literacy in new languages was achieved in scriptural scripts: Indic in Southeast Asia where Buddhism or Hinduism spread; Arabic where Islam prevailed; Roman in the wake of Western Christianity in Sub-Saharan Africa, the Americas, and Oceania.

Politics, too, has been responsible for at least one large swath of new literacy: during the second quarter of the twentieth century, writing systems were devised for a large number of languages of the Soviet Union. Policy changed over the years, sometimes favoring Arabic script for Muslim republics, sometimes Roman, but most often Cyrillic in imitation of Russian, with a multitude of new letters for unfamiliar speech sounds.

Details *(continued)* ──

series of volumes is S. D. Houston, ed., *First Writing* (2004) and *The Shape of Script* (2012), and J. Baines, J. Bennet, and S. D. Houston, eds., *The Disappearance of Writing Systems* (2008); the first of them was anticipated by W. M. Senner, ed., *The Origins of Writing* (1989), which covers a wider variety of scripts and is more popularly oriented, see Peter T. Daniels, review of *The Origins of Writing* by W. M. Senner (1991c).

The quotation by the eminent linguist is from Leonard Bloomfield, *Language* (1933), 21, 282; he adopted the view of the founder of structural linguistics, Ferdinand de Saussure, *Cours de linguistique générale* (1916):

> Language and writing are two distinct systems of signs; the second exists for the sole purpose of representing the first. The linguistic object is not both the written and the spoken forms of words; the spoken forms alone constitute the object. (translated by Wade Baskin [1959], 23)

> A language and its written form constitute two separate systems of signs. The sole reason for the existence of the latter is to represent the former. The object of study in linguistics is not a combination of the written word and the spoken word. The spoken word alone constitutes that object. (translated by Roy Harris [1983], 24)

Contrast the observation of the scholar who occupied a similar niche in British linguistics, J. R. Firth, "Foreword" (1953): "A system of writing and spelling is the foundation of a system of grammar."

Few have been theoretical treatments of writing systems. Other than Peter S. Du Ponceau, *Nature and Character of the Chinese System of Writing* (1838), which however lay fallow for more

The historical spread of writing, however, has been discussed in a number of comprehensive books and in volumes on individual languages and language families. Decipherment has attracted less attention, and I myself have been the first to unearth and describe the methods and achievements of several early decipherers. Here I'm attempting something different: I want to show how writing systems represent their languages, and how relations between language and script have operated and have changed over the centuries. I'm less concerned with the shapes of letters than with what they stand for. This approach to the study of writing systems has attracted very little attention until very recently, and, as sometimes happens throughout linguistics, some of the recent work is hampered by focusing solely on one or a few writing systems rather than standing back and looking at the big picture. In this book I cast my net widely to consider seemingly very disparate scripts that are mutually and perhaps surprisingly revealing, but I neither attempt nor claim to be comprehensive. A few examples must suffice to illustrate a point.

Details *(continued)* ───

than a century until its discovery by Yuen Ren Chao, "A Note on an Early Logographic Theory of Chinese Writing" (1940) and was studied by Peter T. Daniels, "Peter Stephen Du Ponceau and the Typology of Writing Systems" (2009b), the first was Isaac Taylor, *The Alphabet* (1883), which held the field for more than half a century and still merits study.* The first book informed by contemporary linguistics was I. J. Gelb, *A Study of Writing* (1952), which was mostly written in the late 1930s, and it too stood almost alone for almost as long—and it is my teacher Gelb's work, however much I disagree with some of its claims, that always stands as the model for

---

*Taylor wholeheartedly embraced Darwinian evolution ("The Epilogue," 2: 362–73), even using the familiar phrases "struggle for existence" (2: 117, 265), "survival of the fittest" (2: 68), and "natural selection" itself (2: 72 n. 1: "… and the two characters i and j were slowly differentiated out of one primitive symbol, U and V out of another, and then specialized by natural selection so as to denote the vocalic and consonantal sounds")—an attitude a bit startling for an Anglican cleric, subsequently Canon of York ([Anon.], "Isaac Taylor (1829–1901)" [1912]). The word "evolution" occurs nearly sixty times to denote alphabet change. Taylor was, though, occasionally misled by Darwin's emphasis on the slow pace of evolutionary change, apparently declining to recognize individuals' contributions, such as are considered in Chapter 11 below. Thus he writes of

> the specialization of V and U, and of j and i, to denote the consonantal and vocalic sounds …. Originally V was the capital form, and U the uncial and cursive. In the 10th century minuscule we find the capital form used by preference as the initial, and U as the medial. The consonant being more common at the beginning of Latin words, and the vowel in the middle, the initial form seems to have been gradually appropriated as the symbol of the consonant, and the medial form as that of the vowel. Similarly, in the 15th century, the forms j and i, which were originally only initial and medial forms of the same letter, became specialized to denote the consonant and the vowel. (2: 189)

We know, however, that the differentiation "was first suggested by Pierre de la Ramée (Petrus Ramus) in his *Grammatica* (1559). It was generally adopted in France from about 1620, where ⟨j⟩ and ⟨v⟩ became known as 'consonnes Ramistes'" (Abercrombie *apud* David Abercrombie and Peter T. Daniels, "Spelling Reform Proposals: English" [2006], 72).

Jonathan B. Losos, *Improbable Destinies* (2017), is a lively account of the science—both observational and experimental, just like Darwin's—that is showing how quickly evolution can proceed in nature, and that similar evolutionary paths can be followed in different populations in similar circumstances.

Because the compass is limited, I also limit my subject matter to "true writing," a less than ideal term, and pay little attention to what have elsewhere been called "forerunners of writing" or "mnemonic systems" or "discourse systems." "Writing" in my sense is a graphic system that records language rather than ideas, sentences rather than the situations described by sentences. This position is explicated and elaborated in the course of the discussion. The study of writing systems may be called *graphonomy*.

In autumn 2013, I went to a (rare!) lecture on writing systems theory at a well-known linguistics department in the New York City area. After an initial survey of the neglect of writing within general linguistics, the speaker presented some new ideas, touching on a wide variety of the world's writing systems. But during the question period, a linguist in the audience—a syntactician—asked in effect, "But

Details *(continued)* ————————————————————————————————

explorations such as mine. A work by a scholar of Chinese, John DeFrancis, *Visible Speech* (1989), corrected many misconceptions. More recently, it is almost exclusively in textbooks that theoretical outlooks have been expounded, most notably Henry Rogers, *Writing Systems* (2005).

Corporate attention to writing systems within linguistics, at least in North America, can perhaps be dated to the spring of 1988, when conferences were held both in Milwaukee, with some of the presentations published by P. Downing, S. D. Lima, and M. Noonan, eds., *The Linguistics of Literacy* (1992), and a few weeks later in Toronto, represented by I. Taylor and D. R. Olson, eds., *Scripts and Literacy* (1995).* The sorts of questions linguists faced at that time are ably summarized by Henry Rogers, "Optimal Orthographies" (1995).

Meanwhile quite a few books have been aimed at the popular market but almost all are by journalists or by dilettantes believing themselves to have insights that have escaped specialists for generations; all should be avoided. I had high hopes for one published early in 2015, but because on p. 9 it claims that the Rosetta Stone bears a text in "Egyptian hieroglyphs and two varieties of Greek" (rather than Greek and two varieties of Egyptian) and on p. 10, influenced by a sensational newspaper headline, it quotes Wikipedia almost word-for-word for a specious claim that a Medieval Arab writer had deciphered Egyptian, I won't even name it. Such sins are, however, typical, and far from rare; see, e.g., Peter T. Daniels, review of popular books on writing by J. Drucker, G. Jean, M.-A. Ouaknin, A. Robinson, and L. Shlain (2000a).

The term "grammatology" was introduced by I. J. Gelb, *A Study of Writing* (1952), 23 with 267 n. 39, on the basis of *Grammatography* (London, 1861), by Friedrich Ballhorn. The term has become tainted in recent years: some scholars have taken it to refer to a school of writing-systems studies that holds to the Principle of Unidirectional Development (§11.1) and some other notions supported by Gelb; and the French philosopher Jacques Derrida borrowed it (with acknowledgment) to label a certain approach within Postmodern literary criticism. Therefore, I prefer "graphonomy," which was introduced by Charles F. Hockett, review of *Nationalism and Language Reform in China* by J. DeFrancis (1951a), 445, making explicit the

——————————

*The Toronto volume is scandalously underdistributed: OCLC WorldCat registers only 136 copies in libraries worldwide, compared to 735 for the Milwaukee publication, and 781 for the 1963 edition of Gelb's *Study of Writing*—and 1182 for *The World's Writing Systems*. I myself did not see a copy until 2015.

what's the point of all this? Isn't it just a bunch of disparate facts that don't cohere into something that gives us insight into the nature of language or writing?" The speaker didn't really have an answer (after all, facts about writing systems are interesting for their own sake, or you wouldn't have picked up this book), but I *do* have an answer to that question, and I'm taking the opportunity in this book to set out some of those very disparate facts that do in fact contribute to a coherent view of the nature of writing. A prominent sociolinguist who writes prolifically on writing once wrote, "The history of writing, therefore, cannot rely much on universal tendencies, but has to investigate the spread and transmutation of every script in its own right." He was incorrect.

Most recently, area specialists seem to have abandoned questions of how writing relates to language in favor of how writing relates to society. I find this move to be premature: the comparative and typological exploration of the connections between writing and language is far from completed, and that's the course I've set. That's why, in contrast to other surveys of writing, which are organized by historical relations among scripts (such as those by Diringer and Jensen) or geographically (such as *The World's Writing Systems*), this one is ordered by writing system type.

Overall I proceed from more familiar to less familiar, from more concrete to more abstract; the last chapter is addressed more to the linguist than to the general reader

---

Details *(continued)*

analogy *astrology : astronomy :: graphology : graphonomy*. (Graphology is the pseudoscience of divining someone's personality from their handwriting.) The term could have been, but wasn't, popularized by its appearance in his *A Course in Modern Linguistics* (1958), 539. The manuscript of Hockett's "Speech and Writing" (1952), posthumously published in his "Two Lectures on Writing" (1951b [2003]), 169 with 174 n. 46, included the handwritten note "Define graphonomy." It subsequently transpired that a version of the lecture to which the editors there assigned the title "Writing: A Linguistic Technology" was distributed, though not published, in E. J. Gibson and H. Levin, eds., *A Basic Research Program on Reading* (1963), as "The Elements of Graphonomy"; the article is undated but refers to the *Course* by section number rather than page (as though not yet published).

The quotation by the prominent sociolinguist is from Florian Coulmas, *Writing Systems* (2003), 208, cf. Peter T. Daniels, review of *Writing Systems* by F. Coulmas (2006b).

Explorations of the relation of writing to society rather than to language were much in evidence at the November 2014 symposium sponsored by the University of Chicago's Neubauer Collegium, to be published as C. Woods and E. Shaughnessy, eds., *Signs of Writing* (in preparation). Script family relations don't necessarily correspond with language family relations, as exemplified by the disparate backgrounds of the scripts of Indo-European languages; see Peter T. Daniels, "The Writing Systems of Indo-European" (2017c).

From time to time, mention is made of native grammatical traditions of the societies described. Two recent volumes include chapters on them: K. Allan, ed., *The Oxford Handbook of the History of Linguistics* (2013), and L. Waugh and M. Burston, eds., *The Cambridge History of Linguistics* (forthcoming).

but still shouldn't be inaccessible. The "Details" sections shouldn't be skipped over; alongside bibliographic references, they include interesting tidbits here and there.*

No one person can master all the minutiae of the whole wide variety of writing systems that merit attention, and all general books on writing contain errors of fact or misunderstanding—not infrequently due to use of outdated or superseded reference material. I hope that I will have managed to avoid most such traps!

---

*The Details have been placed at the foot of the page because I greatly dislike flipping to the back of the book to find who said something, and the short titles of the references to avoid flipping further to discover where they said it.

1   Syllables and Syllabaries

Some old Egyptian joke is in the air,

1.1 What is a syllable?

I begin with a simple observation that was hard for scholars to make: If you haven't learned to read an alphabet, you don't think of "letters" as the components of words. It's hard, though, for people who do read with an alphabet to imagine that. But before there was modern linguistics, some educators realized it intuitively. Noah Webster (1758–1843), most famous these days as the lexicographer who compiled the first dictionary of the American language, made his name by publishing the "Blue-back Speller" for schoolchildren at all levels. Webster's 1783 book was closely derived from a popular predecessor, but—besides making it far more secular and less religious—he made one highly significant and lasting change: where previously every syllable was made to begin with a consonant, as in Latin, Webster divided words according to sound: *cred-it* rather than *cre-dit*. His book predominated for more than half a century; W. H. McGuffey's "Eclectic Readers" supplanted it beginning around 1840. Both of them taught children to read by means of *syllables*. Here are some excerpts from Webster's "Table I":

Lesson I.					
ba	be	bi	bo	bu	by
ca	ce*	ci*	co	cu	cy*
da	de	di	do	du	dy
fa	fe	fi	fo	fu	fy
ka	ke	ki	ko	ku	ky

Lesson IV.				
ab	eb	ib	ob	ub
ac	ec	ic	oc	uc
ad	ed	id	od	ud
af	ef	if	of	uf
al	el	il	ol	ul

Lesson VII.				
bla	ble	bli	blo	blu
cla	cle	cli	clo	clu
pla	ple	pli	plo	plu
fla	fle	fli	flo	flu
va	ve	vi	vo	vu

Lesson II.					
ga	ge	gi	go	gu	gy
ha	he	hi	ho	hu	hy
ma	me	mi	mo	mu	my
na	ne	ni	no	nu	ny
ra	re	ri	ro	ru	ry
ta	te	ti	to	tu	ty
wa	we	wi	wo	wu	wy

Lesson V.				
ag	eg	ig	og	ug
am	em	im	om	um
an	en	in	on	un
ap	ep	ip	op	up
as	es	is	os	us
av	ev	iv	ov	uv
ax	ex	ix	ox	ux

Lesson XII.					
spla	sple	spli	splo	splu	sply
spra	spre	spri	spro	spru	spry
stra	stre	stri	stro	stru	stry
swa	swe	swi	swo	swu	swy

Details ——————————————————————————————————

1.1 The most useful account of Noah Webster, venturing at times into psychobiography, is Joshua Kendall, *The Forgotten Founding Father* (2010). The background of his spelling books is explored in the most detail by Jennifer Monaghan, *A Common Heritage: Noah Webster's*

Table 1.1 The Cherokee syllabary (in "alphabetical" order)

a	e	i	o	u	v = [ə̃]
Ꭰ a	Ꭱ e	Ꭲ i	Ꭳ o	Ꭴ u	Ꭵ v
Ꭶ ga Ꭷ ka	Ꭸ ge	Ꭹ gi	Ꭺ go	Ꭻ gu	Ꭼ gv
Ꭽ ha	Ꭾ he	Ꭿ hi	Ꮀ ho	Ꮁ hu	Ꮂ hv
Ꮃ la	Ꮄ le	Ꮅ li	Ꮆ lo	Ꮇ lu	Ꮈ lv
Ꮉ ma	Ꮊ me	Ꮋ mi	Ꮌ mo	Ꮍ mu	
Ꮎ na Ꮏ hna Ᏽ nah	Ꮑ ne	Ꮒ ni	Ꮓ no	Ꮔ nu	Ꮕ nv
Ꮖ qua	Ꮗ que	Ꮘ qui	Ꮙ quo	Ꮚ quu	Ꮛ quv
Ꮜ sa Ꮝ s	Ꮞ se	Ꮟ si	Ꮠ so	Ꮡ su	Ꮢ sv
Ꮤ ta Ꮣ da	Ꮦ te Ꮥ de	Ꮨ ti Ꮧ di	Ꮩ do	Ꮪ du	Ꮫ dv
Ꮬ tla Ꮭ dla	Ꮮ tle	Ꮯ tli	Ꮰ tlo	Ꮱ tlu	Ꮲ tlv
Ꮳ tsa	Ꮴ tse	Ꮵ tsi	Ꮶ tso	Ꮷ tsu	Ꮸ tsv
Ꮹ wa	Ꮺ we	Ꮻ wi	Ꮼ wo	Ꮽ wu	Ꮾ wv
Ꮿ ya	Ᏸ ye	Ᏹ yi	Ᏺ yo	Ᏻ yu	Ᏼ yv

Further on: "Table IV. *Easy words of two syllables, accented on the first*" (Ba ker, bri er, ci der, cra zy, plum met—290 examples); "Table V. *Easy words of two syllables, accented on the second*" (A base, a bide, com ply, cre ate, trans late—216 examples); "Table XIX. *Words of three syllables, the full accent on the first, and the half accent on the third*" (Di a phragm, du pli cate, e go tism, fre quen cy, jeal ous y—289 examples); down through "Table XXVIII. *Words of five syllables accented on the first and third*" (Am bi gu i ty, pres by ter i an, mon o syl la ble, in tel lect u al, e qui pon der ant—82 examples).

And this is not due to some quirk of English spelling (§2.1). Decades ago, psychologists asked adult nonliterate people—the community studied happened to be Portuguese fishermen—to identify the parts that words were made from. The subjects didn't identify the "simple" sounds our letters stand for, namely consonants and vowels (a term for such simple sounds is *segment*), but instead broke words into syllables. More recently, psychologists have studied children learning to write languages where the simplest symbols stand for syllables consisting of a consonant (C) followed by a vowel (V)—these were children in India. There, too, it is not segments that the children most easily identify, but syllables (§12.1.2). And even, if you can't think of the right word—if it's "on the tip of your tongue"—do you, like me, find that you mentally run through words that have the same number of syllables and the same accent pattern?

What does all this have to do with the nature or origin of writing? We'll travel around the world and across time for some clues.

Details *(continued)* ———————————————————————————

Blue-Back Speller (1983). I quote, because it's the version that happens to be available online, the 90th(!) printing of Noah Webster, *The American Spelling-Book* (1804).

1.2 Cherokee syllabary

In Chapter 11, we'll look at the origins of writing in (by definition) prehistoric times. So here we start with the most celebrated, though far from the only, invention of writing in modern times. The passing on of writing from a literate community to another community is the subject of the middle chapters; the subject here is the invention of writing by people who could not read any language, whether their own or that of a neighbor or an overlord.

Cherokee is an Iroquois language of Native America, at first contact spoken around the present-day Georgia-Alabama-Tennessee border. Aggression by European settlers led to much of the community departing for Arkansas, and in the late 1830s they were forced even farther west to Oklahoma. The prominent Cherokee leader Sequoyah (ca. 1785–1841) spoke little or no English; he was aware of but could not read written communication between the Americans he served with in the War of 1812, and he resolved to provide such a tool for his people. After initial attempts at logography (compare Chapter 6), he discovered that he could record the sounds of all the words of his language using 86 symbols that designated CV syllables (Table 1.1). In the early 1820s, with the help of his young daughter, he demonstrated the system, and it was rapidly adopted by the Cherokee (ᏣᎳᎩ ⟨tsa.la.gi⟩) communities, especially for sending letters between the eastern and western groups.

A feature of Sequoyah's syllabary that's also found in many other writing systems is that it doesn't record every important aspect of Cherokee speech. For instance, the difference between long and short vowels isn't indicated: ᎠᎹ can be read either *ama* 'water' or *āma* 'salt'. While this means on the one hand that it's not quite so easy for the non-fluent reader to decode a text, it also means that it could be employed by people who spoke different varieties (*dialects*) of Cherokee in different areas.

Some aspects of the syllabary show that it sometimes sacrificed explicitness in favor of economy. The only consonant that can be written without bringing along a following vowel is Ꮝ *s*. It's possible that this is because it's the first sound in Sequoyah's name—he spelled it ᏍᏏᏉᏯ ⟨s.si.quo.ya⟩—but it also just so happens that *s* is by far the most frequent consonant that occurs directly before another consonant: ᏔᎵᏍᎪᎯ ⟨ta.li.s.go.hi⟩ *talsgohi* 'twenty'. Other consonant clusters are spelled by using a CV syllable and ignoring the vowel, as seen in the same example ᏔᎵᏍᎪᎯ ⟨ta.li.s.go.hi⟩ *talsgohi*.

Details *(continued)* ───

1.2 The standard presentation of the life and work of Sequoyah is Grant Foreman, *Sequoyah* (1938). Building on it, Ellen Cushman, *The Cherokee Syllabary* (2011), deals with questions of literacy in the modern Cherokee Nation. Various aspects of the fit of the script to the language are dealt with statistically by Janine Scancarelli, "Aspiration and Cherokee Orthographies" (1992).

Table 1.2 The Cherokee syllabary (in the order used by Sequoyah); old-style font

e	*a*	*la*	*tsi*	*nah*	*wu*	*we*	*li*	*ne*	*mo*	*gi*	*yi*	*si*	*tlv*	*o*	*lu*
le	*ha*	*wo*	*tlo*	*ta*	*yv*	*lv*	*hi*	*s*	*yo*	*hu*	*go*	*tsu*	*mu*	*se*	
so	*tli*	*qui*	*que*	*sa*	*qua*	*no*	*ka*	*tsv*	*sv*	*ni*	*ga*	*do*	*ge*	*da*	
gv	*wi*	*i*	*u*	*ye*	*hv*	*dv*	*gu*	*tso*	*quo*	*nu*	*na*	*lo*	*yu*	*tse*	
di	*wv*	*du*	*de*	*tsa*	*v*	*nv*	*te*	*ma*	*su*	*tlu*	*he*	*ho*	*mi*		
tla	*ya*	*wa*	*ti*	*tle*	*hna*	*quu*	*dla*	*me*	*quv*						

Something similar happened with *aspiration*. This is a little puff of air after a consonant. Voiceless stop consonants in English almost always have aspiration, but they don't have aspiration when they come right after *s*. If you hold your finger in front of your lips when you say *pot*, you can feel the puff of air after the *p*, but when you say *spot* you won't feel it. And it doesn't happen with voiced stops—you won't feel it with *bot*. In English, aspiration doesn't make any difference in the words at all. The technical term for this is *phoneme*: in English, [p] and [pʰ] are *conditioned allophones* of the single phoneme /p/.

In many languages, including Cherokee, however, aspiration does make a difference—it is *phonemic*, and all the Cherokee stops come in aspirated and unaspirated versions: *kōla* is 'winter' and *khōla* is 'bone'—but both are written AW ⟨go.la⟩. Only for the six most frequently occurring aspirated/unaspirated pairs does the syllabary provide separate symbols, such as Ꭷ *ka* and Ꮝ *ga*—as in ꂔꞒꮮ ⟨ka.ga.li⟩ *khāka'li* 'February'. And why aren't they transliterated as ⟨kha⟩ and ⟨ka⟩? Because the consonant-by-vowel chart was created by an English-speaker, not by Sequoyah, and an *unaspirated* stop (even if it's voiceless) tends to sound, to an English-speaker, like a *voiced* stop. The aspirated stops sound like ordinary English voiceless stops, so that's how they're transliterated.

If Sequoyah didn't recognize units smaller than the syllable, and didn't put the same consonants and the same vowels together as his American printer did, then what order did he use? My best guess, for all alphabetical orders (compare Chapter 3, §11.5.2) unless there's some obvious other explanation (see §§ 5.2 and 5.6), is that characters are simply recorded in the order the inventor thought of them. We are fortunate to have two copies of the syllabary in Sequoyah's own hand, as well as a few other early examples, and they use the same order, which appears to be arbitrary, and break the rows in the same places.

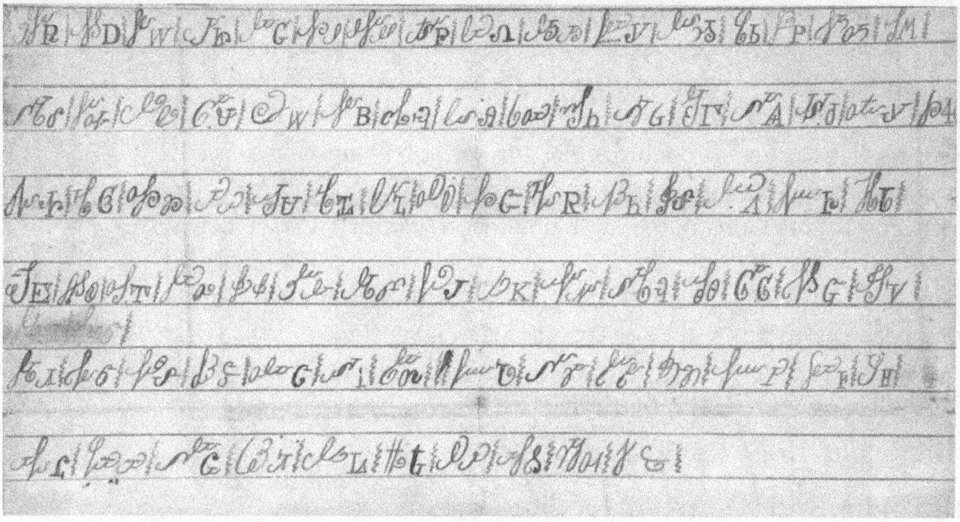

Figure 1.1. Sequoyah's syllabary, believed to be in his hand, showing the original shape to the left of each formal shape

Sequoyah's original designs were quite elaborate (Figure 1.1), bearing no resemblance to the Roman letters he might have occasionally had a look at. It has long been supposed that the printed forms of the Cherokee symbols, which are much more letter-like in shape, were devised specifically for the printing press, but evidence has recently turned up that the simpler shapes were in use before the printing of Cherokee was even thought of. And in a similar, very recent development, the Cherokee Nation has commissioned a font whose curves and shading fit better with today's varieties of Roman type. Compare the words above, which use the new font, with how they used to appear in print (Table 1.2): **ᏣᎳᎩ**, **ᎠᏧ**, **ᏍᏏᏉᏯ**, **ᏔᎵᏍᎪᎯ**, **ᎪᎳ**, **ᎾᏎᎵ**.

1.3 African syllabaries

Shortly after Sequoyah's invention of the Cherokee syllabary, another inventor went to work across the Atlantic Ocean. The territory of the Vai people straddled

Details *(continued)*

The new material is found in Willard Walker and James Sarbaugh, "The Early History of the Cherokee Syllabary" (1993).

1.3 Seemingly everything that can be known about the invention of the Vai syllabary is collected and analyzed by Konrad Tuchscherer and P. E. H. Hair, "Cherokee and West Africa" (2002), which incorporates considerable archival research into unpublished missionary documents. Its twentieth-century use is exhaustively studied by Sylvia Scribner and Michael Cole, *The Psychology of Literacy* (1981)—a curious title, since the investigation is largely ethnographic the future Sierra Leone–Liberia border, and some Vai children and adults had the opportunity of basic education from British or American missionaries. But when Momolu Duwale Bukele chose, probably in 1832/33, to make a script for his people, he rejected anything he might have known of the English alphabet and created a syllabary. The possibility exists that he was aware of Sequoyah's achievement, through the missionary press, but this seems doubtful. The Vai script has survived in use to the present day, alongside both Roman-script and Arabic-script texts.

One occupation for Vai men during the later nineteenth century was as mercenaries over an extensive area of West Africa, and it seems likely that it was knowledge of the existence of an indigenous Vai script, owing nothing to either Muslim or Christian forebears, that prompted more than a dozen inventions of syllabaries throughout the region (some remaining in limited use to this day), all graphically dissimilar but all reflecting the primacy of the syllable in creating a writing system.

1.4 Syllabaries of the ancient eastern Mediterranean

Every so often, archeologists find remains of writing systems of long-gone peoples. Some of them, as we'll see in the next few chapters, are clearly in the lineage of modern scripts, but others are not so easy to place. If we're lucky and sufficient quantites of inscriptions are available, they can be deciphered, though sometimes they remain uninterpreted (Chapter 9, §10.4).

Three syllabaries from the eastern Mediterranean area have been deciphered but have proved to be dead ends in the history of writing. Because these scripts are quasi-pictographic, they may reflect the pervasive Egyptian influence over the entire region during the millennium and a half before the Common Era (see §8.2). In approximate chronological order: Luvian glyphs recorded an Anatolian language close to Hittite: its early forerunners were contemporary with Hittite cuneiform

Details *(continued)* ——

and sociological. Other scripts of West Africa, most of which seem to have been inspired by Vai, are described in a series of articles by David Dalby, "A Survey of the Indigenous Scripts of Liberia and Sierra Leone" (1967), "The Indigenous Scripts of West Africa and Surinam" (1968), and "Further Indigenous Scripts of West Africa" (1969), with a synthesis provided by Konrad Tuchscherer, "Recording, Communicating and Making Visible" (2007); see also Saki Mafundikwa, *Afrikan Alphabets* (2004). The names at least of the half-dozen inventors of the syllabaries that found at least some use deserve to be recorded: after Bukele, Sultan Njoya, Bamum; King Pufong and his retainer Nde Temfong, Bagam; Mohamed Turay, Mende; Chief Gbili, Kpelle; and Wido Zobo, Loma (called Toma in Guinea). In addition, two alphabets were devised by literate inventors, Bassa by Thomas N. Lewis and N'ko by Souleymane Kanté (§3.3.4).

1.4 H. C. Melchert, ed., *The Luvians* (2003), definitively gathers what is known of the people, the language, and the script. Johannes Friedrich, *Geschichte der Schrift* (1966), 63, suggests that aspects of Luvian orthography reflect familiarity with details of Akkadian cuneiform orthography (§7.2) rather than with Egyptian orthography (§8.2). The non-alphabetic Greek

(§7.2), but it continued in use after the demise of that writing system. Linear B was used (as far as we know) only for accountancy by the Mycenaeans of Crete and parts of the Greek mainland in the mid second millennium BCE. Cypriote was used on Cyprus, in competition with the Greek alphabet, during the second half of the first millennium BCE. It seems, from the rather poor way that they fit the Greek language, that both Linear B and Cypriote may have been devised for some other, unrelated language(s) of which not a trace remains.

Details *(continued)* ————————————————————————————————————

scripts have received very uneven coverage, as hinted in the title of John Chadwick, *Linear B and Related Scripts* (1987), a useful introduction. Their fit to the Greek language is discussed, with rather different conclusions, by D. Gary Miller, *Ancient Scripts and Phonological Knowledge* (1994), and Roger D. Woodard, *Greek Writing from Knossos to Homer* (1997); both are discussed in Peter T. Daniels, review of *Ancient Scripts and Phonological Knowledge* by D. G. Miller (1998) and "Some Semitic Phonological Considerations on the Sibilants of the Greek Alphabet" (1999).

Table 2.1 International Phonetic Alphabet (modified)[a]

Consonants[b]

	bilabial	labio-velar	dental	alveolar	post-alveolar	retroflex[c]	palatal	velar	uvular	pharyngeal	glottal
plosive	p b			t d		ʈ ṭ ɖ ḍ	c ɟ	k g *g*	q ɢ		ʔ '
nasal	m			n		ɳ ṇ	ɲ *ñ, ń*	ŋ *ng*	ɴ		
fricative		f v	θ *th* ð *dh*	s z	ʃ *sh, š* ʒ *zh, ž*	ʂ ṣ ʐ ẓ	ç ć ʝ	x *kh* ɣ *gh*	χ ʁ	ħ ḥ ʕ '	h ɦ
affricate			ts *ts* dz *dz* ɬ ɮ (lateral fricative)				tʃ *ch, č* dʒ *ǰ*				
approximant	ʍ *wh* w			r		ɻ *r*	j *y*				
lateral			l			ɭ ḷ		ɫ			

Vowels[d, e]

	front	central	back
close (high)	i *ē* y *ü*	ɨ *ï* ʉ	ɯ u o͞o
close lax	ɪ *ĭ*		ʊ o͝o
close-mid	e *ā* ø *ö*	ə	ɤ o͞o
open-mid	ɛ *ĕ* œ	ɐ	ʌ ɔ *ô*
open (low)	æ *ă*	a *ŏ*	ɑ ɒ

[a] Usual transcriptions are given in italics after phonetic symbols where they differ.
[b] Where symbols are paired, the left one represents the voiceless segment, the right one the voiced segment.
[c] The Semitic "emphatic" series is also marked with an underdot; it represents different pronunciations in different languages.
[d] Where symbols are paired, the left one represents the unrounded vowel, the right one the rounded vowel.
[e] The italic letters (except for the ones with umlauts ü ö ï) show a common US dictionary-style transcription.

2   Segments and Alphabets

An able text, more motion than machines

For a very long time, European scholars have seen all languages in terms of European languages, and one seemingly uncontroversial aspect of that viewpoint is that every language ought to be seen in terms of individual consonants and vowels—*segments*. I mean that literally: *seen*, in the form of a "phonetic alphabet," which provides a character for each segment that might occur in some language. Table 2.1 shows a simplified chart of the most widely used one, the International Phonetic Alphabet. ⟨'⟩ comes before a stressed syllable, ⟨.⟩ comes between syllables, and ⟨:⟩ marks a long segment.

As I'm introducing the symbols used throughout this book, I'll also list a few other conventions. *Transliteration* is the transposition of written symbols into equivalents in another script, typically using the symbols from Table 2.1. They're enclosed in ⟨angle brackets⟩, which are also used when Roman letters are being discussed. *Transcription* is the transposition of the sounds of a language, including ones that happen not to be notated by the writing system, into another script. Sometimes it doesn't matter whether I'm referring to the written or spoken version, and then they're in *italics*. When I need to call attention to details of pronunciation, I enclose a *phonetic transcription* in [brackets]. And once in a while, when I need to refer to speakers' conceptions of the sounds they use, I provide a *phonemic transcription* in /slants/. An asterisk before an item indicates that the item is either an unattested, reconstructed historical form, or else an unattested form that could (or should) not exist in a language.

2.1 English spelling

People love to complain that English spelling is "irrational" and "chaotic," and in the middle of the nineteenth century someone wanting to "prove" this invented

---

Details ──

2 The occasional phonemic transcriptions of American English in this book follow the system devised by Bernard Bloch and George L. Trager, *Outline of Linguistic Analysis* (1942).

2.1 David J. Peterson, *The Art of Language Invention* (2015), 34, facetiously (I think) writes that English orthography

> was devised by a team of misanthropic, megalomaniacal cryptographers who distrusted and despised one another, and so sought to hide the meanings they were tasked with

the non-example *ghoti* "*gh* as in *enough*, *o* as in *women*, *ti* as in *nation*, hence 'fish'" (it wasn't George Bernard Shaw, and there's no evidence that he ever mentioned it). But it's easy to show that *ghoti* for "fish" is simply silly.

Scour the English dictionaries, and you won't find a single example of ⟨gh⟩ pronounced [f] at the beginning of a word. ⟨gh⟩ originally stood for a sound now found only in foreign words like the name *van Gogh* (the phonetic symbol is [ɣ]), which was fairly common in Old English. During the Middle English period, the sound usually got lost, except after a vowel involving lip-rounding (*o, u*), where it turned into [f], which also involves a near-meeting of the lips. *Enough*, *laugh*, and *cough* all had such vowels in the olden days. They're all fairly common words, so they kept the old spelling—but *dwargh* changed the spelling to match the pronunciation, since it isn't that often that one needs to write about a *dwarf*. The few words that begin with ⟨gh⟩ owe that spelling to the fact that when William Caxton (1422?–1491) began printing books in English in 1473 in Bruges, and even when he brought his business to London two years later, he had to employ Flemish craftsmen, and they were accustomed to spelling /g/ with ⟨gh⟩ in their language, and simply carried that habit over into English. It stuck in a few words centering on *ghost*.

In *women*, the problem isn't the spelling, but the pronunciation! *Woman* was originally *wifman*. The [f] eventually disappeared, and the lip-consonants *w* and *m* influenced the vowel to become [ʊ]. But consider the appearance of **wuman**, with no fewer than eight short vertical strokes in a row at the beginning. A plausible suggestion is that in this sort of word—including *come*, *some*, and *won*—an original *u* was replaced by *o* to break up the confusing sequence of vertical lines. But how do we get from *women* to [ˈwɪm.ɪn]? A small number of very common English nouns make their plural in a very old, Indo-European way: *goose/geese*, *foot/feet*, and a few others: the singular has a lip-rounded back vowel, the plural a non-rounded front vowel. The [ʊ] of *woman* is a rounded back vowel, and [ɪ] is the corresponding front vowel, so *analogy* was at work to produce [ˈwɪm.ɪn] while the spelling remained ⟨women⟩.

Lastly, the sequence ⟨ti⟩ has the "sh" sound [ʃ] because of the phonetic process of *assimilation*—specifically, *regressive assimilation*, which means the assimilation seems to go "backwards" with the later sound influencing the earlier one. This particular assimilation is called *palatalization*; it's very common around the world. Compare *assimilate* with *assimilation*. The [t] at the end of the base word is pronounced with

---

Details *(continued)*

encoding by employing crude, arcane spellings that no one can explain. ("*Ha, ha! I shall spell 'could' with an ell! They will be powerless to stop me!*")

The book is, nonetheless, a pretty good superficial introduction to basic concepts in linguistics.

Shaw's lack of connection with *ghoti*, and the possible reasons for the attribution, were investigated by Ben Zimmer, "On Language: Is This Word Really Pronounced 'fish'?" (2010).

The explanation for writing [ʌ] as ⟨o⟩ is given with some hesitation by D. G. Scragg, *A History of English Spelling* (1974), 44, and with considerable certainty by Richard L. Venezky, "Notes on the History of English Spelling" (1976), 358f.

the tongue tip against the gum ridge; the "y" sound [j] at the beginning of the suffix *ion* is made with the blade of the tongue against the hard palate. Anticipation of the tongue's position for [j] brings the tongue tip back from the gum ridge to the palatal place where [ʃ] is made and allows air to escape around it. So [t] becomes [s] before [j]—when the syllable before it is stressed—; and [sj] coalesce into [ʃ]. So ⟨ti⟩ can never be [ʃ] at the end of a word.

So *ghoti* can't have any other pronunciation than *goaty*.

2.1.1 How bad is it?

Okay. So "*ghoti* = fish" is silly. But English spelling really is pretty chaotic, isn't it? We have *beak* and *break*, *teak* and *steak*. We also have *break* and *brake*, *steak* and *stake*. We have *bomb* and *comb* and *tomb*. But there's also *read* and *read* and *red*, *lead* and *lead* and *led*. Not to mention *island* and *debt*. (Never mind *cello* and *khaki* and *gnu*.) More annoyingly, we have *dive* and *give*, *gave* and *have*, *go* and *do*, and most annoyingly, *to* and *two*, too. But how bad is it *really*? In a dictionary of the 5000 most frequent English words, the pronunciation of almost half of the top 50 words violate one or another of the principles that govern the pronunciation of the vast majority of English words, but the proportion falls by and large asymptotically through the list. *People* is on it, but not *leopard* (or *jeopardy*), *yeoman*, or even *luncheon*, and there isn't really a way to choose any pronunciation of ⟨eo⟩ as the basic one.

The idea of "chaos" is due to the notion that each identifiable sound in English ought to have one and only one spelling, and vice versa any spelling should be readable only one way. But is that in fact the ideal situation that spelling reformers—including George Bernard Shaw—make it out to be? Consider these sentences:

Details *(continued)* ───

2.1.1 There have been a number of attempts to catalog the correspondences between sound and spelling of English. The most successful is that of Edward Carney, *A Survey of English Spelling* (1994), who presents both speech-to-text correspondences (pp. 134–255) and text-to-speech correspondences (pp. 280–380, summarized on pp. 381–94) for British spelling. D. W. Cummings, *American English Spelling* (1988), presents the former sort of correspondence for American spelling, though not exhaustively (omitting the spellings of shwa and other unstressed vowels). Richard L. Venezky, *The Structure of English Orthography* (1970b), presents the latter sort, very compactly—but the laurel for compression must go to W. A. Ainsworth, "A System for Converting English Text into Speech" (1973), whose 159 rules for driving a minimal speech synthesizer from written input can be reproduced on a single page (as by Carney on p. 265).

Mark Davies and Dee Gardner, *A Frequency Dictionary of Contemporary American English* (2010), rank 5000 words. Unfortunately for our purpose they list noun and verb usages separately (e.g. *campaign*—at nos. 650 and 4987) and group all the forms of *be* under a single item (no. 2). But the number of "irregularly" spelled words—those whose pronunciation can't unequivocally be determined by general rule—can be charted by counting the ones that appear on specific pages:

Doo yoo see the yoo doo under the yoo by the see yet? If the korister in the quyr (kwyr?) in a hyr wuud pyoo askt the wich wich him to by from the himnl, what wuud shee tel him? Hee reelee wantd too no. Are those preferable to *Do you see the ewe due under the yew by the sea yet? If the chorister in the choir in a higher wood pew asked the witch which hymn to buy from the hymnal, what would she tell him? He really wanted to know.*?

Right off, you can see four of the most important benefits of English orthography being more or less as it is: (a) It keeps apart words that sound the same—homophones:* *by, buy; do, due* (you didn't think I'd write about *ewe-doo* in a scientific book, did you?); *see, sea; hymn, him.* (b) It can be read with different pronunciations by different people: some say *due* as "doo," some as "dyoo" (like *dew*). And (c) it signals the relation between words or parts of words that might not sound the same but are: **chor**ister, **choir**; *hymn, hymnal; asked, wanted.* "Phonetic" spellings of *photograph* and *photography* would be very different!

Another benefit (d) reflects a pattern more than it concerns individual words: compare ⟨doo⟩ and ⟨no⟩ with their standard spellings ⟨do⟩ and ⟨know⟩. Almost every two-letter word in English is a "function word" rather than a "content word"—even ⟨ax⟩ is often spelled ⟨axe⟩. Function words, moreover, are some of the most common words in the English language, meaning they're among the first words to be learned and the ones that are most reinforced by appearing every day. The more common a word, the more likely it is to have an "irregular" spelling because the spelling doesn't get a chance to change in sync with a change in the language.

---

*Some distinguish *homophones*, words pronounced alike, from *homonyms*, words both pronounced and spelled alike, such as *ear* of corn or for hearing, or *quail* verb or noun.

Details *(continued)* ───────────────────────────────────────

page containing item no.		# of irregular words on the page	# of words on the page	percent
1	*the*	7	12	58%
25	*we*	10	25	40%
50	*as*	6	23	26%
100	*well*	8	22	36%
250	*word*	11	22	50%
500	*federal*	5	19	26%
1000	*cause*	2	19	11%
2500	*testing*	1	20	5%
5000	*trim*	1	22	4%

For instance, p. 13 holds the 85th–106th most frequent words, and I deem the pronunciation of the ones I italicize to be not fully predictable: way no *look* first *also* new because day more use man here *find give* thing well *many only* those tell *very one.*

A point that needs to be made is that the "irregularities" or "mismatches" between spelling and sound are much more from the point of view of the writer than of the reader, and as with just about any written language, there are far more readers than writers—many people will have little occasion to write anything throughout their adult life, perhaps beyond filling out forms, so on a practical level, it's the spelling-to-sound correspondences that are most important, and for the most part, determining the pronunciation of written words is quite straightforward for someone who speaks the language fluently.

Consonants, first of all, are almost entirely straightforward. There might be hesitation over whether ⟨g⟩ is [g] as in *gill* (of a fish) or [dʒ] as in *gill* (an old liquid measure, ½ cup), but that's a very exceptional case—probably no one ever pointed out in elementary school that ⟨g⟩ is almost always [g] before ⟨a o u⟩ (back vowels) and [dʒ] before ⟨e i⟩ (front vowels), but if you see a new word, you'll very likely get it right.

It's in the vowels where the help of the orthography is really needed, because English has so many vowels and so few vowel letters. And many of the pronunciations are quite predictable. For instance, the English vowels come in pairs conventionally (in American schoolbooks and dictionaries) called "long" and "short." In a stressed syllable, the vowel letters usually stand for a "short" vowel when they come before two consonant letters (or one consonant at the end of a word): *mad, mat, past.* But they stand for a "long" vowel when such syllables are followed by a "silent *e*"— what one useful analysis calls a *marker*, meaning a letter that provides no sound of its own but marks a difference in the sound of another letter: *made, mate, paste.* The two devices interact when endings are added: *matting, mating*: the double ⟨t⟩ shows that the vowel is short, leaving the single-⟨t⟩ word to have the long vowel so that the marker isn't needed. A different marker—though it's spelled the same—accounts for the *dive/give* conflict. The first ⟨e⟩ makes the *i* long, but the second is there because ⟨v⟩ is hardly ever allowed to appear at the end of an English word. Yet a third ⟨e⟩

Details *(continued)*

In 1952, the National Council of Teachers of English issued a report finding that

> Reading itself was overrated. In fact, people listened most, spoke much more than they read, and wrote very little. But the American school curriculum, NCTE said, made it seem like reading and writing, the least frequently used language skills, were the only ones worth teaching. (summary by David Skinner, *The Story of* Ain't [2012], 181)

The proliferation of texting might alter the findings somewhat today.

Richard Venezky's "marker" concept is presented most fully in his *The Structure of English Orthography* (1970b). Little-known but insightful treatments of various aspects of English spelling include Eleanor M. Higginbottom, "Representation of English Vowel Phonemes" (1962); Robert L. Oswalt, "English Orthography as a Morphophonemic System" (1973); Wayne B. Dickerson, "Decomposition of Orthographic Word Classes" (1975) and "English Orthography: A Guide to Word Stress and Vowel Quality" (1978); and Ralph H. Emerson, "English Spelling and Its Relation to Sound" (1997). Dickerson's approach is almost exhaustively worked out but is published only as a textbook-cum-workbook for advanced students of English as a Foreign Language, *Stress in the Speech Stream* (1989).

marker helps with the pronunciation of ⟨g⟩ as in *singe* vs. *sing*, and here it is kept: *singeing, singing*.

Indicated only rudimentarily in orthography by punctuation marks is *intonation*, the rises and falls of the pitch of the voice: roughly, down at a period, up at a question mark, suspended at a comma.

All the factors seen in §2.1—sound change, foreign influence, nearby sounds ("phonetic environment"), stress assignment, and occasionally scribal whim—are responsible for the supposed "mismatch" between English spelling and pronunciation. But how great a "mismatch" is there really? Noam Chomsky and Morris Halle notoriously proclaimed, in fact, that "conventional orthography is ... a near optimal system for the lexical representation of English words." That statement has caused considerable consternation among users and teachers of English alike, but in a way it's true even at face value.

2.1.2 How did it get that way?

English spelling is quite good at reflecting several unique circumstances that have befallen the language. Old English goes back to the late seventh century, when English interpretations (*glosses*) were added to Latin words in manuscripts; texts originally written in English survive from the time of King Alfred (r. 871–899). Old English absorbed loanwords, and their spellings, from Scandinavian invaders and Greek- and Latin-speaking and -writing Irish missionaries.

Middle English dates from the Norman Conquest of 1066, which brought an influx of Romance (Norman French) words pertaining to more cultivated levels of society—domestic animals have names like those in the other Germanic languages, but their flesh is eaten in French (*cow/beef, calf/veal, sheep/mutton*), for instance. Latin, and later Greek, remained the languages of intellectual endeavor; and ever since, the vocabulary of science, religion, and the humanities has been formed from Classical (Latin and Greek) roots. With all those borrowings, and down to the present

---

Details *(continued)*

American English intonation is studied in two sizable volumes by Dwight Bolinger, *Intonation and Its Parts* (1985) and *Intonation and Its Uses* (1989); for British English and more generally, Alan Cruttenden, *Intonation* (1997).

The notorious proclamation appears in Noam Chomsky and Morris Halle, *The Sound Pattern of English* (1968), 49—but a few pages later, they expand it to "conventional orthography is remarkably close to the optimal phonological representation when letters are given a featural analysis—much closer, in some respects, than standard phonemic transcription" (p. 69), which although it is less quotable, makes clearer what they had in mind. They believed that phonology is best explained by taking into account the history of the language; the genesis of that idea is investigated in Peter T. Daniels, "Chomsky 1951a and Chomsky 1951b" (2010).

2.1.2 An eloquent overview is given by Richard L. Venezky, "How English Is Read" (1995), 113. "English spelling," he writes, whenever words are borrowed from languages that use Roman alphabets, the spellings of the originating language are almost always borrowed as well.

One consequence of the influx of French words is that voiceless and voiced pairs of fricatives started to make a difference—become phonemic. In Old English, [v] and [ð] and [z] and [ʒ] and [ɣ] could only be pronounced when /f/ or /θ/ or /s/ or /ʃ/ or /x/ was between vowels. But French words changed that: *house* still becomes *houses*, but *place* becomes *places*—so both /z/ and /s/ are between vowels; and *face* /feys/ and *phase* /feyz/ are different words.

It turns out that native (Germanic), French, and Classical words in English behave somewhat differently: for instance, *sameness* and *similarity*, not *similarness* or *sameity*; and when you attach *-ness* (a native suffix) to a word, the word stays the same—*pérfect*, *pérfectness*, but *-tion* (a French suffix) makes the stress (accent) change—*perféction*. That's a simple example, but they quickly get complicated, and in the spelling you can usually find a clue to which words will behave differently, and what that behavior is likely to be; and that's what Chomsky and Halle meant by "near-optimal."

The alphabet English took over from Latin had 23 letters (§2.1.4.2), 6 of them for vowels ⟨A E I O V Y⟩, 17 for consonants ⟨B C D F G H K L M N P Q R S T X Z⟩. Old English had considerably more sounds than Latin, but even so, some of the letters are "wasted"—Q, X, Y, and Z didn't have jobs of their own to do! This has been taken care of

---

Details *(continued)*

> has at its core, patterns which originated from Latin orthography of the sixth and seventh centuries, but were heavily modified over a thousand year period, primarily through the influence of sound change. Intermixed with that core, like the swirls of chocolate in a marble cake, are a host of sub-patterns and singularities created through borrowings, spelling reform, and scribal caprice. Nevertheless, by the beginning of the sixteenth century, the counterpoint of morphological and etymological representation with that of the phonological base was firmly established and has undergone little alteration since.

The most useful history of English for us, because of its thorough coverage of orthography, is R. M. Hogg, ed., *The Cambridge History of the English Language* (1992–2001). Two readable histories of English spelling are D. G. Scragg, *A History of English Spelling* (1974), a narrative account; and Christopher Upward and George Davidson, *The History of English Spelling* (2011). The brief synthesis by David Crystal, *Spell It Out* (2012), is readable and informative and remarkably comprehensive. The Early Modern systematization of English spelling was studied by F. H. Brengelman, "Orthoepists, Printers, and the Rationalization of English Spelling" (1980), on the basis of the enormous body of data collected by E. J. Dobson, *English Pronunciation 1500–1700* (1957).*

Kristian Berg and Mark Aronoff, "Self-Organization in the Spelling of English Suffixes" (2017), though, find, by investigating historical corpora of English in 70-year chunks from 1350 to 1710, that certain of the adjective-forming suffixes they studied (-ic*, *-al*, *-el*, and *-ly*) had several coexisting variants for centuries and did not attain standard spellings until the eighteenth century, whereas *-ous* and *-le* were set by 1500. This suggests to me that the concern of the orthoepists, and their influence, was limited to the content words of English and especially the stressed vowels found in them.

in two different ways. First, new letters were borrowed from the native runes (Table 2.5) or even invented: either ⟨þ⟩ (called *thorn*) or ⟨ð⟩ (*edh*) was used for either [θ] or [ð] (because they are simply a voiceless/voiced fricative pair)—both letters could even be used in the same manuscript for either sound. The symbol ⟨ƿ⟩ (*wen*) was [w], and ⟨ȝ⟩ (*yogh*) was [ɣ]. The sound [ʧ] was spelled ⟨c⟩, taking advantage of one of the redundancies. And [ʃ] was spelled with the *digraph* (two letters for a single sound) ⟨sc⟩.

Ushering in Middle English, Norman scribes adapted the Latin way of rendering sounds found only in Greek words and created digraphs using ⟨h⟩—as a diacritic—for English sounds that were unfamiliar: ⟨c⟩ changed to ⟨ch⟩—after a short vowel it was spelled ⟨cch⟩, which became ⟨tch⟩; ⟨ȝ⟩ was ousted by ⟨gh⟩, which as we saw has persisted in spelling long after the sound was lost; ⟨ph⟩ represents [f] in words that came from Greek; ⟨sh⟩ took over from ⟨sc⟩ and was probably simplified from ⟨sch⟩; ⟨th⟩ replaced ⟨θ⟩ and ⟨ð⟩; and ⟨wh⟩ was used for [ʍ], a sound that by the twenty-first century has become [w] almost everywhere English is spoken. The letter ⟨w⟩ came from ⟨vv⟩, spelling the consonantal value of the vowel letter, [u̯] or [w]. The letters ⟨x⟩ and ⟨z⟩ received their current pronunciations in Latin, but ⟨y⟩ simply alternated with ⟨i⟩.

Early Modern English conventionally began with Caxton's introduction of printing. He was largely responsible for establishing norms of spelling, and they were based on the usage of the capital, London. Unfortunately, just when printers had settled on an orthographic system conforming with the general European use of the vowel letters, the vowels were undergoing a change in pronunciation known as the Great English Vowel Shift—whereby the sound spelled ⟨e⟩ everywhere else a Roman alphabet is used became [iː] as its name says, the sound spelled ⟨i⟩ everywhere else became [aj] ("*eye*") in English, the sound spelled ⟨a⟩ everywhere else became [ej], and so on. The spellings remained what they were before the change set in, though, and so English vowel spelling is out of step with the rest of the world.

English was quite a diverse language by the fifteenth century, and scribes in different regions had adopted different conventions for spelling various vowels—but also, the language changed differently in different areas, and variations like *meat* and *meet*, *steak* and *stake* entered the London standard as people came to the capital from throughout the country, bringing their dialects, their traditions, and their manuscripts with them.

Until the seventeenth century, ⟨u⟩ and ⟨v⟩ were the same letter, with ⟨v⟩ at the beginning of a word and ⟨u⟩ elsewhere. The same held for ⟨j⟩ and ⟨i⟩. The assignment of ⟨j v⟩ to the consonant and ⟨i u⟩ to the vowel began a bit earlier in France (see n. * on p. 3), but by the time of John Milton (1608–1674) it had prevailed in English—yet dictionaries didn't list *I* and *J*, *U* and *V* words separately until 1801. The word-final form ⟨s⟩ didn't fully oust ⟨ſ⟩ elsewhere in a word until even later, and the latter persists in German, where ⟨ß⟩ is a *ligature* (joining of letters) of ⟨ſs⟩.* Some examples:

---

* Or of ⟨ſz⟩, as is reflected in the Fraktur form ß, composed of ſ and ȝ, and even in some Roman fonts.

Goe to, let vs go downe, and there cõfound their language, that they may not vnderſtand one anothers ſpeech. (Genesis 11: 7 [1611 spelling; another example on p. 54])

Thou com'ſt to vſe thy Tongue :thy Story quickly. (*Macbeth* V.v. 29 [1623 spelling])

... till one greater Man
Reſtore us, and regain the bliſsful Seat,
Sing Heav'nly Muſe ... (Milton, *Paradise Lost* i.4–6 [1667])

It was the eighteenth century that essentially saw the codification of standard English spelling, when Samuel Johnson (1709–1784) created the first English dictionary that was intended to include the entire vocabulary, not just "hard words"; in the process, he tried to be consistent in his spelling practice, though he did not entirely succeed. It was first published in 1755. A generation later, the birth of the new American nation afforded the rare opportunity to carry out a spelling reform. Led by Noah Webster (1758–1843), it involved mostly the omission of unnecessary letters such as the *u* in *-our* and the change of *-re* to *-er*. This innovation, coupled with a certain conservatism in pronunciation (such as the retention of postvocalic *r* in many American dialects), means that American spelling reflects the pronunciation of English a bit more faithfully than British spelling does, though the removal of ⟨k⟩ from words like *musick* soon made its way back to England. Webster's first dictionary, of 1806, was fairly extreme in its recommendations, but by the 1820s his "Blue-back Speller" was teaching what became the American standard, codified in his big dictionary of 1828.

The lack of obvious agreement of English spelling with the pronunciation of any specific dialect of English, which is tremendously varied worldwide, especially for vowels, is a great advantage: it means that all English-speakers can interpret the orthography without prejudice toward any particular one—and this is due to

Details *(continued)* ────────────────────────────────

First editions: Samuel Johnson, *A Dictionary of the English Language* ... (1755), on which see Allen Reddick, *The Making of Johnson's Dictionary 1746–1773* (1996); Noah Webster, *A Compendious Dictionary of the English Language* (1806) and Noah Webster, *An American Dictionary of the English Language* ... (1828), on both of which see David Mickelthwait, *Noah Webster and the American Dictionary* (2000).

The spoken English language of the 17th–18th centuries, too, is what underlies the great dialectal variety of modern Englishes: English-speakers from around the world recognize the reconstructed Shakespearean "Original Pronunciation" as somehow similar to their own variety and different from twentieth-century "Received Pronunciation" and "Mid-Atlantic Stage English," as explored by David Crystal, *Original Shakespearean Pronunciation* (2016), x with n. 1.*

───────────────

*This was brought out especially clearly by David Crystal and Ben Crystal, interview, "All Shakespeare All the Time" (2016).

the sheer coincidence in time of the standardization of spelling with the spread of English around the world. As regional accents developed from the spoken language in North America, South Asia, and the southern hemisphere, all of them continued to spell with the same orthography, so that somewhat different spelling-to-sound relationships emerged, ensuring that *writers* of different "World Englishes" could successfully communicate even if their spoken varieties verged on the mutually unintelligible.

2.1.3 Should it be fixed?

At the beginning of §2.1.1, I mentioned the spelling reformers' ideal of one letter for one sound, and vice versa. But whose "sounds" should the orthography represent? Enthusiasts for spelling reform have included the American librarian Melville Dewey (1851–1931), who sometimes styled himself Melvil Dui, and his son Godfrey (1887–1977); President Theodore Roosevelt (1858–1919); and the British playwright George Bernard Shaw (1856–1950) and parliamentarians Mont Follick (1887–1958) and James Pitman (1901–1985). But which variety of English would be represented in a simplified orthography? Did Shaw want Americans to be dissuaded from reading his plays?

Section 2.1.2 skipped from Caxton to Johnson. But in the intervening three centuries, orthography was not standing still, or simply at the mercy of the great diversity of scribes and typesetters around the country. There were many scholars at work, who to a great extent systematized the spellings of long and short vowels, of the alternations among them, and so on; but they were also so fully steeped in Classical traditions that they felt that English words borrowed from Latin (or thought to be borrowed from Latin) ought to be spelled like the originals—and they gave us *debt*, which historically was *dett* but was awarded a *b* by analogy with Latin *debitus*—even though the French source of the word had long since lost its *b*.

To the extent that the historic richness of English vocabulary and spelling results in sets like *bomb/comb/tomb* and *cove/love/move*, where each word has to be learned

---

Details *(continued)* ──

2.1.3 Squabbles among the partisans of various spelling reform schemes are aired in W. Haas, ed., *Alphabets for English* (1969), and a sympathetic but dismissive survey of proposals is offered by Josef Vachek, *Written Language* (1973), ch. 8. Nonetheless, the two collections of data by Godfrey Dewey, *Relativ Frequency of English Speech Sounds* (1923) and *Relative Frequency of English Spellings* (1970), are remarkable achievements for the pre-computer age and were used for decades by reading researchers. The most recent entry into the spelling reform lists is Robbins Burling, *Spellbound* (2016), which includes a useful comparative table of reformers' proposals for vowel-spelling but is concerned almost entirely with difficulties for the writer rather than the reader, a relatively minor concern (as we've seen), and does not mention at all the value of spelling different pronunciations of the same morpheme the same.

separately, English writing can be considered logographic. But the spelling never deviates far from the pronunciation— for instance, *tomb* can never be read 'grave'.

2.1.4 Two attempts at fixes

Two interesting attempts were made around 1960 to replace or supplement English orthography, one ultimately unsuccessful and one quixotic. Here's a familiar passage using both schemes:

> ŧhe mock tuɍtl sied deeply, and drω ŧhe back ov wun flappeɍ across hiꞩ ieꞩ. hee lωkt at alis, and tried tω speek, but, for a minit or tω, sobꞩ ȼhœkt hiꞩ vois. 'sæm aꞩ if hee had a bœn in hiꞩ ţhrœt,' sed ŧhe gryfon: and it set tω wuɍk ʃhækiŋ him and punȼhiŋ him in ŧhe back. at last ŧhe mock tuɍtl recuveɍd hiꞩ vois, and, wiŧh teerꞩ runniŋ doun hiꞩ ȼheeks, went on agæn:
>
> 'yω mæ not hav livd muȼh undeɍ ŧhe see—' ('ie havn't,' sed alis) 'and peɍhaps yω weɍ neveɍ eeven introduest tω a lobsteɍ—' (alis began to sæ, 'ie wuns tæsted—' but ȼheckt heɍself hæstily, and sed, 'nœ, neveɍ.') '—sœ yω can hav nœ iedea whot a delietfωl ţhiŋ a lobsteɍ kwadrill iꞩ!'

> 𐑞 ·𐑥𐑪𐑒 ·𐑑𐑻𐑑𐑩𐑤 𐑕𐑲𐑛 𐑛𐑰𐑐𐑤𐑦, 𐑯 𐑛𐑮𐑵 𐑞 𐑚𐑨𐑒 𐑝 𐑢𐑳𐑯 𐑓𐑤𐑨𐑐𐑼 𐑩𐑒𐑮𐑪𐑕 𐑣𐑦𐑟 𐑲𐑟. 𐑣𐑰 𐑤𐑫𐑒𐑑 𐑨𐑑 ·𐑨𐑤𐑦𐑕, 𐑯 𐑑𐑮𐑲𐑛 𐑑 𐑕𐑐𐑰𐑒, 𐑚𐑳𐑑, 𐑓𐑹 𐑩 𐑥𐑦𐑯𐑦𐑑 𐑹 𐑑𐑵, 𐑕𐑪𐑚𐑟 𐑗𐑴𐑒𐑑 𐑣𐑦𐑟 𐑝𐑶𐑕. "𐑕𐑱𐑥 𐑩𐑟 𐑦𐑓 𐑣𐑰 𐑣𐑨𐑛 𐑩 𐑚𐑴𐑯 𐑦𐑯 𐑣𐑦𐑟 𐑔𐑮𐑴𐑑," 𐑕𐑧𐑛 𐑞 ·𐑜𐑮𐑦𐑓𐑩𐑯; 𐑯 𐑦𐑑 𐑕𐑧𐑑 𐑑 𐑢𐑻𐑒 𐑖𐑱𐑒𐑦𐑙 𐑣𐑦𐑥 𐑯 𐑐𐑳𐑯𐑗𐑦𐑙 𐑣𐑦𐑥 𐑦𐑯 𐑞 𐑚𐑨𐑒. 𐑨𐑑 𐑤𐑭𐑕𐑑 𐑞 ·𐑥𐑪𐑒 ·𐑑𐑻𐑑𐑩𐑤 𐑮𐑦𐑒𐑳𐑝𐑼𐑛 𐑣𐑦𐑟 𐑝𐑶𐑕, 𐑯, 𐑢𐑦𐑞 𐑑𐑽𐑟 𐑮𐑳𐑯𐑦𐑙 𐑛𐑬𐑯 𐑣𐑦𐑟 𐑗𐑰𐑒𐑕, 𐑣𐑰 𐑢𐑧𐑯𐑑 𐑪𐑯 𐑩𐑜𐑧𐑯:—
>
> "𐑿 𐑥𐑱 𐑯𐑪𐑑 𐑣𐑨𐑝 𐑤𐑦𐑝𐑛 𐑥𐑳𐑗 𐑳𐑯𐑛𐑼 𐑞 𐑕𐑰—" ("𐑲 𐑣𐑨𐑝𐑩𐑯𐑑," 𐑕𐑧𐑛 ·𐑨𐑤𐑦𐑕)— "𐑯 𐑐𐑼𐑣𐑨𐑐𐑕 𐑿 𐑢𐑻 𐑯𐑧𐑝𐑼 𐑰𐑝𐑩𐑯 𐑦𐑯𐑑𐑮𐑩𐑛𐑿𐑕𐑑 𐑑 𐑩 𐑤𐑪𐑚𐑕𐑑𐑼—" (·𐑨𐑤𐑦𐑕 𐑚𐑦𐑜𐑨𐑯 𐑑 𐑕𐑱 "𐑲 𐑢𐑳𐑯𐑕 𐑑𐑱𐑕𐑑𐑦𐑛—" 𐑚𐑳𐑑 𐑗𐑧𐑒𐑑 𐑣𐑻𐑕𐑧𐑤𐑓 𐑣𐑱𐑕𐑑𐑦𐑤𐑦, 𐑯 𐑕𐑧𐑛 "𐑯𐑴, 𐑯𐑧𐑝𐑼") —𐑕𐑴 𐑿 𐑒𐑨𐑯 𐑣𐑨𐑝 𐑯𐑴 𐑲𐑛𐑾 𐑣𐑢𐑪𐑑 𐑩 𐑛𐑦𐑤𐑲𐑑𐑓𐑫𐑤 𐑔𐑦𐑙 𐑩 ·𐑤𐑪𐑚𐑕𐑑𐑼-·𐑒𐑢𐑩𐑛𐑮𐑦𐑤 𐑦𐑟!"

2.1.4.1 i.t.a.

It was Sir James Pitman, K.B.E., M.P., who stood behind the "initial teaching alphabet" or i.t.a. This was an alphabet, gradually introduced in British schools from 1960 to about 1965, that adapted traditional orthography ("t.o.") to express each phoneme of English with a single character: a Roman letter, a variant, or a newly created ligature (Table 2.2). Larger letters were used in place of the differing capital forms of t.o.

T.o. is largely respected with regard to consonants; no less than three spellings for /k/ are retained (c, k, ck). So are doubled consonants, but "silent" consonants are omitted (sied). A clever device is the use of ꞩ for ⟨s⟩ when pronounced /z/. The "marker" vowel *e* (§2.1.1) is incorporated into the ligatures for the "long" vowels (in the American sense, cf. Table 2.1) æ ee ie œ ue, rather than appearing after an intervening consonant. Reduced vowels keep their spelling: across, eeven, alis, gryfon, upon. The spelling of iedea is surprising.

Details *(continued)*

2.1.4 The i.t.a. transliteration is from John Downing, *The Initial Teaching Alphabet Explained and Illustrated* (1965), 127; The Shavian transcription is from Lewis Carroll, *Alice ... in the*

Table 2.2 i.t.a.[a]

[1]p	[3]t	[5]c,k	[7]f	[9]þh	[11]s	[13]ʃh	[15]ȼh	[24]y	[19]ŋ
pæ	top	cat,kitten	fun	þhin	sit	ʃhip	ȼhurȼh	yellœ	siŋ
[2]b	[4]d	[6]g	[8]v	[10]ðh	[12]z, ʃ	[14]ʒ	[16]j	[23]w	[22]h
but	dog	gæt	vois	wiðh	zœ, aʃ	meʒuer	jam	wet	hat
[20]l	[17]m	[29]i	[27]e	[25]a	[(1+)]a, e, i, o, u	[31]o	[35]ω	[38]ou	[26]a
lip	man	it	egg	appl	about, *etc.*	on	tωk	out	fatheʀ
[21]r,ʀ	[18]n	[30]ɛɛ	[28]æ	[37]ie	[33]u	[34]œ	[36]ω	[39]oi	[32]au
riŋ	not	ɛɛȼh	æbl	ies	up	œpen	mωn	boi	aull
	(ar	aur, or	ær	eʀ	–	ɛɛr	–)	[40]ue	[25/26]a
	ar	waurt, or	ær	eʀ		ɛɛr		uez	graʃʃ

[a] Arranged like Table 2.3 for comparison. The numbers are those used in the sources to mark the order of letters.

Table 2.3 The Shaw Alphabet Reading Key

Tall:	peep	tot	kick	fee	thigh	so	sure	church	yea	hung
Deep:	bib	dead	gag	vow	they	zoo	measure	judge	woe	ha-ha
Short:	loll	mime	if	egg	ash	ado	on	wool	out	ah
	roar	nun	eat	age	ice	up	oak	ooze	oil	awe
Compound:	are	or	air	err	array	ear	ian	yew		

Details *(continued)* ———————————————————————————

Shaw Alphabet (2013), 86, transcribed by Thomas Thurman. Table 2.2, collated from James Pitman and John St. John, *Alphabets and Reading* (1969), 132, and John Downing, *The Initial Teaching Alphabet Explained and Illustrated* (1965), 93–108, follows the arrangement of Table 2.3 for comparison. A report on the use of i.t.a. in one school district is presented by Maurice Harrison, *The Story of the Initial Teaching Alphabet* (1964). Jeremy Hall, "The Initial Teaching Alphabet" (2005), provides an overview of its origin and reception. The Shaw Alphabet Reading Key, imitated in Table 2.3, is from George Bernard Shaw, *Androcles and the Lion* (1962), 151.

John C. Wells named the TRAP, BATH, and PALM types of vowel (among his 27 "lexical sets" of English vowels), discussing the ambivalence of the BATH set in *Accents of English* (1982), 133–35; this book remains the standard reference for worldwide variation in English pronunciation.

Differing phonemic systems were accommodated in two ways. In many British varieties of English, the vowel of words like BATH, such as *last*, is the same as the vowel in words like PALM, but in some British and many American varieties of English, the vowel of words like BATH is the same as the vowel in words like TRAP. An extra variety of ⟨a⟩ was introduced for BATH words that students were expected to interpret as one or the other pronunciation according to their own usage: pɑm bɑʃh trap; it's not clear whether they were expected to write that variety in such words, which they wouldn't be able to distinguish from the PALM words or the TRAP words other than by memorization.

Standard British English omits /r/ after vowels, though ⟨r⟩ appears in the spelling. A distinctive variety ɾ was introduced—but to be used only after the vowels e i u y when they yield the vowel in *her*; all other r's are written even though in such varieties they aren't pronounced, as in *heart*, *fire*, and *sword*: heɾ, but hɑrt fier sord. Note how d is made more distinct from b, two letters that can be confused by learners as well as dyslexics (there's a p but no ⟨q⟩), and the c and t from those in the ʤh and ʧh ligatures.

Extensive research showed positive, or at least not negative, results for children's ability to read t.o. after learning i.t.a., but either the promoters of i.t.a. were not concerned about children's learning to write t.o., or else they suppressed what results they had. I've met a few people whose first reading experiences were with i.t.a., and they never did master t.o. spelling. This is anecdotal but credible information. It's possible that educators recognized that writing isn't a frequent practice for most people (cf. the quotation on p. 19) and so weren't greatly concerned with that skill. I haven't found explicit accounts of why i.t.a. was abandoned after its brief heyday.

2.1.4.2 Shavian

In his will, G. B. Shaw left a considerable sum of money to finance the creation of a phonetic orthography to completely replace traditional orthography. The result was a new design finalized by Kingsley Read (Table 2.3); it achieved just one publication then, Shaw's play *Androcles and the Lion* (1962), as he had instructed, using the pronunciation of King George V (again, following Shaw's direction) as transcribed by Peter McCarthy, of the Phonetics Department, University of Leeds. The volume includes Afterwords by McCarthy, who perhaps not inadvertently lays out a number of drawbacks in using the alphabet (which has come to be called "Shavian," though that term was not used at the time), and Read, who offers guidance in calligraphy. It also has a Foreword by C. R. Sopwith, the Public Trustee in charge of carrying out Shaw's wishes, who outlines the legal problems and the design competition involved—and an Introduction by Sir James Pitman, instigator of i.t.a., who extols Shaw's intent and the result.

The consonant shapes are paired by rotation: voiceless and voiced where applicable, and also for other natural pairs. The vowel pairings are less systematic. To some extent they match the "short" and "long" pairs (of American usage). The

Table 2.4 The Latin alphabet and its ancestors

Greek	Λ	ꓭ	⌐	◁	Ǝ	Y	I	⊟	⊕	⟨	⅄	L	M	Ͷ	Ξ	O	Γ	M	Ϙ	⏌	ꙅ	T	Y	⊕	X	Y
Etruscan	A	ꓭ	◁	◁	Ǝ	⅂	I	⊟	⊗	I	⋋	⌐	M	Ͷ	⊞	O	Γ	M	Ϙ	⏌	ꙅ	T	Y	Φ	X	Y
Latin	A	B	C	D	E	F		H		I	K	L	M	N		O	P		Q	R	S	T	V		X	
	a	b	c	d	e	f		h		i	k	l	m	n		o	p		q	r	s	t	u		x	

"Compound" group appears to be a half-hearted attempt at accommodation of both r-less and r-full dialects of English (§§ 2.1.4.1, 12.3.3); most can be seen as adding an arc to the base vowel shape. No other concession, though, is made to any other variety of the language.

2.2 The Latin alphabet

Let's now look at how the Irish missionaries who brought Christian literacy to Britain learned to write.

Greeks came to the west coast of Italy early in the eighth century BCE, bringing with them one of the local variants of the Greek alphabet. It was quickly taken up by the indigenous Etruscans, who in turn passed it on to the Romans. The shapes of Roman inscriptional capitals were perfected by the first century CE and remain the standard *majuscules* to this day. Our *minuscules* ("small letters") were standardized under the direction of Alcuin of York at Charlemagne's court around 800. They were one of a number of regional hands that became fixed among different European peoples, resulting in the sort of diversity that happened with other scripts (see Chapters 3 and 5). Thanks to Petrarch at the beginning of the Italian Renaissance early in the fourteenth century, they became the ordinary style that prevails today.

On the other hand, because literacy in its early stages was closely linked with the Roman Catholic church, almost all the other variants (which go by such names as Insular Half-Uncial, Visigothic, and Rotunda) were eventually abandoned. Two with a less ignominious end are *italic*, which is now usually used for various kinds of highlighting within ordinary text, and 𝔉𝔯𝔞𝔨𝔱𝔲𝔯 ("Fraktur," familiar from the Gutenberg Bible of 1455, which was usual in German printing until the mid twentieth century). Italic was first cast in type right around 1500 because it was a more compact style than upright letters, thus making the manufacture of printed books more economical.

Etruscan didn't have voiced stops, so it had no need for B, C (i.e., *gamma*), or D, but, fortunately for Latin, kept them in the alphabet—Table 2.4 shows the forms in

Details *(continued)* ————————————————————————————

2.2 The varieties of Roman alphabets that developed over the last two millennia are treated in many handbooks of calligraphy, which also include instructions on how to write them with a pen. See also Stanley Morison, *Politics and Script* (1972).

the earliest abecedary, from Marsiliana—but (for reasons that escape us) spelled *k* three different ways: ⟨K⟩ before *a*, ⟨C⟩ before *e* or *i*, and ⟨Q⟩ before *o* or *u*. Latin took over this last practice, where it made sense because ⟨QU⟩ represented *kʷ*, and used ⟨X⟩ for *k* combined with *s*. But ⟨K⟩ dropped out in favor of ⟨C⟩ quite early and hung on in only a few standard abbreviations. ⟨B⟩ and ⟨D⟩ were revived for *b* and *d*, but ⟨C⟩ represented both *g* and *k*—until, at least according to Plutarch, one Spurius Carvilius Ruga, the first named educator in Roman history, ca. 230 BCE, wanted people to stop pronouncing his name *Ruka* (a nice story, but it turns out ⟨G⟩ was in use before his time, so it has been suggested that it was he who assigned ⟨C⟩ to *k* and ⟨G⟩ to *g*). Y and Z didn't come into Latin until the late second century BCE, when they started being used in words borrowed from Greek. The Latin alphabet thus achieved 23 letters.

2.2.1 The Roman alphabet

Latin literacy reached much of western Europe with the Roman legions. With the demise of the Roman Empire, vernacular languages came to be written, under the aegis of both church and state. We've seen the adjustments made for English; other languages, also with larger inventories of sounds than Latin, found additional sorts of accommodations.

The Bohemian religious reformer Jan Hus (1372–1415) is credited with inventing the *diacritic*, a mark added to a letter to designate a different but similar sound. Latin gets along with the single sibilant *s*, which is very inconvenient for lots of other languages. Hus's solution for Czech was to mark the *sh*-sound with a dot over ⟨s⟩, ⟨ṡ⟩, which eventually turned into ⟨š⟩.

Latin scribes had long been using abbreviations, ligatures like ⟨æ⟩ and ⟨œ⟩, and contractions signaled by diacritic-like marks to economize on expensive time and materials. In German, the ⟨e⟩ in the sequences ⟨ae⟩, ⟨oe⟩, and ⟨ue⟩ could appear on top of the preceding vowel, and eventually this evolved into a pair of strokes and then a pair of dots, ⟨ä ö ü⟩. Hungarian also writes front rounded vowels with umlauts, and long vowels with acute accents—and combines them for long front rounded vowels: ⟨ő ű⟩.

The Scandinavian languages have used diacritics to create new vowel letters—⟨å ø ü⟩—and added them to the end of their alphabets. Icelandic preserves the Runic ⟨þ⟩ and adds ⟨ð⟩ for the two interdentals, representing different sounds, unlike in Old English.

Details *(continued)* ———————————————————————————————

George Heimpl, "The Origin of the Latin Letters G and Z" (1899), gathers much detail, though his conclusions are not very persuasive.

2.2.1 The term "diacritic" is discussed by Peter T. Daniels, "Two Notes on Terminology" (2009c), 277–78.

Table 2.5 Germanic runes

f	u	þ	a	r	k	g	w	h	n	i	j	ï	p	z	s	t	b	e	m	l	ŋ	d	o
ᚹ	ᚢ	ᚦ	ᚠ	ᚱ	ᚲ	ᚷ	ᛈ	ᚺ	ᛏ	ᛁ	ᛞ	ᛃ	ᛕ	ᛜ	ᛋ	ᛐ	ᛒ	ᛗ	ᛘ	ᛚ	ᛝ	◇	ᛯ

Table 2.6 Ogham

b	l	f	s	n	h	d	t	c	q	m	g	ŋ	z	r	a	o	u	e	i	ea	oi	ui	ia	ae
ᚁ	ᚂ	ᚃ	ᚄ	ᚅ	ᚆ	ᚇ	ᚈ	ᚉ	ᚊ	ᚋ	ᚌ	ᚍ	ᚎ	ᚏ	ᚐ	ᚑ	ᚒ	ᚓ	ᚔ	ᚕ	ᚖ	ᚗ	ᚘ	ᚙ

Table 2.7 The Yiddish alphabet *(read the table from left to right)*

-ᵃ	a	o	b	g	d	h	u	v	oy	z	zh	t	tsh	y,i	i	ey	ay	kh	l	m	n	s	e	p	f	ts	k	r	sh
א	אַ	אָ	ב	ג	ד	ה	ו	וו	וי	ז	זש	ט	טש	י	יִ	יי	ײַ	כ	ל	מ	נ	ס	ע	פּ	פֿ	צ	ק	ר	ש

ᵃ Used at the beginning of a word before vowels whose letter is or begins with ו or y.

In French, diacritics are used not only to mark different-sounding vowels, as in *parlé* [par'le] 'spoken' vs. *parle* [parl(ə)] 'speak(s)', but also simply to differentiate homophones: *ou* 'or', *où* 'where', and even *août* 'August', all pronounced [u].

And then there are the diacritics that do different things in neighboring languages: in Portuguese *São Paulo*, the tilde marks the nasal vowel; but in Spanish *cañon*, it marks the palatal consonant. As in Hungarian, in Czech the acute accent marks a long vowel (except that ⟨ů⟩ is long [uː] in the middle of a word), but in Polish it changes ⟨ó⟩ to [u]—and also marks several consonants as palatal (see § 12.3); but Polish nasal vowels are marked with an *ogonek*: ⟨ę⟩.

A very important feature of French orthography results from the fact that many consonants at the end of a word are lost. The most outstanding result of this is seen in the adjectives. Many adjectives distinguish feminine from masculine with an ⟨e⟩ at the end: *verte* 'green' (fem.), *vert* (masc.); *blanche* 'white' (fem.), *blanc* (masc.)—but they are pronounced [vɛrt(ə)] and [vɛr], [blɑ̃ʃ(ə)] and [blɑ̃]. You cannot know how to spell the masculine forms unless you know the corresponding feminine forms. This is not a problem for native speakers of French, but it presents severe problems for theories of writing systems! What do the ⟨t⟩ and the ⟨c⟩ in those two words represent? It's even more daunting when sound change has produced homophonic nouns that don't have corresponding forms: *compte* 'reckoning', *comte* 'earl', and *conte* 'tale' are all [kõt(ə)]; *saut* 'leap', *sceau* 'seal', *seau* 'bucket', and *sot* 'fool' are all [so].

2.2.2 North European alphabets

Northern Europe saw two derivatives of the Latin alphabet, created for use on specific surfaces, largely for ceremonial use, each with its own alphabetical order.

Germanic runes (Table 2.5) are found first in the Danish peninsula in the first century CE; over the centuries they spread throughout Scandinavia and to Great

Britain, and over the centuries, additional runes were created for additional sounds that needed to be noted. Their angular shapes are because they were originally incised on wood. They subsequently appeared in manuscripts but only in, sometimes fanciful, explanations of their reading and use. The similar-looking script devised by J. R. R. Tolkien doesn't share any values with genuine runes.

In Ireland, a "code" (Table 2.6), Ogham, represented the letters with incisions on the edges of standing stone monuments; the horizontal line in the written version represents the vertical edge of the stone. The incisions were on one, the other, or both adjoining faces of the rock; the vowels were notches in the edge. Ogham was occasionally used for brief comments in manuscripts; the last four letters appear only in manuscripts.

It may be surprising to find Yiddish here, but unlike the other "Jewish languages,"* Yiddish is written (right to left) with a true alphabet using the Hebrew script (Tables 3.3, 3.8). In writing Hebrew, indicating the vowels is in many cases optional, and the vowel-indicators can appear with any consonant-letter. But in Yiddish, a Germanic language that was used especially in Slavic-speaking regions of Eastern Europe, the few vowel-indicators that appear are fused with the letters they accompany and cannot be used with any other letters. Table 2.7 presents the letters occurring in words of Germanic and Slavic origin. The five word-final lettershapes are used. Vocabulary borrowed from Hebrew and Aramaic follows the orthography of those languages, including the letters not in this table. In the example, Hebrew-origin words are transcribed in italics.

די וואָס האָבן אַ בטחון אויף גאָט וועלן זיי זיין אַזוי ווי דער באַרג ציון

(Di vos hobn a *bitokhn* oyf Got veln zey zayn azoy vi der barg *Tsien*)

'They that have confidence in God, they will be just like (the) Mount Zion.'

2.3 The Greek alphabet

Probably around 800 BCE, certainly somewhere on an eastern Mediterranean coast, two seafaring peoples met and interacted: the Phoenicians and the Greeks. The Phoenicians used a consonantal writing system (§3.1.1); the Greeks had had no

---

*Jewish languages are language varieties used by Jews and written with a Hebrew script instead of whichever script is used by the surrounding community.

Details (*continued*) ————————————————————————————

2.2.2 The development of Tolkien's scripts is summarized by Arden R. Smith, "Invented Languages and Writing Systems" (2014), 212–14, and the development of Tolkienian linguistics is outlined by Dimitra Fimi and Andrew Higgins, "Coda" (2016).

Jewish languages are described in L. Kahn and A. D. Rubin, eds., *Handbook of Jewish Languages* (2015), and their scripts in Peter T. Daniels, "Uses of Hebrew Script in Jewish

Table 2.8 An Archaic Greek alphabet

	ʔ	b	g	d	h	w	z	ḥ	ṭ	y	k	l	m	n	s	ʕ	p	ṣ	q	r	š	t					
Phoenician	𐤀	𐤁	𐤂	𐤃	𐤄	𐤅	𐤆	𐤇	𐤈	𐤉	𐤊	𐤋	𐤌	𐤍	𐤎	𐤏	𐤐	𐤑	𐤒	𐤓	𐤔	𐤕					
Greek	Α	Β	Λ	Δ	Ε	Ϝ	Ι	Β	⊕	Ι	Κ	Λ	Μ	Ν	Ξ	Ο	Γ	Μ	Ϙ	Ρ	⁵	Τ	Υ	Φ	Χ	Ψ	Ω
	a	*b*	*g*	*d*	*e*	*6*	^{z}*d*	*ē*	*t*^{h}	*i*	*k*	*l*	*m*	*n*	*k*^{s}	*o*	*p*	*900*	*90*	*r*	*s*	*t*	*u*	*p*^{h}	*k*^{h}	*p*^{s}	*ō*

Table 2.9 The Modern Greek alphabet

Majuscules	Α	Β	Γ	Δ	Ε		Ζ	Η	Θ	Ι	Κ	Λ	Μ	Ν	Ξ	Ο	Π		Ρ	Σ	Τ	Υ	Φ	Χ	Ψ	Ω
Minuscules	α	β	γ	Δ	ε		ζ	Η	θ	ι	κ	λ	μ	ν	ξ	ο	π		ρ	σ^a	τ	υ	φ	χ	ψ	ω

^{a} At the end of a word, ς.

Table 2.10 The first Christian alphabets

Greek	Α	Β	Γ	Δ	Ε	Ϝ	Ζ	Η	Θ	Ι	Κ	Λ	Μ	Ν	Ξ	Ο	Π	ϙ	Ρ	Σ	Τ	Υ	Φ	Χ	Ψ	Ω	↗							
																													š	*f*	*h*	*ǰ*	*q*	*ti*
Coptic	Ⲁ	Ⲃ	Ⲅ	Ⲇ	Ⲉ		Ⲍ	Ⲏ	Ⲑ	Ⲓ	Ⲕ	Ⲗ	Ⲙ	Ⲛ	Ⲝ	Ⲟ	Ⲡ		Ⲣ	Ⲥ	Ⲧ	Ⲩ	Ⲫ	Ⲭ	Ⲯ	Ⲱ			Ϣ	Ϥ	Ϩ	Ϫ	Ϭ	Ϯ
					q			*þ*								*j*	*u*	*90*				*w*			*hv*	*o*	*900*							
Gothic	𐌸	𐌱	𐌲	𐌳	𐌴	𐌿	𐌶	𐌷	𐍈	𐌹	𐌺	𐌻	𐌼	𐌽	𐌲	𐌿	𐍀	𐌵	𐍂	𐍃	𐍄	𐍅	𐍆	𐍇	𐍈	𐍉	↑							

writing for several centuries at least, since the demise of the Minoan and Mycenaean realms that had used Linear B (§1.4). Presumably the impetus for the Greek adaptation of their alphabet was mercantile: it's much easier to do business when records don't have to be held in the memory. The Greek alphabet reused for vowels the letters that in Phoenician represented consonants not found in Greek, or indeed in most European languages, as in Table 2.8.

This table shows the alphabet approximately as it was standardized on the Attic (Athenian) practice in 403/2 BCE. Earlier, the largely independent Greek city-states had used their own local ("epichoric") varieties, with varying sorts of additional letters ("supplementals") added after ⟨T⟩, or none. The Latin alphabet was borrowed from an epichoric variety with none. These variations mainly concerned how the aspirated (*t*^{h} *p*^{h} *k*^{h}) and assibilated (*k*^{s} *p*^{s}) consonants were notated.*

---

*In 1877, Adolf Kirchhoff published a map that showed the distribution of the varieties into four color-coded groups, and the colors he chose have named those groups ever since.

Details *(continued)* ————————————————————————————

Languages" (in press d). The Yiddish example is from Howard I. Aronson's contribution to P. T. Daniels and W. Bright, eds., *The World's Writing Systems* (1996), 737.

2.3 The standard reference for the epichoric alphabets is Lillian H. Jeffery, *The Local Scripts of Archaic Greece* (1990). The color nomenclature was introduced by Adolf Kirchhoff, *Studien zur Geschichte des griechischen Alphabets* (1877) in the third edition.

As with Latin, the minuscule letters developed as scribes valued speed and economy of materials, in Byzantine scriptoria. The three accent marks, designating pitch accent (as opposed to the stress—loudness—accent found in English), were sporadically used even in ancient times and eventually standardized; in Modern Greek, they have been reduced to a single all-purpose accent (Table 2.9).

2.4 Eastern alphabets

Unlike with the Roman Church, which retained Latin in the liturgy and scholarly writings, things were different in various Eastern churches. There was no insistence there on maintaining the church's classical language, in those cases Greek, for the Scriptures and other ecclesiastical writings; instead, they were translated into local languages, and eventually new works were composed in those languages. It was felt that each nation deserved a script of its own (Table 2.10).

The first beneficiary of "alphabetogeny" seems to have been Coptic, the variety of the ancient Egyptian language used by the Christian communities of Egypt in the first centuries CE. The Coptic alphabet is simply the Greek alphabet with a number of additional letters, borrowed from the Egyptian demotic script (§8.2), for sounds found in Egyptian but not Greek. The next was probably Gothic, the only known East Germanic language (which was used in the area of present-day Moldova; *ƕ* is the equivalent of English *wh*); the shapes of the letters of the Greek alphabet were altered a bit, and it seems a few letters were taken from the Latin alphabet. For Gothic, the name of the adapter is known: Bishop Wulfila (d. 383).

The next known deviser of alphabets, the Armenian saint Mesrop Mashtoc‘ (d. 440), is credited with no fewer than three new alphabets, for Armenian, Georgian, and Udi (Table 2.11). All three are languages of the Caucasus. Armenian is Indo-European, Georgian is South Caucasian (Kartvelian), and Udi is Northeast Caucasian. Whether the attribution to Mesrop is correct in all three cases may be debated; the modes of adaptation differ. Armenian—its lettershapes are often said to relate to shapes in this or that Iranian abjad—preserves the Greek order but inserts additional letters in what seems to be arbitrary fashion. Georgian for the most part adds its new letters at the end of the alphabet.

Details *(continued)* ————————————————————————————————————

2.4 The alphabets of the Christian East are dealt with by Thomas V. Gamkrelidze, *Alphabetic Writing and the Old Georgian Script* (1994), except for the Udi alphabet, which was deciphered more recently, by Jost Gippert, Wolfgang Schulze, Zaza Aleksidzé, and Jean-Pierre Mahé, *The Caucasian Albanian Palimpsests of Mount Sinai* (2009–10). An earlier view of the origin of the Mesropian alphabets refers it to the Avestan alphabet (Heinrich F. J. Junker, "Das Awestaalphabet" [1925–26]), and this was reflected in some general handbooks. In a study reminiscent of Frank Kammerzell, "Die Entstehung der Alphabetreihe" (2001) (see §11.5.2 Details), Serge Mouraviev, "Les caractères daniéliens"; "Les caractères mesropiens" (1980) reconstructs geometric forms that could underlie the Armenian and Georgian shapes.

Table 2.11 The "Mesropian" alphabets

	a	b	g	d	e	v	z^d	ē	ə	ž	t^h	ć	y	ž	i	ʕ	ł	ń	x
Greek	A	B	Γ	Δ	E		Z	H			Θ				I				
Armenian	Ա	Բ	Գ	Դ	Ե		Զ	Է	Ը		Թ			Ժ	Ի		Լ	Ղ	Խ
Georgian	ა	ბ	გ	დ	ე	3	ზ	ჱ											ი
Udi																			

	d'	ç	ż	K	l'	h	j	l	x̣	å	ć	č	[c'	m	q̇	y	n	[ʒ'	k^s, š
Greek				K				Λ						M			N		Ξ
Armenian		Ծ		Կ			Ձ	Ղ			Ճ			Մ			Ն		Տ
Georgian					ჰ					ღ				მ			ნ		
Udi^a																			

	j, [ž]	o	ṭ	f	ʒ	č', č	p	j̇	ž	ġ	r, ṙ	s	v	t, ṭ	ś	ü	ç'	r	c', c
Greek		O					Π				Ρ	Σ		T					
Armenian		Ո				Չ	Պ	Ջ			Ռ	Ս	Վ	Տ				Ր	Ց
Georgian	ჟ	ო						ჯ			ჟ	ს							
Udi^a																			

	u, w	ou	p^h	k^h	p^s	γ	q̣	š	č	c	j	ç	č	x	q	ǰ	h	ō	f
Greek	Y		Φ	X	Ψ													Ω	
Armenian	Ւ		Փ	Ք														Օ	Ֆ
Georgian	ჳ	უ	ფ	ქ		ღ	ყ	შ	ჩ	ც	ძ	წ	ჭ	ხ	ჴ	ჯ	ჰ	ჵ	ჶ
Udi																			

^a Three of the letters are attested only in the alphabet list but not in the limited amount of known text. They are bracketed.

Table 2.12 The Avestan alphabet

	a		ā		å		ā̊		ą
	i		ī		e		ē		ə
	u		ū		o		ō		

	b		β		p		f		m, m̨
	d		δ		t		θ	t̰	n
	g, ġ		γ		k		x	h	ŋ
	j				c				ń
	Y		y				x̌		ŋ́
	V						x^v		ŋ^v
	r								ṇ
	s		z		š		ž	ś	ṣ̌

We can't be entirely certain about the order of the Udi alphabet, because until very recently it was known only from an alphabet recorded in an Armenian manuscript. Then several pages of palimpsest (reused parchment) were discovered at St. Catherine's Monastery in the Sinai, Egypt, which sufficed for identifying the language (see §9.7). It no longer needed to be known as "Caucasian Albanian."

Still more extensive than the Udi alphabet is the Avestan alphabet (Table 2.12), the alphabet of the Zoroastrian scriptures, the *Avesta*. Some of those scriptures may be as old as the Vedic Sanskrit texts of India, dating from the middle of the second millennium BCE, but they were not written down until the fifth century CE or so. The alphabet is an amalgamation of Pahlavi lettershapes (see §3.3.4) with the principles of the Greek alphabet—at least one letter, ₹ ⟨ə⟩, is taken directly from Greek ε. The large number of letters in the Avestan alphabet is noteworthy: it's a very rare example of a writing system that encodes, as it seems, phonetic detail beyond what is needed to distinguish words—which means that the exact readings of some of the letters cannot be recovered. This is because, in general, historical linguistics is unable to recover the phonetic details of languages that are no longer spoken: only the significant—that is, *phonemic*—distinctions can be determined. For instance, we don't know the difference between ⊂ and ᴨ. Both represent /y/ at the beginning of a word—but /y/ in the middle of a word is written ⊍ (ii).

The ancient letter order is not known.

Here's a sentence in Avestan *(read right to left)*:

⟨hāuuanīm . ā . ratūm . ā . haomō . upāiṯ . Zaraθuštrəm .
ātrəm . pairi . yaoždaθəntəm . gāθåsca . srāuuaiiaṇtəm.⟩

'At the proper hour of the haoma pressing haoma went up to Zarathustra,
who was purifying the fire and reciting the Gathas.'
                              —*From the Avestan Hōm yašt 'hymn to haoma' (Yasna 9)*

The most recent adaptation of the Greek alphabet into a world-class script also had a religious origin (Table 2.13): in the ninth century, the church in Byzantium sent two brothers, Cyril and Methodius, to preach to the Slavic peoples, and they devised an alphabet, based on Greek capital letters, for Old Bulgarian (or Old Church Slavonic). It is called Glagolitic. Toward the end of that century, another alphabet,

---

Details *(continued)*

The Avestan example is from P. Oktor Skjærvø's contribution to P. T. Daniels and W. Bright, eds., *The World's Writing Systems* (1996), 528, lightly revised by Skjærvø.

Peter T. Daniels, "On Beyond Alphabets" (2006a), identifies eight techniques for expanding alphabets: reduction of inventory; addition of letters; combination of letters; alteration of letters; borrowing of letters; additions to letters; diacritics; simplification of letters.

Table 2.13 The Slavic alphabets

	a	b	v	g	d	ʲe	ž	z	i	j	k	l	m	n	o	p	r	s	t	u	f	x	c	č	š	šč	y	ʼ	e	ʲu	ʲa
Glagoliticᵃ	Ⰰ	Ⱛ	Ⱎ	Ⰳ	Ⰴ	Ⰵ	Ⰶ	Ⰸ	Ⰹ		Ⰽ	Ⰾ	Ⰿ	Ⱀ	Ⱁ	Ⱂ	Ⱃ	Ⱄ	Ⱅ	Ⱆ	Ⱇ	Ⱈ	Ⱌ	Ⱍ	Ⱎ	Ⱋ		Ⱐ	Ⱑ	Ⱓ	
Cyrillic	А	Б	В	Г	Д	Е	Ж	З	И	Й	К	Л	М	Н	О	П	Р	С	Т	У	Ф	Х	Ц	Ч	Ш	Щ	Ъ	Ы	Ь	Э	Ю	Я
(Russian)	а	б	в	г	д	еᵇ	ж	з	и	й	к	л	м	н	оᵇ	п	р	с	т	у	ф	х	ц	ч	ш	щ	ъ	ы	ь	э	ю	я

ᵃ Croatian version; showing only the letters corresponding to those in the Russian alphabet.
ᵇ The dieresis on ë (ʲo) is often omitted.

named for Cyril, based on Greek cursive writing, was introduced, and it's the one now used for Russian, for many Slavic languages where Orthodox Christianity prevailed, and for many other languages of the former Soviet Union.

Both the Roman and the Cyrillic alphabets have been used for a great number of languages with sounds that did not occur in Latin or Russian, and over the centuries the churchmen and scholars who created new writing systems tended to use different approaches for creating new letters. Roman alphabets usually got new letters by adding diacritics—⟨à á â ã ä å ā ă ą ç ć ċ č đ è é ê ë ē ĕ ė ę ě ğ ġ ħ ì í î ï ĩ ī ĭ į ķ Ĺ ļ ł ñ ń ņ ň ò ó ô õ ö ō ŏ ő ŕ ŗ ř ś ş š ţ ŧ ù ú û ü ũ ū ŭ ů ű ų ý ź ż ž⟩ (and those are just the first two groups encoded in Unicode)—while Cyrillic alphabets usually got variations of lettershapes—⟨љ њ ѕ ԋ ѡ ү є І қ ә з љ њ ꙅ ε ј⟩ (etc.).

3 Consonants and Abjads

From twenty alphabets—we're still unripe!

In this chapter we'll look at the type of script I call the *abjad*. It's the longest chapter because, well, abjads have been involved in more of the evolution of writing systems than the other types have been. An *abjad* is a script that notates only the consonants of its language.

3.1 West Semitic

The abjads we know go as far back as the first half of the second millennium BCE—to, the archeologists tell us, Egypt's Twelfth Dynasty (ca. 2000–1775). As we saw in §2.3, it was an abjad that underlay all the alphabets in use anywhere in the world—in fact, just about the only pure abjad that ever there was: the Phoenician. Abjads, as I've defined them, have letters only for consonants, and none for vowels. It's natural for us, as English-speakers and -readers, or for readers of any alphabetically written language, to wonder how it was possible for Phoenician scribes (in the ancient world it was almost exclusively scribes who could read and write) to read their language with none of the vowels written.

It's often said that the Semitic languages, which include Phoenician and all its relatives, don't "need" vowel letters because the languages are organized around "(tri)consonantal roots" that carry all the meaning of a word, whereas the vowel sounds "merely" carry "grammatical information." But this isn't so: all the verbs and nouns are based on *stems* that (like the other parts of speech) include both consonants and vowels; and most grammatical inflections and derivations include consonants as well as vowels. Conversely, it is often claimed that languages like English can't get along with no vowels being written. thrs lk t sy t's lmst mpssbl t rd vwllss nglsh, bt s ths xmpl shs, tht's nt tr. 3thrs lk t sy 3t's 3lmst 3mpssbl t rd vwllss 3nglsh, bt 3s ths 3xmpl shs, tht's nt tr—3nd 3t's 3vn 3sr whn 3ntl vwls 3r 3ndctd (Phncn

Details ──

3.1 Still the standard reference for the development of the West Semitic abjads is Joseph Naveh, *Early History of the Alphabet* (1987). The earliest stages in the development of West Semitic writing are elucidated by Gordon J. Hamilton, *The Origins of the West Semitic Alphabet* (2006); and minute detail, with intriguing hypotheses, is offered by Benjamin Sass, *The Genesis of the Alphabet* (1988), *Studia Alphabetica* (1991), and *The Alphabet at the Turn of the Millennium* (2005).

Table 3.1 The Ugaritic and Phoenician abjads *(read the table from left to right)*

	ạ/ʔ	b	g	ḫ	d	h	w	z	ḥ	ṭ	y	k	š	l	m	ḏ	n	ẓ	s	ʕ	p	ṣ	q	r	t̠/š	ġ	t	ị	ụ	s̀
Ugaritic																															
Phoenician																															

wrds ɜnl strt wth cnsnnts). One learns to read whatever system one's language uses. Moreover, nothing has prevented the Arabic script from being adapted to write scores of languages spoken in the Islamic world, belonging to all sorts of language families, that don't rely on "consonantal roots" for their structure.

3.1.1 Phoenician

No literature has survived that is written in the Phoenician abjad. Most of what we have are brief royal proclamations that were erected to impress a public that could not read them, and various burial inscriptions not unlike our headstones and memorial plaques. In fact the earliest known Phoenician inscription (ca. 975 BCE) is one of the latter, on the sarcophagus of King Aḥirom of Byblos (cf. the biblical Hiram of Tyre), and it was even accompanied by a curse scratched into the tomb shaft about halfway down *(read right to left)*:

It's customary to present Phoenician transliterated into the more familiar Hebrew characters:

לדעת : הן יפד לך : תחת זן

The text transliterated into Roman letters *(read left to right)*:

⟨ldʕt . hn ypd lk . tḥt zn⟩

It probably would have sounded something like this, as reconstructed on the basis of related languages as well as the handful of Punic words badly preserved in *Poenulus*, a play by the early Roman author Plautus (*fl.* 205–184 BCE):

lidaʕt hin yupād lika taḥt zin

'Attention! Behold, grief-shall-come to-you below here!'

That pronunciation involves considerable guesswork *for us*, but it would have been perfectly clear to any literate would-be tomb robbers; indeed, the excavator who discovered it in 1924 noted that the graffito used the same lettershapes as the inscription on the sarcophagus itself, indicating that literacy may have been available to more people than just professional scribes. Reading writing is a comfortable activity for people who speak the language involved and have sufficient practice in it.

There is, though, one sizable corpus of abjadic texts—some 200 years older than the earliest Phoenician—that began to be discovered in 1929 and is still coming to light in continuing excavations at Ugarit (Ras Shamra), on the coast of Syria. They survived because they were impressed on clay like Mesopotamian cuneiform (§§ 6.2, 7.2), and they read from left to right, but the resemblance ends there. From abecedaries, lists of the letters of the abjad, we know that there were 30 letters (Table 3.1). All but two of the consonants of Proto-Semitic (the ancestral language that can be reconstructed from the known Semitic languages) are preserved, 27 of them, and there is a word-divider character, ᐧ.

Along with the ordinary sorts of letters and accounts, several extensive literary texts are known, and they are remarkably like some passages in the closely related Hebrew language found in the Psalms and elsewhere. Even more remarkable, from the point of view of writing, at least, is the fact that there is not just one letter for the glottal stop ʔ, but three— ➤ ⟨å⟩ ⧻ ⟨i̇⟩ ⪨ ⟨u̇⟩. These have been described as syllabic signs, but they are not: they do not include the vowel sounds; each represents the glottal stop when it is followed by, or occasionally when it is preceded by, the respective vowel.

3.1.2 South Arabian

Very little known is the other branch of West Semitic abjads, the scripts of the Arabian Peninsula (Table 3.2). Monumental inscriptions from the southern coastlands, from Oman to Yemen, began to be found early in the nineteenth century. Unlike all other West Semitic abjads, they had a separate letter for each reconstructed Proto-Semitic consonant: 29 in total—and as with Phoenician, they offer no indications of vowels at all. Most of them record royal building projects, in particular the erection of dams; they stretched along very broad walls and often have the interesting property of being written *boustrophedon,* 'as the ox plows', reading from right to left for the first line, from left to right for the next line, and so on—a reasonable approach for inscriptions that could extend for several yards/meters. Four somewhat different languages can be identified, with most of the inscriptions in Sabaean, which would have been the language spoken by the biblical Queen of Sheba (Saba).

Because of the nature of the inscriptions, they contained no first- or second-person forms—neither pronouns nor verb forms. And whether those particular forms have a *t* or a *k* in them is an important indicator for classifying the Semitic languages

Details *(continued)* ————————————————————————————————————

3.1.1 Ugaritic is of wider interest than the other ancient West Semitic languages because its poetic texts are eerily similar to corresponding biblical texts, and Pierre Bordreuil and Dennis Pardee, *A Manual of Ugaritic* (2009), is tailored to that approach. Treatments of many topics are in W. G. E. Watson and N. Wyatt, eds., *Handbook of Ugaritic Studies* (1999).

3.1.2 For South Arabian, see Peter Stein, "Ancient South Arabian" (2011), and for the cursive inscriptions, Peter Stein, *Die Altsüdarabischen Minuskelinschriften* (2010). The first steps

Table 3.2 South Arabian abjads *(read the table from left to right)*

	h	l	ḥ	m	q	w	s²	r	b	t	s¹	k	n	x	s³	p	ʔ	ʕ	ḍ	g	d	ġ	ṭ	z	ḏ	y	t̲	ṣ	ẓ
Sabaean	𐩠	𐩡	𐩢	𐩣	𐩤	𐩥	𐩦	𐩧	𐩨	𐩩	𐩪	𐩫	𐩬	𐩭	𐩯	𐩰	𐩱	𐩲	𐩳	𐩴	𐩵	𐩶	𐩷	𐩸	𐩹	𐩺	𐩻	𐩮	𐩼
Dadanite	𐩠	𐩡	𐩢	𐩣	𐩤	𐩥	𐩦	𐩧	𐩨	𐩩	𐩪	𐩫	𐩬	𐩭	𐩯	𐩰	𐩱	𐩲	𐩳	𐩴	𐩵	𐩶	𐩷	𐩸	𐩹	𐩺	𐩻	𐩮	𐩼

and thus investigating their history. This gap began to be filled in the late 1970s, when ancient "batons" began to come out of illicit excavations in Yemen. These are lengths of wood, mostly cypress branches, resembling lengths of broomstick, up to about a foot long. On them are incised all sorts of texts—personal letters, accounts, everything else that people needed to write to each other—in a cursive variety of the monumental script of the inscriptions. A *cursive* or "running" hand is written with speed and economy of materials in mind (writing surfaces were always expensive!), so corners tend to become rounded off, and letters within a word come to be joined together. The cursive South Arabian texts date from maybe the seventh century BCE to a thousand or more years later; the earliest ones closely resemble the monumental letters, and over the generations of scribes they took on more and more cursive characteristics. These developments can be followed closely, so that even the latest ones can be read with comparative ease. The main problem is in identifying the vocabulary, for which reliance on related languages like the Modern South Arabian languages still spoken in the area, as well as Arabic itself, is necessary.

Arabic, too, was written with a South Arabian script, an extremely cursive version known from tens of thousands of brief inscriptions from northern Arabia. From their location they have been called Old North Arabian, but there doesn't seem to be any reason not to recognize them as the pre-Islamic version of Classical Arabic. Among the varieties are Safaitic, Dadanite, and Hismaic. The alphabetical order was initially discovered from markings on a long stretch of paving-blocks, and subsequently identified in a few North Arabian graffiti.

3.2 Aramaic: Vowel letters

The Semitic language subfamily to which the Phoenician language belongs (it's called Canaanite; Hebrew is its best known member) has a sister language subfamily, Aramaic. The Aramaic languages use a sister abjad—and as early as the earliest known example of Aramaic writing, the Aramaic abjad functioned somewhat differently from the Phoenician. The Aramaic innovation is known by the Latin label *matres lectionis* (it means 'mothers of reading', and the singular is *mater lectionis*; texts

---

Details *(continued)*

toward their decipherment were taken in 1977 by Mahmoud Ghul (d. 1983), but he did not live to fully write up his findings. The most accessible description of North Arabian is M. C. A. Macdonald, "Ancient North Arabian" (2004).

using them are written *plene*, 'full' in Latin). In English it's usually referred to as the use of "vowel letters," though this term can be misleading because the letters continued to be used with their original consonant sounds as well. Here's a brief excerpt from one of the earliest known Aramaic inscriptions, the Tell Fekheriyeh inscription, which probably dates to 866 BCE (middle of line 16 to the first word of line 18, the beginning of a rather long curse section):

מן : ילד : שמי : מן : מאניא \ זי : בת : הדד : מראי :
מראי : הדד : לחמה : ומוה : אל : ילקח : מן \ ידה :

⟨mn . yld . šmy . mn . mʔnyʔ / zy . bt . hdd . mrʔy .
mrʔy . hdd . lḥmh . wmwh . ʔl . ylqḥ . mn / ydh .⟩

man . yalūd . šemî . min . maʔnayyâ . zî . bēt . Hadad . marʔî .
marʔî . Hadad . laḥmeh . wmaweh . ʔal . yelqaḥ . min . yadeh .

'Whoever removes my-name from the-movables of the-temple-of Hadad, my-lord, (may) my-lord Hadad his-bread and-his-water not accept from his-hand.'

In the transcription, circumflex accents mark the vowels indicated by *matres*; at that time, only vowels at the ends of words received *matres*. Even in these very early Phoenician and Aramaic inscriptions, the similarity between D, M, and N and their eventual Greek descendants—and so the Roman letters we still use today—can be discerned.

Over about a millennium and a half, the leading languages of most of ancient Southwest Asia were Aramaic. For the first few centuries, the only inscriptions we have are the ones that were carved in rock, and their script is fairly uniform across their geographic range. From later on, though, thanks to the preservative capacities of the desert climate, we have a surprising number of papyri in the Aramaic language, along with ostraca (ink inscriptions on potsherds, the readily available scratch pads of the day), and we can see varying regional developments in the familiar 22-letter abjad (Table 3.3). Informal, cursive, regional hands sometimes came to be used in durable inscriptions as well.

One of those regional hands is what we know as Hebrew—Square Hebrew, what the rabbinic authorities called "Assyrian script," because its use was probably taken up during the Babylonian Exile far to the east, where the Phoenician-origin Old Hebrew script would have looked quite alien. Another is the scripts of Syriac, which

Details *(continued)* ───────────────────────────────────

3.2 The translation of the Fekheriyeh excerpt is after Edward Lipiński, *Studies in Aramaic Inscriptions and Onomastics II* (1994), 49f.

Table 3.3 The Phoenician, Old Hebrew, and some Aramaic abjads *(read the table from left to right)*

	ʾ	b	g	d	h[a]	w	z	ḥ	ṭ	y	k[a]	l[a]	m[a]	n[a]	s	ʿ[a]	p[a]	ṣ[a]	q	r	š	t
Phoenician	𐤀	𐤁	𐤂	𐤃	𐤄	𐤅	𐤆	𐤇	𐤈	𐤉	𐤊	𐤋	𐤌	𐤍	𐤎	𐤏	𐤐	𐤑	𐤒	𐤓	𐤔	𐤕
Old Hebrew	𐤀	𐤁	𐤂	𐤃	𐤄	𐤅	𐤆	𐤇		𐤉	𐤊	𐤋	𐤌	𐤍	𐤎	𐤏	𐤐	𐤑	𐤒	𐤓	𐤔	𐤕
Epigraphic Aramaic	𐡀	𐡁	𐡂	𐡃	𐡄	𐡅	𐡆	𐡇	𐡈	𐡉	𐡊	𐡋	𐡌	𐡍	𐡎	𐡏	𐡐	𐡑	𐡒	𐡓	𐡔	𐡕
Imperial Aramaic	𐡀	𐡁	𐡂	𐡃	𐡄	𐡅	𐡆	𐡇	𐡈	𐡉	𐡊	𐡋	𐡌	𐡍	𐡎	𐡏	𐡐	𐡑	𐡒	𐡓	𐡔	𐡕
Square Hebrew	א	ב	ג	ד	ה	ו	ז	ח	ט	י	ך כ	ל	ם מ	ן נ	ס	ע	ף פ	ץ צ	ק	ר	ש	ת
Palmyrene	𐡠	𐡡	𐡢	𐡣	𐡤	𐡥	𐡦	𐡧	𐡨	𐡩	𐡪	𐡫	𐡬	𐡭	𐡮	𐡯	𐡰	𐡱	𐡲	𐡳	𐡴	𐡵
East Syriac	ܐ	ܒ	ܓ	ܕ	ܗ	ܘ	ܙ	ܚ	ܛ	ܝ	ܟ	ܠ	ܡ	ܢ	ܣ	ܥ	ܦ	ܨ	ܩ	ܪ	ܫ	ܬ
West Syriac	ܐ	ܒ	ܓ	ܕ	ܗ	ܘ	ܙ	ܚ	ܛ	ܝ	ܟ	ܠ	ܡ	ܢ	ܣ	ܥ	ܦ	ܨ	ܩ	ܪ	ܫ	ܬ
Modern Syriac	ܐ	ܒ	ܓ	ܕ	ܗ	ܘ	ܙ	ܚ	ܛ	ܝ	ܟ	ܠ	ܡ	ܢ	ܣ	ܥ	ܦ	ܨ	ܩ	ܪ	ܫ	ܬ
Mandaic	ࠀ	ࠁ	ࠂ	ࠃ	ࠄ	ࠅ	ࠆ	ࠇ	ࠈ	ࠉ	ࠊ	ࠋ	ࠌ	ࠍ	ࠎ	ࠏ	ࠐ	ࠑ	ࠒ	ࠓ	ࠔ	ࠕ
Nabataean	𐢀	𐢁	𐢂	𐢃	𐢄	𐢅	𐢆	𐢇	𐢈	𐢉	𐢊	𐢋	𐢌	𐢍	𐢎	𐢏	𐢐	𐢑	𐢒	𐢓	𐢔	𐢕
Arabic	ا	ب	ج	د	ه ه	و	ز	ح	ط	ي	ك ك	ل	م	ن	س	ع	ف	ص	ق	ر	ش	ت

[a] The letterform to the left is used at the end of a word.

has been a liturgical and literary language for more than 1500 years—the oldest durable inscriptions are in mosaics in second-century churches. At first glance there isn't much similarity between Hebrew and Syriac writing, but as soon as the first decipherment of a dead script and language was accomplished—in 1754 (see §9.1)—Palmyrene was seen to be intermediate between the two. The Arabic script, too, emerged from the Nabataean form of Aramaic writing during the sixth century CE.

Two Aramaic languages have brought the use of *matres lectionis* about as far as they can go, without actually becoming an alphabet—that step was never taken by an abjad-using language, a good indication that the alphabet isn't the "best" or "ultimate" kind of writing system.

One of them is the language of the Babylonian Talmud, the immense collection of Jewish "oral law" that may be a good reflection of the spoken language of the first centuries CE. Both long and short *a* can, but don't have to, be indicated with א ⟨ʔ⟩: סאבר *sāḇar*, באעו *baʕū*, לאחתיה *laḥteh*; ו ⟨w⟩ indicates both *o* and *u*: שבוחי *šabboḥe*, איזול *ʾezūl*; besides the *e* seen in these examples, י ⟨y⟩ can also indicate *i*: איפשוט *ippəšot*, עבדין *ʕāḇədīn*. At the end of a word only, ה ⟨h⟩ can indicate *e* or *ā*: מפנה *mippəne*, פלגה *palgā*; and *ay* is spelled יי, אי, י, or איי.

The other is Mandaic, the language of a Gnostic sect that was at home in southern Iraq and western Iran and still survives, just barely, in exile communities in the United States and Australia. The earlier sounds [ʔ], [ʕ], and [ħ], represented by ه, ڪ, and ح, are lost, leaving those letters free for other uses. Every *a*, *i*, and *u* is written ه, c ⟨y⟩, and ں ⟨w⟩ respectively (is it significant that these three letters are smaller in stature than the others?)—but ں is also used for *o*; *e* occurs only initially, where it appears as ڪ—but so do all other initial vowels. The suffix *eh* is written with ح. The ligature ںc is the prefix *di-*. Hence the Mandaic sentence:

ﻋﺧﺭﺎﺳﺳ ﺐ ﺪﻣﻪ ﺪﻛﻤﻟ ﺎﺭﻟﺎﺪﻟ ﺎﺭﺪﻗﻪ

⟨npaqteh lqiluma ulpagra saria dihuitbeh⟩

'You have left the corruption and the stinking body in which you dwelt'
—*From a Mandaean funerary ritual*

Details *(continued)* ─────────────────────────────────────

The examples of Jewish Babylonian Aramaic are taken from Elitzur Bar-Asher Siegal, *Introduction to the Grammar of Jewish Babylonian Aramaic* (2013), 39–40. I once suggested that an impetus for the use of vowel letters in Aramaic might have been the frequent inclusion of a seemingly redundant vowel sign after a CV sign in Hurrian cuneiform (§7.2 end), which was used in the region where Aramaic is first attested but before there is evidence for the Aramaic languages (Peter T. Daniels, "Toward a Sociolinguistic Prehistory of Aramaic" [1985]), but Frank Moore Cross and David Noel Freedman, *Early Hebrew Orthography* (1952), show convincingly that vowel letters were first used only at the ends of words. Accordingly, Johannes Friedrich, *Geschichte der Schrift* (1966), 86, proposes that Aramaic *plene* writing might have been suggested by *plene* spellings in Akkadian cuneiform (§7.2) such as 𒆠𒄿 ⟨ki-i⟩ *kî* 'as' and 𒆷𒀀 ⟨la-a⟩ *lâ* 'not'.

3.2.1 Syriac

Now we can return to less exceptional scripts. Here are two passages in the Aramaic language Syriac, the first using the eastern Estrangelo script, the second the western Serto script. These two variants arose because of a theological schism that split the churchmen; and also because the split coincided with Byzantine versus Iranian (and later Arab) rule over the ensuing two communities, so communication between them was difficult.

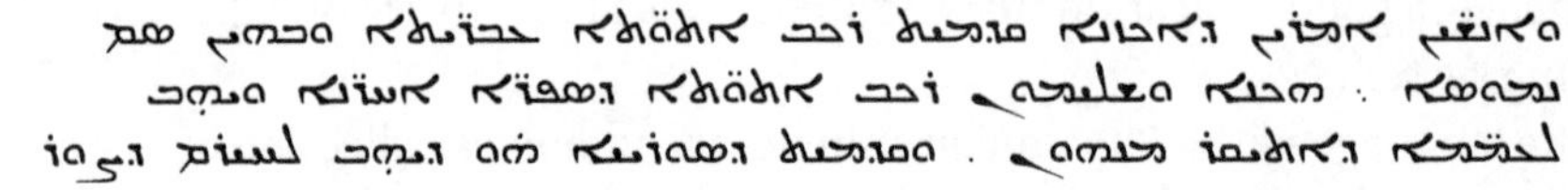

ܐܘܟܝܪ ܐܝܟܕܐ ܕܐܝܟܢܐ ܡܕܡ ܐܚܕ ܐܬܘܬܐ ܕܥܒܪ̈ܝܬܐ ܩܕܡ ܗܘ
ܒܗܝܢ . ܗܟܢܐ ܘܫܠܝܡܘܢ ܐܚܕ ܐܬܘܬܐ ܕܣܦܪ̈ܐ ܐܚܪ̈ܢܐ ܘܝܗܒ
ܠܥܡܡ̈ܐ ܕܐܬܝܩܪܘܢ . ܘܩܕܡܝܬ ܕܣܘܪ̈ܝܝܐ ܗܘ ܕܝܗܒ ܠܚܝܪܡ ܕܨܘܪ

⟨wʔnšyn ʔmryn dʔkznʔ qdmyt rkb ʔtẅtʔ ʕbrïytʔ wbhyn sm
nmwsʔ,hknʔ wšlymwn rkb ʔtẅtʔ dspr̈ʔ ʔḥ̈rnʔ wyhb
lʕm̈mʔ dʔtyqrmnhwn. wqdmyt dswryyʔ hw dyhb lḥyrm dṣwr⟩

*w-nāšîn āmrîn d-aḵznâ qaḏm-āyaṯ rakkeḇ āṯwāṯâ ʕeḇrāyāṯâ wa-ḇ-hên sām
nāmôs-â hāḵannâ wa-šlêmôn rakkeḇ āṯwāṯâ d-seḇrê ḥrānê w-yāḇ
l-ʕammê d-etyaqqar men-hôn w-qaḏm-āyaṯ d-sûryāyâ haw d-yaḇ l-Ḥîrām d-Ṣôr*

'Men say that as (Moses) first devised the Hebrew letters and wrote the law with them, so Solomon devised the letters of other languages and imparted them to the Gentiles in order to be held in honor by them. (He devised) first (the letters of) Syriac, which he gave to Hiram of Tyre.'
       —*From Ishodad of Merv's commentary on Genesis (ninth century)*

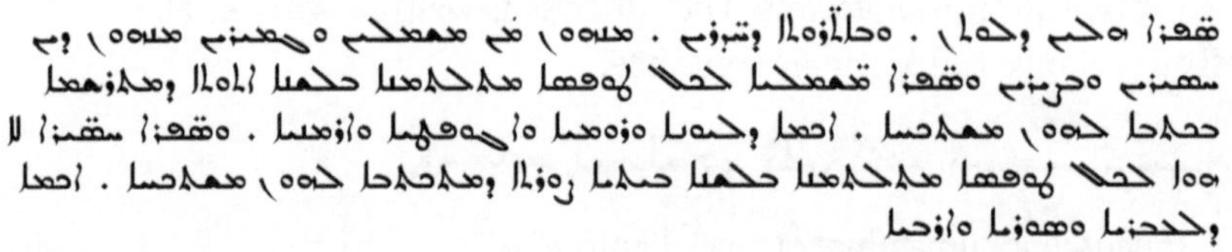

ܣܦܖ̈ܐ ܗܠܝܢ ܕܠܘܬܢ . ܕܒܐܬܪ̈ܘܬܐ ܘܬܒܪܢ . ܡܢܗܘܢ . ܡܢ ܡܫܡܠܝܢ ܘܓܡܝܪܝܢ ܡܢܗܘܢ ܕܝܢ
ܚܣܝܪܝܢ ܘܒܨܝܪܝܢ . ܘܣܦܪ̈ܐ ܡ̈ܫܡܠܝܐ ܠܟܠ ܛܘܦܣܐ ܡܬܠܬܡܢܐ ܒܠܫܢܐ ܐܬܘܬܐ ܕܡܬܪܫܡ̈ܐ
ܒܟܬܒܐ ܠܗܘܢ ܡܫܬܟܚ . ܐܟܡܐ ܕܠܝܘܢܝܐ ܘܪ̈ܘܡܝܐ ܘܐܓܘܦܬܝܐ ܘܐܪܡܢܝܐ . ܘܣܦܖ̈ܐ ܚܣܝܖ̈ܐ ܠܐ
ܗܘܐ ܠܟܠ ܛܘܦܣܐ ܡܬܠܬܡܢܐ ܒܠܫܢܐ ܒܝܬܝܐ ܘܨܘܪܬܐ ܕܡܬܟܬܒܐ ܠܗܘܢ ܡܫܬܟܚ . ܐܟܡܐ
ܘܠܥܒܖ̈ܝܐ ܘܣܘܪ̈ܝܐ ܘܐܪܒܝܐ

⟨šprʔ hlyn dlwtn. dbʔ̈trwtʔ dḥ̇dryn. mnhwn. mn mšmlyn wgmyryn mnhwn dyn
ḥsyryn wbṣyryn. wšprʔ m̈šmlyʔ lkl ṭwpsʔ mtltmnʔ blšnʔ ʔtwtʔ dmtršmʔ
bktbʔ lhwn mštkḥ. ʔkmʔ dlywnyʔ wrwmyʔ wʔgwptyʔ wʔrmnyʔ. wšprʔ ḥṣyrʔ lʔ
hwʔ lkl ṭwpsʔ mtltmnʔ blšnʔ bytyʔ ṣwrtʔ dmtktbʔ lhwn mštkḥ. ʔkmʔ
dlʕbryʔ wswryʔ wʔrbyʔ⟩

*seḇrê hālên da-lwāṯ-an d-ḇ-aṯrawwāṯâ da-ḥḏār-ayn men-hôn man mšamlên wa-ḡmîrîn men-hôn dên
ḥassîrîn wa-ḇṣîrîn w-seḇrê mšamlayyâ l-ḵol ṭûpsâ meṯlaṯmānâ b-leššānâ aṯûṯâ d-meṯrašmâ ba-ḵtāḇâ
l-hôn meštaḵḥâ aḵmâ da-l-yawnāyâ w-rômāyâ w-eguptāyâ w-armānāyâ w-seḇrê ḥassîrê lâ wâ l-ḵol
ṭûpsâ meṯlaṯmānâ b-leššānâ baytāyâ ṣûrtâ d-meṯkaṯbâ l-hôn meštaḵḥâ aḵmâ da-l-ʕeḇrāyâ wa-sûrāyâ
w-arbāyâ*

'As for the scripts (used) by us or our neighbors, some are complete and perfect, but others are incomplete and imperfect. For complete scripts, each distinct sound has its own written letter, as in Greek, Latin, Coptic, and

---

Details *(continued)* ──

3.2.1 The Mandaic and Syriac examples are from my contribution to P. T. Daniels and W. Bright, eds., *The World's Writing Systems* (1996), 512, 502–3.

> Armenian; but incomplete scripts do not have, for each distinct sound, their
> own written form, as in Hebrew, Syriac, and Arabic.'
>
> —*Bar Hebraeus (1225/6–1286), "Book of Rays," tractate 4, chap. 1, sec. 1*

A further development of the Eastern variety, often mistakenly labeled "Nestorian," is the version used for Modern Aramaic languages at least since American missionaries in Urmia in 1852 cast type in it for their Bible translation into a *koine* that could be read in most of the regional varieties.

The first feature of these scripts that we've seen before only in Mandaic is that most of the letters in a word are attached to each other—though some letters don't connect with the letter after them (to the left). And then we notice the dots: even in these bare consonantal texts, they are performing three different functions: one syntactic, one phonological, and one morphological.

From quite early on, several of the West Semitic scripts had used visible "word dividers" between words, but as Aramaic writing tended to become cursive, using joined-up letters, spaces were left between words instead. The dot and a few combinations of two dots were thus freed up to become like what we call punctuation marks, dividing up phrases and clauses.

Over the years, ⟨d⟩ and ⟨r⟩ grew more and more similar, and their shapes finally merged in the earliest Syriac inscriptions. A recourse was soon devised: ܪ is ⟨d⟩, and ܪ is ⟨r⟩. In Serto, the letters ، and ؛ almost disappear into the line when they have a connection, but the dots make sure they're visible and distinguishable: ܝܕܝ ⟨ydy⟩, ܝܪܝ ⟨yry⟩.

Each plural noun is marked by a pair of dots above it, because the consonantal skeletons alone of the singular and plural forms are often indistinguishable: ܣܦܪܐ *sefrâ* 'script', ܣܦܪ̈ܐ *sefrê* 'scripts'. If there is an ⟨r⟩ ܪ/؛ in the word, the dots coalesce with its dot; otherwise it can appear anywhere, even over the tall letters if necessary.

Only ⟨k⟩ and ⟨n⟩ change their shapes greatly at the end of a word. The beginnings of this practice can be seen in the fifth-century Imperial Aramaic script of the papyri from Egypt, which can be almost fully read by those who are familiar with Square Hebrew. It seems to be the result of pausing the pen for a moment before moving on to the next word, so that a downward stroke is slightly prolonged. This has resulted in four of the five Square Hebrew "final forms": ך ⟨k⟩ ם ⟨m⟩ ן ⟨n⟩ ף ⟨p⟩ ץ ⟨ṣ⟩.

3.2.2 Arabic

At first sight the degree of this sort of variance is the biggest difference between Syriac and Arabic script: the Arabic letters seem to vary wildly in their shapes within

Details *(continued)* ───────────────────────────────────────

3.2.2 The resources on Arabic writing are not so extensive as might be expected for the language of a major world civilization; multilingual bibliography, mainly in journal articles and specialist encyclopedias, is gathered in Peter T. Daniels, "The Arabic Writing System" (2013b).

Table 3.4 A portion of the Arabic abjad as found in textbooks

	Isolated	Final	Medial	Initial		Isolated	Final	Medial	Initial
ā	ا	ـا	–	–	*f*	ف	ـف	ـفـ	فـ
b	ب	ـب	ـبـ	بـ	*q*	ق	ـق	ـقـ	قـ
ğ	ج	ـج	ـجـ	جـ	*k*	ك	ـك	ـكـ	كـ
d	د	ـد	–	–	*l*	ل	ـل	ـلـ	لـ
r	ر	ـر	–	–	*m*	م	ـم	ـمـ	مـ
s	س	ـس	ـسـ	سـ	*n*	ن	ـن	ـنـ	نـ
ṣ	ص	ـص	ـصـ	صـ	*h*	ه	ـه	ـهـ	هـ
ṭ	ط	ـط	ـطـ	طـ	w	و	ـو	–	–
ʕ	ع	ـع	ـعـ	عـ	*y*	ي	ـي	ـيـ	يـ

Table 3.5 The Arabic abjad, followed by two supplementary marks *(read table left to right)*

ā	b	t	ṯ	ğ	ḥ	x	d	ḏ	r	z	s	š	ṣ	ḍ	ṭ	ẓ	ʕ	ġ	f	q	k	l	m	n	h	w/ū	y/ī	:	ʔ
ا	بـ	تـ	ثـ	جـ	حـ	خـ	د	ذ	ر	ز	سـ	شـ	صـ	ضـ	طـ	ظـ	عـ	غـ	فـ	قـ	كـ	لـ	مـ	نـ	هـ	و	يـ	ّ	ء

a word—so much so that Arabic textbooks always present the script in a form something like Table 3.4. When presented this way, the script can appear intimidating; the rules for combining the letters into texts may seem overwhelming. But in fact the principles governing the differences in shape of the "four" forms are not difficult, and the principles for joining them are also not daunting.

It therefore makes sense to teach the Arabic script in the form shown in Table 3.5 (only ⟨h⟩ needs special study). These are the shapes known as the "initial" forms, and the "isolated" forms of the letters that don't connect to the left.

Overlooking for the moment the fact that there are six more letters in Arabic than in the ancestral Aramaic abjads, we can see that the Syriac-style use of differentiating dots appears here, too. ⟨d⟩ and ⟨r⟩ had not merged in Nabataean, but ⟨r⟩ ⟨z⟩ had, and also ⟨b⟩ ⟨t⟩ ⟨n⟩, and ⟨g⟩ ⟨ḥ⟩, as well as ⟨f⟩ ⟨q⟩. These are all distinguished with dots: قفحخنتبزر.* The dots don't appear in the earliest, austere, Kufic Qur'ān manuscripts, but they do appear scattered in the earliest surviving secular papyrus (dated to the earliest generation of the Islamic Era, 22 AH = 643 CE), used only where needed but in exactly the positions found in the modern script.

* Before the discovery and decipherment of Nabataean in the mid nineteenth century, this was taken as evidence that the Arabic script derived from the Syriac.

Looking at the letters in the excerpted way shown in Table 3.4 also clarifies the seemingly anomalous order of the letters (compare Table 3.3 with Table 3.5). They are brought together by shape, and they occur in the position of the first letter of each such group—thus ر *r* is in the ز *z* order. The three "glide" letters that have special grammatical functions are taken to the end. It is apparent that Arabic alphabetical order is a rational adaptation of the inherited Semitic order.

What about the six "extra" letters? They reveal something very sophisticated about the first Arabic scribes. Arabic and Nabataean Aramaic are closely related and inherited much vocabulary from Common Semitic. But in Aramaic, some of the more *outré* sounds had merged with more common ones: **ṯ* [θ] (English *th* in *thin*), for example, is [t] in Aramaic but remained [θ] in Arabic, and naturally there were no Aramaic letters for the sounds that continued to exist only in Arabic. Early Arabic scribes naturally wanted to have a way to write their special sounds, and they didn't go the way of the Anglo-Saxon scribes at about the same time (see §2.1.2) by coming up with digraphs; instead they created new letters by dotting existing letters. And how did they choose the letters to base the new letters on? Not, it turns out, by phonetic similarity: the sound closest to [θ] is probably [f], but the θ letter is not an alteration of the *f* letter. In fact, they chose the *etymologically* appropriate letter; *ṯ* is ث, or *t* ت with an extra dot. In parallel, *ḏ* [ð] (English *th* in *this*) ذ is *d* د with an extra dot. So also ⟨x⟩ ⟨ḍ⟩ ⟨ẓ⟩ ⟨ġ⟩ غظضخ. No one has found a really satisfactory explanation for why Nabataean 𐢖 ⟨s⟩ disappeared and the Arabic scribes used Nabataean 𐢝 ⟨š⟩ for س ⟨s⟩ (discarding 𐢖) and dotted it for ش ⟨š⟩.

Now we're ready to look at a brief passage in Arabic. Here's a sentence from the early eighth century (CE) legal scholar al-Shāfiʿi:

ولسان العرب أوسع الألسنة مذهبا وأكثرها ألفاظا

ولا نعلمه يحيط بجميع علمه إنسان غير نبي

⟨wlsān ʾlʕrb ʔwsʕ ʾlʔlsnт mḏhbɴ wʔktrhā ʔlfāẓɴ
wlā nʕlmh yḥīṭ bǧmīʕ ʕlmh ʔnsān ġyr nbyɴ⟩

'For the language of the Arabs is the widest-spread language in extent and most abundant in words;
and we do not know that any man encompasses complete knowledge of it except a prophet.'

The key feature that sets Arabic orthography apart from Syriac and Hebrew orthography is the fact that (with a handful of exceptions) every long vowel must be written, within the line of consonants (ﯜ is و followed by ا).

Details *(continued)* ――――――――――――――――――――――――――――――

The Arabic selection is from Gotthelf Bergsträßer, *Introduction to the Semitic Languages* (1995), 183.

As with Syriac, most of the letters within a word are connected, and likewise a few don't connect on the left with the letters that follow. Compare the singular لسان *lisān^(un)* 'language' with the plural ألسنة *ʔalsinat^(un):** the letter ن ⟨n⟩ stands alone at the end of the word because it follows ا ⟨ā⟩, one of the letters that does not connect with what follows. But (thanks to Arabic morphological patterns), there is no ا in the plural; the ن connects to the preceding ‌س ⟨s⟩, and it reverts to its base shape of a little vertical interruption in the word's penstroke with one dot above it.

The plural ألسنة illustrates two other unusual features of Arabic orthography that originate in its unusual background, the symbol ء *hamza* and the ة *tā marbūṭa* (in its connected form ة). Arabic script was elaborated in the course of recording the utterances of the Prophet and collecting them to form the Qur'ān. The basic consonantal text was recorded by speakers of a variety of Arabic that had lost the glottal stop (with compensatory lengthening of the preceding vowel) and most case-endings, but when it was realized that the vowel sounds needed to be recorded as well, so as to avoid errors in reading and interpretation, the vocalization was carried out by speakers of a more conservative variety that retained those two features (and some others), so they were accounted for, too.

The symbol ء ⟨ʔ⟩ is a small ع ⟨ʕ⟩ (the voiced pharyngeal fricative that is almost unique to Arabic). It is placed on the letter that would otherwise indicate the long vowel that took the place of the glottal stop (*ā*, *ī*, or *ū*). There are several examples in our little text, and they all happen to come at the beginnings of words and all happen to be on ا *ā*—except that in إنسان *ʔinsān^(un)* 'men' it appears *beneath* the ا. This is a cue that the vowel of its syllable is *i* and not *a*, because (see §3.3.3) the symbol for [i] is a little stroke beneath the letter, and the symbol for [a] is a little stroke above the letter.

But not all initial ا's have a *hamza*; in fact, most of them don't—because most initial ا's are the start of the definite article ال *al*, and ال *al* doesn't begin with a "real" glottal stop. It has one when it begins an utterance, simply because (as in German) a word can't start with a vowel, but (unlike in German) the *a* of *al-* gets swallowed up by the vowel that ends the preceding word. A familiar example is in the name *Abdullah* عبد الله *ʕabdu ḷḷāh* 'servant of Allah'. The name we think of as "Abdul" is actually 'Servant-of-the'.†

Another function of ا is to mark the accusative case of a noun that isn't definite, as in مذهبا *maḏhab^(an)*; here it means that the noun is used as an adverb. The innovative variety of Arabic, the one that provided the consonant text, had lost the -n of the indefinite, and then most of the vowels at the ends of words. Those vowels were mostly the noun case endings -u and -i (a was not lost). The final -a was then lengthened, so it was written with ا.

---

* Superscripts in Arabic transcriptions represent endings not recorded in the consonantal script.

† The [l] of the definite article changes, in speech but not in writing, into a duplicate of the following consonant when that consonant is apico-dental (tongue-tip against the front teeth).

The ة *tā marbūṭa* appears because the feminine ending *t*, now at the end of the word, had weakend to *-h*. So in order to mark the *-t* ending, the two dots of ة *t* were added to the ه *h*.

3.2.3 Persian

The technique of dotting letters to produce new letters has made Arabic script a remarkably flexible vehicle for literacy in many languages. As far as we know, the first writing system to augment the Arabic script was the Persian, which added the letters پ *p*, چ *č*, ژ *ž*, and گ *g*, and these are found in most of the Arabic-based writing systems of the Islamic world. A few languages under Western influence have adapted some of the consonant letters to denote vowels, resulting in an alphabet; some languages, especially ones spoken in Africa, use the Arabic-style vowel points but make them obligatory, just as Modern Syriac orthography requires the use of the Eastern Syriac vowel points (§3.3).

We saw in §2.3 that the Greek alphabet developed out of the Phoenician abjad. It is sometimes suggested, though, that an Aramaic script underlies the Greek alphabet. Two reasons are given: First, the names of most of the Greek letters (*alpha*, *beta*, *gamma*, etc.) end in *-a*, and Aramaic nouns often end with the suffix *-a*, which functioned something like a definite article, whereas the Phoenician forms were probably *alp, *bet, *gaml, etc. (Table 11.2). Second, and much more important, Aramaic provided a "model" for letters designating vowels in the *matres lectionis*.

The first argument is easily dismissed. Many of the Phoenician letter names end with two consonants (a consonant cluster), but for the most part word-final clusters aren't possible in Greek, so a vowel sound of some sort was pronounced at the end to make them into plausible Greek words. A similar process is familiar from Spanish, which put a vowel before a word-initial cluster, so that Latin *scola* 'school' became *escuela*.

As for the second argument, we can look at what happened when an Aramaic abjad was adopted or borrowed by another language, a language which is not Semitic, where vowels are supposedly "more important" than in Semitic languages. Persian, a modern relative of Sanskrit, is a good example. It has used Arabic writing since at least the eleventh century, probably earlier. Here's a literary example:

Details *(continued)*

3.2.3 A recent collection on the application of Arabic script to numerous previously unwritten languages is M. Mumin and K. Versteegh, eds., *The Arabic Script in Africa* (2014). The adjustments made to Arabic script when it is adapted to other languages are described by Peter T. Daniels, "The Protean Arabic Abjad" (1997) and "The Type and Spread of Arabic Script" (2014b), though the tables are mangled in the latter. The Persian passage is taken from Alan S. Kaye's contribution to P. T. Daniels and W. Bright, eds., *The World's Writing Systems* (1996), 749.

Table 3.6 East Syriac vowels

î	i	e	ɛ	a	ɔ	ô	oi	û

Table 3.7 West Syriac vowels

i	e	a	ɔ	o–u

خیام اگر ز باده مستی خوشباش \ با ماه رخی اگر نشستی خوشباش

چون عاقبت کار جهان نیستی است \ انگار که نیستی چو هستی خوشباش

xayyām agar ze bāde mastī xošbāš / bā māh roxī agar nešastī xošbāš
čūn ʾāqebate kāre jahān nīstī ʾast / ʾengār ke nīstī čo hastī xošbāš

Khayyam if from wine drunk-you-are happy-be / with moon face-a if sitting-you-are happy-be
since end-of work-of world nonexistence is / suppose that nothing when you-are happy-be

> 'And if the Wine you drink, the Lip you press,
> End in the Nothing all Things end in—Yes—
>   Then fancy while Thou art, Thou art but what
>   Thou shalt be—Nothing—Thou shalt not be less.'

—From the Rubaiyyat of Omar Khayyam, "translated" by Edward Fitzgerald, no. 42

All the long vowels, and some *o*, *u*, and final *e*, are written.

3.3 Vowel (and other) points

Over centuries, languages change while writing systems tend not to—we have already observed this for English (§2.1.2). In writing systems that do not strictly maintain an orthographic tradition, so that for instance *matres lectionis* can proliferate, the writing system can keep up, to an extent, with language change. But there is one important exception: sacred texts must be maintained intact. At some point their linguistic form is solidified, and no matter how much the spoken language changes, the sacred language does not. We met an example where a text was transmitted orally for, possibly, as long as two millennia before the Avestan alphabet was

Details *(continued)* ————————————————————————————

3.3 The classic study of vowel pointing is Shelomo Morag, *The Vocalization Systems of Arabic, Hebrew, and Aramaic* (1961).

devised (Table 2.12). But for the three great abjadic writing systems of the Abrahamic religions— Syriac, Hebrew, and Arabic—the sacred texts were fixed in writing early on in the developments of their respective faiths. However, notating only the consonants and some or all of the long vowels did not suffice to guarantee the accurate recitation of the text from the marks on the visible page. Scholars in Christian, Jewish, and Muslim communities elaborated systems for notating all the vowels, and considerable additional information about the texts as well.

3.3.1 Syriac

The first Semitic abjad for which explicit and specific vowel notation was devised was the Ethiopic (see §5.9). The first one with "points" like those familiar from Hebrew sacred texts was Syriac—and in fact in Syriac they really are further *points* beyond the ones described in §3.2.1: dots above, below, and beside the line of letters. They didn't just appear one day, one for each vowel; their development can be followed in dated manuscripts over the centuries.

Even the earliest dated Syriac manuscript, from 411 CE—which is probably the oldest extant dated codex in any language—sporadically uses a "diacritical point" to distinguish words that are spelled the same but pronounced differently—*homographs*. But this point is not applied arbitrarily: above a letter, it indicates a vowel with a "fuller" sound, meaning more like *a*, or below a letter, it indicates a vowel more like *e*: ܫܐܠ *šaʔal* 'he asked', ܫܐܠ *šaʔel* 'he asks'; ܡܠܟܐ *malkâ* 'king', ܡܠܟܐ *melkâ* 'counsel'. Sometimes three homographs need to be distinguished: ܫܐܠܬ *šaʔalt* 'you (masc. sg.) asked', ܫܐܠܬ *šeʔlet* 'I asked', ܫܐܠܬ *šeʔlat* 'she asked'. And the points could even be transferred to corresponding verb forms where homographs did not exist: ܩܡ *qam* 'he rose', ܩܐܡ *qaʔem* 'he rises'.

Over the next few centuries, these diacritical points became a system for explicitly denoting every vowel, when necessary, as in Table 3.6. Additionally, a dot over a stop consonant marked its plosive pronunciation, a dot below it marked its fricative pronunciation (transliterated with a bar: $\bar{p}\ \underline{t}\ \underline{k}\ \underline{b}\ \underline{d}\ \bar{g}$), which occurs only after a vowel.

In the western, or Byzantine-influenced, area, Greek vowel letters came to be used to denote vowels—at a time that can't really be pinned down because manuscripts using this system are not too common. Unfortunately, though, some of the first Syriac manuscripts that reached Europe were vocalized this way, and it is the Greek vowels that are usually used in elementary Syriac textbooks. They are seen in Table 3.7. They can occur either above or below the line of consonants, wherever they will better fit, and they appear tilted with respect to normal Greek; and this is because of a quirk in the way Syriac was written on the page. To avoid the problem of smeared ink (cf. §11.5.1), the scribes turned the page 90° counterclockwise and

Details (*continued*) ───────────────────────────────────

3.3.1 The evolution and use of pointing in Syriac was thoroughly investigated by J. B. Segal, *The Diacritical Point and Accents in Syriac* (1953).

Table 3.8 Traditional interpretation of Hebrew vowel points

i	.	*ī*	ֹ			*u*	ֻ	*ū*	וּ
e	ֱ	*ē*	ֵ	*ə*	ְ	*o*	ֹ	*ō*	וֹ
		a	ַ	*ā*	ָ	*ɔ*	ָ		
ĕ	ֱ	*ă*	ֲ			*ŏ*	ֳ		

Table 3.9 Linguistic interpretation of Hebrew vowel points

i	.			*u*	וּ
e	ֵ	*ə*	ְ	*o*	ֹ
ɛ	ֶ	*a*	ַ	*ɔ*	ָ
ɛ̆	ֱ	*ă*	ֲ	*ɔ̆*	ֳ

wrote downward. The Greek letters were then written normally, so when the page
was turned back for proper reading, the vowels were askew.

The first lines of the two Syriac samples might look as follows, fully vocalized:

ܘܩܰܬ݁ܶܪ ܐ݇ܡܳܝ ܠܩܰܪ݇ܐܳܙ݁ ܐܝܬ݂ ܕܝܬ݂ ܟܝ݁ܬ݂ܳܢܳܐ ܐܳܗ݁ܳܩ݁ܳܐ ܦܰܪ݁ܚܬ݁ܶܠ ܦ݁ܰܪ݂ܚܡܝ

ܩܰܦ݂ܙܳܐ ܗܶܚܝ ܘܶܟ݂ܳܐ . ܘܓ݂ܶܠܝܳܐܦ݁ܠܳܐ ܘܣܰܪܝ̈ܘ . ܬ݁ܠܘܗܦ ܝܶܦ ܣܩܰܚܠ݁ܝ

The dots between the words in Syriac manuscripts are some of the *accents*, which
act as syntactic punctuation marks. They too underwent considerable elaboration
over the centuries.

3.3.2 Hebrew

There were several schools of Hebrew biblical scholars, known as Masoretes, who
in the third quarter of the seventh century CE standardized the holy text. Probably
influenced by Syriac and possibly by Arabic practice, they came up with several
competing sets of markings added to the traditional consonantal text. Eventually
the one established by the Tiberian Masoretes, centered in Tiberias, in the Galilee,
prevailed. Not many manuscripts using the other systems have survived.

Details *(continued)*

3.3.2 Two recent, accessible books placing the most familiar and most misunderstood writing system of the pre-Classical world in the contexts of society, literacy, and scribal practice are Seth L. Sanders, *The Invention of Hebrew* (2009), and Christopher A. Rollston, *Writing and Literacy in the World of Ancient Israel* (2010), brought down to the present, sensitively describing the social and linguistic conditions of each of the many genres of Hebrew literature,

Most of the marks, usually called points, go beneath the letter for the consonant after which the vowel is pronounced. Some go above or inside the letter. The points for *i/e, u/o*, and sometimes *a* interact with the pre-existing *matres lectionis* in complicated ways.

Interpreting the Masoretic Hebrew pointing is difficult; the Masoretes didn't leave any manuals explaining what they had done. The grammarian David Kimḥi (1160–1235) chose to interpret the pairs of marks as short and long versions of the same vowel. This is the system that has been adopted in most biblical studies, where the exact pronunciation of Classical Hebrew isn't at issue. But note the complication: inside the dashed box in Table 3.8, we see the same symbol used for two different sounds. Can this be right?

As philologists (historical linguists) investigated the closely related Semitic languages—Aramaic, Arabic, Ethiopic, and (later) Akkadian (see §7.2)—they came to realize that what the Masoretes were actually indicating was eight different vowels, any one of which could be either short or long, depending on the surrounding sounds in the word (Table 3.9).

The Hebrew name of the symbol in the middle is שְׁוָה *šəwō*, and that has come into English as the name for the "indistinct" vowel at the end of *sofa*. It's usually spelled ⟨schwa⟩, using the German spelling, but I prefer to write ⟨shwa⟩, which better reflects the source. The shwa symbol is especially puzzling. It appears to serve two different functions (plus a third function of marking vowels as super-short, as seen below the dotted line in the tables): it marks the indistinct or reduced vowel, as in שְׁוָה *šəwō*; but it also marks the absence of any vowel at all, as in פָּעַלְתִּי *pōʕaltī* 'I did'.

Two dots for interpreting consonants are important. A dot inside a letter, *dagesh*, marks a long consonant, and inside one of the stop consonants its absence indicates the fricative pronunciation of the stop, as is found only after a vowel. Hebrew maintained the Proto-Semitic distinction between **s¹*, **s²*, and **s³*, but the Northwest Semitic abjad provided for only two sibilants, שׁ ⟨š⟩ and ס ⟨s⟩. Thanks to the inertia that so often operates in adopting scripts, both /š/ [ʃ] = **s¹* and /ś/ [ɬ] = **s²* were written with ⟨š⟩.* By the time of the Masoretes, Hebrew /ś/ had merged with /s/

---

* An interpretation of **s¹* as [s], **s²* as [ɬ], **s³* as [t͡s], **ṣ* as [t͡s'], and **z* as [d͡z] is due to Alice Faber.

Details *(continued)* ————————————————————————————————

by Lewis Glinert, *The Story of Hebrew* (2017), and more technically by Angel Sáenz-Badillos, *A History of the Hebrew Language* (1993). A full overview of the various Masoretic schools is provided by Aron Dotan, "Masorah" (2007). William Chomsky, *David Kimhi's Hebrew Grammar (Mikhlol)* (1952), translates Kimḥi's text but arranges it according to the structure of a modern grammar.

Alice Faber's series of articles, published in the early 1980s but not synthesized by the author, are summarized by Peter T. Daniels, "Some Semitic Phonological Considerations on the Sibilants of the Greek Alphabet" (1999), and her findings are fully assimilated by John Huehnergard, "Afroasiatic" (2004) (which despite the title assigned by the editor is an overview of Common Semitic grammar).

= *s³, and the two uses of שׁ are marked as שׁ /š/ and שׂ /ś/ = ס /s/ [s]. The biblical passage Judges 12:6 has occasioned a great deal of discussion of how the three sibilants were actually pronounced. Here it is with a bit of context (displaying, incidentally, the 1611 orthography of the King James Version):

> ⁵ And the Gileadites tooke the paſſages of Iordan before the Ephraimites : and it was ſo that when thoſe Ephraimites which were eſcaped ſaide, Let me go ouer, that the men of Gilead ſaid vnto him, Art thou an Ephraimite? If he ſaid, Nay : ⁶ then ſaid they vnto him ,

אֱמָר־נָא שִׁבֹּלֶת וַיֹּאמֶר סִבֹּלֶת

(ʔᵉmɔr-nō šibbṓleṯ wayyṓmer sibbṓleṯ)

Say-now, Shibboleth : and-he ſaid, Sibboleth :

> for hee could not frame to pronounce it right. Then they tooke him, and ſlewe him at the paſſages of Iordan :

Should we take this אמר־נא שבלת ויאמר סבלת at face value and say that Ephraimites said [s] instead of [ʃ]? Or could it be that they said [ʃ] instead of [ɬ], but the scribe had used up שׁ in writing [ɬ] and was stuck with ס for writing [ʃ]?

3.3.3 Arabic

Now, no one has trouble reading Arabic written with the assortment of devices outlined in §3.2.2, but it soon became clear that disputes could arise over the pronunciation of specific words in the Qur'ān, and those disputes could have doctrinal implications. For instance, sura (i.e., chapter) 9 verse 3: أن الله بريء من المشركين ورسوله should be read *'anna ḷḷāha barīʔun min al-mušrikīna wa-rasūluhu* 'that God has nothing to do with the polytheists, and neither does His prophet' (nominative case), but a non-native speaker could read by mistake the blasphemous *wa-rasūlihi* '... nor with His prophet' (genitive case). It therefore became necessary to devise a manner of fixing *all* features of the text, including all the short vowels. After some experimentation, a system was decided on that simply uses ˊ for *a*, ˎ for *i*, and ˈ for *u*—each symbol is placed above or below the consonant its vowel follows, so that the sacrosanct linear skeleton is not interfered with: رَسُولُهٗ *rasūluhu,* رَسُولِهٖ **rasūlihi.* The indefinite endings are doublings of the plain vowels: ˝ *an,* ˌ *in,* ˵ *un;* ˚ marks a consonant followed by no vowel, and ˜ a lengthened ("doubled") ˜ consonant. A few words that were not written with ا do contain a long *ā,* and for them there's a special vowel mark, ˌ. These last two commonly appear in otherwise unvocalized text in الله *aḷḷāh*

Details *(continued)* ───

3.3.3 The example of potential misreading of a Qur'anic passage is from Kees Versteegh, *The Arabic Language* (1997), 49, 50–51.

'Allah'. There are also two special variants of *hamza*, one, آ, for when there's no glottal stop at the beginning of a word; the other, آ, for when a long *ā* follows a glottal stop; both appear in ٱلْقُرْآن *al-qurʔān* 'the Qur'ān'. We can now display our text as it would probably never appear (not being a sacred or poetic text), fully vocalized:

وَلِسَانُ ٱلْعَرَبِ أَوْسَعُ ٱلْأَلْسِنَةِ مَذْهَباً وَأَكْثَرُهَا ٱلْفَاظاً

وَلَا نَعْلَمُهُ يُحِيطُ بِجَمِيعِ عِلْمِهِ إِنْسَانٌ غَيْرُ نَبِي

walisānu 'lʕarabi ʔawsaʕu 'lʔalsinati maḏhaban waʔakṯaruhā 'lfāẓan
walā naʕlamuhu yuḥīṭu biǧamīʕi ʕilmihi ʔinsānun ġayru nabīyin

For-the-language-of the-Arabs (is) widespreadest-of the-languages extent-
    wise and-mostest-its-of the-words
and-not we-know-it encompasses in-full knowledge-its a-man except
    a-prophet

3.3.4 N'ko

A unique postscript to the adaptation of Arabic script to other languages is found in the N'ko script, devised in 1949 by the Guinean Souleymane Kanté. Stung by an insult that his Maninka language was "inferior" because it had no writing system, he resolved to provide a written form for it. After experimenting with both French-based (Roman) and Arabic solutions, he chose to create a distinctive script, called *N'ko*, 'I say'. Like Arabic, it is written from right to left with all the letters in a word connected at the base; but unlike Arabic, the letters represent both consonants and vowels, so that it is a true alphabet: ߒߞߏ (N'ko). Arabic-like, it also uses additional marks above the line of letters—to indicate vowel length, nasalization, and tone. He taught the script at first in his temporary location in Côte d'Ivoire and then at home in Guinea. Over the ensuing decades it came to be used for several related Manding languages in those two countries and Mali as well, with a potential of serving tens of millions of speakers.

3.4 Iranian

In the ancient Iranian empires, a nearly unique and surprisingly persistent practice of writing Iranian languages with Aramaic script developed as the chancery language changed from Aramaic to varieties of Iranian but the records remained readable (Table 3.10).

Details (*continued*) ————————————————————————————

3.3.4 Information on N'ko is provided by Christopher Wyrod, "A Social Orthography of Identity" (2008).

Table 3.10 Some Middle Iranian scripts

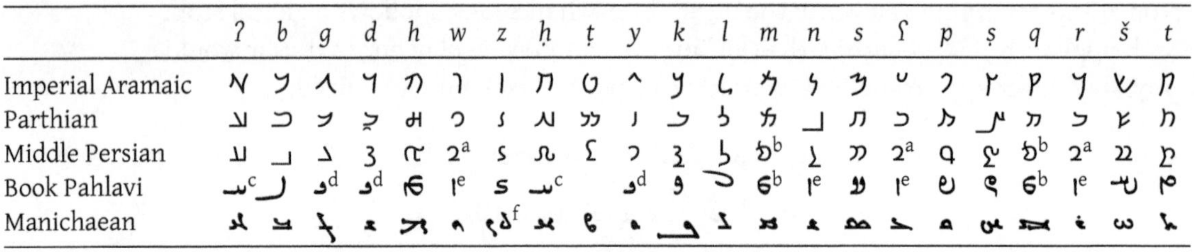
ʔ b g d h w z ḥ ṭ y k l m n s ʕ p ṣ q r š t
Imperial Aramaic
Parthian
Middle Persian
Book Pahlavi
Manichaean

[a] *W*, *ʕ*, and *r* have merged in this shape. [b] *M* and *q* have merged in this shape. [c] *ʔ* and *ḥ* have merged in this shape.
[d] *G*, *d*, and *y* have merged in this shape. [e] *W*, *n*, *ʕ*, and *r* have merged in this shape. [f] Additional letter *ǰ*.

The Achaemenid Empire was succeeded by the short-lived empire of Alexander, which was in turn broken up by his generals. In the east, Seleucus established the Seleucid empire, where Aramaic continued as the chancery language, though Greek was used as well. In 247 BCE, the area was taken over by the Iranian Arsacid (or Parthian) dynasty. It was succeeded in 224 CE by the Sassanian Empire, which also endured for more than 400 years.

Commentaries on the Avesta (§2.4) are composed in Pahlavi, a Western Iranian language that proved to be the end point of several centuries of evolution of Middle Iranian languages—whose script involves a fascinating complication that must be put off to §7.3. East Iranian languages, though, seem to have first been recorded by scribes transmitting the writings of Mani, the third-century CE founder of the Manichaean religion, who wrote at first in Syriac and then, using essentially the same script, a faulty variety of Iranian. The dean of American Iranists, Richard N. Frye (1920–2014), hints that awareness of Mani's voluminous writings, which were translated into many literary languages, might have sparked both the recording of the Avesta (4th c. CE?) and the compilation of the Babylonian Talmud (5th c.).

Manichaean script was in turn adapted for yet another Iranian language, Sogdian. Most of the East Iranian languages and scripts, which were used in early centuries of the Common Era, came to light only in the twentieth century, and therein lies a tale. The first modern scholar of writing, Isaac Taylor, was dissatisfied with the general

Details *(continued)*

3.4 An account of post-Achaemenid, pre-Islamic Iranian history—a much overlooked field of study—that is concise, comprehensive, and comprehensible is Richard N. Frye, "The Sassanians" (2005). For more detail see Ehsan Yarshater, "Introduction" (1983), and the massive volume it introduces. Desmond Durkin-Meisterernst, "Erfand Mani die manichäischen Schrift?" (2000), 165–67, suggests that Mani's native language was Aramaic because an interpreter accompanied him at his audience with the king; but he himself offers other explanations for the interpreter's presence.

The postulation of a Manichaean intermediary in the transmission of the abjad to the Far East is found in Isaac Taylor, *The Alphabet* (1883), 1: 310–11 (though further evidence showed that Sogdian derived from a secular Iranian abjad), and the significance of Taylor's work is discussed by Peter T. Daniels, "The Study of Writing in the Twentieth Century" (2002), 88–91.

view that a distinctive Sogdian script, Uyghur, and Mongolian writing (see §3.5) went back ultimately to some variety of Syriac. He suggested instead a Manichaean intermediary, and this was a remarkable suggestion—since no Manichaean materials would be discovered until some twenty years after Taylor's book was published!

3.5 Inner Asia

The latest adaptation of an Iranian abjad for an Iranian language, before Islam brought Arabic writing to Classical Persian, was the Sogdian, for the language of the sometime province of Sogdiana, east of the Caspian Sea and north of the Oxus River. Sogdian in turn provided the model for the script of the Turkic language Uyghur, which was used in the Uyghur Empire of the eighth-ninth centuries, in the present-day Chinese Autonomous Region of Xinjiang (Sinkiang) (Table 3.11).

Perhaps it was entirely due to influence from Chinese writing, which was done in vertical columns arranged right to left, or perhaps it was a reflection of the Syriac procedure of rotating the page to write downward (§3.3), but Uyghur is both written and read vertically; since the columns are read left to right, the Syriac(-Manichaean-Sogdian) influence may be more salient than the Chinese. The Uyghur abjad was used in turn for writing the language of the Mongol Empire from its very beginning. In 1208, one account has it, Genghis Khan ordered a captured Uyghur scribe, Tatar-Tonga, to improve the script for Mongolian. With subsequent emendations over the centuries, the Mongolian abjad continued in service almost to the present in Mongolia—it was supplanted by a Cyrillic alphabet during the period of Soviet influence, but attempts to revive it after 1991 have been unsuccessful—and to the present time in China's Inner Mongolia region. These two words read *Moŋγol bičig* or (as used in Mongolia proper) Монгол бичиг, 'Mongol script'. The Mongolian abjad was adapted in turn for the Manchu language, by Erdeni Bakshi on the order of Emperor Nurhachi, in 1499. A reform in 1632 resulted in an alphabet (Table 3.12). The Manchu language proper and its script did not survive into the twentieth century in Manchuria, though the Xibe language of the Manchu family (in China) still uses the script.

Details *(continued)* ───

3.5 A classic work on writing system transfer is by an Iranist investigating a Turkic language, Nicholas Sims-Williams, "The Sogdian Sound-system and the Origin of the Uyghur Script" (1981). If only other transfers were, or could be, studied so carefully! The authoritative account of Mongolian writing—covering almost a dozen scripts used over a millennium—is György Kara, *Books of the Mongolian Nomads* (2005), but curiously it doesn't include tables of the letters. A guide going into such complications of Mongolian script as ambiguous consonant letters and vowel harmony can be found at www.cjvlang.com/Writing/writmongol/mongolalpha.html.

Table 3.11 The Sogdian and Uyghur abjads[a]

Sogdian				Uyghur			
(initial)	*(medial)*	*(final)*		*(initial)*	*(medial)*	*(final)*	
			a e				a e
			w				w f
			o ö u ü				o ö u ü
			z ž				z
			t				t
			i y				i y
			i				i
			k g				k g
			g γ q x				g x
			ð				d t
			m				m
			n				n
			s				s
			p b				p b
			č				č ǧ
			r				r
			l				l
			š				š
			v				?
			h				?

[a] After David Diringer, *The Alphabet* (1968), fig. 16.7.
Left to right, initial, medial, and final forms.

Table 3.12 The Uyghur, Mongolian, and Manchu abjads[a]

Uyghur		Mongolian[b]			Manchu	
a e				a		a
				e		e
				i		i
i y o						y
				y		j
						zh[f]
				o u		o
						u
				öü		öü
l				l		l
m				m		m
n				n		n
p b				b		b
						p
				qc		γ
g x				γc		q
						χ
k g				k g[d]		k
						g
						x
č ǧ				(č)[e]		(č)[e]
				č		č
						(č)
r				r		r
				t d		t d
d t				(t d)		d[c]
				t d		t[c]
				t d		d[d]
w f				v w		f
						w f
š				s		s
						š
						s(i)[f]
z				š		z[f]
						c[f]

[a] After David Diringer, *The Alphabet* (1968), fig. 16.9a.
Transliterations provided by Mikael A. Thompson.
[b] *Left group*, rotated 90° counterclockwise for comparison.
[c] In back-vowel words.
[d] In front-vowel words.
[e] In foreign words, especially Tibetan.
[f] In Chinese words.

4 Moras and *Kana*

Come, search the marshes for a friendly bed

In contrast to the syllables and segments that we have looked at so far, a stretch of speech that has been recognized only fairly recently is the *mora*. One (not all that helpful) definition of mora, found in an innovative work on Japanese phonology, is "something of which a long syllable consists of two and a short syllable consists of one." A mora can be a short vowel alone or preceded by a consonant; or length added to a vowel or consonant; or the final consonant of a syllable. The mora isn't a particularly useful concept in relation to English with its complicated syllables and its association of vowel length with quality and consonant length with morpheme boundaries: *bookkeeping* has a long [k:] because it is a compound of *book* and *keeping*.

4.1 Japanese

The word *mora* originally referred to long vowels in Classical Greek, especially in analyzing poetic meter. It was introduced into modern linguistics as useful in describing accent patterns in several Native American languages, and subsequently the phonology of Japanese.

Curiously, the Japanese writing system was not mentioned at all in the work that included the "definition," but it incorporates the purest moraic notation that has been devised anywhere. Japanese writing is so complicated—it is based in the borrowing of Chinese characters—that it is best to describe it in two different places; for the rest of the story, see §7.1.

Both the word order and the morphological type of Japanese differ considerably from those of Chinese (§6.1), and just using one character per morpheme did not work well for recording the Japanese language. Some sort of phonological notation proved necessary, and quite early in the history of writing Japanese, certain characters came to be used for their phonetic values; they are called *kana*. They stand alongside and supplement characters (*kanji*). This is not to say, though, that Japanese *has* to continue to use Chinese script; it *could* have used the purely phonetic writing, as indeed did happen early in the eleventh century. Women were barred from most education, kept from studying classical literature, but they did learn to write, and

Details ──

4 The definition of *mora* is from James D. McCawley, *The Phonological Component of a Grammar of Japanese* (1968), 58 n. 39. For references on Japanese, see Chapter 7.

Table 4.1 The Japanese moraic characters

	hiragana					katakana				
	-a	-i	-u	-e	-o	-a	-i	-u	-e	-o
A. The (C)V characters										
Ø-	あ	い	う	え	お	Ø-	ア	イ	ウ	エ	オ
k-	か	き	く	け	こ	k-	カ	キ	ク	ケ	コ
s-	さ	し	す	せ	そ	s-	サ	シ	ス	セ	ソ
t-	た	ち	つ	て	と	t-	タ	チ	ツ	テ	ト
n-	な	に	ぬ	ね	の	n-	ナ	ニ	ヌ	ネ	ノ
h-	は	ひ	ふ	へ	ほ	h-	ハ	ヒ	フ	ヘ	ホ
m-	ま	み	む	め	も	m-	マ	ミ	ム	メ	モ
y-	や		ゆ		よ	y-	ヤ		ユ		ヨ
r-	ら	り	る	れ	り	r-	ラ	リ	ル	レ	ロ
w-	わ				を	w-	ワ				ヲ

B. The syllable-final characters

-n ん		:(C) っ			-n ン		:(C) ッ		
(V): あ	い	う	え	お	(V): —				

C. Some characters with diacritics

	-a	-i	-u	-e	-o		-a	-i	-u	-e	-o
g-	が	ぎ	ぐ	げ	ご	g-	ガ	ギ	グ	ゲ	ゴ
z-	ざ	じ	ず	ぜ	ぞ	z-	ザ	ジ	ズ	ゼ	ゾ
p-	ぱ	ぴ	ぷ	ぺ	ぽ	p-	パ	ピ	プ	ペ	ポ
b-	ば	び	ぶ	べ	ぼ	b-	バ	ビ	ブ	ベ	ボ
⋮						⋮					

D. Some characters for moras with glides

ky-	きゃ		きゅ		きょ	ky-	キャ		キュ		キョ
gy-	ぎゃ		ぎゅ		ぎょ	gy-	ギャ		ギュ		ギョ
ty-	ちゃ		ちゅ		ちょ	ty-	チャ		チュ		チョ
⋮						⋮					

the classic *Tale of Genji* by Lady Murasaki Shikibu is written entirely without the use of characters.

Old Japanese had a very simple syllable structure, and only CV signs were at first needed. Modern Japanese is slightly more complicated, and the *mora* became the stretch of speech that was symbolized. There are two sets of *kana*, the *hiragana* and the *katakana*, and they serve different functions in the Japanese writing system. The way they represent the sounds of the language, though, is all but identical. *Katakana* function rather like English italics, used for emphasis and for foreign (borrowed) words. *Hiragana* are the symbols for writing the inflections added to roots written with *kanji*, or for *kanji*-less texts, such as *Tale of Genji* or modern books for very young readers.

The simplest mora is a single vowel, or a vowel preceded by a consonant. Each possible (C)V mora has one *kana* in each set (Table 4.1A).

Over the history of Japanese, it became necessary to write a final nasal consonant or nasalization of the preceding vowel, as in *shimbun* 'newspaper'. Long vowels developed, and also doubled consonants. Each of these—nasalization, vowel length, and consonant length—contributes a mora to its syllable. The final nasal mora has a *kana* of its own (linguists transliterate it with -N when necessary), but doubling of any consonant is marked with a diacritic placed *before* the CV character; and this diacritic is a small version of the *kana* for *tu* [tsu]. (It is transliterated -Q.) Long vowels, though, are marked in different ways in *hiragana* and *katakana*. In *hiragana*, the character for the corresponding plain vowel appears after the CV character, but in *katakana*, a diacritic—a long-mark—is placed after the CV character (Table 4.1B).

Another development in Japanese phonology was distinctive voiced consonants. They no longer have *kana* of their own (it is not clear why), but are marked by a two-stroke diacritic (like an umlaut) in the upper right corner. Because early /p/ evolved into /h/, modern *p-* is shown with the *h-* series using a circle diacritic in the same corner (Table 4.1C).

And, thanks originally to some of the vocabulary borrowed early on from Chinese, Japanese also has initial consonants with palatal glides (the *y*-sound). They too don't have *kana* of their own but are written with the *kana* for the consonant-followed-by-*i* plus the *kana* for *y*-plus-the-desired-vowel—again, in miniature—but they do not count as two moras (Table 4.1D).

Here are examples containing all these features of Japanese *kana* writing:

	Nippon 'Japan'	*Hattori*	*Hokkaidō*	*Kyōto*
	⟨ni-Q-po-N⟩	⟨ha-Q-to-ri⟩	⟨ho-Q-ka-i-do-u*/L⟩	⟨ki-yo-u*/L-to⟩
Hi.	にっぽん	はっとり	ほっかいどう	きょうと
Ka.	ニッポン	ハットリ	ホッカイドー	キョート

Japanese continues to assimilate loanwords from foreign languages, and sometimes they include unfamiliar sounds. Similar devices have been pressed into service to render them, as in *sherī* 'sherry' シェリー ⟨si-ₑ-ri-L⟩, *jerī* 'jelly' ジェリー ⟨zi-ₑ-ri-L⟩—using only *katakana* because these are borrowed words.

The various *kana* glyphs do not much resemble the Chinese characters they ultimately derive from. In one case, the two sets use the same shape: *he* へ = へ, from 部 *bù* (recall that Jpn. ⟨h⟩ < **b*). About two thirds of the *kana* pairs represent different simplifications of the same character, and about one third of the *kana* have different origins for the corresponding *hiragana* and *katakana* (Table 4.2).

---

* A few ō's are spelled with ⟨u⟩ instead of ⟨o⟩.

Table 4.2 The origins of some of the *kana*

Type of simplification		hiragana	katakana
		Chinese character(s)	
Simplifications of different parts of the same character	hi	ひ 比 *pí*	ヒ
	ni	に 仁 *rén*	ニ
Simplifications of the whole character	wa	わ 和 *hé*	ワ
	mo	も 毛 *máo*	モ
Simplifications of the same part of a character	ya	や 也 *yě*	ヤ
	to	と 止 *zhǐ*	ト
The two *kana* originate from different characters	a	あ 安 *ān*	ア 阿 *ā*
	mi	み 美 *měi*	ミ 三 *sān*

4.2 Arabic (continued)

Complicated as the discussions of Arabic in §§ 3.2.2 and 3.3.3 were, a recent approach to the theory of writing systems, taking the Japanese system as a model, suggests that virtually all "syllabaries" should actually be considered to write "moras." This is extreme, but Arabic writing, for all its similarity to Syriac writing, can be fruitfully analyzed when it is considered moraically; linguists must note that these are not the moras of recent phonological theory, where only vowels and final consonants are accorded moraic status.

A vocalized Arabic text looks as though it could be considered strictly alphabetic, in that each vowel and each consonant has its own symbol. The vowel and consonant

Details *(continued)* ───────────────────────────────────────

4.2 The "moraography" theory has never been published; it is usually cited from an unpublished talk by William J. Poser, "The Structural Typology of Phonological Writing" (1992), though handouts from prior and subsequent presentations of the talk have been preserved. A similar approach is taken by Robert R. Ratcliffe, "What Do 'Phonemic' Writing Systems Represent?" (2001), and by Amalia E. Gnanadesikan, "Maldivian Thaana" (2012) (see n. ‡ on p. 149). Peter T. Daniels, "Moraic Writing Systems versus Syllabic Writing Systems" (in press c), discusses the question in detail.

symbols are different in kind, for the most part; but so are the vowel and consonant symbols of Korean (§8.1), and we don't hesitate to call it an alphabet. But what about the unvocalized text? We might recognize that historically, it's an abjad, similar in principle to Hebrew or Syriac orthography, but different in obligatorily recording all long vowels, not just those that are of morphological import or that might help with a potentially ambiguous form. Now let's align the unvocalized text used earlier with a transcription done a bit differently:

ولسان العرب أوسع الألسنة مذهبا وأكثرها الفاظا

ولا نعلمه يحيط بجميع علمه إنسان غير نبيّ

wa·li·sa·a·nu ˀl·ʕa·ra·bi ʔaw·sa·ʕu ˀl·ʔa·l·si·na·ti ma·ḏ·ha·ba·n wa·ʔa·k·ṭa·ru·ha·a ˀl·fa·a·ẓa·n
wa·la·a na·ʕ·la·mu·hu yu·ḥi·i·ṭu bi·ǧa·mi·i·ʕi ʕi·l·mi·hi ʔi·n·sa·a·nu^n ǧa·y·ru na·bi·y·yi^n

You can see that for each group of letters set off by dots or spaces in the transcription, there is one letter/symbol in the Arabic text, with a couple of minor exceptions. But where have we seen this sort of letter-group before? They correspond all but exactly with the moras notated in Japanese *kana* writing. The exceptions are the elided \ of the definite article, which doesn't represent a spoken sound, and the indefinite *n*, which is only written when a text is fully vocalized. Unvocalized Arabic script, therefore—especially when the ˝ long consonant mark is included—could well be regarded as moraographic.

5 Clusters and Abugidas

So far, we've seen examples of scripts that passed from place to place, from people to people, more or less by accident or by political or religious impulse. But now we come to a part of the world where grammatical study of texts thrived *before* those texts were written down: India. Scholars of the Indian grammatical tradition tell us that there is no evidence that such masters as Pāṇini and his predecessors and successors were familiar with any writing system (or if they were, it had no effect on their work). There's considerable disagreement as to when Pāṇini and his ilk lived, but the latest era suggested is earlier than the earliest evidence for writing in India. It seems likely that their work had some effect on those who adapted writing to Indic languages.

Note: adapted, not adopted. In Chapter 3 we saw script after script marching across Asia, from chancery to chancery, changing very little in essence for some 3,000 years. But from the very beginning, Indic writing was different. Little is known of Achaemenid activities in the northeast corner of their empire, but in 500 BCE, the satrapies of (from north to south) Sogdiana, Bactria, Gandhara, and India constituted the eastern frontier of Darius the Great's empire, from modern-day southern Kazakhstan down to Pakistan. Administrative records were kept in Aramaic, so

Details

5 The Indic family of scripts hasn't been the subject of a book-length treatment; the books on it either deal with only the early stages of the family, or consider the scripts of only Indic or only Dravidian languages. A concise but comprehensive overview of South and Southeast Asian scripts is in R. F. Hosking and G. M. Meredith-Owens, eds., *A Handbook of Asian Scripts* (1966), 27–41. An attempt at an overview has been made in Peter T. Daniels, "Indic Writing: History Typology Study" (submitted). The fullest, albeit still brief, treatment is in a French handbook, Jean Filliozat, "Paléographie" (1953). Two linguistic collections are available: P. Bhaskararao, ed., *International Symposium on Indic Scripts Past and Future: Working Papers* (2003), and P. G. Patel, P. Pandey, and D. Rajgor, eds., *The Indic Scripts: Palaeographic and Linguistic Perspectives* (2007). An immense chart covering the Indic scripts of South and Southeast Asia was compiled nearly a century and a half ago and was recently made available in English: K. F. Holle, "Table of Old and New Indic Alphabets" (1999). The epigraphy and paleography of the earlier scripts are covered by Georg Bühler, *On the Origin of the Indian Brāhma Alphabet* (1898) and *Indian Paleography* (1904); Ahmad Hasan Dani, *Indian Palaeography* (1986); and Richard G. Salomon, *Indian Epigraphy* (1998). Salomon deals with all aspects of Indo-Aryan inscriptions (but not manuscripts), but explicitly does not go into detail on the history of the shapes of the letters, for which Bühler's and Dani's treatments remain reliable (though Bühler's account of the history of the script has to be updated).

the Aramaic abjad with *matres lectionis* must have reached the banks of the Indus and even a little beyond. The climate has not been conducive to preservation of records from that time in that place, but recently, a precious trove of chancery documents probably from Balkh, Afghanistan—ancient Bactra, the capital of the satrapy of Bactria—has been published. These items date to the time of Alexander and a few years before—roughly the third quarter of the fourth century BCE. We can now see that the specific forms of letters that reached the Subcontinent were essentially indistinguishable from the forms current in Egypt and Mesopotamia a few decades earlier (Table 3.3, fourth row).

Most of the hundreds of languages of India belong to three families: the Indic, the family within Indo-European that includes Sanskrit;* the Dravidian, in the south of the peninsula, with the four literary languages Kannada, Malayalam, Tamil, and Telugu; and the Munda, which is related to many languages of Southeast Asia and with them constitutes the Austroasiatic family. The Munda languages are "tribal." Some are written with Oriya script, a few have developed alphabets of their own.

5.1 Kharoṣṭhi

It has long been clear that the earliest script for an Indic language was built upon an Aramaic framework. This earliest script is called Kharoṣṭhi, and it was used for Gandhara Prakrit. It didn't last long in its homeland, but continued to be used on manuscripts, for instance written on birchbark, along the Silk Road to the north and east, into the first centuries CE. Prakrits were the colloquial languages of early India, as opposed to the sacred, unwritten language Sanskrit, which was the topic of the Pāṇinian grammars. What is clear now, from the Bactra documents, is that the table drawn up by Georg Bühler more than a century ago remains valid (Table 5.1). The earliest Kharoṣṭhi materials are inscribed on rock, but it's now a safe bet that any Aramaic inscriptional models available to the Indians were as similar to the inscriptions we know from western Asia as the handwritten documents from Egypt are to those from Bactra; moreover, Kharoṣṭhi reads from right to left. The *differences* between the Aramaic and Kharoṣṭhi letterforms suggest that several generations of scribes, at least, have intervened between the adaptation of Kharoṣṭhi and its earliest surviving examples.

Those earliest known Kharoṣṭhi documents are inscriptions of Aśoka from the middle of the third century BCE from the far northwest of India. But a similar text

---

* I prefer "Indic" for the language family also called "Indo-Aryan," because Indic and Iranian together constitute the Indo-Iranian branch of Indo-European.

Details *(continued)* ————————————————————————

5.1 Recently discovered Gandhari documents in Kharoṣṭhi have been the province of Salomon and his colleagues; the general articles by Richard G. Salomon, "Gāndhārī and the Other Indo-

Table 5.1 Apparent derivation of Kharoṣṭhī from Aramaic

Aramaic		Kharoṣṭhī					
		Inscriptions	Papyri	Borrowed Letters	Derivatives		
I–II		I	II	III	IV	III	IV
ʔ	1					a	i u e o
b	2					ba	bha$^{×2}$
g	3					ga	gha
d	4					da	dha ḍa ḍha
h	5					ha	
w	6					va	
z	7					ja	jha
ḥ	8					śa	
y	9					ya	
k	10					ka	
l	11					la	
m	12					ma	
n	13					na	ṇa ña$^{×2}$
s	14					sa	
p	15					pa	pha
ṣ	16					ca	cha
q	17					kha	
r	18					ra	
š	19					ṣa	
t	20					ta	ṭa tha ṭha$^{×2}$

Georg Bühler (1898), pl. II   after Hans Jensen (1969), fig. 339

Table 5.2 Some Kharoṣṭhī abugida characters

	-a	-e	-i	-o	-u
–					
k-					
g-					
n-					
m-					
ś-					

was found—in Aramaic—to the *east* of Gandhara, at Taxila. Thus by the time the Greek alphabetical model became available, the Aramaic-based *abugidic* script was already in place. What makes Indic writing so different from its predecessors? What is an abugida?*

An abugida is a writing system in which each basic character represents a consonant *and the "unmarked" vowel that follows it.* "Unmarked" is a term in linguistics for the most common variety of something—the variety that is so common that it doesn't need to be specially *marked* in the language. Thus in English, the singular of a noun is unmarked but its plural is marked: most plurals add an *s* to the singular, and on the whole plurals occur less commonly in speech than singulars. In most of the world's languages, including the ancient languages of India, the most common— least marked or most unmarked—vowel is /a/.

So in Kharoṣṭhi (Table 5.2), each basic character represents a single consonant followed by *a*. The other four vowels found in Gandhara Prakrit, *e i o u*, are marked with strokes added to the *a* forms. Such strokes are called *matras*. Words can also begin with a vowel, so there's a letter for *a*, with the other initial vowels indicated by adding the four *matras* to it.

Why are abugidas like that? Now this is purely speculative: In the Aramaic inscriptions or documents that might have been available to the pandits (Indian scholars) who chose to adapt Aramaic writing to Gandhara Prakrit, no *a*'s, but many *i*'s and *u*'s and some *e*'s and *o*'s were notated (recall the *matres lectionis* from §3.2). They had learned their Pāṇini, from memorizing his verses at their teachers' knee, so they could recognize the vowels in their own language. What they learned from the Aramaic-writing scribes they queried was that most of the consonant letters would be followed by /a/ (and some by /i/ or /u/), but that most *i*'s and *e*'s, *u*'s and *o*'s would be represented by ⟨y⟩ and ⟨w⟩ respectively. This is what suggested that they should use the plain letters for C*a*, and additions to the letters for the other vowels. The decision was made easier by the fact that, unlike in Aramaic, there were no or almost no closed syllables (syllables ending with a consonant).

---

*The term "alphasyllabary" was introduced about the same time as "abugida," and immediately caught on among South Asia scholars, but I reject it because it implies that the abugida is some sort of hybrid between an alphabet and a syllabary. Cf. §12.1 Details.

Details *(continued)* ————————————————————————————

Aryan Languages" (2002) and "Writing Systems of the Indo-Aryan Languages" (2007) have been particularly useful.

The term "abugida" is discussed by Peter T. Daniels, "Two Notes on Terminology" (2009c), 278–80.

Table 5.3 Devanagari vowel characters

	initial/*akshara*			postconsonantal/*matra*		
	short	long	diphthong	short	long	diphthong
unrounded						
low central	अ *a* [ʌ]	आ *ā* [aː]		– प *pa*	ाा पा *pā*	
high front	इ *i* [i]	ई *ī* [iː]		ि पि *pi*	ी पी *pī*	
rounded						
high back	उ *u* [u]	ऊ *ū* [uː]		ु पु *pu*	ू पू *pū*	
syllabic						
vibrant	ऋ *r̥* [r̥]	ॠ *r̥̄* [r̥ː]		ृ पृ *pr̥*	ॄ पॄ *pr̥̄*	
lateral	ऌ *l̥* [l̥]	ॡ *l̥̄* *[l̥ː]		ॢ पॢ *pl̥*	ॣ पॣ *pl̥̄*	
unrounded front		ए *e* [e(ː)]	ऐ *ai* [aj]		े पे *pe*	ै पै *pai*
rounded back		ओ *o* [o(ː)]	औ *au* [aw]		ो पो *po*	ौ पौ *pau*

Table 5.4 Devanagari consonant characters

velar	क *ka* [ka]	ख *kha* [kʰa]	ग *ga* [ga]	घ *gha* [gɦa]	ङ *ṅa* [ŋa]
palatal	च *ca* [ca]	छ *cha* [cʰa]	ज *ja* [ɟa]	झ *jha* [ɟɦa]	ञ *ña* [ɲa]
retroflex	ट *ṭa* [ʈa]	ठ *ṭha* [ʈʰa]	ड *ḍa* [ɖa]	ढ *ḍha* [ɖɦa]	ण *ṇa* [ɳa]
dental	त *ta* [ta]	थ *tha* [tʰa]	द *da* [da]	ध *dha* [dɦa]	न *na* [na]
labial	प *pa* [pa]	फ *pha* [pʰa]	ब *ba* [ba]	भ *bha* [bɦa]	म *ma* [ma]
sonorants	य *ya* [ja]	र *ra* [ra]	ल *la* [la]	व *va* [ʋa]	
sibilants	श *śa* [ɕa]	ष *ṣa* [ʂa]	स *sa* [sa]	ह *ha* [ɦa]	ळ *ḷa* [ɭa]

Table 5.5 Devanagari conjunct formation

omit vertical	त *ta*	+	क *ka*	=	त्क *tka*				
	प *pa*	+	य *ya*	=	प्य *pya*				
stack	द *da*	+	व *va*	=	द्व *dva*				
merge	ह *ha*	+	य *ya*	=	ह्य *hya*				
	त *ta*	+	त *ta*	=	त्त *tta*	+ व	+ *va*	=	त्त्व *ttva*
coalesce	क *ka*	+	ष *ṣa*	=	क्ष *kṣa*	+ म	+ *ma*	=	क्ष्म *kṣma*

5.2 Devanagari

Almost a dozen different Indic scripts are used today for many of the hundreds of languages of the South Asian subcontinent. They all developed from an ancestor, known as Brahmi (§5.3), attested throughout the region from the third century BCE. To display the full working-out of abugidic writing, we use the variety most often used for Sanskrit in the West, known as Devanagari. Three serious differences from Kharoṣṭhi are that Devanagari is written left to right, that vowel length is notated, and that each initial vowel has its own character. Indian scholars systematized the script to such a degree that for the sake of symmetry, they introduced signs for a sound that does not occur in the Sanskrit (or any other Indic) language, long vocalic *ḹ* (Table 5.3).

The first group of characters in the standard order of Devanagari is the vowels. They are conceptualized in short–long pairs and in primary–secondary groups. For each item, the long vowel (or diphthong) character is an elaboration, in some way, of the corresponding short (or long) vowel character. Each vowel *matra* appears after, above, below, or even before the consonant after which its vowel is pronounced.

In order between the vowels and consonants come two symbols of a different sort, the *anusvāra* ं *ṃ* (variant *candrabindu* ँ) indicating nasalization—as in the familiar Buddhist incantatory syllable ॐ *auṃ* [õ] ("om")—and the *visarga* ः *ḥ* [h] at the end of a word.

The consonants too are divided into two groups: the stops and nasals; and the sonorants, sibilants, and "miscellaneous" (Table 5.4).

Spelling Sanskrit begins quite straightforwardly. A series of simple letters indicates a word containing only *a* vowels: वदथ *vadatha* 'you (pl.) speak'. Words comprising open syllables containing other vowels are written with characters to which the *matras* are attached: वदामि *vadāmi* 'I speak'.

It is when *closed* syllables need to be written that Sanskrit orthography begins to get complicated (Table 5.5). If a word doesn't end with a vowel, then a "killer" (*virāma*) ੍ is appended to the final consonant letter: वदामस् *vadāmas* 'we speak'. But within a word, *virāma* is not used—instead, a truncated form of the first in a series of vowelless consonants—a *conjunct*—appears: वदन्ति *vadanti* 'they speak'. Sometimes, it is simply the vertical part of the character that is omitted. Sometimes, the character parts are stacked. Sometimes, the strokes of the character merge to a degree but remain identifiable. And occasionally, the characters merge to such an extent that the included symbols can barely be identified, or even not at all. In all cases, consonants can pile up in an unrelieved sequence of three, four, or once in all of classical Sanskrit literature, five consonants.

With yet one more complication, we can display that unique five-consonant sequence: The consonant *r* combines not within the line of the word, but (if it comes first) above it and always at the far right of the whole sequence, or (if it comes last) below it: र *ra* + प *pa* = र्प *rpa*; प *pa* + र *ra* = प्र *pra*. The Sanskrit word *kārtsnya* 'totality' is spelled कार्त्स्न्य = क *ka* + आ *ā* + र *r* + त् *t* + स् *s* + न् *n* + य *ya*.

Table 5.6 Possible West Semitic backgrounds of Brahmi

I–IV		Archaic Phoenician (I)	Mesa's Inscription (II)	Assyrian Weights (III)	Intermediate forms (IV)	Original letters (V)	Derivatives (VI)	V	VI
ʔ	1							a	ā
b	2							ba	bha
g	3							ga	gha
d	4							dha	da×2 ḍa ḍha×2 da×2 ḍa
h	5							ha	
w	6							va	u dhu×2 ū dhū o×2 ko2
z	7							ja	jha
ḥ	8							gha	
ṭ	9							tha	ṭha ṭa
y	10							ya	
k	11							ka	
l	12							la	ḷa
m	13							ma	ṃ
n	14							na	ña ṇa
s	15							sa, ša	sa×2 ša×3; ke ai thai
ʕ	16							e	i×3 * ki kī ī
p	17							pa	pha
ṣ	18							ca	cha×2
q	19							kha	
r	20							ra	
š	21							śa	
t	22							ta	

Georg Bühler (1898), pl. I

after Hans Jensen (1969), fig. 343

This word provides a spectacular example of why Indic writing systems should not be considered syllabaries: the writing-units do not denote syllables! An entire sequence of up to five consonants followed by a vowel (or a *virama*) is a single writing-unit; the name for such units is *akshara*. Repeating some of our examples, प *pa* is an *akshara*, का *kā* is an *akshara*, मि *mi* and मी *mī* and मे *me* and मू *mū* are *aksharas*, ह्य *hya* is an *akshara*, क्ष्म *kṣma* is an *akshara*, and र्त्स्न्य *rtsnya* is an *akshara*. Clearly, *rtsnya* is not a syllable; the syllables of the word *kārtsnya* are *kārts-* and *-nya*. No matter where a syllable boundary falls in a sequence of consonants, all the consonants combine in a single *akshara*. Several of these properties can be seen in this example:

Details *(continued)* —————————————————————————————————

5.2 The Sanskrit example is from Holger Pedersen, *The Discovery of Language* (1931), 191.

समदिशत्पितापुत्रँलिखलेखँममाज्ञया
नतेनलिखितोलेख:पितुराज्ञानखण्डिता

samādiśat pitā putraṁ likha lekham mamājñayā
natēna likhitō lēkhaḥ pitur ajñā na khāṇḍitā

'The father commanded the son: write a letter after my command!
Bowing wrote he the letter; the father's command was not broken.'

But नतेन 'bowing' could also be read *na tēna* 'he wrote not ...', a problem that came to be avoided by the spelling न तेन.

5.3 Brāhmī

Devanagari did not come out of nowhere. Its historical development can be followed in inscriptions leading back through the centuries to a script known as Brahmi. Like Kharoṣṭhi, Brahmi seems to have first been used during the reign of the emperor Aśoka, in the middle of the third century BCE, for inscriptions publicizing his edicts exhorting his subjects to follow the teachings of Buddhism. These inscriptions are found throughout his realm; those in the northwest are in Kharoṣṭhi, for Gandhari Prakrit, but most of them are in Brahmi and record other varieties of prakrits—Sanskrit would not be written for centuries to come.

Early Brahmi already exhibits the characteristics that distinguish Devanagari from Kharoṣṭhi—written left to right, accommodating both short and long vowels, and distinct *akshara*s for each initial vowel (Table 5.7). A few conjunct forms are even found from early inscriptions. Visually, however, it is quite distinct. The Brahmi characters are severely geometrical (Table 5.8). Georg Bühler's correlations of Brahmi with West Semitic consonantal forms (Table 5.6) are less convincing than in the case of Kharoṣṭhi. During the nineteenth century there was considerable controversy over whether a Phoenician, an Aramaic, or even a South Arabian model served the devisers of Brahmi. During the twentieth century some scholars suggested it was an independent innovation. Some have even tried to trace it to the undeciphered Indus Valley script (§10.4), despite the near-2000-year gap between the demise of the Indus Valley civilization and the first attestations of Brahmi, and despite the extreme unlikelihood that the Indus Valley language was Indic.

Rather, I would see Brahmi as a rationalization and regularization of Kharoṣṭhi. It's not impossible that the shift was prompted by familiarity with the Greek alphabet used in the Greco-Bactrian kingdom, the easternmost part of the Seleucid Empire which seceded from it about 250 BCE. Such familiarity is attested by the bilingual edict inscriptions of Kandahar.

Brahmi served not only the Indo-European (Indic) Prakrits of northern India, but also at least one of the Dravidian languages of the south, Old Tamil. And although Brahmi was gradually superseded by local variants throughout India, it lived on in

Table 5.7 Brahmi vowel characters

	initial/*akshara*			postconsonantal/*matra*		
	short	long	diphthong	short	long	diphthong
unrounded						
low central	*a*	*ā*		*ka*	*kā*	
high front	*i*	*ī*		*ki*	*kī*	
rounded						
high back	*u*	*ū*		*ku*	*kū*	
syllabic						
vibrant	*r̥*	*r̥̄*		*kr̥*	*kr̥̄*	
unrounded front		*e*	*ai*		*ke*	*kai*
rounded back		*o*	*au*		*ko*	*kau*
Tocharian addition				*kə*		

Table 5.8 Brahmi consonant characters

velar		*ka*		*kha*		*ga*		*gha*
palatal		*ca*		*cha*		*ja*		*jha*
retroflex		*ṭa*		*ṭha*		*ḍa*		*ḍha*
dental		*ta*		*tha*		*da*		*dha*
labial		*pa*		*pha*		*ba*		*bha*

velar	*ṅa*
palatal	*ña*
retroflex	*ṇa*
dental	*na*
labial	*ma*

sonorants	*ya*		*ra*	*la*		*va*
sibilants	*śa*		*ṣa*	*sa*		*ha*	

| sibilants | *ḷa* |

| Tamil additions | *ṟa* | *ḻa* | | | | *ṉa* |

Tocharian additions	*kə*					
	tə					*nə*
	pə					*mə*
		rə	*lə*	*wa*		
	śə	*ṣə*	*sə*			

| Uyghur additions | *qa* | | *γa* | *za* | *źa* |
| | | | *δa* | *dza* | |

Central Asia as the script for the two languages of the Tocharian branch of Indo-European—which was unknown and unsuspected before manuscript discoveries around the turn of the twentieth century—as well as for the Turkic language Uyghur, which we have met in §3.5, and the Iranian language Khotanese. These languages thrived during the heyday of the Silk Road, which was not a single highway connecting the Western and Eastern worlds, but a network of routes that skirted the Takla Makan desert, north of Tibet and south of the Tien Shan mountains. The manuscripts in the various languages cover about a millennium beginning around 200 CE.

Three new letters were required for Tamil. For Tocharian, which featured a "high central" vowel not found in Prakrit, represented as ə, a typologically interesting solution was found. On the one hand, a new vowel *matra* was introduced; on the other, new shapes were devised that denote various consonants followed by ə without any *matra*: this is a syllabic component grafted onto an abugida (Table 5.8).

5.4 Descendants of Indic writing throughout India

Devanagari is not restricted to Sanskrit, and Sanskrit is not confined to Devanagari. It can be, and throughout history has been, written with any of the local scripts of India. Over the 2000+ years since Indic and Dravidian languages began to be written, in the absence of frequent written communication between isolated communities that were only occasionally unified into an expansive polity that might have imposed a single script and official language throughout the realm, both language and script diversified across the Subcontinent. A plethora of local varieties emerged, Indic in the north, Dravidian in the south (Table 5.9).

It was only with British sovereignty beginning in the later eighteenth century, and the need to print materials in local languages, that a number of Indic scripts were standardized—at present nine Indic scripts serve the first tier of languages in the nation's official ranking. Devanagari is used for Sanskrit, Hindi, Konkani, and Marathi; and for Nepali. In Hindi, certain sounds not found in Sanskrit are written by adding a dot to a letter: क़ *qa*, ख़ *xa*, ग़ *ya*, ज़ *za*, ड़ *ṛa*, ढ़ *ṛha*, फ़ *fa*, य़ *yya*. Bengali is used for Bengali and Assamese, and Gurmukhi by the Sikh community for Punjabi; together with Gujarati and Oriya, those are the North Indic scripts. South Indic scripts serve the Dravidian languages Kannada, Malayalam, Tamil, and Telugu, as well as Sinhala, the Indic language of Sri Lanka. Kashmiri and Urdu, being primarily languages of Muslim communities, use scripts based on the Arabic (see §3.2.3).

Details *(continued)*

5.3 There are two articles in English on Central Asian Brahmi: Lore Sander, "Brahmi Scripts on the Eastern Silk Roads" (1986) and "Remarks on the Formal Brāhmī Script from the Southern Silk Route" (2005). The archeologist J. P. Mallory, "Bronze Age Languages of the Tarim Basin" (2010), puts the many languages into their sociohistorical context, with a number of illustrations of manuscripts.

Table 5.9 Modern Indic consonants (selected)

		kha	ga	ṭa	ṭha	ta	na	pa	ba	bha	ma	ya	ra	la	sa	ha
	Brahmi	𑀔	𑀕	𑀝	𑀞	𑀢	𑀦	𑀧	𑀩	𑀪	𑀫	𑀬	𑀭	𑀮	𑀲	𑀳
NORHTERN Indic	Devanagari	ख	ग	ट	ठ	त	न	प	ब	भ	म	य	र	ल	स	ह
	Gujarati	ખ	ગ	ટ	ઠ	ત	ન	પ	બ	ભ	મ	ય	ર	લ	સ	હ
	Gurmukhi	ਖ	ਗ	ਟ	ਠ	ਤ	ਨ	ਪ	ਬ	ਭ	ਮ	ਯ	ਰ	ਲ	ਸ	ਹ
	Bengali	খ	গ	ট	ঠ	ত	ন	প	ব	ভ	ম	য	র	ল	স	হ
	Oriya	ଖ	ଗ	ଟ	ଠ	ତ	ନ	ପ	ବ	ଭ	ମ	ଯ	ର	ଲ	ସ	ହ
	Sinhala	ඛ	ග	ට	ඨ	ත	න	ප	බ	භ	ම	ය	ර	ල	ස	හ
SOUTHERN Dravidian	Kannada	ಖ	ಗ	ಟ	ಠ	ತ	ನ	ಪ	ಬ	ಭ	ಮ	ಯ	ರ	ಲ	ಸ	ಹ
	Telugu	ఖ	గ	ట	ఠ	త	న	ప	బ	భ	మ	య	ర	ల	స	హ
	Malayalam	ഖ	ഗ	ട	ഠ	ത	ന	പ	ബ	ഭ	മ	യ	ര	ല	സ	ഹ
	Tamil			ட		த	ந	ப			ம	ய	ர	ல	ஸ	ஹ

The division between North and South refers to the shapes of the letters, not to relationships among the languages they write, and reflects the historical development that can be observed in inscriptions created over at least fifteen centuries—the climate is not conducive to the survival of manuscripts, so older ones are fairly rare. The prominent roundedness of the South Indic scripts arose because the writing was most usually done with a stylus incising on leaves, but is not limited to them: in its details the Oriya script is very like the Bengali script, despite the prominent "umbrella" that tops most *aksharas*.

5.5 *Matra* and *akshara* formation

As they developed from ancestral Brahmi, the many local script varieties gradually evolved different shapes for the vowel *matras* and different techniques of forming the conjunct consonants that indicate vowellessness. The Brahmi *matras* were short single or double strokes attached to the top or bottom of a letter (Table 5.7). Whether for ease of writing or for sheer joy in the beauty of exuberant calligraphy, over the centuries these modest lines turned into curves and swoops that are positioned, as we have seen with Devanagari, not only above and below, but also before and after the consonant letters. The similarity in positioning of the *matras* throughout India shows that the habits were set quite early in their development.

This means that early in the development of the Northern group, the short *i matra* began to curl leftward to help distinguish it from the long *ā* and *ī matras*, so it ended up at the left of its consonant—Brahmi 𑀓𑀺 ⟨ki⟩, Oriya କି, Bengali কি—which ought to interfere with a fluent reading process proceeding from left to right. But the fact that it persisted over many centuries suggests that scribes felt no inconvenience. The left positioning of the *e matra* is less surprising, given the form in Brahmi. The *ai* and *au* *matras* retain their kinship to the *e* and *o* *matras* respectively; ⟨o⟩ is often a combination of ⟨ā⟩ and ⟨e⟩:

	kā	*ke*	*kai*	*ko*	*kau*
Brahmi	ᜀ	ᜀ	ᜀ	ᜀ	ᜀ
Gujarati	કા	કે	કૈ	કો	કૌ
Bengali	কা	কে	কৈ	কো	কৌ

In the Southern group, only the *e* family of *matras* appears to the left of the consonant, but the Dravidian family, and following the Dravidian languages Sinhala, require both short and long ⟨ĕ⟩ and ⟨ŏ⟩; but their ways of notating them diverge to some extent:

	ke	*kē*	*ko*	*kō*
Malayalam	കെ	കേ	കൊ	കോ
Sinhala	කෙ	කේ	කො	කෝ
Kannada	ಕೆ	ಕೇ	ಕೊ	ಕೋ

Kannada uses the same diacritic for making most, but not all, vowels long: ಕಿ *ki* ಕೀ *kī*, ಕೆ *ke* ಕೇ *kē*, ಕೊ *ko* ಕೋ *kō*; but ಕ *ka* ಕಾ *kā* and ಕು *ku* ಕೂ *kū*—but ಕೊ ⟨ko⟩ is already an elaboration of ಕೂ ⟨kū⟩. Sinhala also adds *matras* for කැ *kæ* and කෑ *kǣ*.

In Tamil, the *matras* for *u* and *ū* combine in four different ways, about equally distributed among the consonants:

ப	*pa*	ம	*ma*	ர	*ra*	ஜ	*ja*
பு	*pu*	மு	*mu*	ரு	*ru*	ஜு	*ju*
பூ	*pū*	மூ	*mū*	ரூ	*rū*	ஜூ	*jū*

Malayalam also had impressive variation in *u* and *ū* *matras*, but it is difficult to find patterns; in a recent innovation to accommodate typewriters, for which traditional subscripts were difficult, Malayalam *u* and *ṛ* *matras* are now postscripts: കു *ku* കൂ *kū*, കൃ *kṛ* കൄ *kṝ*—all the scripts that can be used for Sanskrit include *matras* for *ṝ*, *ḷ*, and even *ḹ*, although those sounds do not occur in the modern languages. An ancestral Tamil script, called Grantha, could be used to write Sanskrit for Tamil-speakers. Perhaps the exuberance of the Tamil *u* *matras* is to make up for its poverty in the other distinctive aspect of Indic scripts: Tamil does not use conjuncts to form consonant clusters. Instead, it marks with a dot above the letter every consonant that isn't followed by a vowel: போர்களளாத் *pōrkaḷḷat* 'battlefield'.

The other most distinctive Indic script is the Gurmukhi, which is used for Punjabi by the Sikh community.* This was adapted from a Nagari-like script in the first half of the sixteenth century by the second Guru, Angad (hence the name *gurmukhi* 'from the mouth of the guru'). Its vowel *aksharas* are created by adding the *matras* to base forms: ਅ for the low vowels ਅ *a* ਆ *ā* ਐ *ai* ਔ *au*, ੲ for the high front vowels ਇ *i* ਈ *ī* ਏ *e*,

---

*Punjabi-speaking Muslims in Pakistan use an Arabic-derived script, and Punjabi-speaking Hindus in India use Devanagari.

and ੳ for the high back vowels ੁ *u* ੂ *ū* ੋ *o*. In each case, the differentiator is the *matra* used within words. Moreover, it uses only a handful of conjunct forms—*r, w, h, y*—because of the dearth of closed syllables in the language; but it marks nasalization and consonant length with diacritics on the preceding *akshara*: ਮੁੰਡਾ *muṃḍā* 'boy', ਪੱਕੀ *pakkī* 'ripe' (compare the Japanese *kana* for the moras of nasalization and length in §4.1).

The other Indic scripts use a plethora of devices for creating conjuncts. By the time Sanskrit began to be written, so that a real need arose for indicating vowellessness, Brahmi was on its last legs, and scribes in different parts of India found different ways to build on the few examples of conjuncts found in Brahmi. The almost unrecognizable "diacritic" shapes for *r, y,* and *w* are found in several scripts. Sinhala has such forms for *-r, r-,* and *-y* but mostly uses the vowellessness mark for consonant clusters. As if to make up for this lack, Sinhala has a set of prenasalized consonants: ඟ *ŋg,* ඬ *ṇḍ,* ඳ *ṇd,* ඹ *ṃb.* Malayalam uses a true diacritic to mark lengthening ("doubling") of some consonants with a particular conformation: ച്ച *cca,* ബ്ബ *bba,* വ്വ *vva*—but other double consonants with the same feature are simply written below: പ്പ *ppa,* ള്ള *lla.*

Several ways of dealing with consonant sequences were devised over the centuries. Malayalam puts the second consonant beneath the first one in a few combinations besides doubling—such as ക്ല *kla*—and it's the usual practice in Kannada (ದ್ಘ *dgha,* ಬ್ಧ *bdha*) and Telugu (స్త *sta,* ట్ఠ *ṭṭha*). Gujarati follows the Devanagari practice of reducing the first consonant. Usually the sequence is horizontal, but sometimes it's vertical: શ્લ *śla,* હ્મ *hma*; દ્દ *dda,* દ્વ *dva.* In Bengali the sequence is more often vertical than horizontal (ক্ক *kka,* ঙ্ক *ṅka,* ক্ত *kta*), and in Oriya, the outcome of a combination seems quite unpredictable: କ + ଷ = କ୍ଷ *kṣa,* ଷ + ପ = ଷ୍ପ *spa,* ଣ + ଠ = ଣ୍ଠ *ṇṭha,* ବ + ଦ = ବ୍ଦ *bda,* ଦ + ଭ = ଦ୍ଭ *dbha,* ଙ + କ = ଙ୍କ *ṅka,* ନ + ଦ = ନ୍ଦ *nda.*

Malayalam's may be the most difficult system to master, because although in the 1970s–80s for the typewriter's sake some of its clusters were simplified into full-size sequences employing the vowellessness mark the way Tamil does, as in ല്‍ക *lka,* ട്‍ന *ṭna,* on the other hand, letters that merged horizontally still do so, giving up more or less of their individual identities: ക + ഷ = ക്ഷ *kṣa,* ട + ട = ട്ട *tta,* ന + ന = ന്ന *nna,*   ഞ + ഞ = ഞ്ഞ *ñña,*   ജ + ജ = ജ്ജ *jja,*   ക + ക = ക്ക *kka,* ക + ത = ക്ത *kta,* ശ + ച = ശ്ച *śca,* ണ + ട = ണ്ട *ṇṭa*—and there's at least one vertical combination, ട + ട = ഷ്ട *ṭṭa.*

5.6 Southeast Asia

There seem to have been two phases in the arrival of writing in the Southeast Asian mainland and the offshore archipelagos. The process of "Indianization" of Indochina is not well understood, but the earliest inscriptions, from present-day Vietnam, Malaysia, and Thailand, are in Sanskrit and date to the 2nd–5th centuries CE. The scripts exhibit South Indic affinities. Local languages were being written, and local script varieties were developing, by the seventh or eighth century; these are largely associated with Hindu scribal practice, but a North Indic script reached Cambodia with Mahayana Buddhism. At a later period, greatly simplified characters came into use in various areas of Indonesia and the Philippines, and very recent investigation suggests that they reached those areas with Indian merchants who habitually used Gujarati-like simplified scripts (often omitting vowel *matras*) for everyday use. Islam came late to Malaysia and Indonesia, and there, Arabic-based scripts mostly supplanted Indic varieties. Indonesian, a development of Malay, uses a Roman alphabet.

The present-day national scripts of Burma, Thailand, Laos, and Cambodia (Table 5.10) serve languages representing three major language families with very different phonological properties. Burmese is Tibeto-Burman, distantly related to Chinese in the Sino-Tibetan family; Thai and Lao are very similar Tai languages; and Khmer, the national language of Cambodia, is Austroasiatic. They reuse the resources of their Indic forebears in distinctive ways.

Burmese, Thai, and Lao are tonal, and each has developed different means of notating the tones on its syllables. In the case of Thai, at least, the orthography has not been reformed in nearly a thousand years, and pronunciation has diverged from spelling even more than is the case for English orthography. Lao, on the other hand, has greatly simplified its consonant inventory and no longer takes an *a* to be inherent in the bare consonant—that is, Lao orthography is alphabetical. In both Thai and Lao, the contemporary readings of the consonant characters differ greatly from those of their Indic ancestors. In all three of these orthographies, the interlocking representations of vowels and tones are too complicated to reduce to a cogent summary.

As for Khmer, it has no need for the voiced vs. voiceless pairs of letters inherited from Brahmi, but instead uses the pairs of consonants to distinguish the very large number of vowels and has an enlarged set of vowel *matras* as well. Khmer also has a full set of reduced consonant characters, which notate the second consonant in an initial cluster—not crossing syllable boundaries; they can also write the "double" consonants in borrowed words.

The languages of Indonesia and the Philippines are Austronesian. The moribund (at best—sadly, because it is one of the most beautiful of all) Javanese script is interesting for having given up the phonetic order of the letters otherwise found

Details *(continued)* ——————————————————————————————————————

5.6 Even less information is generally available on the Southeast Asian scripts, and we can do no better than to recommend the surveys, with technical bibliography, by Christopher Court, "The Spread of Brahmi Script into Southeast Asia" (1996), and Joel C. Kuipers and Ray McDermott, "Insular Southeast Asian Scripts" (1996). Christopher Ray Miller, "Devanagari's Descendants in North and South India, Indonesia and the Philippines" (2014), is an intriguing overview. A beginning has been made in *Proceedings … Endangered Scripts of Island Southeast Asia* (2014); it's a welcome sign that this volume includes contributions in Indonesian and Tagalog, showing that users of such scripts are participating in their study.

Table 5.10 Modern Indic consonants in mainland Southeast Asia (selected)

	kha	*ga*	*ṭa*	*ṭha*	*ta*	*na*	*pa*	*ba*
Burmese	ခ [ká]	ဂ [gá]	ဋ [tá]	ဌ [tʰá]	တ [tá]	န [ná]	ပ [pá]	ဗ [bá]
Thai	ข [kʰa]	ค [kʰa]	ฏ [ta]	ฐ [tʰa]	ต [ta]	น [na]	บ [ba]	พ [pʰa]
Lao	ກ [kʰ]	ຄ [kʰ]			ຕ [t]	ນ [n]	ປ [b]	ບ [p]
Khmer	ខ [kɒː]	គ [kɔː]	ដ [dɒː]	ឋ [tʰɒː]	ត [tɒː]	ន [nɔː]	ប [ɓɒː]	ព [pɔː]

	bha	*ma*	*ya*	*ra*	*la*	*sa*	*ha*
Burmese	ဘ [bá]	မ [má]	ယ [já]	ရ [já]	လ [lá]	သ [θá]	ဟ [há]
Thai	ภ [pʰa]	ม [ma]	ย [ja]	ร [ra]	ล [la]	ส [sa]	ห [ha]
Lao		ມ [m]	ຍ [ɲ]	ຮ [h]	ລ [l]	ສ [s]	ຫ [h]
Khmer	ភ [pʰɔːʼ]	ម [mɔː]	យ [jɔː]	រ [rɔː]	ល [lɔː]	ស [sɒː]	ហ [hɒː]

Table 5.11 Javanese "capital" letters

	na	*ka*	*ta*	*sa*	*pa*	*ga*	*Ba*
regular	ꦤ	ꦏ	ꦠ	ꦱ	ꦥ	ꦒ	ꦧ
"capital"	ꦟ	ꦑ	ꦡ	ꦯ	ꦦ	ꦓ	ꦨ

Table 5.12 Hanunoo script

ka	ga	ṅa	ta	da	na	pa	ba	ma	ya	ra	la	wa	sa	ha
ᜃ	ᜄ	ᜅ	ᜆ	ᜇ	ᜈ	ᜉ	ᜊ	ᜋ	ᜌ	ᜍ	ᜎ	ᜏ	ᜐ	ᜑ

in the Brahmi-based scripts, using instead a pangrammatic sentence representing a summary of a folktale:

> ꦲꦤ ꦕꦫꦏ ꦢꦠ ꦱꦮꦭ ꦥꦢ ꦗꦪ�season ꦩꦒ ꦧꦠꦤ
> *Hana   caraka,   data   sawala   paḍa jayaña,   maga   baṭana*
> 'There were (two) emissaries, they began to fight, their valor was equal, they
> both fell dead.'

It also has a reduced form for each letter, and some of them go after rather than beneath the consonant they follow. The vowel characters aren't included in that sequence: ꦄ *a* ꦏ *ka*, ꦏꦴ *kə*, ꦅ *i* ꦏꦶ *ki*, ꦏꦸ *u* ꦏꦸ *ku*, ꦌ *e* ꦏ *ke*, ꦏ *o* ꦏꦴ *ko*.

Javanese has another interesting property, unique among Indic scripts, of a group of "capital" letters—not a full set, as in the Roman alphabet, but for only some of the letters—which can appear anywhere in a word to mark the word's special status

(Table 5.11). Some of these, too, have sub- or postscript forms. Finally, Javanese has a series of introductory symbols to be used when writing to a personage of higher ᰀ, equal ᰀ, or lower ᰀ social status, a perhaps unique reflection of diglossia in a writing system (see Dimension V on p. 176 below).

Hanunoo is one of the several Philippine languages for which scripts were devised at some time before Spanish contact early in the sixteenth century. The scripts record their typically few consonants (Table 5.12) and their three vowels. They were incised on bamboo stalks, and this led to the notion that they were read "from bottom to top." The vocalization continues to use the *matra* system: 𝒱 a 𝒱 i 𝒱 u, 𝒱 wa 𝒱 wi 𝒱 wu.

5.7 Tibet

Tibet too, like India, possessed a grammatical tradition, and it may well have played a part in adapting an Indic abugida to the specifics of the Tibetan language, in the mid seventh century CE, apparently on the basis of a North Indic, specifically Nepali, model. The Indic languages have inflections, just like any other Indo-European language, but Tibetan is "isolating," like the other Sino-Tibetan languages, including Chinese. This means that it expresses the relations among the parts of a sentence not with case-endings, but solely by their order and by "grammatical morphemes," things like the prepositions and conjunctions of English. The rest of a language's lexicon, the words with specific meanings, are "content morphemes." In Tibetan, these morphemes tended to be a single syllable and to have sequences of consonants at both the beginning and the end. Successive syllables tend not to blend into each other.

The Tibetan writing system (Table 5.13) caters to this characteristic. Each word/morpheme/syllable is separated from the next with a dot at the shoulder of its last letter. For the most part, Tibetan does not use conjunct forms like the Indic scripts; instead, one consonant serves as the heart of the syllable with the others ranged below, left, above, right, or far right of the radical. A word displaying all the possibilities is བསྒྲུབས. *bsgrubs* 'established'—where the radical is ག *g*. Before it is བ *b*; above it is ས *s*; below it are ྲ, which is the combining form of ར *r*, and the vowel ུ *u*; and after it are another *b* and *s*. Not surprisingly, also before a consonant an ར *r* takes a truncated form, as in རྒ *rga*. The only other letters with combining forms are ྱ *y*, ླ *l*, and ྭ *w*, which may have been the only ones found in the putative Nepali model.

Details *(continued)*

5.7 Linguists will be interested in Roy Andrew Miller, *The Tibetan System of Writing* (1956), while the importance of Tibetan script in Buddhist spirituality is stressed by John Stevens, *Sacred Calligraphy of the East* (1988). The first detailed investigation in decades into the origins of Tibetan writing is Sam van Schaik, "A New Look at the Tibetan Invention of Writing" (2011).

Table 5.13 Tibetan consonants[a]

ka	kha	ga	ṅa
ca	cha	ja	ña
ṭa	ṭha	ḍa	ṇ
ta	tha	da	na
pa	pha	ba	ma
tsa	tsha	dza	
wa	ža	za	
'a	ya	ra	la
ṣa	ša	sa	ha	a

a. Dashed boxes, additions for Tibetan; dotted boxes, additions for Sanskrit.

Table 5.14 'Phags pa consonants[a]

[1]ka	[2]kha	[3]ga	[4]ṅa	[35]qa	[38]gga
[5]ca	[6]cha	[7]ja	[8]ña		[36]ya
ṭa	ṭha	ḍa	ṇa		[37]fa
[9]ta	[10]tha	[11]da	[12]na		[42]va
[13]pa	[14]pha	[15]ba	[16]ma		[46]fha
[17]tsa	[18]tsha	[19]dza			[44]ḥa
[20]wa	[21]ža	[22]za			[40]-wa
[23]'a	[24,45]ya	[25]ra	[26]la		[41]-ya
[43]ẓa	[27]ša	[28]sa	[29]ha	[30]a	-ra

a. Characters 1–35, 39, and the three subscript forms at lower right, Mongolian and Tibetan; 36//46, additions for Chinese; unnumbered, Sanskrit. Numbers designate the order in the principal Chinese source.

Table 5.15 'Phags pa vowels

[31]i	[39]ï	ü	[32]u
[33]e		ö	[34]o

Four letters for Tibetan sounds not found in Prakrit receive differentiated rather than invented shapes, as when Hindi provides for sounds not found in Sanskrit by adding a dot beneath a letter. Tibetan script provides for sounds found in Sanskrit but not Tibetan—the retroflexes *ṭ, ṭh, ḍ, ṇ,* and *ṣ*—with mirror images of letters. Since models for these letters were readily available, my inference is that transcribing Sanskrit texts wasn't a concern at the time Tibetan writing developed.

Vowels are added above or below. Tibetan doesn't have separate letters for initial vowels. Reverting to the Kharoṣṭhi pattern—could Kharoṣṭhi still have been known, or was this an independent reinvention?—the four *matras* are added to ཨ *a* or འ *'a:* ཨི *i* འི *'i,* ཨུ *u* འུ *'u,* ཨེ *e* འེ *'e,* ཨོ *o* འོ *'o.* The long vowels needed in loanwords, not only from Sanskrit but also from Chinese and even English, are signaled with a འ beneath: ཨཱ *ā,* འཱ *'ū.*

The well-known mantra *oṃ ma ṇi pad me hūṃ* is written ཨོཾ་མ་ཎི་པད་མེ་ཧཱུྃ.

It should be noted that the pronunciation of Modern Tibetan has diverged mightily from the Classical orthography, which is still in use—the example བསྒྲུབས་ ⟨bsgrubs⟩ is pronounced [ḍùp].

5.8 Mongols

Alongside the Mongolian script proper, which we met in §3.5, Emperor Qubilai, or Kubla Khan, commissioned a script that could be used for all the languages of the Mongol empire. The scholar he approached was the Tibetan monk 'Phags pa Blo gros rgyal mtshan (1235–1280), and not surprisingly the ensuing script takes its forms from Tibetan (Table 5.14); it bears his name, the 'Phags pa script. It was in use for exactly a century, from 1269 to 1368, and as it happens, mostly for Chinese rather than Mongolian, Tibetan, or Uyghur.

Like Tibetan, 'Phags pa is an abugida; unlike Tibetan, it is written vertically, left to right—probably in imitation of Chinese like Uyghur and Mongolian—and each vowel symbol (Table 5.15) follows its consonant(s) rather than appearing to the sides or above:

jar liq jiṅ gis q'a nu
'edict of Genghis Khan'.

Details *(continued)* ————————————————————————

5.8 There is not, as far as I know, any popularly oriented discussion of 'Phags pa. The biography of its creator is reconstructed by Miyoko Nakano, *A Phonological Study* (1971), 24–35; the fullest discussion is by W. South Coblin, *A Handbook of 'Phags-pa Chinese* (2007); and its use for Mongolian is described by Jan-Olof Svantesson, Anna Tsendina, Anastasia Karlsson, and Vivan Franzén, *The Phonology of Mongolian* (2005), esp. §8.4.

Table 5.16 The basic Ethiopic letters[a]

ha	la	ḥa	ma	śa	ra	sa	qa	ba	ta	xa	na	ʔa	ka	wa	ʕa	za	ya	da	ga	ṭa	ṗa	ṣa	ẓa	fa	pa
ሀ	ለ	ሐ	መ	ሠ	ረ	ሰ	ቀ	በ	ተ	ኀ	ነ	አ	ከ	ወ	ዐ	ዘ	የ	ደ	ገ	ጠ	ጰ	ጸ	ፀ	ፈ	ፐ

[a] For the order, compare Table 3.2 and see §11.5.2.

Table 5.17 The first few Ethiopic characters

	-a	-u	-i	-ā	-e	-ɨ/Ø	-o
h-	ሀ	ሁ	ሂ	ሃ	ሄ	ህ	ሆ
l-	ለ	ሉ	ሊ	ላ	ሌ	ል	ሎ
ḥ-	ሐ	ሑ	ሒ	ሓ	ሔ	ሕ	ሖ
m-	መ	ሙ	ሚ	ማ	ሜ	ም	ሞ
ś-	ሠ	ሡ	ሢ	ሣ	ሤ	ሥ	ሦ
⋮							

5.9 Ethiopic

It is probably not a coincidence that vowel marking first appeared in Ethiopic inscriptions at the very moment when King Ezana converted to Christianity. A few monuments in the South Arabian script and language, Sabaean, have been found near the Red Sea coast opposite Yemen. A development of South Arabian script was used for several centuries for the local administrative language, Giʻɨz, but suddenly, in the middle of the fourth century CE, the script grew vowels. The vowels were not written with letters between the consonant letters, as might have been expected if they had been introduced by Greek missionaries, or with dots accompanying the letters, as might have been possible if the missionaries were accustomed to Syriac (and had arrived some 200 years later).

Instead, they are written with appendages to or modifications of the basic consonant letters, and the former plain consonant letters now stand for the consonant plus short *a* (sometimes transliterated *ä*; Table 5.16). This suggests to me that the missionaries who visited the kingdom of Aksum came from the venerable Christian

Details *(continued)*

5.9 The Ethiopic script is generally treated (briefly) in accounts of West Semitic writing. Siegbert Uhlig, *Introduction to Ethiopian Palaeography* (1990), is condensed from his massive German reference work. In preparing Peter T. Daniels, "Contacts between Semitic and Indic Scripts" (1992a), I relied on Auguste Toussainte, *History of the Indian Ocean* (1966). Recent archeological work that illuminates the trans-oceanic trade is summarized by Elvind Heldaas Seland, "Archaeology of Trade in the Western Indian Ocean" (2014).

community in India, crossing the Arabian Sea with the monsoons, which had been mastered a century or two earlier. They didn't teach the Aksumite scribes to write their language, however, since the details of the vocalization system differ; they must simply have known that the scribes back home didn't leave the consonants to fend for themselves (compare §9.6).

In the Ethiopic writing system, each of the 26 consonants has seven shapes ("orders") for the seven vowels. For most of the orders, the vowel additions are easily recognizable (Table 5.17). The greatest difference from the Indic system is that there is no means of indicating that a consonant is not followed by a vowel: the symbols that represent the *i* vowel* are *also* used for consonants without vowel. Nor does it mark the long ("double") consonants that play an important part in the morphology of the Ethiopian Semitic languages. Provision is made, however, for the four *labiovelar* consonants—ቈ *q*ʷ*a*, ኈ *ḫ*ʷ*a*, ኰ *k*ʷ*a*, ጐ *g*ʷ*a*—that can occur before vowels other than *o* and *u*, for example ከ *ka*, ኰ *k*ʷ*a*; ኪ *ki*, ኲ *k*ʷ*i*; ካ *kā*, ኳ *k*ʷ*ā*; ኬ *ke*, ኴ *k*ʷ*e*; ክ *ki*, ኵ *k*ʷ*i*.

The classical Giʻiz script has been enhanced for Amharic, the principal Semitic language of modern Ethiopia, to express a number of palatalized consonants. ከ is *ka*, and ኸ is *ha*; ተ is *ta*, and ቸ is *ča*; ጠ is *ṭa*, and ጨ is *ča*; ነ is *na*, and ኘ is *ña*; ዘ is *za*, and ዠ is *ža*; and so on.

---

* Usually transliterated *ə*, but because of the phonetic symbol [ə], this is often mistakenly thought to represent a reduced vowel, a shwa. In fact it's a full-strength "high central" vowel. I. J. Gelb, *A Study of Writing* (1952), 149f., was misled by the symbol into equating the sixth order with the Hebrew symbol ְ and using this to support a mistaken hypothesis on the nature of West Semitic writing (see §11.1).

6   Morphemes and Morphograms

The keyboard no more offers an escape

We've seen (Chapter 1) that when writing systems are invented in modern times, by people who know that writing exists, the result is always a syllabary. It's then no surprise that when writing systems were invented thousands of years ago, by people who had no idea that writing *could* exist, the result was also always a syllabary. It happened three times. Here, as earlier, we'll take the three cases in the order of familiarity, considering in detail only the one that's still in use today.

6.1 Chinese

The one thing everyone knows about Chinese is that it's a tonal language. This is absolutely true, and has absolutely nothing to do with the nature of Chinese writing. The other one thing everyone knows about Chinese is that Chinese characters are ideograms. This is absolutely false, and has absolutely everything to do with the nature of Chinese writing.

We only need to mention two things about Chinese tones. First, they are just as much elements of words as consonants and vowels are. The Mandarin (Standard Chinese) words *mā*, *má*, *mǎ*, and *mà* are not one word pronounced with four different tones;* they are four completely different words, meaning 'mother', (question particle), 'horse', and 'scold' respectively. You can't replace one with another any more than you could say *She rode the horse to the funeral* when you meant *She rode the hearse to the funeral.*

---

*Those are the symbols used in *pinyin*, the transliteration system of the People's Republic of China; the Wade-Giles transliteration system, formerly popular among Western scholars, numbers them as *ma*[1], *ma*[2], *ma*[3], and *ma*[4] respectively. In order, they mark "high level," "high rising," low dipping," and "high falling" tones on the syllable.

Details ———————————————————————————

6.1 The best introduction to the nature of Chinese writing remains John DeFrancis, *The Chinese Language* (1984). His long-time associate J. Marshall Unger, *Ideogram* (2004), carries on the campaign against the misunderstandings of Chinese (and Japanese) writing; together they discuss the typology of writing systems in J. Marshall Unger and John DeFrancis, "Logographic and Semasiographic Writing Systems" (1995). Moira Yip, *Tone* (2002), is a comprehensive survey of the various lexical and grammatical uses of tone in languages throughout the world.

The second thing to know about tones is that they have not always been there: due to the physical nature of the energy produced as the sound of a consonant that follows a vowel (see §12.1.2), the noise of the consonant can move backward to become a change of pitch of the vowel it follows; the consonant as a result becomes redundant, so the tiny bit of extra effort it takes to say it is basically wasted, and over time speakers stopped wasting the effort, so that the distinctive information that used to be carried by the consonant is now carried by the change in pitch of the vowel—the *tone* of the syllable.

Scholars of Chinese—Sinologists—have devoted a great deal of effort to reconstructing what Chinese might have sounded like before the evolution of tones, and several proposals have been published in great detail; they take into account the sounds of words in the various modern Chinese languages such as Cantonese and Shanghainese, the ways Chinese words were borrowed into neighboring languages long ago, and the "rhyme tables" mentioned on page 89. But none dare take their reconstructions back to the earliest known Chinese writing, around 1250 BCE, let alone to however many centuries earlier when Chinese might first have been written. It is thus conventional in most circumstances to use the modern sounds of words even when referring to much earlier stages of Chinese. Traditionally, Chinese (as well as Korean and Japanese) texts are written (with a brush) in columns, top to bottom, the columns proceeding right to left. When written horizontally, the lines are read left to right.

6.1.1 Characters

With a few exceptions, each Chinese character represents one syllable, and that one syllable is almost always the sound of a *morpheme* (a minimal unit of meaning, like *horse* or *hearse*). The name for this type of writing system is *morphography*; the older, more familiar term is *logography*, referring to the word (*logos* in Greek). Taking into account the form of the words or morphemes gives us *logosyllabary* or *morphosyllabary*.

Examples are 媽 *mā* 'mother', 嗎 *má* 'hunh?',* 馬 *mǎ* 'horse', and 罵 *mà* 'scold'. In the most recent reconstruction of Old Chinese, the last two were pronounced

---

* One dictionary offers 'what (colloquial)' as a meaning of this "question particle" with tone 2—this is one of a few particles that only take their tone from surrounding syllables. It's hard to find examples of the same phonetic with tones 1 and 2 for reasons having to do with the history of the Chinese language, and this is a more satisfactory set: 巴 *bā* 'hope', 疤 *bā* 'scar', 耙 *pá* 'rake', 靶 *bǎ* 'target', and 爸 *bà* 'dad' (pers.comm., William H. Baxter, 13 November 2015).

Details *(continued)* ————————————————————————————————

William G. Boltz, *The Origin and Early Development of the Chinese Writing System* (1994), deals with the earliest phases. The latest reconstruction is by William H. Baxter and Laurent Sagart, *Old Chinese* (2014). Qiu Xigui, *Chinese Writing* (2000), is a dense but surprisingly lucid account of the full compass of the subject. Tsien Tsuen-hsuin,

Table 6.1 Some compound Chinese characters

Radical/Semantic	Phonetic 丁 dīng			工 gōng			堯 yāo			番 fān		
人 MAN	亻	仃 dīng	'left alone'	仜 hōng	'paunch'		僥 jiǎo	'lucky'		播 bō	(a name)	
手 HAND	扌	打 Dǎ	'strike'	扛 káng	'bear'		撓 náo	'scratch'		播 bō	'strew'	
水 WATER	氵	汀 tīng	'spit of land'	江 jiāng	'river'		澆 jiǎo	'sprinkle'		潘 pān	'ricewater'	
糸 SILK	糸	紅 zhēng	——	紅 hóng	'red'		繞 rào	'roll up'		繙 fān	'translate'	

mˤraʔ and *mˤra-s* when they were first written down. Tens of thousands of different characters and variants have been created over the 30+ centuries the Chinese writing system has been in use, but the vast majority might have only been used a few times and survive only in the great medieval and later dictionaries. Three thousand characters suffice for ordinary reading, and specialist scholars nowadays probably command as many as 5,000. How, then, is it possible to represent a full normal vocabulary of 25,000–30,000 words?

The word "word" is tricky when dealing with Chinese. 字 zì signifies both 'character' and the thing represented by a character, which is almost always a single syllable, one morpheme. It's the ordinary Chinese word for talking about units of language bigger than a sound and smaller than a sentence; as such it has been called the "sociological word." 詞 cí is a technical grammatical term that has been interpreted as "syntactic word"; it corresponds to a considerable extent to 'dictionary entry', so is closest to what we mean when we say an English word is 'a sequence of letters between spaces'—but there are no spaces between words in Chinese texts.

Chinese dictionary entries, or words, are mostly two characters long, so if you know 5,000 characters, you could spell 25 million words; 3,000 get you 9 million. Here are some examples from a medium-sized Chinese–English dictionary (listing 4,000 characters and 23,000 "words and phrases"):

Details *(continued)* ——————————————————————————————

Written on Bamboo and Silk (2004), describes the pre-modern texts and writing materials. The rhyme tables are investigated in D. P. Branner, ed., *The Chinese Rime Tables* (2006).
6.1.1 Jerome Lee Packard, *The Morphology of Chinese* (2000), provides an introduction to the nature of "words" in the modern language; and the observations of one of the founders of American descriptivist linguistics, Yuen Ren Chao, *Language and Symbolic Systems* (1968), are especially valuable as he combined the insights of a native speaker of Chinese with technical sophistication and a brilliant command of English style. The mid-sized dictionary mentioned is Yu S., Sheng P., Yin P., Ding F., Yu R., and Chen Y., eds., *Quaille's Practical Chinese–English Dictionary* (1999). I also used Bernhard Karlgren, *Analytic Dictionary of Chinese and Sino-Japanese* (1923); Rita Mei-Wah Choy, *Read and Write Chinese* (1990); and Go Ping-gam, *What Character Is That?* (1995).

媽媽	*māma*	'mommy' (compare 爸爸 *bàba* 'daddy')
馬鞍	*mǎān*	'saddle'
罵街	*màjiē*	'shout abuse in the street'
馬車	*mǎchē*	'carriage'
馬達	*mǎdá*	'motor'

Does even 3,000 separate items seem like an excessive memory burden? (Not really; we saw in §2.1.2 that there might be that many words in English whose spelling is sufficiently "irregular" that they need to be memorized.) This is still not a problem, because the 3,000 essential characters are not, in fact, 3,000 different graphic entities. All but a few hundred characters are *compound* characters (Table 6.1), composed of a part that clues the meaning (the *radical* or the *semantic*) and a part that clues the pronunciation (the *phonetic*). When the character set was first systematized, around the turn of the Era, the pronunciation part did more than clue the pronunciation; it actually gave it. But that's useful nowadays only to the scholars who attempt to reconstruct the ancient sounds.

You'll see assertions that Chinese characters do not help with pronunciation because in only 39% of them does the sound of the phonetic agree with the sound of the character ("even when tone is disregarded"); they simply overlook the fact that the sounds are similar enough to suggest the appropriate word, whose meaning is suggested by the radical: after all, anyone reading a text in Chinese already knows the language and thus already knows the word in its context. Moreover, it is quite illegitimate to "disregard tone," as tone is as essential a part of the morpheme as the consonants and vowels.

Look closely at our four examples of morphemes involving the sound [ma]. The simplest of them is 馬 'horse'. Many "guides to Chinese characters" will tell you that the shape of 馬 is a stylized picture of a horse—in this case, that observation is historically accurate, but many such "pictures" are the product of imagination rather than historical development. As with other ancient writing systems, the origin is indeed in representations of observed things (*pictograms*). Even in the earliest known Chinese inscriptions, the Oracle Bone Inscriptions (OBI) of the late second millennium BCE through which the gods were addressed, however, the script had been in use for so long that most of the glyphs are unrecognizable as representations.

Throughout the history of writing, there is a continual battle among (i) the energy it takes to inscribe a character involving multiple movements of the writing instrument, (ii) the need to preserve recognizability, (iii) conformity to a prevailing aesthetic, and (iv) visual distinctiveness. Less than half of the known inventory of maybe 4,000 distinct OBI characters can be securely read. They are identified by tracing the shapes of modern characters, which were codified nearly 2,000 years ago, back through time.

But there are only so many picturable objects in the world, and Chinese scribes soon hit on a way of writing words for things that could not so easily be pictured (about one quarter of the identified OBI characters are of this type): they combined into a single character two existing characters, which became the radical and the phonetic. Often the components are compressed horizontally or vertically, and sometimes these condensed forms don't look much like the full forms. Eventually the inventory of radicals was standardized at 214 (though various modern dictionaries now reduce them to fewer—174, 182, 189), and three of them are at work in our [ma] words: in 媽 we see 女 WOMAN (its pronunciation *nǚ* is irrelevant), combined with 馬 *mǎ* (its meaning 'horse' is irrelevant), written within one square space, to yield *mā* 'mother'. Similarly, 嗎 contains 口 MOUTH (ignoring *kǒu*) and 馬 *mǎ*, giving *ma* (question particle); and in 罵, 网 NET (ignoring *wǎng*; in its condensed form 罒) above 馬 *mǎ* produces *mà* 'scold'.

The other characters in our examples of 詞 *cí*'s take us a little further. (詞 *cí* itself is 言 [*yán*] SPEECH [considered a radical itself, despite containing 口] with 司 *sí* ['manage'].) 街 *jiē* 'street' places the radical 行 (*xíng*) WALK *around* the phonetic 圭 *guī* ('jade tablet'). 鞍 *ān* 'saddle' contains the radical 革 (*gé*) LEATHER and the phonetic 安 *ān* ('peaceful'). But 圭 *guī* and 安 *ān* are in turn composite characters. The obsolete 圭 is a stack of two 土 (*tǔ*) EARTH, said to refer to the jade token used in conferring fiefs, or else 土 LAND and 禾 CROPS, or else a 木 TREE on a 土 MOUND (all three interpretations leading to 'fief' and then 'scepter' as the sense of the character). In 安 *ān* 'peaceful', 女, meaning WOMAN, which we have already met in 'mother', is under a 宀 ROOF (which does not occur as a separate character), supposedly illustrating "domestic tranquility." Early treatments explain 字 *zì* 'character', 宀 ROOF over 子 *zǐ* (SON), not as a radical with a phonetic, but as 'to have a child in a house' > 'a brought-up person who takes a name at age 20' > name > word > character; or as "to have children under one's roof ... to shelter, nurse, bear, ... the characters produced or born by combining the simple 文 into compound characters, 字, either by logical composition or phonetic combination." The multiplicity and fancifulness of some of these "explanations" of semantic–semantic compounds have led some scholars to posit that virtually all such characters are ordinary semantic–phonetic compounds, sometimes involving component phonetic readings that have been completely forgotten.

There are, though, a few characters where the "semantic composition" is undeniable, such as 林 *lín* 'forest' and 森 *sēn* 'bushy' that do not have phonetic components alongside the radical 木 *mù* TREE. And this is a good example of a character whose pictographic origin remains recognizable. Can we say the same for 日 *rì* 'sun', 月 *yuè* 'moon', 田 *tián* 'field', 目 *mù* 'eye', 耳 *ěr* 'ear'? For the sake of completeness, we should note that traditional Chinese scholarship also recognizes a category of sign origin distinct from the last, in which a character depicts a relationship rather than an object: 上 *shàng* 'above' and 下 *xià* 'below' are the standard examples.

Details *(continued)* ———————————————————————————————————

The "explanations" of *zì* are from Bernhard Karlgren, *Analytic Dictionary of Chinese and Sino-Japanese* (1923), 310 #1089, and G. D. Wilder and J. H. Ingram, *Analysis of Chinese Characters* (1934), 1 #1, respectively.

Returning to the list of 詞 *cí* entries, 馬車 *mǎchē* 'carriage' shows a sort of limitation in the construction of characters. 車 (*chē*) alone is the radical for VEHICLE, so there *could* be a character with radical VEHICLE and phonetic *ma*—but because there isn't a single morpheme for 'horse-drawn carriage', there isn't one.

Thus it's not possible for Chinese writing to be "ideographic," readable in any or no language, with units invented on the fly for any concept whatsoever.

But this is not to say that pairs of characters can't be ambiguous: 紅花 *hónghuā* 'safflower' can also be read as *hóng huā* 'red flower' (compare English *blackbird* and *black bird*—except that the two Chinese expressions are not pronounced differently). There are also a few items that are but one morpheme in two syllables, written with two characters, such as 蝴 蝶 *húdié* 'butterfly'; both characters contain 虫 INSECT. Some polysyllabic characters have been created in modern times, most famously 圕 *túshūguǎn* 'library', a character created in Japan by condensing 圖書館 (but in Chinese the pronunciation is contracted into *tuān* from the first and last sounds and the tone of the middle syllable).

Finally, 馬達 *mǎdá* 'motor' illustrates a light-hearted but pervasive practice in assigning characters to borrowed words according to their sound but with an eye to a punning meaning: 馬 *mǎ* by itself, as we have seen, is HORSE, but 達 *dá* by itself is 'extend, reach, attain'; so a motor is, probably subconsciously, a thing that surpasses horses. In olden times, such punning was popular, for instance *Utopia* 烏托 邦 *wūtuōbāng* 'fabricated country', and it is still done today: the name Obama is rendered as 奧 巴馬 *Àobāmǎ*, where the characters translate as 'profound sincere-hope ma'; and, according to Wikipedia, one translation of *World Wide Web* is 萬維網 *Wàn Wéi Wǎng* meaning '10,000 dimension net'.

Naturally, the inventors of Chinese versions of foreign names needed to have a way of identifying suitable characters by their pronunciation—and much more importantly, so did poets (whose lines would rhyme) and other authors generally. The method eventually hit upon for explaining the pronunciations of characters involved analyzing each one into its *initial*—the opening consonant sound—versus everything else, the *final*, comprising the vowel and the closing consonants (that later morphed into tones). A limited set of familiar characters was chosen to identify each initial and each final, and charts—*rhyme tables*—placed them at the heads of rows and columns, with the characters being explained placed in the cells of the grid.

This system, though, was not particularly useful if you had an unfamiliar character before you and didn't know its pronunciation (or meaning). A scheme was needed, therefore, for organizing lists of characters, and that scheme is to order them by the number of brushstrokes employed in writing them. Uniformity is additionally preserved in that the strokes within any character are always written in the same order; this also makes possible extremely cursive forms of characters that can be written quickly but that do not present problems in reading later on.

First, the radical is identified. Characters are always analyzed into just two parts: there is always a radical and almost always a remainder. The remainder is either the

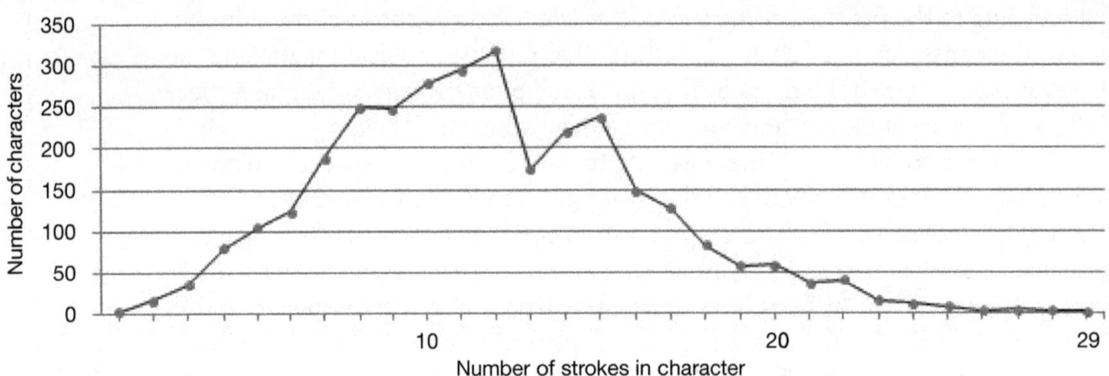

Figure 6.1. Number of characters per stroke count (from a 3200-character guide)

phonetic (the phonetic may itself be complex, but complexities within the phonetic are not taken into account), or else some additional component(s) suggesting the meaning. All the characters with the first 1-stroke radical come first, ordered by the number of strokes in the residue (whether it be a phonetic, as in most cases, or a semantic component), then those with the next 1-stroke radical, and so on; then the first 2-stroke radical, and so on; all the way down to some characters involving the 17-stroke 龠 *yuè* FLUTE radical: 龡 *chuī* 'blow', 龢 *hé* 'harmonious', 龣 *jué* (a musical instrument or its sound, associated with 'east' in cosmography), 龤 *xié* 'harmonize', and 龥 *yù* 'beg'. A complication is that dictionaries don't agree on the order of the radicals within each stroke-count group.

Just as a matter of curiosity, the most complex characters included in Unicode appear to be the 64-stroke 龘 *zhé* 'verbose' and 𪚥 *zhèng* [unknown], but those are merely quartets of 龍 *lóng* 'dragon' and 興 *xīng/xìng* 'flourish' respectively; 36-stroke 齉 *nàng* 'snuffle' is uncommon, and the champion that is actually used is 32-stroke 鬱 *yù* 'implore' (Figure 6.1).

6.1.2 Simplification

Overall, of course, Chinese writing is not nearly so complicated as those extreme examples, but it has been seen (both inside and outside China) to be a barrier to "progress," and the twentieth century was rife with proposals for supplementing or even replacing characters with some sort of phonetic notation. In 1949, the success of the Revolution provided an opportunity to impose a thoroughgoing script reform.

Details (*continued*)

6.1.2 Many of the documents surrounding the debate over Simplification and the introduction of *pinyin* are translated in P. J. Seybolt and G. K.-k. Chiang, eds., *Language Reform in China* (1979), including one by the principal architect of *pinyin*, Zhou Youguang (1906–2017; he lived until the day after his 111th birthday).

At first, Mao Tse-tung favored a phonetic script that would retain visual similarity with traditional characters, and hundreds of schemes were proposed, but ultimately a Roman-based alphabet was devised, the 漢語拼音 *Hànyǔ Pīnyīn* system (officially adopted in 1958) that even in Western scholarship has largely supplanted the "Wade-Giles" transliteration (so that Chairman Mao is now spelled Mao Zedong).

Nonetheless, even the most forward-thinking revolutionaries realized it would be folly to cut off all future generations from nearly two millennia of literature and calligraphy (Mao's own calligraphy was admired, apparently not just sycophantically), and reforms were proposed to the inventory of characters. By and large the new "simplified" characters made use of forms that were already widespread in informal use, and by no means were all characters replaced (only about 2,000); these examples from a couple of names cited above show some correspondences: *Utopia* 烏托邦 *wūtuōbāng* becomes 乌托邦—only the first character is simplified—and *World Wide Web* 萬維網 *Wàn Wéi Wǎng* becomes 万维网.

All four of the changed characters in these examples have something to tell us. 烏 *wū* 'crow, dark' is listed under ⺍ (the combining form of 火 FIRE), but the remainder does not occur separately; so the character is also taken as an old simplification (by one stroke) of 鳥 *niǎo* BIRD. 烏 is now simplified as 乌, with the FIRE radical replaced by a horizontal line. Compare the simplification of 馬 *mǎ* HORSE as 马, with the same replacement of the four dots at the bottom—which were never taken as FIRE in this character. This is an example of how the entire apparatus of radical+phonetic, which aided mnemonically in the identification of characters, has been abandoned. The dots at the lower left of 維 have also turned into a line in 维. Compare 23-stroke 變 *biàn* 'change', where the radical, taken to be 言 SPEECH, appears in the upper part flanked by SILK (this combination appears in a few characters as a phonetic), with the lower part 夊 *zhi* 'walk slowly'; it becomes 10-stroke 変—but this is an old *Japanese* simplification (which we will meet again in §7.1).

In 萬 '10,000' becoming 万, the simplification is extreme—in one way it assimilates to the simplicity of the traditional numerals 一 二 三, but in another it betrays the system of "complicated" numerals devised to forestall fraudulent alteration of economic documents, where '1, 2, 3' are respectively 壹 貳 參.

And 網 *wǎng* 'net' becoming 网 is the adoption of the (somewhat) simplified radical form that we have seen above in place of the fuller character, where 糸 SILK is joined by 罔, which on its own is not *wǎng* NET—so this is not a semantic–semantic compound—but *wǎng* 'not'. This description is summarized in Table 6.2.

The simplification of Chinese characters—despite the possible cost in memorizability—appears to have won the day. The Republic of China continues to use traditional characters, as do Hong Kong and Macao, but a recent perusal of bookstore shelves showed that not one of the assortment of popular-audience Chinese-English dictionaries on hand employs traditional characters. And the two sets of characters appear to be tossed together in the Unicode ordering. When I first met a linguist from the PRC—a graduate student at a conference in Canada in 1994—who had never been exposed to traditional characters, I asked him whether he could read them.

Table 6.2 Examples of character simplification

Character		Simplified	Component(s)
鳥	*niǎo* 'bird'	鸟	火 FIRE in its combining form 灬
烏	*wū* 'crow, dark'	乌	–
馬	*mǎ* 'horse'	马	–
維	*wéi* 'hold together'	维	糸 SILK; 佳 *jiā* 'good'
變	*biàn* 'change'	変	糸 SILK 言 SPEECH 糸 SILK; 夂 *zhi* 'walk slowly'
萬	*wàn* '10,000'	万	–
網	*wǎng* 'net'	网	糸 SILK; 罔 *wǎng* 'not'

He pointed to the masthead of the *New York Times*, with its elaborate "black-letter" elaborations, and said they were like that: the text was readable, but there was a lot of extra decoration.

6.2 Sumerian

The first language that we know to have been written is Sumerian. And we know it was written because of the material it was written on: not some vegetal or animal product, like papyrus or palm leaves or paper, like leather or parchment; but simple clay. Clay that was deposited by the powerful waters of the Land Between the Rivers (the Tigris and Euphrates)—Mesopotamia. Clay that could be scooped from their banks, patted into handy sizes and shapes, and while moist incised or impressed with marks made using a stylus. Clay that would then dry solid and nearly indestructable. Tens of thousands of documents—we call the inscribed objects *tablets*—have survived across two to five thousand years and more. At first it was drawings—pictograms—that were incised. Each pictogram represented a Sumerian word. The need for speed and readability soon led to the pictograms being stylized and abstracted into patterns of wedges impressed with the touch of a rectangular corner of a stylus. It is the wedge, *cuneus* in Latin, that gave its name to this *cuneiform* writing.

Details *(continued)* ──

6.2 A convenient overview of cuneiform writing is C. B. F. Walker, *Cuneiform* (1987), but the current understanding of Sumerian can be found, beyond the primary technical studies, in Piotr Michalowski, "Sumerian" (2004), and Christopher Woods, "The Earliest Mesopotamian Writing" (2010). G. R. Driver, *Semitic Writing* (1976), 8–17, gathers much information about the materials and shapes used for cuneiform writing, and (17–31) much speculation about the nature of the stylus. The stylus has been reconstructed—because no examples have been found in the archeological record—by Michele Cammarosano, "The Cuneiform Stylus" (2014). An

Sumerian was not related to any known language. This doesn't mean that it had no relatives, only that none of its relatives happened to get written down on durable materials before they or their descendants died out. The earliest documents—this term has come to be used for any texts that aren't *belles lettres* or creative writing—, which date from about 3400 BCE, come from administration. They are lists: lists of people, of professions, of things in categories; they are records of transactions, for instance concerning sheep or barley. They are not connected texts; there is no Epic of Creation or Story of the Flood in the early cuneiform materials.

Some of those lists continued to be used and copied and elaborated for thousands of years. They provided the basis of Mesopotamian scribal education, indeed made the cuneiform writing system possible, because they included the hundreds of characters (in cuneiform studies, each is called a *sign*) a scribe needed to know.

But wait: any language must have tens of thousands of words in it. How could just a few hundred signs be adequate for representing an entire language? There are two complementary ways. One way is by use of the *rebus* principle. This means using a pictogram only for its sound but not for its meaning: in an English rebus, you can use a picture of an eye (not so hard to draw) to represent the word "I" (almost impossible to draw). This principle is at work to a very limited extent even in the earliest Sumerian tablets; for instance, the sign 𒄀 for *gi* 'reed' is also used for *gi* 'to return'. The other way is by using a pictogram for its meaning but not for its sound. This principle is very common even in the earliest Sumerian tablets: a picture of a leg can be used for 'leg' but also for 'walk'.

Unlike Chinese, Sumerian writing sometimes differentiated the same pictogram used for different words not by marking different pronunciations, but by marking different meanings: *ka* 'mouth' was represented by adding "shading" markings to the mouth area of the *sag* 'head' pictogram, and *gu$_7$* 'eat' was represented by a bowl adjacent to the face of the 'head' pictogram. Eventually these signs took on these forms (the head in the pictogram faced up): *sag* 𒊕 *ka* 𒅗 *gu$_7$* 𒅥.

Usually, syllabograms represent CV syllables, but Sumerian cuneiform is unique in including VC and CVC symbols in its inventory, such as 𒂗 *en* 'lord' and 𒁺 *gub* 'put'.

In the earliest lists, a few signs appear that seem to incorporate phonetic complements, indicating that the sign had a pronunciation that we can recognize from

---

*In cuneiform studies (Assyriology, Sumerology, etc.), the transliterations of different signs with (we assume) the same pronunciation are differentiated with numerical subscripts, assigned long ago according to rough frequency of occurrence. *gu$_2$* and *gu$_3$* are often spelled *gú* and *gù* instead.

Details *(continued)* ————————————————————————————————

illustration of how a stylus could be cut from a hollow cylindrical reed (alongside stunninng photographs of a variety of tablets) is found in Irving Finkel and Jonathan Taylor, *Cuneiform* (2015), 75.

The phonetic complements in the earliest Sumerian texts were recognized by Piotr Steinkeller, review of *Zeichenliste der archaischen Texte aus Uruk* by M. W. Green and H. J. Nissen (1995), but his interpretation has not been fully accepted by other Sumerologists.

later developments as specifically Sumerian, a good indication that the script was developed for Sumerian, rather than taken over from another language. The earliest suggested example is 𒂠𒂗 *ezen^{en}*, where 𒂗 *en* 'lord' may be there only to guarantee the reading of 𒂠 as *ezen* 'to sing' and not as the alternative reading *bad* 'wall, fortress'.

A further important feature of Sumerian orthography is the use of *semantic determinatives*: a limited number of signs regularly preceded—or in a few cases followed—the sign(s) for a word indicating what category it belonged to. Names of gods were preceded by 𒀭 *dingir*, names of men by 𒁹 *diš*, names of women by 𒊩 *sal*, wooden items by 𒄑 *giš*; and names of places were followed by 𒆠 *ki*.

Only later—after cuneiform writing had been borrowed for writing the Semitic language Akkadian (see §7.2)—were the grammatical suffixes of Sumerian written. One reason might be that when you're simply listing things, you don't need to know about grammatical relations like subjects and objects. Another might be that the base words of Sumerian generally didn't change with their inflections—they were more like English *dog/dogs* than like *man/men*—but the inflections did—like that [z] in *dogs*, the [s] in *cats*, and the [ɪz] in *horses*. But the principle was that one morpheme always has the same sign, and it was difficult for the first scribes to abstract

---

Details *(continued)*

An enigmatic text, most fully and reliably studied by Miguel Civil, "Remarks on AD-GI₄" (2013), whose earliest examples date well before 3000 BCE, appears to be nothing but a list of words—in part it even overlaps a text that *is* known to be a list of vegetables—but it can also be interpreted as the first known example of a narrative text. Civil

> postulates the existence of a simpler, more archaic stage in the evolution of the cuneiform writing system. When the scribes attempted for the first time to write down narrative texts, they simply enunciated the participants of the narrated event, leaving out the representation of predicates and [other elements that] give continuity to a narrative. The bare enumeration of the core arguments of the predicate …, but without making explicit the predicate itself, can only function as a mnemonic trigger that evokes the full plot in the addressee's mind. The addressee must therefore know beforehand the story because in such a system of writing a text carries practically no new information. (17f.)

The text was copied and recopied over at least a thousand years, and it may have received many explanations during that time. If this interpretation or a kindred one is on the right track, then this is a precious, perhaps unique, exemplar of a graphic system captured at a mnemonic stage (Chapter 10) interpretable because it was soon to be a writing system. The archeologist Denise Schmandt-Besserat, "Writing after Accounting in the Ancient Near East" (2015), suggests that a several-generation sequence of Sumerian votive statues found in a temple cella with increasingly elaborate inscriptions on the shoulder (first just a name, then a phrase, then a full sentence) reflects the progression from list-writing to prose-writing.

The example is from Jerrold S. Cooper's contribution to P. T. Daniels and W. Bright, eds., *The World's Writing Systems* (1996), 44.

See also §7.2 Details.

a single sound, to be represented by a single sign, for a varying morpheme. Not until the twentieth century—when linguistic analysis was devised—did anyone think of writing the English plural mark as something like {S}, so this is not surprising.

A Sumerian proverb was written down in this form ca. 2500 BCE:

dumu engar níg na-ra

son farmer thing do. not-beat

and in this form ca. 1800 BCE:

dumu engar-ra-ra níg nam-mu-ra-ra-an

son farmer-of-to thing do.not-(prefix)-beat-beat-you
'do not beat a farmer's son'.

6.3 Mayan

When the *Conquistadores* arrived in Mexico from Spain shortly after 1500 in search of gold, they encountered two literate cultures, the Aztec and the Maya. It's not entirely clear that Aztec pictography had yet developed from ideograms to writing; post-Conquest materials using the old images indubitably represent the sounds of the names that were the only things that were written. The Aztecs were concentrated in a small area around present-day Mexico City.

On the Yucatan Peninsula—easternmost Mexico, and Guatemala and Belize—were and are magnificent ruins of tomb and temple complexes, many of them covered with intricate carvings in columns of squared glyphs. The conquerors had no interest in these pagan remains, though they took care to extirpate almost every bark-paper manuscript that had been preserved by the remnant of traditional scribes who presumably could have interpreted both them and the stone monuments, had the Spaniards not assumed that they were nothing but worthless heathen foolery.

The Spaniards were also unable to imagine a writing system that wasn't an alphabet, so when Bishop Diego de Landa actually did take an interest in the native culture, he had a scribe write down the Spanish alphabet in Maya glyphs. But the result was

---

Details *(continued)*

6.3 Aztec writing is described by Gordon Whittaker, "The Principles of Nahuatl Writing" (2009).

Mayan studies proceed so quickly that any treatment for the general public is outdated before it is published, but Stephen D. Houston, *Maya Glyphs* (1989), provides the basics. Early interpretations by a visionary scholar are set forth in Linda Schele and Mary Ellen Miller, filed away in an archive for nearly 400 years, unconsulted, forgotten. Eventually, with its rediscovery it became the first evidence used in recovering the script (§9.3). Maya writing proved to be a morphosyllabary, with great complication that was introduced no doubt to make its mastery as difficult as possible, evidence of the intellectual and social superiority of the few who could boast such an achievement.

In the most ordinary Maya writing, each of the squarish glyphs has at its center a syllabogram whose reading is based on the word for the item depicted, often functioning as a logogram. Around all four sides of it, condensed or abbreviated versions of signs can be attached, like intricate little sausage links, each with its own reading to be added as a prefix or suffix to the central sign's morpheme, or else as phonetic complements just as in cuneiform:

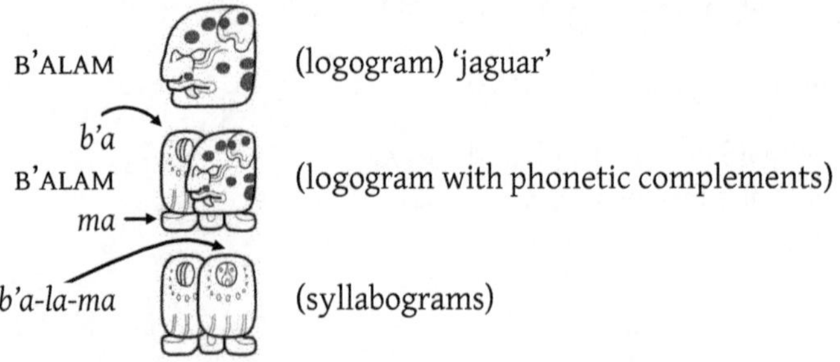

Details *(continued)*

The Blood of Kings (1986); Linda Schele and David Freidel, *A Forest of Kings* (1990); and Linda Schele and Peter Mathews, *The Code of Kings* (1998). The drawings and explanations of Maya glyphs are from Scott A. J. Johnson, *Translating Maya Hieroglyphs* (2013). The Rabbit Vase is celebrated as one of the finest examples of Mayan iconography, but since the vase was first published by Michael D. Coe, *The Maya Scribe and His World* (1973), the inscription has received little attention: the analysis of selected portions of it in Johnson's textbook is the only treatment that's widely available.

Remnants of a dozen or more probable writing systems have been discovered in Mesoamerica, a culture-area covering most of Mexico and northern Central America. None of those besides Mayan has been satisfactorily deciphered, and the oldest known one, associated with the Olmec culture of the Gulf Coast states of Veracruz and Tabasco, Mexico, and dating to perhaps 1000 BCE, appears itself to be the result of considerable development. The shapes of the characters in all of them are so similar as to suggest that they share a common ancestor, and Olmec is the currently available candidate to be that ancestor. An overview of Mesoamerican writing with its connections to the calendrical system is provided by Joyce Marcus, "Mesoamerica: Scripts" (2006). She offers the following criteria "to distinguish Mesoamerican writing from its iconographic precursors":

1. There must be at least three glyphs, arranged in a row or column.
2. The arrangement must determine reading order.
3. The set of glyphs must show a correspondence to the spoken language.
4. As a consequence, the arrangement must follow grammatical rules.

Iconographic precursors earlier than Zapotec are thus excluded. The earliest writing systems of Mesoamerica—or, as the author carefully notes, "probably four notational systems in which

The glyphs are normally written in vertical columns of horizontal pairs, the columns of two glyphs proceeding from left to right. Here's a rare text that isn't mostly year-dates:

pu-lu	*a-*JOL	*u-c'u*	*a-wi-ti*		…	…	*ni-bu-ku*
			…		ha-ta		

This is the first scene from the so-called Rabbit Vase. The evil rabbit steals God L's things and insults him: *pul-u a-jol uc'-u aw-it* 'hit your head, smell your anus'. On the right, God L complains (the interpreted glyphs read *hat* 'you' and *ni-buhk* 'my clothes'); *a(w)-* is 'your', *ni-* is 'my'.

But there are many additional features. Various categories of concepts—month names, god names, individuals, and so on—are often represented by glyphs in the form of human, animal, or monster shapes. As is well known, elaborate calendar

Details *(continued)* ————————————————————————

symbols were deployed in part in relation to a spoken language: Olmec, Zapotec, epi-Olmec (Zoque), and Mayan"—are concisely and cogently described by John S. Justeson, "Early Mesoamerican Writing Systems" (2013). The next four chapters in the same volume discuss the later scripts and colonial-period literature. Alfonso Lacadena, "Historical Implications of the Presence of non-Mayan Linguistic Features in the Maya Script" (2010a), brings linguistic evidence to bear on assessing the antecedents of Maya writing, and Martha J. Macri and Matthew G. Looper, "Nahua in Ancient Mesoamerica" (2003), conversely show that borrowed Aztec words can be identified in Maya inscriptions.

notation was very important, and calendrical and mathematical notation had been recorded at least in part by the Spanish, and were well understood long before the script could be read—including the use of the numeral zero:

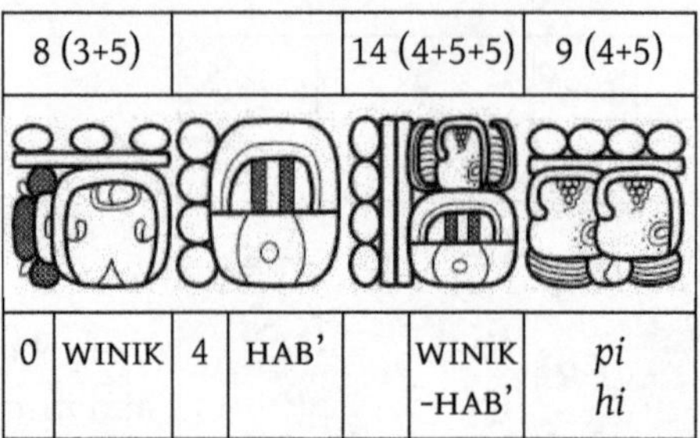

8 (3+5)			14 (4+5+5)	9 (4+5)
0	WINIK	4	HAB'	WINIK-HAB'	pi hi

All glyph drawings © 2014 University of Oklahoma Press.

wašak (k'in) mih winik čan haab' čan haab' čamlaxu'n winikhaab' b'olon pih

'8 (days), 0 [20-day] months, 4 years, 14 score [of years], 9 eras [of 144,000 days]'

In discussions of Maya chronology, *k'atun* is often used for 'score' and *b'aktun* for 'era'.

7 Words and Heterograms

At least three times that we know of, cultures that owed much of their development to an older culture have tried to use the older writing system for their own language but have run into various problems, usually involving a mismatch in their "morphological typology." We've seen examples of all three of the traditional types. Indo-European and Semitic languages, such as Sanskrit and Syriac, are *inflecting*—words change according to their functions in a sentence; endings can signal several different things at once, such as number, gender, and case of nouns, or person, number, and tense of verbs. Turkic languages are *agglutinative*—words have suffixes, as in Indo-European languages, but the morphemes are just strung out in a row without changing at their edges, and each one indicates only one thing: a morpheme for person, a morpheme for number, a morpheme for tense, and so on.* Sumerian until recently was thought to be strictly agglutinative, but it is now understood that the morphemes did in fact change their shape according to preceding or following suffixes—I suggested that this contributed to their not being written in earliest Sumerian (§6.2). Chinese and Tibetan are *isolating*—they use few to no grammatical prefixes or suffixes at all. English retains its Indo-European inflectional heritage to a small extent but has nearly become a fully isolating language, relying to a remarkable degree on word order to communicate the relationships among the parts of sentences.

As it happens, two of the most senior and influential cultures in human history used isolating writing systems, early Sumerian and Chinese, and when successive or surrounding peoples tried to write their languages with the existing scripts, they ran into difficult problems because they couldn't easily express their grammatical morphemes with characters that each carried along a meaning of their own: how could the reader know when a particular character was to be read for its sense, and when only for its sound? The solutions ultimately hit upon around the world were surprisingly similar: develop characters for their sounds, but also use characters for their meanings. In the latter use, the characters are called "word-signs," or *logograms*. The term *heterogram* appears sometimes in Iranian studies (§7.3). Since it's noncommittal as to the level of grammatical analysis involved—it doesn't specify "word" or "morpheme," just "otherness"—it might be convenient to adopt it for general use.

---

*The Turkish language itself switched from Arabic script to Roman script in 1928, as part of President Atatürk's "secularization" program (§12.3.1), and we've mentioned the Uyghur abjad (§3.5).

Even English uses a few heterograms left over from when scholarship was based in Latin. We see ⟨e.g.⟩ and read "for example." We see ⟨et cetera⟩ or ⟨etc.⟩ and read "and so on." We even see ⟨&⟩ and read "and"—because the ampersand is a ligature of the letters ⟨et⟩, Latin 'and'. (Admittedly, ⟨&⟩ is really an ideogram, since the ⟨et⟩ origin is rarely visible in the character.) Signs or characters that indicate a morpheme or word in one language (Sumerian or Chinese or Latin) are used when writing another language; in this second language, they indicate morphemes or words of similar meaning in the second language, without regard for the sound of the morpheme or word in the originating language.

7.1 Japanese

Japanese began to be written with Chinese characters—the *kanji*—toward the middle of the first millennium CE. Unlike Korean (§8.1), Japanese shows no sign of giving up its use of Chinese characters even though it has a fully functional sound-based script (§4.1). Most *kanji* in fact represent at least two different and unrelated Japanese words, both the Chinese word(s) that the character was borrowed along with, and some native Japanese word(s) of similar meaning. The term *logogram* hasn't been used in Japanese studies, but *heterogram* would be a convenient label for the system. The Chinese readings are known as *on*, the Japanese readings are known as *kun*, and one scholar of writing has adapted this terminology to other writing systems, so that native English *faze* could be said to exhibit a *kun* spelling, and *phase*, borrowed from Greek via Latin, an *on* spelling.

That parallel is not exact, however, because the words *faze* and *phase* are unrelated and only coincidentally homophonous. The situation in Japanese can be illustrated with a few characters: the Chinese character 變 *biàn* 'change' represents (simplified, 変) the native Japanese words *kawaru* 'to change (intransitive)', *kawari* 'a change', and *kaeru* 'to change (transitive)'; these are its *kun* readings. The character 変 *biàn* also represents the Japanese word *hen* 'unusual event', which was borrowed long ago from Chinese and is thus its *on* reading. (The change of *b* and *p* to *h* in Japanese postdated the borrowing.) Both kinds of reading can enter into multi-*kanji* words, such as *kawari-mono* 変わり者 'eccentric person' (that's Chinese 者 *zhě* [pronoun]), and *henshin* 変心 'change of heart' (that's Chinese 心 *xīn* HEART.)

But, aside from context, how can the reader know whether any particular occurrence of 変 should be read as any of the *ka-* words, or as *hen*? Notice the *hiragana*

Details ──

7.1 Now fundamental for Japanese is Bjarke Frellesvig, *A History of the Japanese Language* (2010). Timothy J. Vance, *The Sounds of Japanese* (2008), is a very useful guide for the reader with no training in linguistics or phonetics. The history of Japanese writing is set forth in great detail by Christopher Seeley, *A History of Writing in Japan* (1991). The *on/kun* approach to writing systems other than the Japanese is suggested by Henry Rogers, *Writing Systems* (2005).

(§4.1) in the middle of *kawari-mono* 変わり者. They are the *hiragana* for *wa-ri-*. The *kana* represent the grammatical endings and particles that Japanese has and Chinese doesn't, which really need to be represented if a Japanese text isn't to be interpreted purely by guessing at the writer's intent. So the words I've mentioned look like this:

変わる	KA-wa-ru	'to change'
変わり	KA-wa-ri	'a change'
変える	KA-e-ru	'to change something'
変	HEN	'unusual incident'
変な	HEN na	'strange' (the Japanese particle na creates an adjective)
変心	HEN SHIN	'change of heart'

There's a further complication. A more skilled reader can handle less "help" with identifying the reading of the character and so can do with fewer *kana*:

変る	KAWA-ru	'to change'
変り	KAWA-ri	'a change'

Thus *kanji* and *kana* work together to notate the Japanese language in a way that keeps it in touch with many more centuries of cultural heritage than English orthography does.

Less than thirty years ago, there were suggestions that the intricate writing system of Japan would be a barrier to the nation's entering the modern computer-based Information Age, which appeared to be limited to inputting a restricted set of 128 Roman-alphabet letters, numbers, and a few additional characters—then supplemented by a further 128 that could handle most of the scripts of Western Europe—but in a very short time, unprecedented cooperation among the two Chinas, South Korea, and Japan brought about the development of input systems and astonishingly large character sets that could handle the full variety of modern East Asian character-based scripts. And shortly after that, the Unicode Consortium established (different!) standards that, adopted by computer manufacturers worldwide, now make it possible to enter text in any of the languages on just about any computer.

7.2 Cuneiform

Sumerian (§6.2) was the literary language of southern Mesopotamia when writing was first used. Some time in the mid third millennium (ca. 2500 BCE), Semitic-speakers began to use cuneiform writing to record their language, Akkadian. They had no hangups about including the grammatical prefixes and suffixes, they retained

Details *(continued)* ───────────────────────────────────────

7.2 A sweeping overview of the culture revealed in cuneiform documents, though somewhat outdated, by one of the great masters of Assyriology of the twentieth century, is A. Leo Oppenheim, *Ancient Mesopotamia* (1977). Up to date, ranging well beyond its titular subject, and addressed to a more general audience is Irving Finkel, *The Ark before Noah* (2014); its the determinatives device, they occasionally used comparable *phonetic complements* that identified a sound or two in the word, and for a few common words, they used signs for their sense rather than their sounds—Sumerograms in Akkadian, or heterograms, which have long been known as *logograms*.

Semitic languages have more consonants than Sumerian, and this led in part to multiple readings—thus ⊨⊨ could be used for all of *ad*, *at*, and *aṭ*, for instance. As with Japanese, the corresponding words of the borrowing language became attached to the signs, so that they could be used for the sounds of Akkadian words as well as Sumerian words: thus ⊨ could be read either *giš*, as in Sumerian, or *iṣ* from the Akkadian word *iṣu* 'wood'—and still served as the determinative for wooden things.

By the time King Hammurapi caused a lengthy series of his decisions to be incised on a stela to be used as precedents, ca. 1800 BCE, the writing system was fully established, and it continued in use virtually unchanged save for the shapes of the signs, which underwent the usual sort of variation across space and time. Babylonia was southern Mesopotamia, Assyria was northern Mesopotamia, and the Akkadian language and script diverged somewhat according to the two regions. More technical scientific texts would use a much higher proportion of logograms, probably for both concision and confidentiality. Although there were probably no native speakers of Akkadian after the middle of the first millennium BCE, its use in academic circles continued into the first century CE and perhaps even beyond.

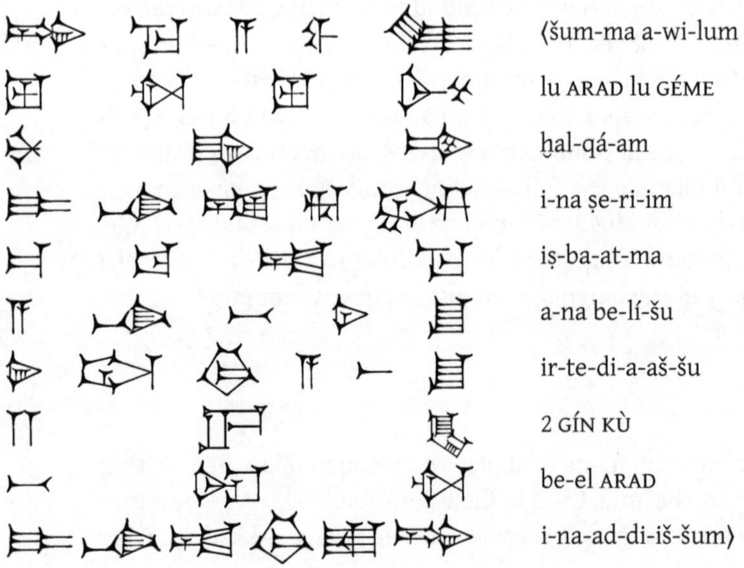

	⟨šum-ma a-wi-lum
	lu ARAD lu GÉME
	ḫal-qá-am
	i-na ṣe-ri-im
	iṣ-ba-at-ma
	a-na be-lí-šu
	ir-te-di-a-aš-šu
	2 GÍN KÙ
	be-el ARAD
	i-na-ad-di-iš-šum⟩

šumma awīlum lu wardam lu amtam ḫalqam ina ṣērim iṣbatma ana bēlišu irtediaššu
2 šiqil kaspam bēl wardim inaddiššum

'If a man seizes a fugitive slave or slave woman in the open country and leads him back to his owner, the slave owner shall give him 2 shekels of silver.'
                                                    —*Laws of Hammurapi, col. viii, lines 49–58 (§17)*

Cuneiform writing was also used by a number of peoples in surrounding areas. We have found large quantities of texts in the Hurrian, Urartian, and Elamite languages—all of them with minimal employment of heterograms—and especially Hittite, which soon after its discovery proved to be an archaic form of Indo-European. Hittite uses heterograms for both their Sumerian and Akkadian readings, so that there are both Sumerograms and Akkadograms among the heterograms in Hittite.

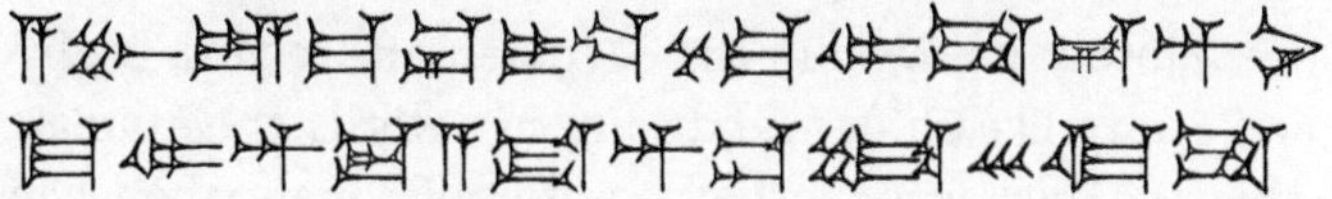

(*A-BU-YA*-ma-kán *I-NA* KUR ^{URU}Mi-it-ta-an-ni
ku-it an-da a-ša-an-du-le-eš-ki-it)

father.my-but-there in land Mittanni
because in camp.iterative.he(past)

'But because my father remained camped in the land Mittanni' ...
—*from the Annals of Mursili II (ca. 1353–1325 BCE)*

Sumerograms are transliterated with small capitals, Akkadograms with italic small capitals, and semantic determinatives with superscript sign names. Some of the most common words in Hittite texts are almost never written phonetically, and we still do not know the Hittite words for notions like 'son', 'daughter', and 'sheep'.

7.3 Middle Iranian

The most interesting development of heterograms is also the least well known: words written in Aramaic are pronounced in Iranian. Part of what makes it so interesting

---

Details (*continued*)

Appendix 1 elucidates intricate—but deadly serious—"wordplay" by which Mesopotamian scholars exploited the polyphony, the bilinguality, and even the shapes of cuneiform signs to evoke esoteric concepts.

The longevity of the use of cuneiform, and much else, is discussed by M. J. Geller, "The Last Wedge" (1997).

The interpretation of Hammurapi's law (not Code!) is from Martha T. Roth, *Law Collections from Mesopotamia and Asia Minor* (1997). The Hittite example is from Gene B. Gragg's contribution to P. T. Daniels and W. Bright, eds., *The World's Writing Systems* (1996), 69.

7.3 After planning this chapter in what I took to be an innovative way, bringing together for the first time the three writing systems that employ heterograms, I discovered that I had been anticipated—by nearly a century and a half! Martin Haug, *Essay on the Pahlavi Language* (1870), 120–25, uses both Japanese and the as yet little-understood Assyrian cuneiform in his attempts to clarify the nature of Middle Iranian writing, which he appears to have been the first European scholar to grasp.

Table 7.1 Book Pahlavi

Iranian	', h	b	g, d, y	–	w, n, r,'	z	k	l	m	s	p	c	š	t
heterograms	A, H	B	G, D, Y	E	W, N, O, R,'	Z	K	L	M, Q	S	P	C	Š	T

is that its development can be closely followed in the documentary record, beginning in the fourth century BCE. But unlike Chinese and Sumerian words, the Aramaic words were spelled with an abjad, so there was a sort of cognitive dissonance between what was seen in the text—actual pronunciations—and what was understood in the mind—totally different words. Nonetheless, these writing systems were the only ones for their languages for more than 800 years, and they are still read to this day by the Zoroastrians—the Parsees—of India and the diaspora.

As mentioned in §3.3.4, commentaries on the Zoroastrian scriptures, the Avesta, were written in the Middle Iranian language Pahlavi,* whose abjad had shrunk to 14 letters (Table 7.1; compare Table 3.10). (Fortunately for Westerners, Pahlavi was occasionally written with the Avestan alphabet, Table 2.12, so that all the sounds were expressed. This hybrid is called Pazand.)

The first Europeans to see this language were mystified: it appeared to be a "mixed language," comprising Aramaic and Iranian elements in seemingly equal measure,

---

*The term "Pahlavi" properly refers to a specific language and script but by non-specialists is sometimes used for the whole group of Middle West Iranian languages between the Old Persian stage and Modern Persian, as in the general histories of writing by Marcel Cohen, James-G. Février, Johannes Friedrich, David Diringer, and Hans Jensen, and the *Encyclopedia* of Florian Coulmas.

Details *(continued)* ———————————————————————

Iranian orthography is described by W. B. Henning, "Mitteliranisch" (1958). Discussions specifically of the scripts and writing systems are found only in edited volumes: by P. Oktor Skjærvø in P. T. Daniels and W. Bright, eds., *The World's Writing Systems* (1996), 515–35, and in G. Windfuhr, ed., *The Iranian Languages* (2009), 196–204; and by Dieter Weber in A. S. Kaye, ed., *Phonologies of Asia and Africa* (1997), 601–10. The importance of Manichaean and even Early Modern Persian orthography for the interpretation of the phonology of Middle Persian as a whole was recognized by D. N. MacKenzie, "Notes on the Transcription of Pahlavi" (1967), and the diacritic-less transliterations of the heterograms in Iranian follow his *Concise Pahlavi Dictionary* (1971). The last word by their initial editor on the great inscriptions of Shapur I is found in Martin Sprengling, *Third Century Iran* (1953); the interpretations of the excerpts are P. Oktor Skjærvø's, pp. 522–23. Werner Sundermann, "Schriftsysteme und Alphabete im alten Iran" (1985), notes that, by and large, the scripts employing heterograms were those serving the state, while those using alphabets and abjads (Avestan, Manichaean, etc.) served religions, but he does register some exceptions.

though its true nature was never lost to its own scholars—what to Westerners looked like Aramaic words were to them simply arcane representations of Iranian words. The Europeans, who could read Aramaic, thought they were reading a text in weird Aramaic. Not until extensive inscriptions in earlier phases of Middle West Iranian were interpreted, in the middle years of the twentieth century, did the writing system become clear, but it is still remarkable that a system harboring so much ambiguity could have succeeded for so long: D. N. MacKenzie gives the example that the sequence of Pahlavi letters ࣟ (lhyk ') represents either *rahīg* 'child' in Pahlavi or the heterogram *LHYK'*, representing Aramaic ࣟ (i.e., ࣟ (rḥyk)), for Pahlavi *dūr* 'far'. The origin of the system appears to have been scribal practicality (and perhaps inertia): records had been kept in Aramaic for centuries (it remains under discussion whether to read a collection of brief third-century economic documents from Parthian Nisa, Turkmenistan, in Aramaic or Iranian), and as the chancery began to switch over to Iranian, it made sense to follow prior practice, however much incremental work it took new recruits to acquire the old spellings— that reflected a language they knew nothing of.

Just as in Akkadian and as in Japanese *on* vs. *kun* readings, there's nothing graphically distinctive about the stretches of text that are heterograms; the scribes simply knew which words were not pronounced as they were spelled. They were common words, belonging to frequent, basic vocabulary; recall (§2.1.1) that it is the most frequent words that are most likely to retain archaic spellings, because they are among the first words one learns to write. In modern studies, heterograms are transliterated with capital letters, but it must be stressed that this reflects no characteristic of the original orthography.

Toward the end of the reign of the second Sassanian king, Shapur I (r. 242–272), a trilingual inscription was incised at Naqš-i Rustam, near Persepolis. Its first editor found the Parthian text to be the original, representing the traditional administrative language left over from Arsacid rule, with the Middle Persian the language of the new rulers; and he observed that the Greek version differs in detail and may have been composed by someone who didn't fully understand the original. The conclusions of the two Iranian versions show how the heterograms functioned in both the earlier Parthian and the later Middle Persian writing systems *(read the inscriptions right to left, the transliterations and transcriptions left to right).*

Details *(continued)*

The two corpora of Achaemenid Aramaic leather documents were published by G. R. Driver, *Aramaic Documents of the Fifth Century B.C.* (1957), and by Joseph Naveh and Shaul Shaked, *Aramaic Documents from Ancient Bactria* (2012). Their relevance to Achaemenid scribal training was brought out by Peter T. Daniels, "Aramaic Documents from Achaemenid Bactria" (2014). The discussion of the earliest heterograms is from W. B. Henning, "Mitteliranisch" (1958), 25.

Table 7.2 Middle Iranian inscriptional and manuscript characters

Parthian — Iranian heterograms

A	B	G	D	E	W	Z	H	Θ	Y	K	L	M	m	S	O	P	C	Q	R	Š	T
ʾ	b, w	g, ɣ	d, δ	h	w	z, ž	h, x		y	k, g	l	m	n	s		p, b	č		r	š, ž	t, d

Middle Persian — Iranian heterograms

A	B	G	D	E	W, O, R	Z	H	Θ	Y	K	L	M, Q	N	S	P	C	Š	T
ʾ	b, w	g, y	d, y		w, r	z	h, x		y, j	k, g	l, r	m	n	s, h	p, b, f	č, j, z	š	t, d

Book Pahlavi — Iranian heterograms

A, H	B	G, D, Y	E	W, N, O, R, ʾ	Z	K	L	M, Q	S	P	C	Š	T
ʾ, h	b	g, d, y	–	w, n, r, ʾ	z	k	l	m	s	p	c	š	t

⟨LHWyš MNW BATR MN LN YHYE W prnhw HWYt LHWyš ʾpr yʾztn CBW
W krtkny twhšywd AYK yʾzt ʾdywr YHYEnt W dstkrty OBDWnt⟩

hawiž kē paš až amāh bawāδ ud farrox ahād hawiž abar yazdān īr
ud kerdagān tuxšāδ kū yazd aδyāwar bawānd ud dastkerd karānd

'He too who shall be after Us and shall be lucky, may he too be diligent in the matters
and services of the gods so that the gods will be his helpers and make him their property.'
—*Shapur I, inscription at Naqš-i Rustam, Parthian, lines 29–30*

⟨AYK MNW AHR LNE MROHY YHWWN ZK yztʾn hwplstʾtly Whwkʾmktly
YHWWNd AYK OLEc yzty ZNE ʾwgwn hdbry YHWWNd cygwn LNE YHWWN⟩

kū kē pas amāh xwadāy bawād ān yaz(a)dan huparistātar ud-hukāmagtar
bawād kū ōy-iz yazd ēn-ōwōn hayār bawānd čiyōn amāh būd

'So that whoever shall become lord after Us he will be more obedient and of
better will toward the gods so that the gods will be his helpers too the way
they have been Ours!'
—*Shapur I, inscription at Naqš-i Rustam, Middle Persian, line 35*

In both languages, ⟨W⟩ (Common Semitic *w-* 'and') represents Iranian *ud* 'and'
(compare Latin *et*). Parthian ⟨YHYE(nt)⟩ and Middle Persian ⟨YHWWN(d)⟩
both represent forms of 'to be' in Aramaic—respectively (singular imperfect) and (plural)—but with only the plural endings added in their
respective Iranian readings, *baw-āδ/d* 'he will be' vs. *baw-ānd* 'they will be' (compare
Latin *-t* sg., *-nt* pl.).

The difficulty in interpreting especially the Middle Persian script is pointed up
especially clearly in the two words ⟨MROHY YHWWN⟩ *xwadāy bawād*
'lord shall.become', where the letter must be read in each of its three possible ways,
and the presumably long-forgotten 'his.lords are' isn't relevant to the
Persian interpretation.

The differences between Parthian and Middle Persian are not due to historical
change—Middle Persian is not a development from Parthian—but to geographic
diversity; the Sassanids came from a different region than the Arsacids. But essentially the same system is used throughout the Iranian-writing region. Why is it so
similar throughout the former Achaemenid area, even after it split into a number of
jurisdictions, despite its awkwardness?

The explanation may be sought in the clash between religion and politics. Recall
that when Mani began to write in Iranian, he didn't use the script of the bureaucracy but adopted almost unchanged the Syriac abjad he was familiar with (§3.3.4).
About this same time, Silk Road Kharoṣṭhi was used by Buddhists, Brahmi by Hindus,

and—in the Greco-Bactrian kingdom that controlled far more than the old province of Bactria—the Greek alphabet was used by Zoroastrians for their Iranian language.

But all the areas that used the heterogram system had previously been united in a single polity. We happen to have a precious handful of letters and documents written on leather in Aramaic during the later years of the Achaemenid Empire. One group, dating to the late fifth century BCE (some can be attributed fairly securly to 410–404 BCE) was from an administrator in Babylon to recipients in Egypt; the other, from the third quarter of the fourth century (one is actually dated to the reign of Alexander, June 8, 324 BCE), is from far to the east in Bactra (modern Balkh), present-day Afghanistan. Both the officials who sent the letters and the scribes who wrote them have Iranian names; Aramaic was probably not their native language.

Already in these texts there are slight hints that the officials dictated in their own language so that the scribes might have translated them on the fly. But what is most significant is that these items, from farthest east and from the center of the empire, are essentially identical in both language and format to those written (on papyrus) by native speakers of Aramaic far to the west in Egypt, namely the materials from Elephantine, present-day Aswan (§3.2.1 end). This indicates that scribal training was very carefully regulated and standardized throughout the vast Achaemenid realm.

It is all but certain that by the time the Arsacids (Parthians) had taken over from the Seleucids, in 247 BCE, the coin legends (just about all there is to go on) were being read in Parthian, even though they appear to be written in Aramaic—because the Aramaic words aren't properly inflected for the grammar of the phrase. W. B. Henning offers this evidence: Toward the end of the second century BCE, coins bear the legend דאריו מלכא ברה ותפרדת מלכא ⟨D'ryw MLK' BRH wtprdt MLK'⟩* 'Darius the King, son of Autophradates the King'—every word either Aramaic-looking or a name. But in Aramaic, the word *brh* would have to be רב ⟨br⟩ 'son-of'; the *h* makes no sense. But the later Middle Persian heterograms were often frozen forms that did not reflect the grammar of the sentence they appeared in. Thus, for Henning, "ברה ⟨BRH⟩ 'son' is the oldest 'Aramaic ideogram' on Persian soil, and the legend proves that the changeover to ideographic writing was now complete."

---

*When the range of exotic type fonts was very limited, it was usual to transliterate all sorts of epigraphic Semitic abjads into the familiar Hebrew forms.

8 Hybrids and Innovations

—stampede it with fresh type

Only two or three writing systems that were devised by people who were literate in an existing script, unlike those described in Chapter 1, are in widespread use today, and they too reveal things about the nature of writing. The work of these people was generally informed by whatever theory of linguistics prevailed in their day; they were not constrained to representing any particular stretch(es) of speech that they were aware of; and they tended to arrive at writing systems that pervasively combined representations of different-sized units—thus these innovative systems can be considered hybrid.

8.1 Korean

For many centuries, the language of Korea was written with the script of its powerful neighbor, China (§6.1). But Korean differs in both syntactic and morphological type from Chinese, so the fit of a script recording only content morphemes—and not grammatical endings or particles—was not good, and reading was difficult and limited to a small class of scribes. Then, in the middle of the fifteenth century, King Sejong (r. 1418–1450) announced that he wished to bring literacy to the people (and, not coincidentally, he wished to introduce a form of Buddhism, bypassing the intellectual class). Tradition holds that he himself devised the *Hunmin chŏng'ŭm* 'Correct Sounds for the Instruction of the People', though it seems likely that he assigned the task to a committee of scholars and might have become involved in detail work only at the final stages. It didn't find much use until the late nineteenth century; it has been known since 1910 as *han'gŭl*, 'Han [Korean/great] script'.

Clear in the surviving documents that accompanied the promulgation of the script in 1446 is the reliance on the Chinese phonological theory, embodied in the

Details ───

8.1 For Korean, Y.-K. Kim-Renaud, ed., *The Korean Alphabet* (1997), covers all the relevant material, especially in the chapter by Gari K. Ledyard, "The International Linguistic Background of the Correct Sounds for the Instruction of the People" (the only legitimate published version of the author's [1966] University of California, Berkeley, dissertation, which set forth in great detail the origin, background, and early history of the Korean alphabet). Some of the examples and some information on the teaching of Korean came from Insup Taylor and M. Martin Taylor, *Writing and Literacy in Chinese, Korean and Japanese* (1995), but this volume is not reliable as to the other two languages it deals with.

Table 8.1 The Korean consonant letters

putative origin ('Phags pa)	ꡂ g	ꡊ d ꡙ l	ꡛ s	ꡎ b		
base	ㄱ k[a]	ㄴ n	ㅅ s[b]	ㅁ m	ㅇ ng/Ø	
+1 stroke		ㄷ t	ㅈ ch	ㅂ p		(stop/affricate)[a]
+1 stroke	ㅋ k'	ㅌ t'	ㅊ ch'	ㅍ p'	ㅎ h	(aspirate)[c]
double	ㄲ kk	ㄸ tt	ㅆ ss	ㅃ pp		(tense unaspirate)
"			ㅉ tch			(" " affricate)
"		ㄹ l[d]				
anatomical representation						

[a] Voiced between vowels
[b] *t* at the end of a word
[c] Not aspirated at the end of a word
[d] *r* between vowels

rhyme tables, that divided syllables into the intial and the final. In Korean, though, a syllable can have one or even two final consonants, and a syllable can begin with a vowel. The Korean inventors were able to go a step beyond Chinese theory: they identified syllable-final consonants with syllable-initial consonants. Having letters for both consonants and vowels, *han'gŭl* is thus an alphabet. It is also all but certain that the inventors were familiar with some variety of an Indic abugida, most likely the Tibeto-Mongolian 'Phags pa (§5.8). Most of the basic forms of the letters of the Korean alphabet can be related to corresponding shapes in 'Phags pa. The original documents mention a model for the shapes that cannot be securely identified; the model might also be a specific calligraphic form of Chinese.

Moreover, from the beginning the basic shapes of the consonant letters were said to reflect the shapes of the organs of speech involved in articulating them. I suspect,

Table 8.2 The Korean vowel letters

ㅣ	i	[i]				ㅟ	wi	[wi]	ㅚ	oe	[we]
ㅓ	ŏ	[ʌ]	ㅕ	yŏ	[jʌ]	ㅝ	wŏ	[wʌ]			
ㅔ	e	[e]	ㅖ	ye	[je]	ㅞ	we	[we]			
ㅏ	a	[a]	ㅑ	ya	[ja]						
ㅐ	ae	[æ][a]	ㅒ	yae	[jæ][a]				ㅘ	wa	[wa]
ㅡ	ŭ	[ɨ]	ㅢ	ŭi	[ɨj][a]				ㅙ	wae	[wæ][a]
ㅗ	o	[o]	ㅛ	yo	[jo]						
ㅜ	u	[u]	ㅠ	yu	[ju]						

[a] The vowel *ae* is pronounced [e] in Seoul, and *ŭi* is prounounced [je] in Seoul.

though, that this reflects wishful thinking more than a design choice, stimulated perhaps by a perceived similarity in one or two of the 'Phags pa letters, offering a *post hoc* justification for all the shapes. What is especially interesting is that the further consonant letters were formed in a fairly systematic manner with changes in shape reflecting fairly regular phonetic similarities across the script (Table 8.1).

The basic vowel letters respond to philosophic considerations, with the vertical *i* shape representing Man, the horizontal *ŭ* shape representing Earth, and the dot (which in modern calligraphy has become a short stroke at the middle of the other vowel shapes) representing Heaven (Table 8.2).

The Korean alphabet has not, however, completely abandoned its Chinese roots, because the letters are not strung out in rows or columns, but are grouped into square blocks denoting complete syllables, so that at first glance a passage of Korean might look like a passage of Chinese. Chinese characters have been almost completely abandoned in modern Korean writing; in South Korea 1800 of them are taught, but it is said that for many modern Koreans, the only character they can write is the one that represents their own name.

Each Korean syllable contains a vowel. A consonant may precede the vowel. One or sometimes two consonants may follow the vowel, making a *closed syllable*. The shape of the vowel letter in a syllable determines how the letters in that syllable are arranged into a block. With a horizontal vowel, for instance — *ŭ*, the consonant before it goes above it, and with a vertical vowel, for instance ㅣ *i*, the consonant before it goes to its left. Thus 'writing' *ssŭgi* is 쓰기. In a closed syllable, the final consonant goes beneath the first two letters, so that 'to speak' *marhada* is 말하다. If a syllable doesn't begin with a consonant, then the no-consonant letter ㅇ precedes the vowel—and at the end of a syllable the same letter is *ng*: 'alphabet' is *alp'abet* 알파벳; 'Seoul' is *Sŏul* 서울; 'Hong Kong' is *Hongk'ong* 홍콩.

As with English, nowadays the orthography is not strictly phonological, and the morphology of the word is taken into account: 'price' *kap* is not spelled 갑 ⟨kap⟩ but 값 ⟨kaps⟩ with silent *s*, because of 값이 *kaps·i* (with postposition -*i*); compare English *hymn ~ hymnal*. Similarly, the pronunciation [nat] can have many different spellings—낫 ⟨nas⟩ 'sickle', 낮 ⟨nach⟩ 'daytime', 낯 ⟨nach'⟩ 'face', 낟 ⟨nat⟩ 'grain', 낱 ⟨nat'⟩ 'piece', and 낳 ⟨nah⟩ 'be born'—because when endings are added, each word has a different pronunciation.

In the early days of computerizing East Asian languages, it was simpler to design a separate glyph for every possible written Korean syllable than to come up with an algorithm for sizing and positioning the letters, and Unicode accommodates more than 11,000 such glyphs (though perhaps only about 20% of them occur in texts). But typing Korean on a modern computer is done simply by typing the letters, and the software selects the properly composed syllable blocks.

Traditionally, children were taught to read by introducing syllable blocks as wholes, and they were left to discover for themselves that the parts of the syllable blocks were used consistently for the sub-sounds. At least as of 1989, a chart of "basic" CV syllable blocks—the 14 "simple" consonants versus the 10 "simple" vowels—was given at the beginning of the first of two reading primers for first grade, but "actual learning of the chart—reading aloud the syllable blocks in the chart after their teacher—does not begin until page 39." The volume for the second half of first grade has charts for the 5 "double" consonants with the 10 simple vowels and for the 14 simple consonants with 5 of the compound vowels. CVC(C) syllables are not explicitly taught yet, but some of them occur in the first-grade reading passages.

8.2 Egyptian

If you're wondering why this section isn't in Chapter 6 with the other inventions of writing where no writing was known before, you'll have to wait until §11.4.1!

Almost everyone has a mental image of Egyptian writing: rows of stately hieroglyphs, pictures—not even pictograms—of just about everything that figured in Egyptian culture: carved in stone or painted on lovingly prepared surfaces, adorning tombs and their furnishings in brilliant, varied colors. It's almost no wonder that for some 2000 years, the West was under the impression—misled by none other than the Father of History, Herodotus—that they were mystic symbols, communicating with gods, their secret long buried with the civilization that produced them.

But when, thanks to François Champollion in France and Thomas Young in England,* it became possible in the 1820s to read the "sacred characters" (the translation of Greek *hieroglyphs*), the content of the inscriptions began to become clear. Some papyri found by the early explorers, or treasure-hunters, were also written with hieroglyphs, but more often they were written in *hieratic*, a cursive interpretation of hieroglyphs that was much easier and faster to write; the decipherment of hieratic was completed by about 1850.

These two Egyptian scripts are functionally the same. Any hieratic text can be converted to hieroglyphic, and vice versa.† They are abjad-like, in that they denote

---

*The Rosetta Stone alone, with its Greek, hieroglyphic, and demotic text, was not in itself sufficient to begin the decipherment, because only a single royal name was preserved in the hieroglyphic text, that of Ptolemy. Young provided Champollion with a Greek–Egyptian text including the name Cleopatra; the overlaps and differences within the names sufficed for him to understand that Greek names were written phonetically. But only when Champollion guessed that the Coptic word for 'sun' might represent the sound of a "sun" hieroglyph could he recognize the name of Ramses, and understand that Egyptian, too, was written phonetically and not with mystical "ideographic" signs.
† The third variety of Egyptian script, demotic, 'popular' in Greek, is a highly cursive development of hieratic, recording a late stage of the Egyptian language, and is not interconvertible with hieroglyphic/hieratic.

Details *(continued)* —————————————————————————————————————

8.2 The essentials of Egyptian writing are set forth in Alan H. Gardiner, *Egyptian Grammar* (1957), and Antonio Loprieno, *Ancient Egyptian* (1995).

only consonants—one, two, or three consonants each.* Anything we think we know about Egyptian vowels comes only by retrojecting from the Coptic language, which was spoken almost into modern times and which was written with an augmented Greek alphabet (§2.4); or by identifying Egyptian loanwords in languages written with cuneiform scripts, the only ones that notated vowels in the heyday of ancient Egypt, which reached an acme about 1500 BCE.

But the Egyptian scripts are also *morphographic*. Egyptian writing is usually lumped together with Sumerian and Chinese as "logographic." The term is appropriate for those two languages, because there, at least in the early days, each character stood for an individual word. But in Egyptian, what the characters stood for, before their use for their consonant sounds only, were morphemes—because Egyptian, like its relative Semitic, is an inflecting language. Words are built of bases, prefixes, and suffixes, and the bases would not be written alone. Thus the most precise terms for the two subtypes of writing system would be *logosyllabic* and *morphoconsonantal*. Some signs, though, were used only for specific words, so they can be understood as a fairly minor logographic component of the writing system.

Egyptian was usually written from right to left, though sometimes the direction was reversed for the sake of artistically complementing an architectural feature—when flanking a doorway, for instance. The characters always face toward the beginning of the line; in modern print, arranged from left to right for the convenience of the Euro-American reader, they face left. The characters within a word don't necessarily appear in the exact order of pronunciation. Broad low signs may be stacked, and divine or royal elements will be moved to the start of the word. Royal names are enclosed in cartouches, rounded-rectangle frames, and this feature proved helpful in the decipherment of hieroglyphs (see footnote * on p. 112), enabling researchers to connect names in the Greek texts with names in the Egyptian.

Egyptian scribes recognized that their morphograms could be ambiguous, just as did their counterparts in the other two realms. Like the Sumerians, they used semantic determinatives. Thus 𓏞, representing a scribal kit, denotes the consonants *sš*; 𓏞𓏲, with a scroll determinative, is *sš* 'writing', and 𓏞𓀀, with a seated man determinative, is *sš* 'scribe'; presumably the two words had different vowels, but we can only guess what the difference might have been. Egyptian scribes use the determinatives more systematically than the Sumerian or Akkadian scribes: so much so, that the limited set of determinatives, which normally come at the ends of words, function also as word dividers. Like the Chinese, they used phonetic complements (though they never incorporated them into the characters as in Chinese); indeed they used phonetic complements much more freely and frequently than the Akkadian scribes: 𓅱𓊃𓋴 (*w3.3.s.DET*) *w3s* 'scepter'; 𓋹𓈖𓐍 (*ʿnḫ.n.ḫ*) *ʿnḫ* 'life' ("ankh").

---

*At no point were the single-consonant signs used as a separate subsystem for writing texts "alphabetically"; the charts of the "Egyptian alphabet" available in many museum gift shops are misleading.

Table 8.3 Cree Syllabics (original version)

	-e	-i	-o	-a	final[a]
–	▽	△	▷	◁	
p-	ᐻ	ᐱ	ᐳ	ᐸ	ᑊ
t-	ᑌ	∩	ᑐ	ᑕ	⁄
ch-	ᒉ	ᒋ	ᒍ	ᒐ	
k-	ᑫ	ᑭ	ᑯ	ᑲ	ᕁ
m-	ᒣ	ᒥ	ᒧ	ᒪ	ᒼ
n-	ᓀ	ᓂ	ᓄ	ᓇ	ᐣ
s-	ᓭ	ᓯ	ᓱ	ᓴ	ᐢ
y-	ᔦ	ᔨ	ᔪ	ᔭ	

[a] Evans included additional finals: ˉ *-h*, ‖ aspirate, · *-w*, ˃ *-r*, ˂ *-l*, ○ *-ow*, × Christ.

8.3 Canadian Syllabics

General books on writing often place the discussions of Cherokee and Cree writing side by side, but they are very different in nature and in origin. The Cherokee syllabary, as we have seen (§1.2), was invented by a brilliant innovator who knew of writing only that it existed. Cree Syllabics, on the other hand, was invented by an educated Methodist missionary, James Evans (1801–1846), for Hudson Bay Cree people of what would become Ontario, in Canada. Evans had seen that attempts to "alphabetize" Native (or First Nations) languages of Canada had met with litle success, in part at least because the people were not sedentary, so they were unable to attend classes for months at a time to learn the system. He may have read of Sequoyah's Cherokee, or he may have known some language(s) of India; be that as it may, he decided to create a CV syllabary. But because he was alphabetically educated, he thought of making his characters quite regular in representing both their consonants and their vowels (Table 8.3). Evans worked before "scientific" phonetic alphabets were widely known, so his columns were labeled *ā ē ō ŭ*—alphabetical order for him. He provided visually distinct characters for final consonants.

The first column of characters is the base form, and the other columns are rotations or reflections of the base forms for the other vowels, consistently in each of the columns. Some of the words Evans used as examples: ᒪᓂᑖ ⟨manita⟩ 'spirit', ᓂᐱᐟ ⟨nipin⟩ 'summer', ᑫᓀᐻᐠ ⟨kenepek⟩ 'a snake'. Over the years, the character inventory has been expanded to accommodate many other Canadian First Nations languages, representing all the Native language families that remain in use.

Details *(continued)*

8.3 A number of treatments of First Nations Syllabics are found in B. Burnaby, ed., *Promoting Native Writing Systems in Canada* (1985). The life of the inventor is piously told by John McLean, *James Evans* (1890).

8.4 Two missionary scripts of Southeast Asia

Two British missionaries, Samuel Pollard (1864–1915) and James O. Fraser (1886–1938), working independently in Yunnan, southeast China, early in the twentieth century, devised scripts that represent two approaches to combining existing conceptions for how writing systems could or should work. Both languages have only CV syllables, and both languages employ lexical tone—both features are as in Chinese, but Chinese isn't a factor in those languages having the features.

Pollard, working with the Western Hmong language, explicitly had in mind Cree Syllabics, but from Evans's system he took only the idea of writing syllabically, but not the idea of using different orientations of letters to indicate different vowels—not least, surely, because the language has 15 vowels. His script is like the Korean, treating consonants and vowels differently. For the problem of notating the four tones, he adapted the Pitman Shorthand device of indicating difference in quality by differences in position of the little vowel symbol: placing it above the letter indicates high tone, below to the right a low tone, and so on. Pollard used geometric shapes; there is some similarity in the letters for similar sounds, and a few of them resemble corresponding Roman letters:

Ɔₙ C˷ Ɉ̆ Ā†ʳ Ɉ̈ Tᵁ Ʇ" Ɔ" Č̊ Ꞇ꜒ T˳'

⟨mì nà kú žá tsɤ kú tu ṭau mau nió tṣû thà⟩

'see, I am sending my messenger ahead of you'

Fraser, on the other hand, took the practical approach of using the Roman type he had on hand, for the Tibeto-Burman language Lisu. Most of the consonant letters have their usual values, and inverting them usually indicates aspiration. The vowels other than *a* are given full-size letters, so the script is abugida-like; tones are represented by punctuation marks (and punctuation by combinations of punctuation marks):

NY.. N.꞊ NU MI: ⊥Ɐ: SI˷ KW ᴧW FI DU FI ſU KO LO꞊

⟨nyā ná, nu mì thæ̀ sī kwa ŋwa tsì du tsi fu kʋ lo,⟩

'see, I am sending my messenger ahead of you,'

Details *(continued)* ⸻

8.4 The descriptions of the Pollard and Fraser scripts were pieced together from a variety of sources by Peter T. Daniels in P. T. Daniels and W. Bright, eds., *The World's Writing Systems* (1996), 580–82.

Table 8.4. Old Persian script

		a		*i*	*u*
		k(a)		–	*k*u
		g(a)		–	*g*u
h					
x					
č					
		j(a)		*j*i	–
			t(a-i)		*t*u
		d(a)		*d*i	*d*u
θ					
s					
š					
ç					
z					
			r(a-i)		*r*u
l					
y					
			n(a-i)		*n*u
p					
b					
f					
		v(a)		*v*i	–
		m(a)		*m*i	*m*u

'king'	'earth'		'god'
Ahuramazda	'land'		
" (genitive case)	(word divider)		

8.5 Old Persian

Perhaps the oddest writing system ever devised is the Old Persian. Its characters are composed of wedges, so it counts as cuneiform (Table 8.4). But it was never regularly impressed on clay, but was only incised on walls, cliffs, and display panels. It's mostly segmental, thus taking its inspiration from Aramaic, but there are characters

Details *(continued)* ————————————————————————————

8.5 There are usually brief mentions of Old Persian cuneiform in references on cuneiform in general. The standard treatment remains Roland G. Kent, *Old Persian* (1953). The suggestion about the limited audience for the inscriptions, and much other speculation, comes from Ilya Gershevitch, "The Alloglottography of Old Persian" (1979).

for the vowels and for some CV syllables, thus taking its inspiration from the moribund Babylonian cuneiform. There are even seven logograms—which are not heterograms, since there is no resemblance at all between Old Persian characters and corresponding characters in the model scripts.

The word divider, unusually, seems to be conceptualized as marking the beginning of each word, since when a gap is left before a new thought, the divider then appears; but it is not needed when a word happens to begin at the left end of a line of tbe inscription.

All evidence suggests that it was devised solely so that King Darius I could erect a magnificent annalistic inscription on a cliff at Behistun in 480 BCE, detailing his expansion of the Achaemenid Empire. Old Persian was almost always placed as the most prominent of three languages used in Achaemenid royal inscriptions for about 250 years, the other two being Elamite and Babylonian—Elamite and Aramaic were actually the administrative languages.* The interesting suggestion has been made that at any one time only a handful of scribes in the entire empire could write or even read the script; and the script as we have it does not give evidence of having been carefully thought out, even though there are only a handful of CV syllables of whose spelling we aren't entirely certain.

$$\langle\bullet\ \theta^a\text{atiy} \bullet D^a\text{ar}^a\text{y}^a\text{v}^a\text{uš} \bullet \text{xš}^a\text{ay}^a\theta\text{iy}^a \bullet \text{v}^a\text{šn}^a\text{a} \bullet \text{Au}^{89}\text{r}^a\text{m}^a\text{zd}^a\text{aha}$$

⟨• θᵃatiy • Dᵃarᵃyᵃvᵃuš • xšᵃayᵃθiyᵃ • vᵃšnᵃa • Au⁸⁹rᵃmᵃzdᵃaha
• i(yᵃ)m • dipⁱimaiy • tyᵃ(am) • adᵃm • akᵘunᵃvᵃm • pᵃtišᵃm
• ariyᵃa • ahᵃ • utᵃa • pᵃvᵃst⁹⁰ ayᵃa • utᵃa • čarmᵃa • grᵃθitᵃa⟩

*θātiy Dārayavauš xšāyaθiya vašnā Auramazdāha
i(ya)m dipīmaiy ty(ām) adam akunavam patišam
ariyā āha utā pavast āyā utā čarmā graθitā*

'Saith Darius the King: By the favor of Ahuramazda
this is the inscription which I made. Besides,
it was in Aryan, and on clay tablets and parchment it was composed.'
—*Behistun inscription iv 88–90 (§70)*

---

*A copy of the Behistun inscription translated into Aramaic was found among the papyri from Elephantine.

9 Recoveries and Decipherments

This hieroglyph is no dumb, deaf mistake.

The texts of a few ancient languages—Chinese, Greek, Latin, Sanskrit, Avestan, Hebrew, Syriac—continued to be studied down to modern times without interruption. All others had to be deciphered, and while every case was different, all decipherments do have certain features in common, and all decipherments rely on certain assumptions about the natures of writing systems. The glamorous decipherments of the nineteenth and twentieth centuries—most notably Egyptian and Linear B, and also Luvian and Ugaritic—have been described many times. Here I focus on less well known decipherments, including the earliest and the most recent, plus perhaps the most important of all, whose account fell afoul of a powerful publicity agent at the end of the nineteenth century.

9.1 Palmyrene

Ancient and mysterious scripts captured the imagination of adventurers whenever they came upon them, but not until the middle of the eighteenth century did anyone succeed in reading one whose interpretation had been forgotten with the culture that created it. The script that received this honor was not a specially worthy one; it was the Palmyrene (Table 3.3), which was used during the early centuries of the Common Era. The rulers of Palmyra, a trading city in the Syrian desert, would place inscriptions in both Greek and Palmyrene Aramaic on the monumental columns that lined the public spaces. In 1754, accurate copies of several such pairs were published in London and Paris as engravings.

Virtually overnight, the abbé Jean-Jacques Barthélemy (1716–1795) was able to interpret the Palmyrene. His method exemplified many of the principles that have been used in decipherments many times since: identify a bilingual text; locate proper names; compare known scripts; guess what language is represented; determine from the number of different characters the likely type of script.

Details

9.1–2 The necessaries for decipherment are exemplified in Peter T. Daniels, "'Shewing of Hard Sentences and Dissolving of Doubts': The First Decipherment" (1988), which reproduces a number of early representations of Palmyrene inscriptions. The best account of decipherment is Maurice Pope, *The Story of Decipherment* (1999), except that even in the second edition, account is not taken of Peter T. Daniels, "Edward Hincks's Decipherment of Mesopotamian

In short order, Barthélemy also deciphered Phoenician and Imperial Aramaic; he had almost nothing but coin legends to work from for those scripts.

Prior to all the steps in the actual decipherment, however, and so obvious that it is often overlooked—when one doesn't have coins in the palm of one's hand—is the necessity of accurate reproductions of inscriptions in the unknown script. For a century and a half, photography has been available, but many important decipherments were accomplished in the century before that. Before Barthélemy, there had been publications of Palmyrene inscriptions going all the way back to 1616, none of them amenable to decipherment—yet no one who had not visited the inscriptions *in situ* could know that!

9.2 Cuneiform

The most important decipherment recovered Mesopotamian cuneiform. The basic materials here came from a brief span of ancient history, the Achaemenid Empire. From the late sixth to the mid fourth centuries BCE, kings Darius, Xerxes, and their successors inscribed on the walls of their constructions, their monuments, and on a cliff at Behistun, propagandistic annals and dedications in three cuneiform scripts. The most prominent was the simplest, comprising a few dozen different characters, the other two considerably more complicated.

The prominence suggested to a junior faculty member in Göttingen, Georg Friedrich Grotefend (1775–1853), that the simplest script represented the rulers' own language, Persian (§8.4). On the basis of Antoine Isaac Silvestre de Sacy's (1758–1838) recent decipherment of some Sassanian inscriptions (§3.3.4), he expected to find introductory expressions along the lines of "X, great king, son of Y, great king." The names of the Persian kings were known, in Greek guise, from the Classical historians. Sure enough, Grotefend found the repetitious pattern, plausibly interpretable as "Xerxes, great king, son of Darius, great king, son of Hystaspes"—who was not a king. His discovery was announced in 1802, and over the next several years, scholars were able to clarify the characteristics of Old Persian.

Note that the initial breakthrough did not involve a bilingual; it was achieved through the insight that names known elsewhere could be expected in the unknown text. Such a correspondence can be called a *virtual bilingual.* The names in the Persian trilinguals did provide the initial clue to the other two languages, but they were soon superseded by a wealth of inscriptional material that became available during the first decades of the nineteenth century.

Details *(continued)* ——————————————————————————————————————

Cuneiform" (1994); the evidence against Rawlinson's claim is presented in Peter T. Daniels, "Rawlinson, Henry. ii" (2008). Fuller discussions of a number of decipherments are provided in Peter T. Daniels, "The Decipherment of Ancient Near Eastern Scripts" (1995), "The Decipherment of Ancient Near Eastern Languages" (in press a), and "Indic Scripts: History Typology Study" (submitted).

Edward Hincks (1792–1866), an Irish clergyman, applied himself first to the trilinguals (coming up with an initial list of values for the signs of the "second script" in 1846), and then turned to annalistic materials coming from Babylonia; he used Semitic grammatical patterning to locate signs involving constant root consonants and affixes. His most useful source, though, proved to be a massive annalistic inscription in yet a fourth language, Urartian, where repetitious formulae provided spelling variants permitting the identification of the vowels of many syllables.

By 1852, Hincks had succeeded in reading the "third script," the language now called Akkadian (§7.2), and moreover had identified the first of thousands of fragments of ancient dictionaries that made the study of both Akkadian and Sumerian (§6.2) something other than decipherment. Meanwhile H. C. Rawlinson (1810–1895) had, with great effort, made a copy of the huge, virtually inaccessible Behistun inscription of Darius. This accomplishment, plus his edition of the Persian and parts of the Akkadian versions, have generally gotten him the credit for deciphering cuneiform, but he was kept abreast of Hincks's findings and incorporated them into his own work; and Behistun was not published until the decipherment was virtually completed, and had little or no impact; and he was never able subsequently to explain how he had achieved his decipherment. Rawlinson was, however, in his youth an intrepid explorer and in his maturity a commanding figure, a diplomat, and a fixture at the British Museum and the Royal Asiatic Society. He was blessed with a brother, the prominent ancient historian George Rawlinson, who published a posthumous biography; and with a champion in the Museum's Keeper of Western Asiatic Antiquities, E. A. Wallis Budge, whose history of Assyriology is shamelessly chauvinistic, belittling the contributions of the Irishman Hincks and of the German and French scholars who had done the most to further the field.

9.3 Mayan

The decipherment of Maya glyphs (§6.3) has proceeded in two separate phases. The interpretation of the numerical, astronomical, and calendrical information included on the monuments was the achievement of the nineteenth century; primary credit goes to Ernst Förstemann (1822–1906), whose work was based on the few surviving pre-Conquest astronomical codices.

Details *(continued)* ───

9.3 The account of the decipherment of Maya glyphs is adapted from Peter T. Daniels, "Methods of Decipherment" (1996a), where similar accounts of the more familiar decipherments omitted here may be found, with full references to the key publications by the decipherers. Those for the decipherment of Mayan are registered by Michael Coe, *Breaking the Maya Code* (2012); though this book is useful for historical information, it doesn't go into the details of methodology. Study of the monuments was facilitated by the superb illustrations by Catherwood—all the more remarkable because he could not know what detail was significant and what was not, and there was of course no photography—accompanying two

Virtually all knowledge of Maya script was extirpated by the *Conquistadores*, along with those who commanded such knowledge. The Spanish bishop Diego de Landa's "alphabet" of the Maya glyphs went unknown until 1864, and meanwhile Americanists, like the Europeans who had been faced with Egyptian hieroglyphs, convinced themselves that the impossibly ornate glyphs could be at best an ideography, and despaired of ever understanding it.

Over the decades, order was brought to the overwhelming variation in sign appearance, and equivalences established between completely different signs (various items could be expressed by distinctive heads, or by full-square glyphs, or by appendages to glyphs, for instance). This kind of information was codified in the works of J. Eric S. Thompson (1898–1975). It fell to a Soviet linguist, Yuri Knorosov (1922–1999), who became aware of Maya literature when he rescued a sumptuous edition of the surviving codices from the ruins of a burning Berlin library in 1945, to take seriously Bishop Landa's "alphabet." Knorosov tried reading some words as (modern) Mayan using the handful of values Landa assigned to glyphs, comparing them with pictures in the codices; he realized that the glyphs actually represented syllables—the names of the Spanish letters, in fact—and his results were encouraging enough to convince some scholars (though never Thompson) that actual language might be concealed in the Maya inscriptions.

The next step was taken by Heinrich Berlin (1915–1987), who discovered that particular "emblem glyphs" are associated with specific sites; when a different site's emblem glyph turns up in an inscription, presumably some sort of interaction between the places is described. About the same time, Tatiana Proskouriakoff (1909–1985) discovered that certain inscriptions bore dates that did not obviously relate to astronomical cycles, and she noted that they often occurred in triplets, spaced suitably to number birth, coronation, and death of a ruler. These discoveries constituted the first evidence that the monuments could concern mundane as well as celestial events.

Finally, it was the linguist Floyd Lounsbury (1914–1998) who led in linguistic interpretation of the glyphs as syllabic and logographic. It is difficult to point to

Details *(continued)* ───

volumes that rank among the great travel narratives, since there was considerable unrest in the region at the time: John Lloyd Stephens and Frederick Catherwood, *Incidents of Travel in Central America, Chiapas and Yucatan* (1841) and *Incidents of Travel in Yucatan* (1843). The monumental work that makes the continuing decipherment possible is J. Eric S. Thompson, *A Catalogue of Maya Hieroglyphs* (1962). Invaluable for everything *except* its insistence that the glyphs are not phonographic writing is his *Maya Hieroglyphic Writing* (1971). The renowned linguist Benjamin Lee Whorf (1897–1941) wrote far more on the topic than "Decipherment of the Linguistic Portion of the Maya Hieroglyphs" (1942 [1956])—many of his manuscripts were made available in microfilm by Norman McQuown (1914–2005) at the University of Chicago Libraries. Unfortunately Whorf chose an invalid virtual bilingual. Additional interpretations of individual signs continue to be posited, and progress increases in interpreting texts as knowledge of the twenty-odd modern Mayan languages is increasingly taken into account.

Table 9.1 The Iberian scripts

Northeast *(left to right)*

		-a	-e	-i	-o	-u
–		ᚹ	Ⴋ	Ⴖ	H	↑
k/g-		Λ	⟨	ſ	⊠	◇
t/d-		X	◇	Ψ	Ш	△
b/p-		I	⋊	Γ	✳	□
ś	M					
đ	Ƨ					
ŕ	◇					
r	△					
l	Γ					
n	ᴎ					
m	Ѱ					
m̄	Y					

Tartessian *(right to left)*

		-a	-e	-i	-o	-u
–		Λ	O	⅄	‡	Ч
k/g-		Λ	⋊	?	⋈	ᛖ
t/d-		X	⧻	Φ	◭	△
b/p-		Ƹ	9	?	□	⋈
ś	M					
s	Ŧ					
ŕ	Ⲭ					
r	9					
l	⇑					
n	Ꙗ					
m	Ⱶ					
?	Ⴞ					
?	Φ					
?	↑					
?	◖					
?	⎏					

South Iberian *(right to left)*

		-a	-e	-i	-o	-u
–		Λ	O	⅄	‡	Ч
k/g-		Λ	⋊	⌐	⋈	?
t/d-		X	Φ	Φ	?	△
b/p-		⊃	Ⴝ	↑	⋈	?
ś	M					
s	Ŧ					
ŕ	Ⲭ					
r	4					
l	⇑					
n	Ꙗ					
m	Ѱ					
m̄	Y					
?	Ψ					
?	□					
?	◖					
?	Ⴌ					

a single breakthrough article; he would publish in great detail on a single glyph or group of glyphs at a time. This is the pattern of progress in Maya research, to which numerous scholars continue to contribute. One cannot help thinking that if Edward Hincks's methods and achievements had not been eclipsed by the partisans of H. C. Rawlinson, they might have provided some guidance to the Mayanists who were faced with essentially the same problem, of a copiously attested script that presumably recorded a language with known descendants but for which no text with a corresponding translation into a known language existed.

9.4 Iberian

Between the mid sixth century BCE and the early first century CE, a small group of related scripts was in use in Iberia. Nearly two centuries of study culminated in the definitive decipherment by Manuel Gómez Moreno (1870–1970), who made the surprising discovery that the scripts (Table 9.1) incorporate both syllabic characters,

Details *(continued)* ———————————————————————————

9.4 For Iberian, James M. Anderson, *Ancient Languages of the Hispanic Peninsula* (1988), provides a general introduction. Gómez Moreno's achievement is synthesized by Julio Caro Baroja, "Historia del desciframiento de las escrituras hispánicas prerromanas" (1954), and the importance of the abecedary was recognized by Ignacio-Javier Adiego, "Algunas reflexiones sobre el alfabeto de Espanca y las primitivas escrituras hispanas" (1993).

for the five vowels and their CV combinations with each of the three stops, and segmental characters, for the continuants. The question has been whether Phoenician or Greek writing was more prominent in the development of the scripts. New evidence came with the 1987 discovery of an "abecedary" of the Tartessian (southwest) variety, in which the first 14 characters are those that correspond in shape, sound, and order to Greek letters, *alpha* to *upsilon*. The language written with the Northeast variety is Celtic, and the Tartessian may be; the third remains mysterious.

9.5 Carian

About half a dozen kingdoms that arose in Anatolia after the demise of the Hittite empire wrote their own languages with alphabets related to, presumably derived from, the Greek alphabet. These include Lycia, Lydia, and Phrygia.* There are on the whole no problems in interpreting the scripts (Table 9.2), though because the inscriptional material is so scarce, understanding the languages is not always so easy. They belong to the Anatolian family within Indo-European, like Hittite.

The language of Caria, on the other hand, proved to be highly problematic. It appeared to be unrelated to any known language. But Carian soldiers were apparently highly valued, and they served as mercenaries as far away as Egypt, where they wrote graffiti on the statues and temples of pharaohs, among other places. It occurred to the Egyptologist John Ray to compare names written in Egyptian and Carian, and he had the insight that the Carian letters largely do *not* have the same readings as the corresponding Greek letters; when these new readings were imported into the Carian isncriptions, it turned out that Carian is an Anatolian language just like its neighbors.

9.6 Meroitic

About the same time as the Anatolian alphabets, far to the south, in present-day Sudan, the Meroitic civilization flourished, and their language was written with a grossly simplified adaptation of Egyptian hieroglyphics; and also with a cursive

---

* Due to some uncertainty in the dating of Phrygian remains, it has been suggested that the Phrgyian alphabet in fact came first and the Greek alphabet was an adaptation of it; but the shapes of some of the letters make this unlikely.

Details *(continued)* ————————————————————————————————

9.5 For Carian in particular, see Ignacio-Javier Adiego, *The Carian Language* (2007); Benjamin Sass, *The Alphabet at the Turn of the Millennium* (2005), puts the Anatolian alphabets into their wider context.

Table 9.2 Anatolian alphabets

(Greek)	Phrygian		Lydian		Lycian		Carian	
Α	Λ	*a*	A	*a*	Ⱂ	*a*	A	*a*
					↑	*e*	C	*d*
Β	B	*b*	B	*b*	B	*b*	Δ	*l*
					ᛉ	*β*	E	*y*
Γ	Γ	*g*	Ɔ	*g*	Y	*g*	F	*r*
Δ	Δ	*d*	⅄	*d*	Δ	*d*	I	*λ*
Ε	E	*e*	⅃	*e*	E	*i*	⊕	*q*
F	F	*υ*	⅂	*v*	F	*w*	Γ	*b*
Ζ	ʃ	*z*			I	*z*	N	*m*
Η					+	*h*	O	*o*
Θ					Χ	*θ*	Ϙ	*t*
Ι	I	*i*			*i*			*y*	ꟼ	*š*
			ᗡ	*y*			M	*s*
Κ	Κ	*k*	ꓘ	*k*	Κ	*k*	T	*?*
					⋇	*q*	Y	*u*
Λ	Λ	*l*	⌐	*l*	Λ	*l*	Φ	*ñ*
Μ	Ϻ	*m*	Ϻ	*m*	Ϻ	*m*	Χ	*ḱ*
Ν	Ν	*n*	Ϟ	*n*	ᴎ	*n*	Υ	*n*
					Χ	*m̃*	⋀	*p*
					Ŧ	*ñ*	Φ	*ś*
Ξ							ⱺ	*i*
Ο	Ο	*o*	o	*o*	Ο	*o*	□	*e*
Π	Ρ	*p*			Π	*p*	ᑫ	*ý*
Ϙ			+	*q*	◇	*κ*	▽	*k*
Ρ	Ρ	*r*	ᑫ	*r*	Ρ	*r*	⋀	*δ*
Σ	Ƨ	*s*	Ŧ	*s*	ς	*s*	⊓	*w*
			ᒿ	*ś*			⊠	*γ*
Τ	Τ	*t*	Τ	*t*	Τ	*t*	)(	*z*
					Υ	*τ*	Ж	*ŋ*
Υ	Υ	*u*	Ⴘ	*u*			Ⱶ	*j*
Φ	Φ	*pʰ*	8	*f*			ᴣ	*?*
Χ							↑	*τ*
Ψ	Ψ	*kʰ*			V	*χ*	6	*ŕ*
Ω								
			Ŧ	*τ*			ꝡ	*β*
			Ϻ	*ã*	Ѱ	*ã*	Ρ	*β₂*
			Υ	*ẽ*	Ƴ	*ẽ*		
			⅄	*λ*				
			ᒉ	*v*				
			↑	*c*				

Table 9.3 The Meroitic abugida

	a	b	d	e	x	h	i	k	l	m	n	ne	o	p	q	r	s	se	t	te	to	w	y
cursive																							
hieroglyphic																							

script that corresponds letter for letter. Early in the twentieth century, the archeologist Francis Ll. Griffith was able to assign readings to each of the letters (Table 9.3), but the language remained uninterpretable. Only very recently did Claude Rilly realize that Meroitic writing is actually an abugida (with four syllabic signs added)—only the vowels other than *a* are written. Moreover, the cursive letters predate the pictographic letters and cannot have derived from them. ⲉϤⲱ⚊/⚌ (pwrite) 'life' is read *pawarit*.

Meroitic writing is attested into the fourth century CE, or just when Ethiopic writing flipped from abjad to abugida (§5.9). There's a slight possibility that a Meroitic scribe somehow made his way to Aksum, bearing the notion of notating vowels other than *a*; but there would be no spur for doing so with appendages on the letters rather than with separate vowel letters.

9.7 Udi

The alphabet that used to be called "Caucasian Albanian" (Table 2.11) has been known since 1937 from a listing in an Armenian manuscript, which also provided the names and pronunciations of the letters (written in Armenian). Nothing was known of what language it had been intended for, and no manuscripts that used it were known. But during the cataloguing and study of the unimaginable manuscript riches of St. Catherine's Monastery in the Sinai, a palimpsest—a volume written on reused parchment with the underwriting washed off—was discovered whose earlier text was in Caucasian Albanian. Sophisticated photographic techniques were able to recover the earlier text well enough for it to be read and analyzed.

There had been reason to suppose that "Caucasian Albania" related to the Udi people. As far back as Herodotus, a group called *Oudi* was said to occupy a region north of Armenia; some of the month names in a list found in several Armenian sources could be interpreted with the help of Udi, as could parts of the few inscriptions that used the alphabet; and local tradition related the present-day Udis to the ancient Albanians (no connection with Albania, the Balkan country).

The available texts, about half of St. John's Gospel and a few other New Testament excerpts, comprise about 15,000 words. It was the writings of proper names in the texts that confirmed the readings in the manuscript list—just as with the first decipherments, so also with the most recent.

Details *(continued)* ————————————————————————————

9.6 The Meroitic language is presented in its linguistic and cultural context by Claude Rilly and Alex de Voogt, *The Meroitic Language and Writing System* (2012).
9.7 The full presentation on Udi is Jost Gippert, Wolfgang Schulze, Zaza Aleksidzé, and Jean-Pierre Mahé, *The Caucasian Albanian Palimpsests of Mount Sinai* (2009–10).

10   Pictograms and Mysteries

It's Titicaca till we've trod it through

Most histories of writing begin with brief, or not so brief, chapters on so-called "forerunners of writing," which are pretty much anything involving visual communication that isn't strictly representational and is found in non-literate societies. They carefully distinguish between visual communication devices that are essentially illustrations and those that convey messages using a series of images, usually representational, sometimes symbolic; a useful term for the latter is *semasiography*, which "expresses meanings and notions loosely connected with speech."* Curiously, though, the authors of those introductory chapters rarely agree on how to characterize and how to categorize the various semasiographic systems they discuss. When such devices are discovered by archeologists or ethnographers (a term for cultural anthropologists who used to investigate "exotic" cultures), it's often clear that they don't represent language, and so aren't writing. Some of them, such as the Rongorongo of Easter Island and the Naxi (*dongba*) pictographic signs of Yunnan, China, serve(d) to guide a storyteller in recalling the details of a narrative, without providing the text to be recited or recreated (compare §6.2 Details). In some cases, we don't know how to interpret them at all; and in every case, they did not "forerun" writing.

** Such communication systems are frequently labeled "writing," perhaps in an attempt to impute some sort of cultural superiority to the communities that use them, but as a term is needed for those visual communication systems that* do *represent language, the existing term "writing" should be retained for the latter.*

Details ————————————————————————————————

10. Pre-writing is discussed by I. J. Gelb, *A Study of Writing* (1952), 24–59, who distinguishes the two kinds as "descriptive or representational" and "identifying-mnemonic"; David Diringer, *The Alphabet* (1968), 4–11, "picture-writing"/"ideographic writing"; Marcel Cohen, *La grande invention de l'écriture* (1958), 13–35, "intellectual representations"/"proto-writing or pictography"; James-Germain Février, *Histoire de l'écriture* (1959), 20–53, "mnemotechnic"/"synthetic"; Johannes Friedrich, *Geschichte der Schrift* (1966), 15–24, "object writing"/"pictorial ideography"; and Hans Jensen, *Sign, Symbol and Script* (1969), 24–49, "object-writing"/"idea-writing (pictography)." *Semasiographic system* was introduced by Gelb (1952), 11. Reasons for excluding non-linguistic visual communication systems from the category "writing" are set forth in J. Marshall Unger and John DeFrancis, "Logographic and Semasiographic Writing Systems" (1995). Compare the passage by Joyce Marcus quoted on p. 96.

10.1 Mesopotamian "tokens"

A big splash was made about a third of a century ago by the claim that the "origin of writing" had been found in the so-called "tokens," small deliberately-shaped clay objects that archeologists had been finding at many sites across and around Mesopotamia, especially from prehistoric—which means simply "pre-writing"—times. A few examples were known of a small group of these tokens encased in a hollowish ball of clay, and a few of them had impressions of the tokens on the outside, so that the number and kind of tokens within could be known without breaking it open. It was hypothesized that such balls constituted a "primitive accounting device," representing, say, a corresponding number of sheep and goats entrusted to a shepherd for a time. A single example was found with not impressions of tokens on the outside, but an actual list of items, whose numbers corresponded to the number of tokens that had been enclosed. Sadly, before their potential importance was realized, those tokens became separated from the envelope, and it was impossible to correlate any different shapes they might have had with the quantities in the list, so there is no way of knowing what the various shapes may have stood for at that time.

It has been suggested that the shapes of these tokens corresponded with the shapes of some of the non-representational pre-cuneiform Sumerian signs whose interpretations are known from their later forms. It turns out, however, that the quantities of tokens that under that interpretation were associated with specific commodities are utterly unrealistic in terms of the probable presence of those commodities in the economy of the time. Moreover, there is no guarantee that any particular shape had the same interpretation over the vast stretches of time and space in which they were found.

10.2 Yukaghir "love letters"

One of the favorite so-called "forerunners of writing" is the "love letters" created in the 1890s by Yukaghir girls, who belonged to a people in eastern Siberia. John

---

Details (*continued*) ──

10.1 The clay-enclosed tokens were first studied by A. Leo Oppenheim, "On an Operational Device in Mesopotamian Bureaucracy" (1959), and the interpretation as the forerunner of cuneiform writing first appeared and attracted great attention in Denise Schmandt-Besserat, "The Earliest Precursor of Writing" (1978). Her numerous articles on the topic were collected in Denise Schmandt-Besserat, *Before Writing* (1992), with the database she interpreted included in the second volume. By reanalyzing these data, Paul Zimansky, review of *Before Writing* by D. Schmandt-Besserat (1993), showed conclusively that they did not support the admittedly attractive hypothesis.

10.2 The "Yukaghir love letters" were reproduced and interpreted by Waldemar Jochelson, *The Yukaghir* (1926), but he himself knew only one, fig. 149 on p. 455. The discussion is in John DeFrancis, *Visible Speech* (1989), 24–35.

DeFrancis devotes more than ten pages of *Visible Speech* to showing how the claim that these were "writing" was copied from writing-book to writing-book over decades—as well as to showing that they aren't "writing" at all. The definitive publication was by Waldemar Jochelson (1855–1937), a Russian-American ethnographer, who reprinted six "letters" and their explanations that had been collected by a colleague, and also presented the one he had collected himself. Jochelson interprets this one as follows:

> Each of the figures resembling folded umbrellas represents in a conventional way a human being. The inner pair of lines indicates the legs, the outer two lines the arms, and the dots show the joints of the legs and parts of the body. The dotted line extending from the side of the second figure, from right to left, indicates a braid, i.e., the figure is a girl or woman. The contents of the letter are as follows: Above the central figure (a) is an object like a hat which represents a deserted dwelling, i.e., one which figure *a* is leaving. The minds or the desires of the two female figures were directed towards the central figure, *a*, but the latter is too important a person for the Yukaghir girls who composed this letter. Their minds stop on the way, not daring to go to their original destination, turn around for a great while, and go back. The mind of *d* goes to figure *b* and the mind of *e* goes to figure *c*. The figures *c* and *e* and *b* and *d* are united by bands of love, but the bands of *b* and *d* are of a more durable nature than those of *e* and *c*. This is shown by the diagonals uniting the heads of both pairs. In the first case we have two diagonals, and in the other only one.

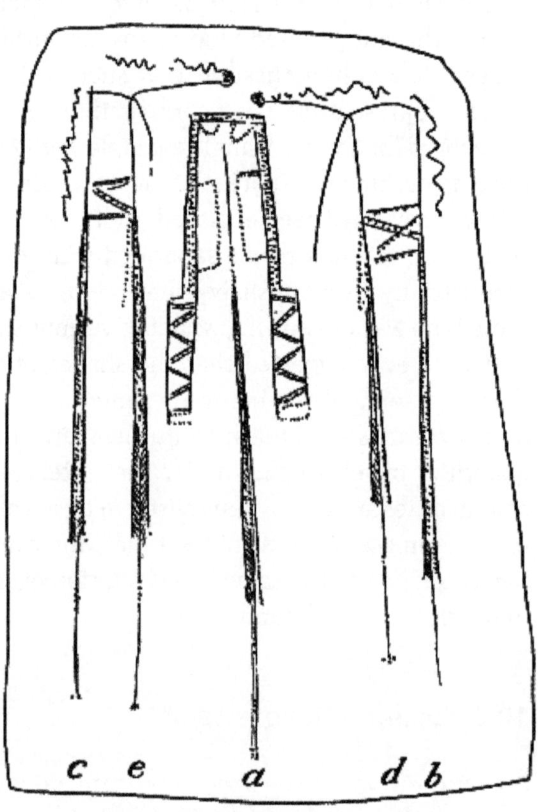

Fig. 149.   Yukaghir love letter on birchbark.

What DeFrancis missed, though, is that this "letter" *was written to Jochelson about himself*. The reproduction and description quoted above are found on p. 445 of the very large book. But, way back on pp. 64f., Jochelson had described his "participant-observer" activities:

> [Jochelson's young Yukaghir interpreter] Dolganoff said to the host in my presence, "Where am I going to sleep, old man?" — "Lie down with the children" (that is, with the daughters), answered the host. As a matter of fact, the two girls had one sleeping-tent, and the young men used to visit both sisters at one time. Such visits of young men to sisters who have a common tent I observed also in other places. ... On my first journey to the Yukaghir in the years 1895–96, on behalf of the Russian Geographical Society, I travelled

alone, without my wife; and the Yukaghir, as I learned to understand later, felt obliged to be hospitable to me in every respect. Once I was at the house of the elder ..., with whom I staid for about four months to study the Yukaghir language. ... My interpreter and a Cossack (a young man who was very successful among Yukaghir girls, to the great annoyance of the Yukaghir young men) had to sleep in other houses. The elder ..., besides his old wife, had with him only an adopted daughter, a distant relative, a girl of seventeen or eighteen years. I noticed that, as soon as I settled in the house, the nightly visits of the young men were discontinued. Afterwards I learned ... that the girl was offended at my indifference to her, and that her girl friends and the young men made fun of her. ...

The youngest [daughter of another family] was considered to be the prettiest on the river Yassachna. For a long time I intended to take her photograph in her holiday dress, ... but as she was then staying with her relatives in another settlement, I asked the old man to send a boat for her. In spite of the fact that I explained to the old man what I wanted his daughter for, my request was understood in another way. The girl arrived late in the evening, and I put off taking the photograph till the next morning. My canvas tent was standing near the skin tent of Shalugin [her father]. Imagine my astonishment next morning, when, stepping out of my tent, I noticed between it and that of Shalugin a separate small tent, which the girl was just then taking away! She was in a very angry mood, and my photographs were not successful. Afterwards my interpreter told me that the young men laughed at the girl for having uselessly put up a separate tent. When I left the river Yassachna, I received a love-letter written on bark, in ideographic characters, by both the above-mentioned girls, without any sign of jealousy; but in this letter I was also told that their unsatisfied feeling towards me was reconciled by their more happy relations with my Cossack and interpreter.

Perhaps Jochelson was reluctant to share the racy, even salacious, details when he first published the love-letter in St. Petersburg just after he returned; but, even more than a quarter-century later, and safely in New York, while he did describe his experience, he didn't explicitly draw the connection with the document. Jochelson also considered two further categories of document to be "writing," namely maps depicting journeys that incorporated a variety of pictograms, and fairly realistic depictions of events or adventures of daily life.

10.3 Peruvian *quipus*

In the Inca Empire of the Andes Mountains along the west coast of South America, elaborate records were kept using assemblages of knotted cords, known as *quipus*.

Details *(continued)* ————————————————————————————————

10.3 The classic account of *quipus* is Marcia Ascher and Robert Ascher, *Code of the Quipu* (1981); their survival into near-modern times is documented by Frank Salomon, "Late Khipu Use" (2008).

No key to their interpretation has survived, and we can only marvel at the elaboration and intricacy of the branching, color-coded precision of these creations.

10.4 Undeciphered scripts

From time to time, archeologists come across what appear to be inscribed objects, objects that seem to bear texts in an unknown script (occasionally, as with Etruscan, the script is known but the language is extremely puzzling), but the seeming inscriptions defy decipherment. By far the most notorious is the Phaistos Disk, a clay disk discovered on Crete around the turn of the twentieth century, stamped (not incised with a stylus) on each side with a spiral of pictograms that look as though they might be writing. Dozens of interpretations have been published, with no particular plausibility, but unless some further use of the pictograms turns up somewhere against which proposals can be checked, it is impossible to verify any interpretation. No purpose would be served by listing a few of the attempts.

A slightly less implausible candidate for an undecipherable writing system is incised graphic marks from what has come to be known as the Vinča culture of the Balkan peninsula, named for a Serbian site. The culture dates between 5300 and 4300 BCE. Some of the marks resemble random characters from known writing systems, but no examples have yet been found of any sequences of marks repeated on different objects.

The largest undeciphered corpus is of the script on seals from the Indus Valley in present-day Pakistan, whose best-known sites are Harappa and Mohenjo-Daro, dating to the third millennium BCE; exemplars have been found as far afield as Mesopotamia. Most of the symbols are pictographic, and many appear to be composed of a base shape with additions that might represent phonemes or morphemes. Of current languages in the area, the most likely candidate family for the language they record is Dravidian; but it is far from impossible that the Indus language has no living relatives. A claim that the Indus materials do not represent writing received considerable attention, but upon publication of the data involved in arriving at that

Details *(continued)* ———————————————————————————————————

10.4 The Vinča materials are illustrated and placed in their cultural context by Marija Gimbutas, *The Civilization of the Goddess* (1991); they were catalogued by Shan M. M. Winn, *Pre-Writing in Southeast Europe* (1981). A profusely illustrated introduction to undeciphered scripts, and also to some of the more celebrated decipherments, is Andrew Robinson, *Lost Languages* (2002). The journal *Kadmos* has been devoted to the more obscure scripts of the Mediterranean area, both deciphered and undeciphered, since 1962.

The fullest introduction to the Indus Valley script is Asko Parpola, *Deciphering the Indus Script* (1994). The claim that the Indus pictograms do not represent writing was set forth by Steve Farmer, Richard Sproat, and Michael Witzel, "The Collapse of the Indus-Script Thesis" (2004), and elaborated by Richard Sproat, "A Statistical Comparison of Written Language and Nonlinguistic Symbol Systems" (2014).

conclusion, it became clear that what had been compared with various non-writing semasiographic systems was the full list of more than 400 unanalyzed signs rather than any attempted list of the presumably significant components of the signs.

Other fairly large corpora of undeciphered texts include the "Linear A" materials from Crete that predate the Linear B that proved to record archaic Greek, and the Byblos "hieroglyphs" that have been claimed as ancestral to the West Semitic abjads. Other undeciphered materials are usually found in very small numbers, and they may tantalize but do not provide sufficient data to create testable hypotheses.

11 Origins and Characteristics

An old Egyptian jest has cramped the tape.

You may have surmised, from what I have and haven't said about the beginnings and dispersals of various writing systems, that I've come to some general conclusions about how such things have operated over the course of human history. I'll set them forth here, and how I arrived at them, and in the final chapter I'll explain what lies behind the conclusions. Now that we've drawn samples from the sea of writing systems that compasses the world of languages, we can see how their essence determines their whole course of development.

Charles F. Hockett (1916–2000) crafted this conspectus of the development of human language:

> At the beginning, since human communities were still small, all languages were still of the tribal or local type, each with a few hundred to a few thousand speakers. But after people started domesticating plants and animals, say some 12,000 years ago (in the Old World; several millennia later in the New), some communities grew first into city-states and then into empires. Thus came about the substage of urban or classic languages, each spoken by tens or hundreds of thousands of people, ultimately even by millions. It was in the classic substage that writing was invented, and many classic languages, though not all, had accompanying writing systems. Then in the last few centuries, especially with the expansion of Europe, we have entered the substage of metropolitan or world languages, each spoken by tens or hundreds of millions of people. All world languages have not only writing but also printing.

But why was writing invented only in *some* urban communities?*

----

*Observe that the term "civilization" has fallen far out of favor. It is too much associated with notions of cultural superiority to illuminate the place of writing in urbanization, or of urbanization in the development of writing.

Details

11 My understanding of the nature and origins of writing was first set forth in a talk at a symposium at the University of Wisconsin – Milwaukee in 1988, published as Peter T. Daniels, "The Syllabic Origin of Writing" (1992b), and its fullest previous exposition was in my *"Littera ex occidente"* (2007). The quotation is from Charles F. Hockett, "In Search of Jove's Brow" (1978), 252, in the guise of a summary of the outlook of Morris Swadesh, *The Origin and Diversification of Language* (1971).

11.1 Unidirectional development

It all started with I. J. Gelb (1907–1985). For hundreds of years, everyone talked about the Roman, the Greek, and the Hebrew alphabet. In 1952, Gelb changed all that. He decreed that the Hebrew alphabet and its relatives like Phoenician, Syriac, and Arabic were *not* alphabets, but syllabaries consisting of a small number of letters that stood for CV syllables with "undetermined" vowels. This seemed like an odd thing to say, but since Gelb's book was the first in more than half a century to embody a scientific approach to writing systems, and it incorporated concepts from the modern science of descriptive linguistics, and linguists had been being told for most of that half-century that only spoken language was important and writing was secondary, it was essentially the *only* thing being said about writing, and what it said was simply copied into textbooks and reference works for several generations.

But that didn't make sense. Many Hebrew (etc.) letters in a text do represent CV syllables, but many don't—those are the ones at the ends of syllables. The first word in the Hebrew Scriptures, בראשית ⟨brʔšyt⟩ *bərêšîṯ* 'in the beginning', shows this clearly: the ⟨t⟩ at the end of the word carries no vowel at all; the ⟨b⟩ at the start of the word doesn't "really" carry a vowel ([ə] doesn't count as making a syllable in biblical poetry, for instance); the ⟨y⟩ is a *mater lectionis*; and the ⟨ʔ⟩, thanks to changes over the history of the Semitic languages, stands for nothing at all! Only the ⟨r⟩ and the ⟨š⟩ stand for CV syllables, and the Masoretic pointing (§3.3.2) makes all this clear: בְּרֵאשִׁית. Gelb's decree is thus counterintuitive at best.

Why, then, did Gelb insist that Hebrew is written not with an alphabet, but with a syllabary? The sole reason was so that the development of the Greek alphabet from Phoenician could be fitted into a schema that he called the "Principle of Unidirectional Development." Now one of the overarching principles of I. J. Gelb's scholarship, from his first contributions—the decipherment of the Luvian hieroglyphs beginning in 1931—through his reconstruction of Proto-Semitic that for the first time fully took into account the Akkadian language, his pioneering studies of the Semitic language of Ebla in the late 1970s, to his posthumously published work on the earliest boundary-markers known to history—was the search for patterns and the construction of frameworks into which the data could be fitted, or on occasion massaged. The Principle of Unidirectional Development, unfortunately, is an extreme case of massaging.

Details *(continued)* ————————————————————————————————————

11.1 The Principle of Unidirectional Development is presented in several passages of I. J. Gelb, *A Study of Writing* (1952). The fullest, nearly word-by-word, refutation is in Peter T. Daniels, "Syllables, Consonants, and Vowels in West Semitic Writing" (2000b). A refutation by one who does promote the superiority of the alphabet is G. R. Driver, *Semitic Writing* (1976), 253–59. Gelb's mentioned systematizing works are, among many others, I. J. Gelb, *Hittite Hieroglyphs I–III* (1931, 1935, 1942), *Sequential Reconstruction of Proto-Akkadian* (1969), and "Thoughts about Ibla" (1977); and I. J. Gelb, Piotr Steinkeller, and Robert M. Whiting, Jr., *Ancient Kudurrus* (1989–91).

The Principle states that "in reaching its ultimate development writing ... must pass through the stages of logography, syllabography, and alphabetography in this and no other order." Gelb was able to list a number of syllabaries that did develop from logographies, such as Akkadian cuneiform and Japanese *kana*. But he did not list syllabaries that did *not* develop from logographies, such as Cherokee—which falsify the first part of the Principle. Since Gelb had ruled Phoenician out of the category of alphabets, there was of course only one example of the origin of an alphabet, namely, the Greek from the Phoenician. Thus either the Principle is entirely circular—Phoenician is called a syllabary so that the alphabet can derive from a syllabary—or else the second part of it is just as invalid as the first part.

There is, moreover, a second group of scripts that derived from a (supposed) syllabary, the Indic and Ethiopic ones. Gelb was aware of the structure of these scripts; they were traditionally called syllabaries, because their characters do in fact stand (for the most part) for syllables. But Gelb couldn't call them syllabaries, because they patently didn't develop from a logography, but from a "syllabary." Therefore he labeled them "problematic" alphabets and essentially didn't discuss their development.

The first difficulty with the Principle, then, is the counterintuitive labelings of the Phoenician alphabet as a syllabary, and the Indic syllabaries as alphabets. The second is that the claims it makes are simply not factually accurate.

What could be done about it? First, I recognized that Gelb was quite right to recognize that the Phoenician script is not an alphabet. If it was not an alphabet, *and* not a syllabary, what else could it be? Aren't there only three possibilities—logographies, syllabaries, and alphabets? Until about 1987, that's all there were. But why couldn't there be more than three? Why couldn't the strictly consonantal script be a whole other basic type? And so the notion of an additional basic type, the consonantary, was born.

Gelb was also right to recognize that the Indic scripts aren't exactly syllabaries— oh, sure, their characters designate CV syllables (and CCV, etc., things that aren't exactly syllables), but not by randomly shaped symbols; the same consonants and the same vowels use the same shapes, whichever syllables they appear in. It turned out when I really looked at specialists' articles on these scripts, that several of them had made this point, but they always considered them either a special kind of syllabary or a special kind of alphabet. But their places in the history of writing suggested that that isn't what they are. They're a further basic type of script that deserved a label of its own.

Casting around for catchy labels for my two new writing-system types, I noticed that the Greek-derived term *alphabet* and the Hebrew word *alephbeth* are both simply the names of the first two letters. But the two words were too similar for me to want to bring the Hebrew word into English. Happily, the Arabic word *abjad* was already in existence for a similar concept, and it came gracefully into English. At first I adopted one of the existing terms for the Indic-style writing system, but the eminent *éthiopisant* Wolf Leslau (1906–2006) suggested the Ethiopic word *abugida*, which exists in Giʻiz and Amharic for a purpose different from that of Arabic *abjad*, and it fit my pattern and my purpose well (the names are explained in §11.5.2). *Alphabet* was thus reserved for scripts in which all segments—both consonants and vowels—are individually notated: both the prototypical Greek kind, and those where consonants and vowels are visually distinct, such as Korean and the Semitic abjads when they're fully vocalized.

The second step was a little less obvious. Was there any sort of Principle of Development at all? It occurred to me, when I started looking at the origins of writing systems, that there was a real difference between the Cherokee (§1.2) and the Cree (§8.3) experiences—which is why I've put them about as far apart as I could here, even though histories of writing usually treat them together. Both were "syllabaries," since their characters denoted CV syllables, but that was about all they had in common. The symbols of one were quite a miscellany; those of the other were regularly arranged. The one's creator was linguistically naive; the other's was an educated man.* This led me to label the former activity *unsophisticated grammatogeny*, the latter *sophisticated grammatogeny*.

As I looked into the various modern inventions of writing, and eventually discovered the work of Alfred Schmitt (1888–1976), I found that this was quite a robust pattern: unsophisticated grammatogenies always resulted in syllabaries, and sophisticated grammatogenies did not. Dare I apply this principle to the original, prehistoric grammatogenies—all two of them,† Sumerian and Chinese? The question was settled on April 23, 1984, when I learned both that considerable progress had been made in recent decades on the decipherment of Maya glyphs—and that the Maya writing system was of the same type as the other two, a logosyllabary. Three independent grammatogenies *ex nihilo*. All of the same type. There was a pattern.

And then I realized what it was that all three languages had in common, which incidentally Egyptian did not share.

---

*The inventor of the Bassa alphabet, Thomas N. Lewis (mentioned in §1.3 Details), in fact resided in Plainfield, New Jersey, when he devised his script and subsequently earned a Ph.D. at Syracuse University, New York.

†Egyptian hieroglyphics was sometimes viewed as a third, independent grammatogeny, but more usually it was felt to have some sort of relationship to cuneiform writing. Which came first was a question for quite a while.

Details *(continued)* ————————————————————————————————

The fullest source for modern origins of writing is Alfred Schmitt, *Entstehung und Entwicklung von Schriften* (1980). The symposium "The Language of Writing in the Mayan Region" held at the University of Chicago, April 23–24, 1984, was published for the most part in W. F. Hanks and D. S. Rice, eds., *Word and Image in Maya Culture* (1989).

11.2 Origin of writing

Many nonliterate, "tribal or local," peoples keep graphic records that perhaps operate on the level of the word, with each pictogram representing a word. But these records don't turn into writing; the "reader" can't determine exactly what sentences the recorder had in mind. In Sumer, China, and the Yucatan,* pictograms turned into logograms. What did these three places have in common? Well, they were developing agricultural cultures where economic exchange was coming to be important; society was becoming complex, and it was useful to be able to keep records of exchanges and of the control of workers—of who paid (bartered) what to whom for what.

But there were many ancient societies on a similar path of development to complexity, where writing did not appear: in India, Iran, and Europe, where many different peoples spoke Indo-European languages; in Africa, where many different agricultural peoples spoke a host of different languages; in the Andes of South America, where the Inca empire thrived and spoke Quechua. All such peoples devised ways of keeping economic records—best known is the Inca *quipu* (§10.3)—but not writing systems that recorded language in all its detail.

Why in those three—not even "many, though not all"—"urban or classic" places? Could it be something about the Sumerian, Chinese, and Mayan languages that led to the invention of writing—to *grammatogeny*—for those three languages in particular, and not for Sanskrit of India or Hittite of Anatolia or Quechua of the Andes?

As we saw in Chapter 1, all new writing systems invented by nonliterates who know that writing exists are syllabaries: Cherokee, Vai, and about a dozen others I haven't described. This suggests that syllables might be paramount in grammatogeny: that there might be something special about syllables. This was already familiar to anthropologists and field linguists early in the last century:

> Non-literate peoples have again and again been found able to syllabify their words on request, that is to break them up without difficulty into their constituent syllables, but are in general unable to break up the syllables farther into the constituent elemental sounds or phonemes. They can of course be taught to do the latter, but rarely if ever make the analysis spontaneously.

---

* Or in some other part of Mesoamerica (see §6.3 Details).

Details *(continued)* ————————————————————————————————

11.2 The monosyllabic nature of the morphemes that gave rise to the Maya glyphs is brought out especially clearly in two articles by David Mora-Marín, "The Origin of Mayan Syllabograms and Orthographic Conventions" (2003) and "Consonant Deletion, Obligatory Synharmony, Typical Suffixing" (2010), and by John S. Justeson, "Early Mesoamerican Writing Systems" (2013), 836. The anthropological quotation is from Alfred L. Kroeber, "Stimulus Diffusion" (1940), 3.

As we can now infer from Chapter 6, all three languages involved in creations of writing systems from nothing share a typological similarity: their morphemes are essentially monosyllabic; most morphemes are just one syllable long. With languages that are monosyllabic in this sense, the drawing of a picture to represent a thing is tantamount to recording the word that names the thing. Thus each pictogram representing a word usually also represented a single syllable, so that it was easy to reuse a pictogram to record a similar-sounding word that did not lend itself to pictography (as in the children's game of *rebus*).

But why the need for monosyllables? Consider English *eye* and *I*, *pea* and *peace*. It's easy enough to make a pictogram of *eye* or *pea*. But how can you make a pictogram of *I* or *peace*? By listening to its sound. You can draw an eye to mean *I*. You can draw three peas to mean *peace*. But when a lot of your words are not simple syllables, a problem arises. You can sketch *finger* or *tomato*, but the sounds of those words will not be particularly useful in writing other words you can't draw pictures of! That seems to be why writing began only for languages where almost everything you draw a picture of also has a pronunciation that is a single syllable and so can be or be part of a similar-sounding word.

The usual example for Sumerian, due to I. J. Gelb, is the word 卅 *ti* 'arrow' reused for *ti* 'life'. Bernhard Karlgren (1889–1978), the first scholar to attempt a reconstruction of the ancestry of Chinese, put it this way:

> We have a word that in Mandarin is pronounced *k'iu* [in 20th-century *pinyin*, *qiú*] and means 'fur-coat', another, also pronounced *k'iu*, meaning 'to seek'. The two must have been homonymous already in very early times, for when the scribe wanted to write the abstract *k'iu* 'to seek', which was difficult to represent by means of a picture, he wrote 求 instead (originally a picture of a fur).

Maya writing includes examples such as a depiction of the head of a snake *kan* to spell *kan* 'to guard' and *b'ak* 'bone' for *bak(i)* 'captive'.

Details *(continued)* ———————————————————————————————

The example of Sumerian rebus is from I. J. Gelb, *A Study of Writing* (1952), 104.

The Chinese rebus is from Bernhard Karlgren, *Philology and Ancient China* (1926), 34; readers might be interested in a contemporary view of this character:

> [preceded by drawings of attested shapes, beginning with the Oracle Bone form] The proto-form of "裘" *qiú* "fur garment" was a pictograph; later the phonetic symbol "又" *yòu* was added. Still later the pictographic symbol that represented a fur garment was changed to the component "衣" *yī* "clothing" and it became an ordinary phonogram. Probably in order to accommodate a change in pronunciation, "又" *yòu* was later changed to "求" *qiú* "seek." (Qiu Xigui, *Chinese Writing* [2000], 222)

The Mayan examples are from John S. Justeson, "The Representational Conventions of Mayan Hieroglyphic Writing" (1989), 32b.

The most salient unit of speech, the syllable, thus coincides with the most salient unit of language, the word or morpheme—and it becomes all but inevitable that such a drawing could be reused as a rebus for another word of the same or similar pronunciation—a word that could not so easily be pictured. *Monosyllabicity*, then, seems to be a necessary, though not sufficient, condition for a writing system to develop out of pictography.* And I can even explain why the syllable is so important; and I put it off once again, to §12.1.2.

I mentioned that developing cultural complexity spurred the need to keep simple records. We cannot (yet?) know whether the need to communicate with entities that do not respond in immediately perceptible ways—such as the gods of ancient China—is a sufficient condition to prompt the development of writing. Perhaps it is, and perhaps the Mayan need to keep track of long expanses and cycles of time also was. But perhaps in those cultures, too, it was a need to keep track of each buy and sale and trade.

11.2.1 A mystery solved

Where did my view of the syllabic understanding of the nature and origins of writing come from? It came from a confluence of half a dozen streams of evidence—four concerning writing and speech (graphonomic or linguistic evidence), one concerning mind and speech (psycholinguistic evidence), and one concerning body and speech (phonetic evidence). Here's how I can recall them after some thirty years.

First came the rejection of "syllabary" to describe West Semitic writing. Only later were *abjad* and *abugida* identified as additional basic types of script.

Second was the decipherment of Maya glyphs, providing the third independent invention of a morphosyllabary for a monosyllabically-organized language, alongside Sumerian and Chinese.

---

*The monosyllabic hypothesis adds some weight to the supposition that the language underlying the Indus Valley script (see §10.4) may be a form of Dravidian (and not Munda or Indo-Aryan).

Details *(continued)* ———————————————————————————————————

The special salience of the syllable is noted by the distinguished phonetician Peter Ladefoged, *A Course in Phonetics* (1982), ch. 10.

11.2.1

> A mystery solved is even more ravishing than the ignorant fantasies it replaces.
>
> Daniel C. Dennett, *From Bacteria to Bach and Back* (2017), 10

The successive stages of my discovery were not laid out in individual presentations as I came upon them. I find that in "Toward the Linguistic Study of Writing Systems" (1986), I rejected the label "syllabary" but retained the label "alphabet" for Aramaic scripts. The first presentation of essentially the full understanding was at the aforementioned 1988 Milwaukee Symposium on the Linguistics of Literacy, but it was not published until 1992b; its first appearance in print, however marginal the publication, was thus as "'Proto-Euphratic' and the Syllabic Origin of

Third, the Cherokee and the Cree ways of denoting syllables were then seen to be essentially different, leading to the refinement of the definition of *syllabary*.

Fourth, every other nonliterate script invention in modern times had by then been found to operate like the Cherokee, as a syllabary. If this held for modern grammatogeny, wouldn't it also hold for ancient grammatogeny?

From those observations flowed the realization: Whereas all modern inventors of writing who did not know writing had encountered the *idea* of writing, so that all they had to do was "merely" to discover the stretches of speech they could write down individually, the three ancient inventions had no such model, so they had to be the incidental result of something else that just happened to provide the opportunity to denote a sound, namely, drawing pictographs to represent things-and-hence-words, and hence the sounds of words, and in turn the sounds of words for the unpicturable. This worked *because* the words were usually only a single syllable, and syllables are how people naturally subdivide their speech, so the sounds of the syllables could be reused to represent the same or similar sounds in other words.

But why?

Why syllables and not (phonemic) segments or (phonetic) features?

The whys are provided by classic observations of, on the one hand, the importance of syllables in the mind (the psycholinguistic evidence) and, on the other, the nonexistence of acoustic consonants in the "speech code" (the phonetic evidence). Both are set forth in §12.1.2.

11.3 Diffusion of writing: Historical sequence

Particularly in Chapters 2, 3, 5, and 7, we have seen writing spreading to neighboring peoples: (i) around the West Semitic area—Phoenician to the Greeks, and South Arabian to some extent; but the real winner being the Aramaic varieties: the Indic scripts throughout South and Southeast Asia; (ii) Chinese through East Asia; and (iii) cuneiform in Mesopotamia and then to the languages of neighboring regions. Several times, entirely new shapes clothed the skeletons of the Greek alphabet. The Roman alphabet and the Arabic abjad went round the world with missionaries, and the Cyrillic alphabet throughout eastern Europe and northern Asia with Russian conquest. All these routes of transmission of writing systems explain why families of script descent often don't correspond with families of related languages.

Writing systems "spread" through time, as well; there is chronological diversity within the unity of, for instance, English orthography (§2.1.2), which over the ages was nourished by its Latin and Anglo-Saxon origins, Irish missionaries,

Details *(continued)* ───

Writing" (1989). The most up-to-date and complete summary—essentially a condensation of this book—will be found in "Writing Systems" (2017b).

11.3 A similar approach is taken independently by Alfonso Lacadena, "Historical Implications of the Presence of non-Mayan Linguistic Features in the Maya Script" (2010a), and:

French-speaking Norman conquerors, and the various authorities who attempted to historicize and then regularize the orthography. Especially interesting are the cases where cultures make alterations to existing writing systems, as opposed to receiving new clothing as did Armenian, Georgian, and Cyrillic, to fit their own languages. We have seen two essentially different kinds of alteration in the diffusion of writing across Asia: adoption and adaptation.

11.3.1 Diffusion of writing: Adoption

The simpler is *adoption.* Let's simply list the astonishing sequence followed by the West Semitic abjad that was laid out in a little detail in Chapter 3: Imperial Aramaic; Syriac; Manichaean; Sogdian; Uyghur; Mongolian; Manchu. From early in the first millennium BCE almost to the third millennium CE—a stretch of 3000 years—the orthographic principles, and hence the skeleton of the writing system as a whole, remained essentially the same; but the styling of the fabric that clothed it changed, sometimes more, sometimes less gradually, as it was communicated from scribal school to scribal school, from chancery to chancery, from fashion to fashion, all across northern Asia to the Pacific coast. The essential type of the script never fundamentally changed.

11.3.2 Diffusion of writing: Adaptation

The second kind of alteration proceeded across southern Asia, but in a different mode. I've mentioned, but did not stress, that mode already. It seems to have operated three times. The first was when Indian pandits encountered the Aramaic writing system that was brought by the Achaemenid would-be conquerors around 500 BCE (§5.1) and *adapted* it to at least one of their languages, Gandhari Prakrit. The rich grammatical tradition associated with the name of Pāṇini was already well developed by the time writing appeared in India, and it fully understood syllables, vowels, and consonants. It was that grammatical tradition that took and improved the Aramaic abjad-with-*matres-lectionis*, turning it into the abugida known as Kharoṣṭhi. It was that same grammatical tradition that further refined Kharoṣṭhi into Brahmi, which could record a language in more detail and which provided the basis for the luxuriant flowering of the scripts of South and Southeast Asia.

Tibet, too, supported a grammatical tradition, which grew up simultaneously with the Tibetan writing system, and it was presumably Tibetan grammarians who

---

Details *(continued)*

1. Writing was invented only once in Mesoamerica, by the Olmec. 2. All the Mesoamerican writing systems come from the original writing (or subsequent ones) through (a) evolution: Olmec—Isthmian; (b) borrowing (and adaptation): Maya; (c) imitation/inspiration: Aztec. (Alfonso Lacadena, "On the Origins of Maya Script" [2010b], slide 8)

realized that it could be advantageous for a Tibetan script not to merge adjacent morpheme-final and -initial consonants as was done in the Indic scripts. The abugidic principle continued in use, so that the individually recorded vowels are those other than *a*, but syllable boundaries are marked with the dot at the shoulder (§5.7). Mongolian culture, on the other hand, did not support a grammatical tradition, and the morphological type differs yet again: explicit syllable boundaries are less important for an agglutinative language like Mongolian, so the refinement of the Uyghur abjad sufficed (§3.5).

The 'Phags pa script commissioned by Kubla Khan in 1269 (§5.8) was adapted from Tibetan but did not retain the marking of syllable boundaries; its importance at this point is that it was probably part of the input to the Korean alphabet (§8.1). But the designing of the Korean alphabet was suffused by familiarity with the Chinese phonological theory that distinguished a syllable's initial consonant from all the rest of the syllable, the rhyme. What Korean grammarians contributed was the recognition that consonants at the end of the rhyme could be identified with the initial consonants, so that letters could be devised to notate consonants as such and vowels as such.

Every script reflects some degree of "native speaker analysis." Usually, the degree of analysis in an adoption is limited to the (subconscious) awareness of the phonemes of one's language. But the lesson of the Asian sequences of transmission, as much as of the "informed" modern inventions exemplified in §§ 8.3 and 8.4, is that real innovation in an adaptation must be primed by grammatical understanding of the language that is to be written—metalinguistic knowledge of one's language: the result of deep study, not simple copying.

11.4 Diffusion of writing: Misunderstandings

It is a third mode of script transmission, however, that accounts for the three transitions that actually led to the vast majority of writing systems, all those that emerged from the Aramaic and Phoenician abjads. We must recognize three episodes of *misunderstanding* that led to revolutionary innovations in writing.

11.4.1 First misunderstanding: Egyptian

If the "monosyllabic" theory of §11.2 is on the right track, it is apparent that Egyptian hieroglyphs (§8.2) cannot be an original grammatogeny, for the signs do not denote

Details *(continued)* ───

11.3.2 The concept of "native speaker analysis" was introduced by M. O'Connor, "Writing Systems, Native Speaker Analyses, ..." (1983), and elaborated by Peter T. Daniels, "The History of Writing as a History of Linguistics" (2013c).
11.4.1 My understanding of the origin of Egyptian hieroglyphs is set out in Peter T. Daniels, "Three Models of Script Transfer" (2006c). The phrase "stimulus diffusion" is associated with

syllables. As we saw, each hieroglyph denotes either one, two, or three consonants, or is a true logogram representing only one word, or is a determinative. A further example will help clarify the situation, and set the stage for the next act in the drama of writing. The sign ⊡ is *p*, ⌒ is *r*, and ⊐ is *pr*; but ⊡⌒ is ambiguous. However, ⊏⌐*pr* (with the "miscellaneous" determinative ǀ) is 'house' and ⊐⌒ℳ *pr*[rLEGS] is 'go forth'—presumably the two words had different vowels, but those are lost to us.

How, then, did Egyptian writing come about? By "stimulus diffusion" from Sumerian. Archeologists have demonstrated contacts between pre-Dynastic Egypt (late fourth millennium BCE) and Mesopotamia. An Egyptian could have seen, or heard of, this "writing" thing the Sumerians were doing, inquired, and learned that one made a mark for each separate word. In Sumerian, those words didn't change when suffixes were added—recall that I suspect (§6.2 end) it was the changeability of the suffixes that might have hindered Sumerian scribes in coming up with notation for them. Egyptian, however, accomplished inflection both by adding prefixes and suffixes and also by changing the vowels within words (like its distant relative Semitic), so what didn't change for the Egyptian scribes was only the consonants of the morphemes. Thus the signs, for them, represented only the consonants.

The shapes of the Egyptian signs were already in existence, used on labels that have not yet been satisfactorily interpreted. These labels were discovered only late in the twentieth century—a few examples had been found more than a century ago but were simply reported and filed away (Figure 11.1). Some of them may represent place names and some may identify commodities contained in long-lost packages they might have been attached to. The first Egyptian scribe, then, put together an existing accounting(?) system with a vague idea of the workings of cuneiform orthography, and hieroglyphic writing came about.

11.4.2 Second misunderstanding: West Semitic

The second accidental advance in writing yielded the abjad. In Egypt (probably) were speakers of a Semitic language (probably) who wanted to be able to compose

---

Details *(continued)*

the work of I. J. Gelb, *A Study of Writing* (1952), but as he explains, the term was not his, but was coined by the anthropologist A. L. Kroeber; see Peter T. Daniels, "'Look with thine ears'" (in press b), Excursus. The notion was "in the air" in the 1930s (when Gelb was preparing his manuscript), leading him to suggest the possibility that some awareness of Mesopotamian cuneiform might have stimulated Chinese grammatogeny; but the natures of the two writing systems make this unlikely in the extreme: cuneiform had long left its pictographic stage behind when Chinese pictography probably began; see Peter T. Daniels, "What Do the 'Paleographic' Tablets Tell Us?" (1992c). The pre-writing "labels" are published by Günter Dreyer, Ulrich Hartung, and Frauke Pumpenmeier, *Umm el-Qaab I* (1998); the photographs are from W. M. Flinders Petrie, *The Royal Tombs of the Earliest Dynasties, Part II* (1901), pl. III, nos. 9–18. Interpretations are offered by John Baines, "The Earliest Egyptian Writing" (2004).

Figure 11.1. The ivory labels discovered a century before they could be understood

prayers in their own language (probably). Back in the eighteenth century BCE or so—the Twelfth Dynasty—they didn't have the luxury of attending Egyptian scribal school for the years it took to master Egyptian writing; but someone did find out that what the hieroglyphs stood for was the consonants of the language. This innovator did not learn to associate the Egyptian sounds with the shapes—and perhaps reused the shapes becasue they had already proved to be efficacious at recording the sounds of a language—but instead used the initial sounds of Semitic words that named the items shown by the pictograms (§3.1). Thus ⌒ is not *r* as in Egyptian, but *p* as in Akkadian *pû*, Hebrew *pê* 'mouth'—the ancestor of ◊ and *4.* and *)* and *פ* and *�* and *ف* and even Π and P.

11.4.3 Third misunderstanding: Greek

Third, there was an encounter between a Greek and a Phoenician. Most likely it occurred in some mercantile center, probably in the eastern Mediterranean, where the two peoples interacted and traded. It has been suggested that the place was Al-Mina, on the Lebanese coast near Beirut, possibly because at one time that was

Details *(continued)* —————————————————————————————

11.4.2 The earliest West Semitic materials come from Serābîṭ el-Khâdem, in the Sinai peninsula. Discovered early in the twentieth century, they were soon recognized as ancestral to the West Semitic abjads. They're known as "Proto-Sinaitic" because a large corpus of inscriptions in what came to be recognized as Nabataean were already labeled "Sinaitic." The "(probably)s" are because two inscriptions were discovered nearly a century later in Egypt proper that use the same lettershapes but cannot be clearly interpreted as either Semitic or Egyptian: John C. Darnell, F. W. Dobbs-Allsopp, Marilyn J. Lundberg, P. Kyle McCarter, and Bruce Zuckerman, "Two Early Alphabetic Inscriptions" (2005).

the only site that had been sufficiently investigated to demonstrate the presence of both Greeks and Phoenicians. The most likely time is ca. 800 BCE. A Greek merchant saw a Phoenician merchant making records of sales, and wondered what was going on. The Phoenician—perhaps a good friend—may have violated trade secrets principles by explaining the abjad: that each of the 22 letters represented the first sound of its name: *ʔalp, bayt, gaml*, etc. (Table 11.2 on p. 150), and that by sounding out the word, you could make a note of it. The Greek grasped the principle easily enough—but wasn't very good at Phoenician; hadn't learned to pronounce [ʔ], or several other consonants that are found in Phoenician but not Greek: [h ħ j ʕ w]. Thus what the Greek heard was the *a* of *alp*, and also, at the starts of the names of the letters for those other consonants, *e* (not *hê*), *ē* (not *ḥēt*), *i* (not *yôd*), *o* (not *ʕayn*), and *u* (not *wāw*). The Greek quite happily sounded out words and found both consonants and vowels that matched up with the beginnings of the letter names.

It has been suggested that the Greek alphabet had an Aramaic rather than a Phoenician origin, because several of the letter names end with *a* (*alpha, beta*, etc.), which would reflect the Aramaic "emphatic state" of the names (*ʔalpā, bēṯā*, etc.). But if Greek had encountered a writing system with *matres lectionis*, it's unlikely that the letters that served that function would have been assigned a very different sort of use in an alphabet; nor does that "Aramaic" theory explain why ⟨ḥ⟩ and ⟨ʕ⟩ would have been incorporated into the *matres* system. ⟨ḥ⟩ never became a *mater*, and ⟨ʕ⟩ did so only rarely and long after the transmission of the alphabet to the Greeks.

As the descendants of abjad and abugida enriched the northeast and southeast, so did the descendants of alphabet enrich the west.

11.5 External characteristics

In the first half of this chapter, I described the commonalities I've observed in the origin and diffusion of writing systems. Now I'll talk about several commonalities that apply to all or most writing systems in general. These pertain to the direction of writing, the regular order in which a set of characters is presented, the names they have, and the factors that affect the characters' graphic shapes.

11.5.1 Script direction

The elements of a script cannot be tossed randomly onto a surface: as the speech stream proceeds unidirectionally through time, so also does the writing stream progress linearly through space—though the continuing availability of the written text marks a profound difference between written and spoken language—and many orientations have been used: horizontal rows (almost always top to bottom) read left-to-right, right-to-left, or back-and-forth; vertical columns (top to bottom), either right-to left or left-to-right; even outward spirals.

All the Phoenician and Aramaic scripts are written from right to left (*sinistrograde*); it takes special circumstances for that to change. In two cases, the circumstance was *boustrophedon* writing (Greek for 'as the ox plows'), in which alternate lines are read in opposite directions. This made sense in the South Arabian inscriptions, which were sometimes engraved into very long stone walls: you could read them without traipsing all the way back to the beginning for each line. Perhaps it was the existence of half the lines reading from left to right—*dextrograde*—that licensed the Ethiopic offshoot to settle on dextrograde exclusively.

The other example is Greek. The earliest Greek inscriptions are sinistrograde like the parent Phoenician, but longish ones could be done in boustrophedon. A preponderance of right-handed writers, for whom, given the choice, left-to-right writing is preferable—less danger of smearing ink, and more visibility of the line of writing—may have sufficed to overcome the inertia of tradition (in this case an alien tradition, after all), so that the dextrograde prevailed. But this must have been a gradual process; Etruscan happened to come upon the alphabet early enough that it was always written sinistrograde.

But why would the earlier scripts—beginning with Egyptian—have been written from right to left in the first place? Could it be that the first scribe to write Egyptian was left-handed? A left-handed inventor might have naturally written from right to left for exactly the two reasons just mentioned—to avoid smearing, and to see the line clearly. The inventor of a writing system might have been accorded great prestige, and the invention imitated precisely, even its less than convenient direction. But as the existence of Islamic calligraphy demonstrates, sinistrograde writing is not a handicap to those who have been accustomed to it from the beginning of their education.

Script direction proves to be a tenacious attribute of a writing system: so long as a tradition remains unbroken, the direction does not change. The Aramaic-through-Sogdian sequence all remained sinistrograde. As we noted (§3.3.1), however, Syriac scribes, would avoid the mechanical problems in such a script by rotating the page 90° counterclockwise and writing downward and left to right, turning the page back for reading in the traditional direction. Perhaps this practice was maintained for Sogdian and along with the dominant Chinese culture accounts for the columnar (and left-to-right) writing of Uyghur, and thence the Mongolian and Manchu traditions. 'Phags pa, too, doubtless imitates this tradition.

Kharoṣṭhi maintained Aramaic sinistrograding, but the refinement into Brahmi reversed it. Another local script derived from Tibetan besides 'Phags pa, the Lepcha of Sikkim, was written in columns from right to left—as if Tibetan was rotated *clockwise* to attain columns in imitation of the right-to-left columns of Chinese.

11.5.2 Letter order

A property possessed by many writing systems with a limited inventory of signs is a canonical order in which the signs are learned and which becomes an organizing principle for lists of words and for other things as well. Such orders may be *arbitrary* or *motivated* (that is, there may be reasons for the order).

Virtually the only motivated sign-order is phonetic. There are two exceptions. In Japanese, the classical arrangement of the 47 *kana* spells out a poem, known as "*Iroha*," in the traditional 7–5-mora lines.*

いろはにほへと	*i ro ha ni ho he to*	'The colorful [flowers] are
ちりぬるを	*chi ri nu ru (w)o*	fragrant, but they must fall.
わかよたれそ	*wa ka yo ta re so*	Who in this world can live
つねならむ	*tsu ne na ra mu*	forever? Today cross over
うゐのおくやま	*u (w)i no o ku ya ma*	the deep mountains of life's
けふこえて	*ke fu ko e te*	illusions and there will be
あさきゆめみし	*a sa ki yu me mi shi*	no more shallow dreaming,
ゑひもせす	*(w)e hi mo se su*	no more drunkenness.'

Translations of the poem are legion, because the limitation on spelling the words requires them to be highly allusive, albeit not nonsensical like most *pangrammatic* sentences in English: *The quick brown fox jumps over the lazy dog*, with nine duplicate letters, pales before *Cwm fjord-bank glyphs vext quiz* (the only one in a list of six perfect ones that doesn't involve initials or proper names—plus, it might have something to do with writing systems).

The other non-phonetic, motivated order is Javanese, where the 20 *Ca* letters spell out a sentence summarizing an etiological tale (as seen in § 5.6).

Table 5.1 shows the Kharoṣṭhī letters using the Aramaic order, and Table 5.2 shows a few letters following the phonetically based order that would become standard in future centuries. The order of the consonants used by Kharoṣṭhī scribes has recently been identified (Table 11.1). Its inclusion of both simple and compound *aksharas* suggests it was based on some specific text that it might not be possible ever to identify. The order of the vowels was recognized even more recently: (*a*) *e i o u*. This is both the order found in the Greek alphabet, and the order of the four vowel markers from

Table 11.1 Kharoṣṭhī *akshara* order

a	*ta*	*śa*	*gha*
ra	*ya*	*kha*	*ṭha*
pa	*ṣṭa*	*kṣa*	*ṇa*
ca	*ka*	*sta*	*pha*
na	*sa*	*jña*	*ska*
la	*ma*	*rtha*	*ysa*
da	*ga*	*bha*	*śca*
ba	*tha*	*cha*	*ṭa*
ḍa	*ja*	*sma*	*ḍha*
ṣa	*śva*	*hva*	
va	*dha*	*tsa*	

---

*Observe that the lines comprise 7 or 5 *kana*, or moras, rather than the syllables counted in the English adaptation of the *haiku* form.

Details *(continued)* ───

11.5.2 The translation of the *Iroha* poem is from John Stevens in P. T. Daniels and W. Bright, eds., *The World's Writing Systems* (1996), 250. A collection of English pangrams may be found at http://www.fun-with-words.com/pang_example.html. The definitive statement on the top to bottom of the writing space. Could either or both have played a role in deciding the vowel order?

The motivated order of the Indic scripts follows the Indian grammatical tradition, placing the vowels (in two groups) before the occlusives (back to front of mouth; within each place of articulation voiceless, voiced, and nasal; for each stop unaspirated and aspirated), which are followed by the continuants (Tables 5.3 and 5.4). The Sanskrit order also provides the order now usually used for Japanese (Table 4.1).

What can be said about the familiar order *a, b,* c, ...? Despite centuries of conjecture—involving lettershape, phonetics, the names of the letters, and doubtless other considerations—no convincing account has ever been suggested; it is *arbitrary.* This order can be traced back nearly to 1200 BCE, when it is attested in a number of Ugaritic abecedaries (Table 3.1)—and any speculation must take into account that five letters were dropped from the original 27. Greek then kept most of the 22 Phoenician letters and, in a very typical fashion, when it needed some new letters, added them at the end. Latin, in turn, rejected some of the Greek letters but when it needed to reintroduce ⟨Y⟩ and ⟨Z⟩ for spelling words borrowed from Greek, it, too, added them at the end.

What seems to me the most likely explanation for the ancestral order is simply that it was the order in which the devisers happened to think of the sounds being memorialized. Coupled with the acrophonic principle, this accounts for occasional adjacencies like *yōd* 'hand' / *kap* 'palm of hand', by semantic association of the objects that lent their names to the signs for their initial sounds. The apparent phonetic association seen in the sequence *mēm* 'water' / *nūn* 'fish' had to be abandoned when the Ugaritic order was discovered. My surmise seems also to serve for the order Sequoyah used for his syllabary (Table 1.2).

When it comes time for an alphabet to be adapted to a new language, letters may be inserted according to graphic similarity (as in Arabic; Table 3.5) or sometimes phonetic (as in Cyrillic; Table 2.13). Armenian represents an exception, where the framework of the Greek order is discernible but no principle can be found for the placement of the additions (Table 2.11).

It's natural that when missionaries adapt old scripts—Greek, Roman, Cyrillic, Arabic, Devanagari—for the languages of their converts, in preparation for translating the Scriptures, they employ the familiar order. But there are also cases where the order of an existing script is used, in preference to some motivated order, for unrelated scripts: we've seen this in play for Japanese (Table 4.1), Cherokee (Table 1.1), and Cree (Table 8.3).

Details *(continued)*

orders of the consonants and of the vowels in Kharoṣṭhī is Richard G. Salomon, "Kharoṣṭhī Syllables Used as Location Markers" (2006).

Countless explanations for the familiar *a, b, c,* ... order attested as far back as 1200 BCE have been proposed; many are discussed, and refuted, by G. R. Driver, *Semitic Writing* (1976), 179–85, 269–73.

Since the fifteenth century, when the Ethiopic languages—literary Gɨʿɨz, modern Amharic—came to the attention of Europe, the distinct order of its letters, beginning *h l ḥ m*, has been known (Table 5.16). Only in the 1950s was it discovered that the ancient South Arabian letters were learned in an order fairly similar to the Ethiopic—and a few inscriptions that had seemed to be gibberish were recognized as abecedaries (or rather, halḥamaries; Table 3.2). In the 1980s, a clay tablet was discovered at Ugarit bearing the Ugaritic letters—but in the South Arabian order; a few of the rather crudely written letters resemble South Arabian forms, and I suspect it was the work of a scribe from the south who was trying to learn to write Ugaritic.

In both Ethiopic and Arabic, the ancestral Northwest Semitic order is known to users of the script alongside the one they usually see. It's known in Ethiopia because the Hebrew letter names appear as headings to the 22 stanzas of Psalm 119 (118) in the Septuagint, the Greek translation of the Hebrew Bible, dating from about the second century BCE, which underlies all the ancient versions of the Old Testament. Each stanza in the Hebrew original contains eight verses, each beginning with the same letter. The names of the letters are transliterated into Greek, and the Greek forms are rendered in the Ethiopic version. This አቡጊዳ: *abugidā* order, used in liturgical contexts, is named from the first four rows of the liturgical sequence and the first four "orders" of vowels (*a u i ā*).*

For modern Arabic-speakers, the ancestral order remains familiar because of the "organizing principle" mentioned at the beginning of this section. It's known as the أبجد *abjad* order. The sequence of letters, being fixed, could label any sequence of

---

*Now that the ancient order of both the consonants (Table 11.1) and the vowels of Kharoṣṭhi is known, if I were naming my types today I might use *arepiconu* instead, since the great preponderance of abugidas come from South and Southeast Asia rather than from Ethiopia.

Details *(continued)* ───

The Ugaritic halḥamary is interpreted in Peter T. Daniels, "The Further Quest for Ugaritic" (2017a).

The significance of the use of letters as numerals for the letter counts in adapted alphabets is proposed by Thomas V. Gamkrelidze, *Alphabetic Writing and the Old Georgian Script* (1994).

The origins of alphabetical order are considered by Frank Kammerzell, "Die Entstehung der Alphabetreihe" (2001), who proposes that both the familiar Northwest Semitic order and the South Arabian order are derived from an Egyptian order that he reconstructs from several sources but is not explicitly found in full. More soberly, Joachim Friedrich Quack, "Die spätägyptische Alphabetreihenfolge" (2003), reconstructs an order corresponding almost exactly with the South Arabian, on the basis of seven papyri, none datable earlier than the fourth century BCE; more recently, a much earlier possible example has been discovered (Ben Haring, "*Halaḥam* on an Ostracon of the Early New Kingdom?" [2015]). All the witnesses, though, suggest that the original was a West Semitic list, the Egyptian exemplars a transcription of it: for all the Egyptian examples begin *h-r-ḥ-m*, because Egyptian had no /l/—and there's another *r* further down in the list, corresponding to the "real" *r* of the Semitic list.

things. This is equivalent to a sequence of ordinal numerals—and even after dedicated characters for numerals were introduced,* letters have continued to be used as numerals in limited contexts in Greek, Greek-derived, and Semitic scripts. Even though the Arabic letters are learned in a different order from the inherited sequence, the inherited numerical values are not altered.

The use of ordered sequences of letters as numerals seems to have in turn had an effect on the sets of letters. Each ennead of Phoenician or Aramaic letters correlates with an order of numbers—the first nine letters represent the numbers 1–9, the next represent 10–90, and the last four, 100–400. Arabic assigns the values 500–900 to the five letters added to the Aramaic set.†

Several descendant alphabets have retained letters unneeded for any phonetic value because of their already associated numerical values: three examples are indicated in Table 2.8, where the values of symbols preserved in Greek are given as 6, 900, and 90. It is possible to see the ennead relation as a guiding principle in the creation of the Greek-based Eastern Christian alphabets, which do suspiciously contain multiples of nine letters. However, this principle wasn't in operation from the beginning, or there would be five empty-letter numerals in Phoenician and Aramaic script, preserving the earlier total of 27.‡

11.5.3 Letter names

For letters to be learned in an order, they need to have names (Table 11.2). Names of letters either are words in the language they record (Northwest Semitic, Runes, Ogham, Armenian, Old Slavic), or they refer in arbitrary patterns to their sound

---

*Dedicated symbols for numbers appeared first in India in the first half of the first millennium CE, then in the Islamic world, including zero, around 800, and thence to Europe around 1000. Mayan numerical notation had included a character for zero all along.

†Modern charts of the Hebrew script often show 500–900 assigned to the five word-final forms of letters. There is no evidence that they were ever used as such at the time when the letters served as numerals in, for instance, treatises on astronomy.

‡A unique inversion of the use of letters as numerals is the use of numerals as letters, in the alphabet, known as Thaana, for the Indic language Dhivehi of the Maldives, beginning early in the seventeenth century. (The Maldives converted to Islam in the twelfth century.) Written right to left, its first nine letters developed from the Arabic forms of numerals, its second ennead from earlier Indic numerals, and the remaning six letters (used mainly in Arabic loanwords) are taken from Arabic script. All vowels are written, using marks above and below letters, based on the Arabic ones.

Details *(continued)* ───

The study of Thaana has become the special province of Amalia Gnanadesikan; see, for example, "Maldivian Thaana" (2012).

11.5.3 We turn again to G. R. Driver, *Semitic Writing* (1976), 152–71, 253–66, for discussions of the letter names. The reconstructed Phoenician letter names are from Gordon J. Hamilton, *The Origins of the West Semitic Alphabet* (2006). The cuneiform Aramaic letter designations

Table 11.2 Letter names (*most column orders rearranged to match Ugaritic*)

Ugaritic	Phoenician (reconstructed)	Aramaic	Hebrew	Arabic	Ethiopic	Greek	Latin	Runes	Ogham
á (A)	*ʾalp 'ox'	A	ʔāleṗ	ʔalif	alf	A alpha	A ā	fehu 'wealth'	beithe 'birch'
b (BE)	*bēt 'house'	BI	bēṯ	bāʔ	bet	B bēta	B bē	ūruz 'aurochs'	luis 'blaze'/'herb'
g (GA)	*gaml 'throwstick'	GI	gīmel	jīm	gaml	Γ gamma	C cē	þurisaz 'giant'	fern 'alder'
ḫ (ḪA)				xāʔ	xarm		G gē	ansuz 'god'	sail 'willow'
								raþiō 'riding'	nin 'fork'/'loft'
d (DI)	*dalt 'door'	DA	dāleṯ	dāl	dant	Δ delta	D dē	kaunaz 'ulcer'	(h)úath 'fear'?
h (Ú)	*hiʔ 'lo!'	E	hē	hāʔ	hoi	E e psilon	E ē	kēnaz 'torch'	dair 'oak'
						(F digamma)	F ef	kanō 'skiff'	tinne 'metal rod'
w (WA)	*waw 'mace'	Ú	wāw	wāw	wawe	Y u psilon	V uē	gebō 'gift'	coll 'hazel'
							Y ī Graeca	wunjō 'joy'	queirt 'bush'
z (ZI)	*zayn 'weapon'	ZA	zayin	zāy	zai	Z zēta	Z zēta	hagalaz 'hail'	muin 'neck'
ḥ (KU)	*ḥēt 'fence'	ḪE	ḥēt	ḥāʔ	ḥaut	H ēta	H hā	nauþiz 'need'	gort 'field'
ṭ (ṬI)	*ṭēt '?'	ṬÈ, ṬU	ṭēt	ṭāʔ	ṭait	Θ thēta		isa- 'ice'	(n)gétal 'wounding'?
y ([)	*yōd 'hand'	IA	yōd	yāʔ	yaman	I iota	I ī	jeíra- 'year'	straif 'sulfur'
k	*kapp 'palm of hand'	KA	kāp̄	kāf	kāf	K kappa	K kā	eihwaz 'yew tree'	ruis 'red(ness)'
š	*šin 'bow'	ŠI	šīn	šīn	śaut	(ϡ san)		perþ- '?'	ailm '?'
l	*lamd 'coil of rope'	LA	lāmeḏ	lām	lawi	Λ la(m)bda	L el	algiz 'sedge'?	onn 'ash-tree'
m	*mēm 'water'	ME	mēm	mīm	māi	M mu	M em	sōwulō 'sun'	úr 'earth'
ḏ				ḏāl				teiwaz Tiw	edad '?'
n	*nūn 'fish'	NU	nūn	nūn	nahās	N nu	N en	berkana- 'birch twig'	idad '?'
ẓ				ẓāʔ				ehwaz 'horse'	ébad '?'
s	*samk 'pillar'	SA	sāmek	sīn	sāt	Ξ xi	X ix	mannaz 'man'	ór 'gold'
ʕ (])	*ʕayn 'eye'	A-A-NU	ʕayin	ʕayn	ʕain	O o micron	O ō	laguz 'water'	uilen 'elbow'
p (PU)	*pi 'edge'	PI, AP	pē	fāʔ	af	Π pi	P pe	inguz Ing	pín/iphín 'pine'
ṣ (ṢA)	*ṣadē 'papyrus'	[A]ṣ	ṣādē	ṣād	ṣadat	(Ϙ qoppa)		ðagaz 'day'	emancholl 'double c'
q (QU)	*qop 'monkey'	QU	qōp̄	qāf	qāf	P rho	Q qū	ōþila 'inherited land'	
r (RA)	*riʔš 'head'	RI	rēš	rāʔ	riʔis	Σ sigma	R er		
ṯ (ŠA)				ṯāʔ			S es		
ǵ (ḪA)				ǵayn					
t (TU)	*taw 'mark'	TA	tāw	tāʔ	tawi	T tau	T tē		
i (I)					ṗait	Φ phi			
u (U)						X chi			
s̀ (ZU)					psā	Ψ psi			
						Ω omega			

(Greek; Latin). It is not clear which came first—what may be the earliest list of letter names (incompletely preserved) gives a single syllabic Mesopotamian cuneiform sign opposite each Ugaritic letter (Table 11.2, first group). Many of these correspond to the beginnings of the names known much later for Hebrew and Aramaic, but some do not; and it is not easy to imagine why a scribe would not have recorded the letters' full names if they had existed. Recently a cuneiform tablet has been identified that provides two sets of cuneiform labels for the Aramaic letters, and it's clear that they do reflect the familiar names of the letters (Table 11.2, middle of the second group).

Most of the Hebrew/Aramaic names are words in Northwest Semitic, but a few are not. Their earliest attestation is the psalm headings in the Septuagint mentioned in the previous section. Most of the Arabic names preserve reminiscences of the earlier forms. Some of the Ethiopic letter names are words only in Hebrew, not in Ethiopic, suggesting that these names (which are not used in Ethiopia) were first assigned by European scholars in the fifteenth or sixteenth century when Giʻiz first came to their notice.

The Greek letter names are meaningless in Greek: they are simply borrowed from the Semitic source. The earliest complete list, though, is from around 200 CE (Athenaeus 453d), in what is purportedly but dubiously supposed to reproduce a fifth-century-BCE text. But the Latin names, which prevail in Europe, are simply phonetic (including CV for stops, VC for continuants), as are those in Georgian and modern Russian, and in the Indic tradition.

11.5.4 Lettershapes

All writing systems have properties relating to their physical existence that have no bearing on their function and so can vary widely. On this concrete level, changes in the shapes of signs, characters, and letters reflect a constant struggle between economy of material and effort on the one hand, and ease of legibility on the other. More abstractly, letterforms are likely to conform to the visual esthetics prevailing more generally in the culture concerned.

The ways people's hands interact with writing implements place certain constraints on the shapes of characters, and there seem to be some general principles

---

Details *(continued)*

were discovered by Irving Finkel, "A Babylonian ABC" (1998), and discussed by M. J. Geller, "The Aramaic Incantation in Cuneiform Script" (1997–2000), 144. The significance of the Ethiopic letter names and the supposed Ugaritic ones is considered by Peter T. Daniels, "Ha, La, Ḥa or Hōi, Lawe, Ḥaut? The Ethiopic Letter Names" (1991a). The Latin letter names were studied by Arthur E. Gordon, *The Letter Names of the Latin Alphabet* (1973).

11.5.4 The only published study, outside a calligraphic context, of the interaction between pens and lettershapes through history that I know of is Herbert Brekle, *Die Antiqualinie* (1994).

of what happens when a scribe starts to write fast, what happens when penstrokes cross, what happens when loops are looped. There are also visual constraints on the shapes of characters—though as we have seen from time to time, there seem to be few limits on how complex or how simple individual characters may be. But one constraint that I think has not been previously noticed is that naturally developed scripts, as contrasted with the missionary scripts noted in §§ 8.3 and 8.4, seem not to contain characters that are mirror images of each other. An apparent exception, Roman ⟨p q b d⟩, has only become one in recent years when some type designers tried (unsuccessfully, if I do say so) using the same shape for all four letters; they're noticeably different in any sort of manuscript hand or in a traditional font.

The shapes of characters can be influenced by the materials on which and with which they are written. The wedges of cuneiform result from the use of a reed stylus on clay—where the surface was not conducive to curving lines. Runes are angular because they were scratched into wood; Ogham is straight lines because it was carved on the edges of blocks of stone; and many scripts of India, Inner Asia, and Southeast Asia are curved because they were incised with a stylus—a rigid pointed burin—on a palm-leaf or birchbark surface.

Pigmented liquid (ink, paint) is probably the most common writing medium around the world, applied to surfaces with brushes made from vegetal fibers or hairs, or with pens cut from hollow reeds or feathers or forged in steel. The surfaces

Details *(continued)* ——————————————————————————————

Paleographic and epigraphic studies of the development of scripts continue to overlook this subject; see Peter T. Daniels, "A Calligraphic Approach to Aramaic Paleography" (1984). An article that has received an inordinate amount of attention is Mark A. Changizi and Shinsuke Shimojo, "Character Complexity and Redundancy in Writing Systems over Human History" (2005), but from a graphonomic point of view, it is severely flawed. Characters are decomposed into "strokes" not according to the practice of scribes, but by visual inspection of typographic forms—the only example of such a decomposition that's provided is the capital letters of English, a "writing system" that has never been used as such for extended text— so that ⟨V⟩ is said to comprise two strokes but ⟨U⟩ one, even though a scribe writing ⟨U⟩ would lift the pen after writing the left stroke from top to bottom center and then add the right stroke meeting the first one at the bottom. Moreover, logosyllabic scripts are entirely excluded from consideration, as are at least two abugidas with especially complicated characters, Malayalam and Sinhala. Doubt is thus cast on the validity of the conclusions for writing systems in general. Finally, how fully were the 114 scripts (they counted numerical systems separately) considered? Another study, cited in the earlier one, takes into account 1442 characters representing 96 scripts—or an average of only 15 characters per script (and further abstracts from unrealistic "strokes" to topological deformations of character components): Mark A. Changizi, Qiong Zhang, Hao Ye, and Shinsuke Shimojo, "The Structures of Letters and Symbols throughout Human History" (2006). Was the earlier study based on a similarly limited sample of characters?

can be any convenient wall (whether natural as of a cave or cliff, or built), or more portably a clay pot or a potsherd (inscribed sherds are called *ostraca*), or even a clay tablet that is also impressed with cuneiform signs.

The earliest known flexible writing surface is papyrus, prepared from the split pith of a reed native to the Nile Valley. Animal skins appear subsequently: leather, prepared by tanning, found from the first millennium BCE, and parchment, somewhat later, prepared by liming. A reusable medium was wooden boards hinged together, their inner surfaces coated with wax, on which Mesopotamian scribes impressed wedges and Greek and Roman scribes scratched letters with a stylus (few of these fragile items have survived, so we cannot be certain how long they were in use). Paper, which is made from macerated, compacted vegetal fibers, was invented in China early in the Common Era and came west with Muslim contact, eventually superseding the other candidates.

Moreover, any and all signs can be imitated by carving or molding all sorts of materials.

Printing from movable type was devised in East Asia—probably Korea—in the Common Era, and (perhaps not independently) by Johannes Gutenberg in Mainz, Germany, in the 1450s. Gutenberg's techniques merged the skills of the goldsmith (for casting type), the vintner (for the press), and the chemist (for the ink). Quick, identical reproductions of texts made possible both religious reformation and the development of science, but widespread literacy awaited mechanical papermaking, printing, and typesetting in the nineteenth century.

Individual mechanical aids for writers followed: typewriters, cheap pencils, fountain pens, ballpoint and fiber-tip pens. A feared post-literate society of broadcast media has been forestalled first by the worldwide network of personal computers,

Details *(continued)* ───

The finest work on the relation between the forms of writing and its surrounding cultures is Donald M. Anderson, *The Art of Written Forms* (1969); see also Albertine Gaur, *Literacy and the Politics of Writing* (2000). For papyrus, see Naphtali Lewis, *Papyrus in Classical Antiquity* (1974). The technologies involved in writing, printing, and texting are discussed in many places—Keith Houston, *The Book* (2016), offers a particularly handsome—designed by Judith Stagnitto Abbate (interior) and David High (cover)—and commendably well documented history (worldwide) of the technologies and crafts of making books. Otto Schroeder, "Gesetzte assyrische Ziegelstempel" (1922), discovered that "movable type" of cuneiform signs was used in preparing the dies with which mass-produced bricks were stamped in the thirteenth century BCE (see G. R. Driver, *Semitic Writing* [1976], 32–33). Douglas C. McMurtrie's classic *The Book* (1943) discusses (Western) typography and design as well. Especially important on the development of paper is Jonathan M. Bloom, *Paper before Print* (2001). The apotheoses of the book arts are described by Sheila S. Blair, *Islamic Inscriptions* (1998) and *Islamic Calligraphy* (2006). Elizabeth L. Eisenstein, *The Printing Press as Agent of Change* (1979), was among the first and most influential works on the significance of the new technology.

on which international communication is again achieved in writing—with the international Unicode enterprise ensuring that electronic literacy is not limited to the Roman alphabet, and without which preparing this volume would have been virtually impossible—and subsequently by texting devices and whatever might come next.

Details *(continued)*

Quite a bit has been published on the interaction between humans and personal electronic media, doubtless almost all of it doomed to almost immediate obsolescence. David Crystal, *Txtng* (2008)—though many of the technical details he provides were indeed obsolete after less than a decade—reassures educators, parents, and alarmists that there is no sign of "contamination" of students' Standard English by textisms; he cites a study that "found strong positive links between the use of text language and the skills underlying success in standard English in a group of pre-teenage children" (p. 161). Meanwhile, a doting great-uncle, using the name Perce P. Cassidy, on March 19, 2015, posted this anecdote (reprinted with permission) to the newsgroup alt.usage.english:

> Our 7-year-old great-niece comes home from school and tells her mother, "We were texting each other in class today." Mother responds, "But you don't have a cell phone, and I don't think any of your friends do either; how could you have been texting each other?" She replies, "We were writing our texts on pieces of paper."

12 Graphonomy and Linguistics

Throughout this book, I've been using certain terms and avoiding certain others, and I've inserted definitions here and there. Now it's time to bring them together with strict definitions and show how they fit into a comprehensive understanding of what writing is and how it works.

12.1 Some definitions

Some terms carry theoretical weight, but in at least some cases, that burden may have been dropped because of their use in ordinary language as well; I deal with them in separate subsections below. Here are some basic, hopefully uncontroversial terms.

(1) orthography   conventional spelling of texts, and the principles therefor
(2) script   a particular collection of characters (or signs), used to avoid specifying abjad, alphabet, etc.
(3) writing system   a script together with an associated orthography

A number of terms are used for the characters or signs that make up a writing system.

(4) pictogram   a stylized representation of an object
(5) ideogram   a symbol (often a pictogram) representing an idea rather than a linguistic expression of that idea
(6) logogram   a symbol (often a pictogram) denoting the meaning but not the pronunciation of a word or morpheme [cf. (20), (22)]
(7) phonogram   a symbol used to represent a unit of speech (typically a syllable or a segment)
(8) syllabogram   a symbol used to represent a syllable
(9) letter   a symbol used to represent a speech segment (a vowel or consonant)

The first three, (4)–(6), are often confused but need to be kept strictly apart. *Any* (quasi)representational component of a graphic communication system is a pictogram, whether it is an ideogram with no particular connection to the name of the item depicted, such as ☺ and ♥, or whether it is a logogram, such as Chinese 口 *kǒu* 'mouth' and 上 *shàng* 'above' (compare 下 *xià* 'below'), or a letter, such as ⟨M⟩, in which the ripples of the ancestral Phoenician letter 𐤌 which depicted **mēm* 'water' can still be discerned.

The five basic types of writing system can be summed up thus.

(10)	logography	a writing system comprising logograms
(11)	syllabary	a writing system whose characters denote syllables with no deliberate graphic similarity between phonetically similar syllables
(12)	abjad	a writing system denoting consonants only
(13)	alphabet	a writing system denoting all consonants and vowels
(14)	abugida	a writing system in which the basic shapes denote a consonant plus /a/ and the other vowels are designated by attachments to the basic shape

"Morphography" would actually be preferable to "logography" (cf. §8.2, p. 113), and historically two subtypes are known: *morphosyllabaries*, such as Chinese, and the *morphoconsonantary* of Egyptian.

And then there's the most important of all.

(15)	writing	a system of more or less permanent marks used to represent an utterance in such a way that it can be recovered more or less exactly without the intervention of the utterer.

Details

12.1 My new typology and nomenclature were first published in Peter T. Daniels, "Fundamentals of Grammatology" (1990), where I gathered from the literature quite a few labels for what I call the *abugida*; the main remaining competition is Bill Bright's *alphasyllabary* (unsatisfactory because it suggests it is a hybrid rather than a distinct type), and in William Bright, "A Matter of Typology" (2000), he makes it clear that the two terms differ slightly: *alphasyllabary* refers to *formal* properties of scripts, and *abugida* to *functional* properties: the test case is 'Phags pa (§5.8), which is an abugida but not an alphasyllabary. The typology and nomenclature were first used in accounting for the origins of writing in the 1988 talk published as Peter T. Daniels, "The Syllabic Origin of Writing" (1992b).

The first group of 15 definitions is adapted from the glossary of P. T. Daniels and W. Bright, eds., *The World's Writing Systems* (1996), xxxix–xlv. On what is not writing, see John DeFrancis, *The Chinese Language* (1984) and *Visible Speech* (1989).

Other typologies of writing systems have been offered over the years, and I discussed them in Peter T. Daniels, "The Study of Writing Systems" (1996b). Geoffrey Sampson, *Writing Systems* (2015), proposed in the 1985 original a sixth basic type, "featural," to account for Korean *han'gul*, shorthand systems like Pitman and Gregg, and Alexander Melville Bell, *Visible Speech* (1867), in which features of characters correspond to phonetic features (Table 8.1). However, neither *han'gul* nor shorthand is taught or learned with reference to the phonetic

The crucial point of this definition is that writing represents *language*; that is, the "pre-writing" or "forerunners of writing" that were glanced at in Chapter 10 are not writing. And, as stressed by John DeFrancis, the crucial feature of writing is that it represents the *sounds* of language. Any writing system *is* or *includes* a means of representing the vocal expression of speech. However,

> Spelling ... only needs to provide enough cues to pronunciation to enable a reader with the necessary linguistic knowledge to combine converging contextual and lexical information to achieve the desired match.

12.1.1 Word and morpheme

A second group of terms concerns the units of language that are relevant to the discussion of reading and writing. Surprisingly difficult is *word*. One linguist writes, "Before I start, you may expect a definition of 'word'. There are actually strong theoretical reasons for avoiding definitions"—such as his long lists of "properties of a typical word": *meaning, realization, word-class, valency, language, frequency, speaker, addressee, time,* and *place* and of "other properties available to some words": *style-level, speaker type, social relation, emotion, etymology, lexical relations, cognates,* and *translation equivalents.*

Quite aside from all those complications, the intuitive "string of letters between spaces" is quite obviously problematic. There is no reasonable reason to claim that, in English, *ice cream* is any less a single word than *bookcase* is. In Thai, and in the languages of India using scripts with a top bar (Devanagari, Bengali)—before British printers changed the conventions—, entire clauses are written without spaces, even though native speakers easily identify words within such stretches. One mid-century descriptive linguist raised eyebrows when he transcribed French verb phrases as, e.g., /vumdɔne/ *you give me* (cf. ⟨vous me donnez⟩), /kɔ̃dɥizelezi/ *take them there* (cf. ⟨conduisez-les-y⟩), and /nunlɥiɑ̃parlərɔ̃pɑ/ *we won't speak to him about it* (cf. ⟨nous ne lui en parlerons pas⟩); as mentioned in the Introduction, a grammatical description was based solely in the spoken language, and in principle that remains true to this day.

Details *(continued)* ————————————————————————————————

correspondences (and Bell's proposal for use in speech sciences found little acceptance); nor is Canadian Syllabics, according to Suzanne McCarthy, "The Cree Syllabary" (1995), 64. It's thus not clear what's gained by the additional category. A little-known catalog of putative universals of writing merits close attention: John S. Justeson, "Universals of Language and Universals of Writing" (1976).

The quotation at the end of the section is from Share *apud* Peter T. Daniels and David L. Share, "Writing System Variation" (2017).

12.1.1 The list of properties of "words" is from Richard Hudson, *An Introduction to Word Grammar* (2010), 114. The French examples are from Robert A. Hall, Jr., *French* (1948), 49.

The most useful definition of "word" goes back a long way—ironically, to the very linguist who, a few years later, would articulate the famous words that relegated writing to, at best, second-class status in linguistics, Leonard Bloomfield (1887–1949). In the second volume of the journal of the newly founded Linguistic Society of America, he carefully worked up to the definition we are seeking.

(16)	utterance	an act of speech (§1 of his article)
(17)	form	a recurrent vocal feature which has meaning (§6)
(18)	meaning	a recurrent stimulus–reaction feature which corresponds to a form (§6)
(19)	minimum X	an X which does not consist entirely of lesser X's (§8)
(20)	morpheme	a minimum form (§9)
(21)	free form	a form which may be an utterance (§10)
(22)	word	a minimum free form (§11)

A word is thus the shortest thing someone can say in a language. In English, *be* and *-ing* are morphemes, *be* and *being* are words, but *-ing* isn't a word.

12.1.2 Syllable and segment

Throughout this book, syllables have kept popping up: in the origins of writing, whether ancient or recent; and in the types of writing systems, whether syllabaries, abjads, abugidas, or hybrids. Why should syllables be so prominent in scripts?

As I was pondering that question, I began finding other places where syllables seemed to be important. Here are a couple of the cases I found in the 1980s. James D. McCawley (1938–1999) told me of watching a doting aunt interact with a toddler: the aunt read out the title of *The Important Book* and tried to get the child to associate the words of the title with their representations. First the child said the three words, pointing to the letters T, H, E. The aunt read the title again, tracing across the words with a finger; then the child said the words, pointing to the letters T, H, E, I, M with the five successive syllables. (A Gelbian might interpret this as logography preceding syllabography!)

The psychologist José Morais with his colleagues, taking up a suggestion by Isabelle Liberman and her colleagues, investigating in Portugal, found that illiterate

Details *(continued)* ───────────────────────────────────────

The definitions leading up to *morpheme* and *word* are from Leonard Bloomfield, "A Set of Postulates for the Science of Language" (1926).

12.1.2 Studies of syllables in various situations were reviewed by Peter T. Daniels, "The Syllabic Origin of Writing" (1992b), 90–93; I refer to José Morais, Luz Cary, Jésus Alegria, and Paul Bertelson, "Does Awareness of Speech as a Sequence of Phones Arise Spontaneously?" (1979), and Isabelle Y. Liberman, Donald Shankweiler, F. William Fischer, and Bonnie Carter, "Explicit Syllable and Phoneme Segmentation in the Young Child" (1974) (the quotation adults—mentioned in §1.1—were unable to manipulate phonemes, while comparable people with even rudimentary reading instruction could do so. They also cited a study that directly compared phoneme and syllable segmentation by the same population: [veʃa] could be reversed to [ʃave] much more easily than [aʃ] to [ʃa]; That article of Liberman's showed that English-speaking children of ages 5–7 could segment words into syllables more readily than into phonemes, and that both abilities improve with age and schooling. But the authors assumed that the ability to segment into phonemes ought to arise eventually, suggesting that

> the possibility that changes with age are relatively independent of instruction could be tested by a developmental study in a language community such as the Chinese, where the orthographic unit is the word and where reading instruction does not demand the kind of phonemic analysis needed in an alphabetic system.

As it happens, the first steps in Chinese education now involve training in sub-syllabic scripts—*pinyin* in the People's Republic, another system in Taiwan—so no "purely" logosyllabic-learning community is available to observe any longer, even though those scripts are soon abandoned and usually turn out to be unusably forgotten by literate Chinese adults. But not long after the study of Portuguese fisherfolk, a team in China was able to study members of the last generation of literate Chinese-readers not started off with *pinyin* and found the same result as in Portugal.

In recent years, happily, the attention of reading specialists has finally been turning away from almost complete fixation on English literacy, and even from Roman-alphabet literacy, focusing especially on the achievement of abugidic and abjadic reading by Indian and Israeli children (Hindi, Kannada, Hebrew, and Arabic have been the objects of the most research). David Share digests a number of these studies, which tend to show that children learning only a non-alphabetic writing system are not necessarily aware of sub-syllabic stretches of speech. For example, one study reported that among fifth-graders in schools using only Oriya, syllable

Details *(continued)* ───

from p. 210). The article from which I first learned of such studies is Alvin M. Liberman, Franklin S. Cooper, Donald P. Shankweiler, and Michael Studdert-Kennedy, "Perception of the Speech Code" (1967). The Chinese study is described by Charles Read, Zhang Yun-fei, Nie Hong-yin, and Ding Bao-qing, "The Ability to Manipulate Speech Sounds Depends on Knowing Alphabetic Writing" (1986). The concentration on English by scholars of reading was decried by David L. Share, "On the Anglocentricities of Current Reading Research and Practice" (2008): both the atypicality of its orthography and its alphabetic type suggest that conclusions drawn from the study of the achievement of literacy in English might not transfer well to other literacies. The digest of studies appears in David L. Share and Peter T. Daniels, "Aksharas, Alphasyllabaries, Abugidas, Alphabets, and Orthographic Depth" (2015); the Oriya and Eritrean studies are, respectively, R. Mishra and R. Stainthorp, "The Relationship between Phonological Awareness and Word Reading Accuracy in Oriya and English" (2007), and Yonas Mesfun Asfaha, Jeanne Kurvers, and Sjaak Kroon, "Grain Size in Script and Teaching" (2009).

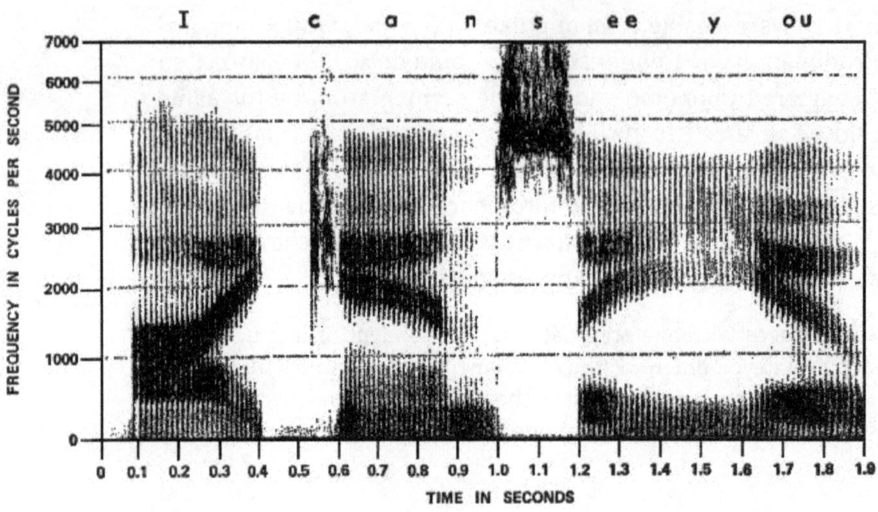

Figure 12.1. Spectrogram of "I can see you."

awareness but not phoneme awareness correlated with reading Oriya; but in a comparable school that taught in English, only phoneme awareness correlated with reading Oriya. ("Awareness" is psychologists' jargon for the ability to recognize and manipulate syllables and phonemes respectively.) An especially significant study indicates that it is not necessarily true that even an alphabet is best taught and learned alphabetically: according to a comparative study of grade-one reading instruction in four languages of Eritrea—Tigre and Tigrinya using the Ethiopic abugida (§5.9); Saho and Kunama using the Roman alphabet—, for languages with simple syllable structures, learning a true alphabetic script may be easier if it is taught as a syllabary: the Saho primer begins by introducing *ka, ku, ki, ke, ko* (compare §1.1), while the Kunama primer teaches letter–sound correlations of the letters individually. Results for Saho were far better than for Kunama.

What, then, are these "syllables" and "segments" that are so important in the nature and history of writing?

This is a question of *phonetics*, the science of speech sounds. There are two kinds of phonetics, corresponding to the two people involved in an occasion of talking: the speaker and the hearer. *Articulatory phonetics* investigates how people "articulate" language—that is, perform the various activities that result in speech sounds coming out of their mouths. These activities include the lungs pumping air, the vocal cords vibrating, and the lips and tongue changing shape and making contacts in the mouth. *Acoustic phonetics* deals with what it is that people hear: the nature of the speech sound waves that reach the ear and that the brain interprets as language.

Let's admit up front that articulatory phoneticians do not yet actually know what a "syllable" is, physiologically. (A pulse of air from the lungs? A resting-point for the muscles of the vocal tract? Each time a phonetician offers a suggestion, other

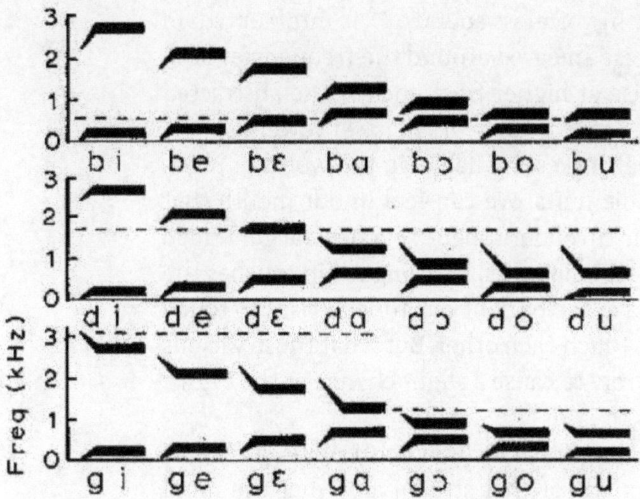

Figure 12.2. Idealized CV formants

http://home.cc.umanitoba.ca/~krussll/phonetics/acoustic/spectrogram-sounds.html

phoneticians show why the proposed definition doesn't work.) But, by and large, we know syllables when we say them or hear them. We can almost always say how many a word contains. We can usually agree on how to divide a word into syllables.

It is acoustic phonetics that we turn to for insight into the prominence of syllables. Toward the end of the nineteenth century, when it became possible to view representations on paper of the energy patterns—the pitch and loudness—of speech sounds, it was discovered that the various simple vowel sounds are the result of changes in shape of two parts of the vocal tract, the pharynx (above the vocal cords) and the oral cavity (the mouth). The noise made by the vibration of the vocal cords resonates in those two chambers—just as any sound is altered by the space it's issued in: a closet, an echoey room, a concert hall. Sometimes a third resonator, the nose, is involved as well.

The resonances show up as *formants* on the paper record of the sound, a *spectrogram*: bands of energy at discrete frequencies and increased intensity, representing pitch and loudness respectively. They aren't tied to specific pitches and volumes; the pitches vary with the pitch of the speaker's voice. But for all speakers, the relationship between the two formants is the same, and it is this relationship that's processed by the brain as representing the various vowels. The "first formant," F^1, is the resonance of the pharynx. The "second formant," F^2, is the resonance of the mouth. The "fundamental frequency," the pitch of the voice that is perceived—the pitch that figures in lexical tone, intonation, and singing—is labeled "F^0."

If we take a spectrogram of a stop consonant (*p t k, b d g*) before or after a vowel, we make the surprising (to someone used to an alphabet!) discovery that the consonants don't have formants of their own: what we hear as a consonant is nothing but the deformation of a vowel's formants. As seen in Figure 12.1, the formants are altered to "point toward" specific pitches. In voiceless sounds, F^0 is interrupted; in aspirated stops, there's a short burst of noise smeared around the frequencies of F^1 and F^2. In fricatives, there's sustained noise at higher frequencies. The abstracted diagram in Figure 12.2 shows F^1 and F^2 but not F^0. F^3 appears in nasal vowels.

In other words, whatever it is we do that makes a syllable, in the world of physical, acoustic reality, syllables are indivisible units. We can feel in our mouth that whenever we English-speakers make a *t*, the tip of our tongue touches the gum ridge just above our front teeth. (Though for most languages, the tongue-tip touches the backs of the front teeth.) When we make a *k*, the back of our tongue rises to touch the soft palate. When we make a *p*, our lips touch each other. But what those various "gestures" do to the stream of sound is merely to cause a slight change at the beginning or end of the adjacent vowel.

Acoustically, there is no such thing as a segment, only a continuous stream of speech, and the constrictions or interruptions of that stream are what the mind interprets as syllables. One characterization is: "loosely, acoustic energy bounded by minima of amplitude." Without awareness of articulatory procedures, nothing smaller enters the consciousness.

12.1.3 Phoneme

What, then, is it that the letters of an alphabet represent? *Phonemes.* "Phoneme" is one of the earliest and most basic concepts in modern linguistics, and once again we can do no better than return to one of its founding documents, Bloomfield's 1926 "Postulates."

(23)		Different morphemes may be alike or partly alike as to vocal features. (§15)
(24)	phoneme	A minimum same of vocal feature (§16)
(25)		The number of different phonemes is a small sub-multiple* of the number of forms. (§17)
(26)		Every form is made up wholly of phonemes. (§18)

In the discussion of these four items, Bloomfield notes, "The morphemes of a language can thus be analyzed into a small number of meaningless phonemes." This

---

* "Sub-multiple" is an old-fashioned term for a factor of a number.

Details *(continued)* ───

The closing characterization of the syllable is from Robert J. Scholes, "Orthography, Vision, and Phonemic Awareness" (1995).

is the essence of the notion of "duality of patterning," which C. F. Hockett lists as the only defining property of human language shared by no animal communication system; succinctly, "Phonemes do nothing but keep morphemes (and sequences of morphemes) apart." The suffix *-eme* marks units that enter into such a relationship and applies in many realms outside language.

It's precisely this function of distinguishing morphemes that causes stretches of speech smaller than a morpheme to enter into the awareness of speakers. Once speakers have learned a writing system, it's the speech-stretches denoted by its units that are most available to that awareness—most salient—while stretches smaller than those units are hard to notice. People from Chicago call the state to their north "Wis-consin," but people from that state call it "Wi-sconsin," and when the difference is pointed out, both groups of people can recognize it. But probably not one person in ten thousand knows that the physical difference between the pronunciations is that English stops are unaspirated after /s/, aspirated at the start of a syllable. If we were writing the two pronunciations in Devanagari, they would be विस्खोन्सिन् (viskhonsin) and विस्कोन्सिन् (viskonsin) respectively—because aspiration was and is phonemic in the languages for which the Indic scripts are used.

Two historical phenomena further make the point. We know of only two alphabets that attempted to record sub-phonemic information, Avestan (Table 2.12) and vocalized Hebrew (Tables 3.8 and 3.9), and in both cases, there's perpetual argument over what some of the symbols stand for. Similarly, it's said that the Roman emperor Claudius tried to introduce into the Latin alphabet a letter, a reversed digamma ⟨Ⅎ⟩, to write the labial glide [w]. However, [w]—the equivalent [u̯] is another transcription—is simply an allophone of /u/ in Latin, and no one saw a use for the letter.

To be sure, the notion of *phoneme* is to some extent obsolete in contemporary linguistics. In Russian, certain phonetic features distinguish morphemes when they are part of some phonemes but not of some others. That is, /t/ and /d/ are separate phonemes, but [ts] and [dz] are merely allophones of a single phoneme /c/ (see Dimension II on p. 176; for allophones, §1.2). This led to the influential—albeit false—conclusion that the concept of phoneme served no purpose at all. You won't find modern phonological analyses making use of the notion—but in fact they *assume* a phonological analysis and start their accounts there. Bloomfield and his school of

---

Details *(continued)*

12.1.3 The definitive presentation of the "design features of language" is the amplifed 1977 reprint of Charles F. Hockett, "Logical Considerations in the Study of Animal Communication" (1960) (the quotation from p. 154).

Sources for the anecdote about Claudius are given by Giovanna Marotta, *The Phonology of Latin* (in preparation), ch. 4, as Suetonius, *Claudius* 41; Quintilian, *Institutes* 1.7.26; and Tacitus, *Annals* 11.24.

Evidence against the usefulness of the phoneme as a tool in analysis began to be offered by Morris Halle, *The Sound Pattern of Russian* (1959).

Descriptive Linguistics were concerned with *describing* languages, not with explaining them.*

Sometimes, though, conclusions can be jumped to on the basis of phoneme theory: when psychologists showed that infants could distinguish between [pa] and [ba], they did not in fact show, as they claimed, that the infants could distinguish between [p] and [b] (or between /p/ and /b/), but only that they could distinguish between [pa] and [ba]. And perhaps it is the alphabet itself that leads the Western linguist to believe that speech is most fruitfully analyzed into segment-sized chunks. Martin Joos quotes W. Freeman Twaddell, whose *On Defining the Phoneme* (1935) was a key document in the development of classic phonemic theory:

> Guess what! Alfred[Senn] has just seen the light: Phonemes, he said to me yesterday, were what makes it possible to write a language alphabetically, and was that a fair statement? Nothing could be fairer, I said, and thanked him for the formulation.

An important concept in describing orthography is the *morphophoneme*, a device invented so that phonological systems could be described without "mixing levels," i.e. without taking into account *morphemic* information in a *phonemic* analysis. The forms *strife/strifes* and *dive/dives* show that the bases of the words end with /f/ and /v/ respectively. But this won't do for *wife/wives*; the base has to be represented as something like |wiFe|—where the capital letter acknowledges the alternation between /f/ and /v/ in the singular and plural forms. This proved to be an analytical conundrum—does the base change because the morpheme {PLURAL} is added?—but it acknowledges that the base of *houses* is spelled with ⟨s⟩ even though the sound it represents is /z/, so it's needed for describing writing systems.

12.1.4 "Grapheme"

If a phoneme is the basic linguistic unit that makes a difference between morphemes, and the morpheme is the basic meaning-bearing unit, shouldn't the *grapheme* be

---

* Martin Joos famously wrote, "Children want explanations, and there is a child in each of us; descriptivism makes a virtue of not pampering that child." The statement (taken in its context) was praised by his contemporaries and (taken out of context) ridiculed by the subsequent generation.

Details *(continued)* ──

A summary of infant "phoneme" experiments is provided by Peter D. Eimas, "Speech Perception in Early Infancy" (1975).

The footnote Joos quotation is from *Readings in Linguistics* [I] (1957), 96; the text quotation is from *Notes on the Development of the Linguistic Society of America* (1986), 134. The history of the morphophoneme is described by James Kilbury, *The Development of Morphophonemic Theory* (1976).

the basic unit of writing? Unfortunately, it isn't that simple.* Recall that the suffix *-eme* identifies units that enter into the "duality of patterning" relationship that is central to language and to so much else in human behavior [§12.1.2 at (23)–(26)]. But duality of patterning is a coping device of the human brain for making sense of the countless stimuli it encounters every day, every minute. Duality of patterning is imposed unconsciously by every human brain.[1]

Writing, however, as we have been seeing throughout this book, is *not* unconscious. Everyone learns to talk simply by being born into a speaking community (or several speech communities), automatically acquiring the language(s) around them. But no one learns to read or write simply by being among people who read and sometimes write. Reading and writing must be *taught*.

This is the first hint that "grapheme" might not be a particularly useful term. But it's far from the only one. The leading scholar of English orthography, Richard Venezky, made this observation:

> Orthography from the time of Alfred to the present day has been delimited by the letters and their powers.[2] So ingrained has this principle become that some contemporary linguists have attempted, by substituting *grapheme* for *letter*, to sanctify it with the countenance of linguistic science without examining how unsound it is.[3]

All too often, in grammars of a language the units of its writing system are called its "graphemes," without regard to what that term might or ought to mean.

12.1.4.1 Use of the term "grapheme"

What, then, might or ought to be meant by "grapheme"? It seems to follow naturally from such terms as *phoneme* and *morpheme*, but there's a big difference.[4] The morpheme *-eme* implicates duality of patterning, the strategy used—unconsciously—by the human brain in all sorts of situations. Writing, being a conscious human invention, need not and does not necessarily conform to it.

---

* Because of the historical nature of this section, references are given in footnotes rather than in the Details portion of the chapter.

1 However, in anthropology "emic" and "etic" seem to be used in a sense inverse to their meaning in linguistics. The opposition was elaborated by Kenneth L. Pike, *Language in Relation to a Unified Theory of the Structure of Human Behavior* (1954–59), the anthropological interpretation was created by Marvin Harris, "History and Significance of the Emic/Etic Distinction" (1976), and their differences are debated in T. M. Headland, K. L. Pike, and M. Harris, eds., *Emics and Etics* (1990).

2 Venezky might as well have named the ancients as Alfred—see David Abercrombie, "What Is a 'letter'?" (1949), esp. 81–83, and William Haas, *Phono-Graphic Translation* (1970), 27f. n. 1, on the Late Classical establishment of *figura*, *potestas*, and *nomen* (shape, sound, and name) as the properties of *litterae*.

3 Richard L. Venezky, "The Basis of English Orthography" (1966), 145. Nonetheless, this didn't stop him from subsequently writing "English orthography contains ... the classes of letters (graphemes)," in "English Orthography" (1967), 77.

4 I began to investigate these matters in Peter T. Daniels, "Is a Structural Graphemics Possible?" (1991b). This subsection largely treats aspects not discussed there.

The term has been "fuzzy" since it began to be used (as opposed to simply being included in a schema of linguistic terminology, §12.1.4.3). The psychologist Leslie Henderson attempted to bring some order to the concept. He had felt constrained to add a footnote in his introduction to a chapter by Max Coltheart registering his objection to Coltheart's usage:

> I employ the term 'grapheme' in the manner of many commentators on writing systems, to denote the minimal functional distinctive unit of any writing system and not in the phoneme-representing sense adopted by Coltheart.[5]

In a subsequent article, he quoted that passage and surveyed "the psychological literature" and found "at least three distinct and conflicting senses":

> "a jargon word for the more homely 'letter'";
> "the minimal contrastive unit in a writing system" (*Sense 1*); and
> "a letter or letters that refer to or correspond to a single phoneme in speech" (*Sense 2*).[6]

Like Venezky, he rightly dismisses the first of these—but does not explain how *Sense 1* differs from it. He claims that no one but Coltheart uses *Sense 2*, which, however, seems to me [see (27) below] the only sensible interpretation the term could have.[7]

Nonetheless, *Sense 1* is what is found in works either by theoreticians who wish to exploit the "phoneme" parallel or by analysts whose familiarity extends primarily to segmental (alphabetic or abjadic) scripts where a one-to-one correspondence of "grapheme" (letter) to phoneme is possible. I know of one major and a few minor attempts to put *Sense 1* to work in analyses of a writing system,[8] and of none devoted to more elaborate ones.

---

5 L. Henderson, ed., *Orthographies and Reading* (1984), 15.

6 Leslie Henderson, "On the Use of the Term 'grapheme'" (1985).

7 It is also the approach found in Eleanor M. Higginbottom, "Representation of English Vowel Phonemes" (1962), a pioneering but premature attempt at devising rules for text-to-speech synthesis that would have benefited greatly from Venezky's concept of the "marker" (§2.1.1). C. E. Bazell, "The Grapheme" (1966 [1956]), appears to attempt to reconcile *Sense 1* and *Sense 2* and assigns the grapheme level to the components of letters: the stem and the bowl of ⟨b⟩ are two graphemes that recur in ⟨d⟩.

8 Earl M. Herrick, *A Linguistic Description of Roman Alphabets* (1966), uses this approach in his "graphemic analysis" of a Roman-alphabet font; see Peter T. Daniels, "Is a Structural Graphemics Possible?" (1991b), 532 n. 2. (Herrick's two rejoinders, "Of Course a Structural Graphemics Is Possible!" [1994a] and "Reply to Daniels's Reply" [1994b], seem to miss the point.) Similar analyses have been carried out by Murray Eden, "On the Formalization of Handwriting" (1963); Giovanna Marotta, "The Features of the Roman Alphabet" (2000); and Beatrice Primus, "A Featural Analysis of the Modern Roman Alphabet" (2004). Herrick ([1994a], 416) introduces the term *graphemic grapheme* for that sort of analysis and *phonological-fit grapheme* for the kind discussed in §12.1.4.2 but immediately replaces the latter with *graphic image of a phoneme* (the symbol that represents speech-sounds) and *phonic image of a grapheme* (the sounds represented by a symbol). David G. Lockwood, "Phoneme and Grapheme"

General dictionaries have had to try to deal with the term. Henderson rightly lights into[9] the *OED*'s

> The class of letters and other visual symbols that represent a phoneme, as e.g. the grapheme ⟨f⟩ consists of the allographs *f, ff, F, Ff, gh, ph*, and *Ph* which represent the phoneme /f/ in *fun, huffy*, ...

(it first appeared in the 1972 Supplement), rightly observing that it's not supported by any of the quotations cited. Henderson didn't note that it seems to have been based on

> the sum of all written letters and letter combinations that represent one phoneme <the *p* of *pin*, the *pp* of *hopping*, and the *gh* of *hiccough* are members of one ~>

in the Merriam-Webster *Third International Dictionary* of 1961,[10] which doesn't provide evidence for its definitions, but he wrongly claimed that it conforms to *Sense 2*! I'm not aware of any scholar of writing systems who has subscribed to such a definition. A *Sense 2* user would consider *each* of the correspondences listed to be a separate grapheme—on the model of Pike's (e.g. n. 1 above) definition of "tagmeme," his unit of syntactic analysis, as a 'slot/class correlation', a correlation of form and function.

12.1.4.2 Why shouldn't "grapheme" be used?

If "grapheme" is to parallel "phoneme," we might expect that a grapheme is "a minimum same of written feature" [cf (24)]. But since this definition is identical to the definition of "phoneme" (differing only in modality), it would seem to imply an exact equivalence of the terms. It is clear, however, that the smallest units of writing do not necessarily correspond to the smallest units of speech that make a difference in meaning: English *cease* /siys/ and *case* /keys/ differ by only one letter, but by two phonemes.

Or, if phonemes are the components of the spoken aspect of morphemes, then what are graphemes the components of? To maintain the parallel, they should be the written components of minimal written units of meaning. But some units of writing *are* minimal units of meaning, namely, logograms. Does this mean that logographic writing systems do not include a graphemic level? If we admit this possibility, for even some writing systems, it's a clear difference between graphemics and phonemics.

(2000), 307, revives the terminology introduced by Manfred Kohrt, "The Term 'Grapheme'" (1986): "The *analogical view* ... makes the grapheme–allograph relation parallel to that between phoneme and allophone. The alternative is called the *referential view*, because it is based on the phonological reference of the various graphemes." Lockwood endorses the analogical view—and then shows that it is inadequate for analyzing, at least, Chinese writing.

9 Leslie Henderson, "On the Use of the Term 'grapheme'" (1985), 140.

10 Followed also by Merriam-Webster's principal American competitors, the *American Heritage Dictionary* and the *Random House Dictionary*. All the dictionaries also provide for the 'letter'/'minimal unit of a writing system' senses.

More concretely, take Chinese. In §12.1 we saw three characters, 口 上 下, which happen to be pictographic, ideographic, and logographic all at once; but this sort of character is fairly uncommon in the full inventory of Chinese characters—fewer than one in five. More than 80% of the 8,075 characters in a popular dictionary are composite,[11] comprising a semantic (or radical) and a phonetic (§6.1). By using both parts, any native-reader of a Chinese text (who by definition already speaks the language perfectly) encountering an unfamiliar character can assign a reading to it on the basis of the two clues and the context in the passage. The question for graphemics is, Which are the graphemes: the thousands of characters, or the hundreds of components? One scholar appears to endorse the view that it's the components that should be the graphemes.[12] But then there would be two entirely different kinds of grapheme in the writing system, the semantic ones and the phonetic ones, and they would only achieve specific reference in combination. This also leaves the residue of non-composed characters to get some sort of separate description.

And again: if the characters are considered the graphemes, there is the dilemma that they constitute ultimately an open class (there isn't a limited number of them)—not only are tens of thousands of characters catalogued that were innovated perhaps once, never to be used again; but there is nothing to stop someone from creating still more new characters. A phonemic system is a small, fixed class—not a closed class; in §2.1.2 we saw that the voiced fricatives went from allophones to phonemes in Middle English—typically numbering around 30–40 phonemes. But if Chinese writing is to be analyzed as graphemes, then the number will be nearly 1000 if the components are counted, and in the tens of thousands if the characters are counted—in both cases open to increase. Open-endedness is a characteristic of lexicons, not of grammatical inventories.

Futhermore: if characters are taken to be graphemes, then the "graphemic" level exhibits no duality of patterning, the very essence of the emic concept.

There is one unsatisfactory solution to the "Chinese character problem": let the canonical eight brushstrokes, which all appear in the character 永 *yǒng*—with its auspicious meaning 'eternal'[13]—plus the order in which they are written to create each character, be the graphemes! The strokes have no inherent meaning, save their differentiation function; their class is closed; they exhaustively constitute the components or characters; their order of writing in each character is fixed.[14] But there is then no connection between the graphemic level of individual strokes and the morphological level of complicated characters which it is supposed to analyze—no stroke contributes some definable essence to the identification of the characters it

---

11 Victor H. Mair, "Modern Chinese Writing" (1996), 201

12 Eric Scott Albright, "Design of an Electronic Method for Describing Writing Systems" (2001).

13 Peter Charles Sturman, *Mi Fu* (1997), 15.

14 The order information might not be found in major reference dictionaries, but it is included in learners' dictionaries such as Yu S., Sheng P., Yin P., Ding F., Yu R., and Chen Y., eds., *Quaille's Practical Chinese-English Dictionary* (1999).

appears in—so this *Sense 1* approach seems less than useful in studies of reading or of writing systems.

And what of multiple components of a single writing system? Brahmi-derived abugidas have distinct forms for independent and dependent forms of characters. Most alphabets have majuscule (capital) and minuscule (lowercase) forms for each letter, and many use italics (or an equivalent), with both of those features used for varying purposes across languages—in eighteenth-century English, nouns were capitalized (as in modern German) and proper names were italicized. Russian novels, such as Tolstoy's *War and Peace*, that contain passages in French naturally use Cyrillic for Russian and Roman for French. But in past times, German used Fraktur for ordinary German text but "Antiqua" (Roman type) for foreign words that happened to occur—Fraktur was seen not (as it is today) as a variety of Roman, but as a distinct script not suited for Latin, French, or English. In contemporary English, it's useful to consider the orthography of French-, Classical-, and native Germanic-origin vocabulary separately. There are no parallels in emic systems for these features, except for the last, where borrowed words in English sometimes follow different stress patterns from native words. Many alphabets use diacritics or optional ligatures (⟨æ œ⟩ etc.). Do these correspond to anything in language?

And even more so: the anomalies noted in the last paragraph can be ignored and all alphabetic text can be presented in plain minuscules. But this isn't an option in Japanese (§§ 4.1 and 7.1). Not only are there both *kana* and *kanji*, but there are two different kinds of *kana*. Where are the graphemes? The relationship between *hiragana* and *katakana* is like the relationship between upright and italic type in English, but unlike in English, it is obligatory. And more: is there one kind of relation between *kana* representing the same mora that happen to derive from the same *kanji* and another for those that derive from different *kanji* (Table 4.2)? Japanese raises problems for "grapheme" with a vengeance!

In still other cases, the notion of "grapheme" is simply redundant. Czech and Finnish are frequently cited as examples of (nearly) "perfect" orthographies in the spelling reformers' sense: letters correspond to phonemes and vice versa, so there is no need for any term beyond "letter" for describing them.

It is questions like these that lead me to suggest that the term "grapheme" should not be used in the study of writing systems.[15]

The one piece of grapheme theory that remains useful is the term *allograph*, which designates variants of a character that are conditioned by its surroundings: the word-final variants of one letter in Greek and five in Hebrew; the syllable-final variant ⟨s⟩ of the normal ⟨ſ⟩ in German and earlier English; the shapes of Syriac and Arabic letters when connected to their neighbors in a word. In the Indic scripts, the vowel *matras* are post-consonantal allographs, but even here there are

---

15 David G. Lockwood, "Phoneme and Grapheme" (2000), suggests ways of rescuing the term, in particular as regards non-alphabetic writing systems.

complications: the reduced consonant shapes for the most part represent C and not *Ca*, so they're not simply positional variants.

It is only for describing orthographies like those of English, French, Thai,[16] Tibetan, and a few other languages with long written traditions where spelling is preserved while language changes, that "phoneme–grapheme correspondences" tend to drift apart. Only then do principles need to be discovered for the historically modulated relationships between spelling and sound. Only then would something like (27) find some use:

(27)   grapheme   a correlation between a phoneme and a spelling

Thus in English, ⟨ee⟩:/iy/, ⟨ea⟩:/iy/, and ⟨e-e⟩:/iy/ (etc.), as in ⟨meet meat mete⟩ (etc.), would each be a grapheme, and so would ⟨eo⟩:/iy/, ⟨eo⟩:/e/, ⟨eo⟩:/ow/, and ⟨eo⟩:/i/, as in ⟨people leopard yeoman luncheon⟩.

One little-known approach, that of Nina Catach.[17] takes the notion of (27) further, because in French there are complications even beyond those of English.

Catach brings the concept back to Ferdinand de Saussure's notion of the *sign*— Saussure had spoken of *graphies* ('writings'), not of *graph⁽è⁾mes*—comprising the *signifiant* and the *signifié* (the *signifier* and the *signified*); and to André Martinet's notion of *double articulation*, the equivalent of Bloomfield's/Hockett's "duality of patterning." For Catach, morphemes are *signs*, but graphemes, like phonemes, are only *figures*. The phoneme is not the signified of the grapheme;[18] graphemes can be one or more letters (the French examples include *e, o, an, in, eau*); and, most noteworthily, the grapheme does not always represent the phoneme: some graphemes—she calls them *morphograms*—carry morphological information only. Among her examples are the consonant doubling in *immaculé* 'spotless' vs. *imaginer* 'imagine' with their homophonous initial sequences, and the many silent final consonant letters in French [§2.2.1 end]).[19] Her definition, then, is:

(28)   grapheme   the smallest unit of the written channel having a phonic
                       and/or semantic correspondence susceptible to linguistic
                       analysis[20]

---

16 There is a comprehensive treatment of the development, or lack thereof, of the relation of Thai orthography and phonology in J. Marvin Brown, *From Ancient Thai to Modern Dialects* (1985).

17 Nina Catach, "Le graphème" (1979).

18 Catach thus diverges from the frequently cited Angus McIntosh, "'Graphology' and Meaning" (1961), which holds the phoneme to be the "meaning" of the grapheme. McIntosh's position is justly criticized in great detail by William Haas, (1970), 9–16. Noam Chomsky, review of *Verbal Behavior* by B. F. Skinner (1959), 50, long ago defended "the important difference between reference and meaning."

19 Catach also invokes some terms and concepts from Louis Hjelmslev's *glossematic* approach to linguistics, filtered through William Haas, *Phono-Graphic Translation* (1970) and "Writing: The Basic Options" (1976). The latter, often cited but largely impenetrable, is vitiated by its insistence on including nonlinguistic graphic communication as "writing."

20 Nina Catach, "Le graphème" (1979), 27 (my translation).

In a subsequent programmatic article, she applies her views to writing systems more generally, but with little detail.[21] It seems to me that hers is the most generally applicable account of "graphemics," making the concept appropriate for all sorts of writing systems, but it is unlikely to find many adherents among modern practitioners.

12.1.4.3 Where did "grapheme" come from?

Current research indicates, not unreasonably because writing isn't inborn, that it piggybacks, rather consistently across speaking populations, not on brain structures devoted to language, but on structures that had evolved primarily for visual functions.[22]

But this neurolinguistic perspective hasn't been around for long, and it's not surprising that the few people who had thought seriously about writing wanted to see in it patterns like those they saw in speech and language.

Accordingly, the word "grapheme" was devised independently at least four times:[23] by Jan Baudouin de Courtenay in 1901; by Benjamin Lee Whorf in 1932; by W. Freeman Twaddell in 1935; and by R. H. Stetson in 1937. Only Stetson generally gets the credit in the literature on writing systems. Until recently, his was the earliest usage registered in the *OED*.

Baudouin de Courtenay (1845–1929) is celebrated for having introduced the concept "phoneme" to the West; it was developed by his student Mikołai Kruszewski in Kazan' around 1880.[24] As part of Baudouin's general program to rejuvenate linguistic terminology, he included "grapheme" in 1901. The first occurrence has been rendered as follows:

> The connection of language enunciation and writing reduces to the associations of phonetic representations with graphic representations, i.e. of phonemes as well as their parts and combinations with graphemes as well as their parts and combinations.[25]

---

21 Nina Catach, "The Grapheme" (1986).

22 Stanislas Dehaene, *Reading in the Brain* (2009). A less parochial view (see §12.4) is taken in Stanislas Dehaene, Laurent Cohen, José Morais, and Régine Kolinsky, "Illiterate to Literate" (2015).

23 A fifth inventor, Aarni Penttilä, used the term quite idiosyncratically and is dismissed by Manfred Kohrt, "The Term 'Grapheme' in the History and Theory of Linguistics" (1986), 82f.

24 See Roman Jakobson, "The Kazan' School of Polish Linguistics" (1971), for as much of the development as can be reconstructed. The term "phoneme" was a few years older but had not been defined in a modern sense or used rigorously, as shown by Joachim Mugdan, "On the Origins of the Term *Phoneme*" (2011).

25 Jan Baudouin de Courtenay, "Wskazówki dla zapisujących materiały gwarowe na obszarze językowym polskim" (1901), 116, translated by Piotr Ruszkiewicz, "Jan Baudouin de Courtenay's Theory of the Grapheme" (1978), 118—who shows that Baudouin had been concerned with the topic for at least 35 years.

In 1908:

> The discourse peculiar to Russian school grammars of "soft vowels" is due to the confusion of letters with sounds, of graphemes with phonemes. Russian writing has vowel graphemes, i.e. representations of vocalic letters, which are associated with the representation of the "softness" of preceding consonants; as a result, this label "soft" is transferred to the vowels corresponding to these graphemes by the so-familiar path of psychological misattribution and confusion, so that the consonants preceding these vowels are not understood at all as "soft."

> We have for the most part divested ourselves of the commingling of letters with sounds, of graphemes with phonemes. But next within the realm of phonetics itself comes the distinction of the acoustic from the physiological, the centripetal from the centrifugal. Accordingly, our scientific jargon must also undergo a thorough revision. [26]

In 1910:

> The *confusion* of letters with sounds, of *graphemes* (representations of letters) with *phonemes* (representations of sounds), is responsible for:

> 1) conclusions about the difference and identity of sounds based on the difference or identity of letters;
> 2) the transfer of the notion of homogeneity and indivisibility from graphemes to phonemes.[27]

This passage continues with a characterization of the phoneme showing that Baudouin extended the use of *-eme* in a way that would not be perpetuated, and *grapheme* may at that time have gone the way of his *kineme* and *acousmeme*.

Much later, he anticipated many of the observations to be made by scholars of writing and written language in succeeding decades. Most importantly, "In order to pronounce correctly a written word ..., one must first understand the word. To the speaker of a given language this presents no special problem."[28]

The use by Whorf (1892–1941) of the term "grapheme" likely went unnoticed[29] because it appeared in an article in the context of his attempted decipherment of Maya glyphs, not a topic of compelling interest to the linguists of his day (§9.3)—astonishingly, the article has long been readily available in the well-known collection *Language, Thought, and Reality*:

---

26 Jan Baudouin de Courtenay, "Zur Frage über die 'Weichheit' und 'Härte' der Sprachlaute" (1908), 586f., 590 (my translations).

27 Jan Baudouin de Courtenay, "Phonetic Laws" (1910 [1972]), 271.

28 Jan Baudouin de Courtenay, "The Influence of Language on World-View and Mood" (1929 [1972]), 287f.

29 The OED reported Stetson's as the first use of the term in English, as does the literature on writing systems and on reading. The 1932 antedating was uncovered by Fred R. Shapiro, "Contributions to the History of Linguistic Terminology" (1995), 26, to which I was directed by Joanne Despres of Merriam-Webster, Inc., whose dictionaries carry the earlier date. Meanwhile, Ross Clark reports (Usenet newsgroup sci.lang, January 6, 2017) that the *OED* now contains Twaddell's 1935 use.

> Grapheme is a word formed on the analogy of morpheme, semanteme, to denote any written symbol, especially as a linguistic factor, in place of "ideogram," "pictograph," or the ambiguous "character." In discussing hieroglyphs it is desirable to have a term that does not presuppose anything about the nature of the denotative process employed.[30]

Twaddell's (1906–1982) coinage seems jocular, intended to mock certain linguists he disagreed with:

> For many linguists, it appears, the phoneme functions as a unit to be represented by a symbol in so-called phonetic transcriptions. It appears that the unit these linguists require cannot sufficiently take into account either phonological or phonetic facts; it would clarify the issue if these units might be called 'graphemes', 'transcribemes', or even 'letters'.[31]

R. H. Stetson (1872–1950) was a phonetician. He was interested in movement and had devised the field of "motor phonetics":[32]

> [The phoneme] is an articulation … essentially a movement pattern.
> There are many movement patterns like it and a comparison may help in understanding the phoneme. The unit of writing may be called the grapheme; although often used to represent phonemes, it is not a mere parallel to speech. Much is written that is not pronounced, in music, in the formulae of mathematics and of the physical sciences …. In English the same character may represent several different phonemes and a well defined phoneme may be represented by two graphemes as in the case of "th" and "ph."
> The grapheme proves to be the standardized character of writing, with certain conventions as to its meaning in combinations which is extremely varied through the range of music, mathematics, symbolic logic, physical sciences, and language.[33]

It is perhaps not surprising to find him veering into matters of handwriting—and the pattern of a symphony conductor's baton marking time, and "the podeme derived from the step or stride in locomotion." These applications of emic theory were perhaps a step too far for language scholars of his time.

12.2 Orthographic depth

Despite all the—mostly unacknowledged—difficulties with the notion of "grapheme," the associated notion of "phoneme–grapheme correspondence" has exercised

---

30 Benjamin Lee Whorf, "A Central American Inscription Combining Mexican and Maya Day Signs" (1932 [1956]), 45 n. 5.

31 W. Freeman Twaddell, *On Defining the Phoneme* (1935), 54 (= 1957: 76b).

32 R. H. Stetson, *Motor Phonetics* (1928).

33 R. H. Stetson, "The Phoneme and the Grapheme" (1937), 353.

a powerful hold on psychologists of reading. While they may not endorse the "one-for-one" obsession of spelling reformers, they seem to have been convinced that there's just one way of teaching reading: to be specific, the way that has been developed for English.

Well, actually, two ways, which often go by the names "phonics" and "whole-word," and for decades these were seen as mutually exclusive. *Phonics*, broadly, follows the premise that the learner must first master the correlations between spellings and sounds; *whole-word* believes that since words aren't read by sounding them out letter by letter (or "grapheme" by "grapheme"), they should simply be taught as wholes of sound and meaning without special attention to the letters they're made up of. Cooler heads seem to have prevailed and recognize that aspects of both techniques are necessary for a language like English.

But in order to teach all writing systems using methods developed for English, it's necessary to fit them all to a Procrustean English bed. When the few other languages mentioned by reading researchers were those like Spanish, Finnish, and Czech, which come close to the one-letter-one-phoneme "ideal," it was easy to say that they were at the easy end of a continuum, English was at the hard end, and French was somewhere in the middle. But then it was suggested that Hebrew fitted alongside English at the hard end—or should we say the deep end.

The term "orthographic depth" was developed in the context of European alphabets and referred to the fact that English orthography does not reflect the *surface* phonemics (or phonetics) of the English language particularly well, but rather a *deep* layer (playing on the by then already superseded Chomskyan notions of "deep" and "surface" structure in syntax), whereas the orthography of Serbo-Croatian (as it then was)* does reflect the surface structure. English was labeled a "deep" orthography

---

* Before the dissolution of Yugoslavia, a single literary language that had been created early in the nineteenth century served both Serbs and Croats. The former (Eastern Orthodox) used a Cyrillic alphabet, the latter (Roman Catholic) a Roman alphabet (but all children were taught both, and interesting inquiries into biscriptalism were made). Nowadays four languages are recognized, not only Serbian and Croatian, but Bosnian and Montenegrin as well—for identifying "languages" is a political, not a linguistic, endeavor.

Details *(continued)* ──

12.2 The notion of orthographic depth was developed by several scholars associated with the Haskins Laboratories for basic research on spoken and written language, in New Haven, notably Leonard Katz and Laurie B. Feldman, "Linguistic Coding in Word Recognition" (1981) and "Relation between Pronunciation and Recognition of Printed Words" (1983), but it was adumbrated in one of the first interdisciplinary conferences on the psychology and linguistics of reading, by Edward Klima, "How Alphabets Might Reflect Language" (1972), and Samuel E. Martin, "Nonalphabetic Writing Systems" (1972). It is associated most prominently with Ram Frost and found its fullest expression in his "Orthographic Systems and Skilled Word Recognition Processes in Reading" (2005). "Biscriptal" education in Yugoslavia provided a rare opportunity to investigate two alphabets that share a number of symbols—some representing and Serbo-Croatian a "shallow" orthography. But does the concept of orthographic depth have value in the description of orthographies other than European alphabets? Casting a broader net across the sea of writing systems suggests that no, there isn't a single continuum on which all writing systems can be placed. The few examples under each of these ten "dimensions" represent only a small selection.

I. *Retention of historical spellings despite pronunciation change*
Words can be spelled the same but pronounced differently. Language change in English accounts for the many pronunciations of ⟨ough⟩ exemplified by the words *bough/cough/dough/through/tough*, which once all rhymed.

Conversely, words can be spelled differently but pronounced the same: In English, *meat/meet/mete*, *peak/peek/pique*, even *relieve/receive*, reflect dialect differences within the language, which are sometimes retained in local pronunciations; or borrowing both spellings and pronunciations from different sources. In Hebrew, ancient spellings with ע ה א, ת ט, ק כ, and שׂ ס ⟨ʕ h ʔ, t ṭ, q k, ś s⟩ are retained even though in the modern language those groups of letters have merged to ø, /t/, /k/, and /s/ respectively. Many languages influenced by Sanskrit retain letters for three sibilants श ष स ⟨ś ṣ s⟩ for spelling loanwords from that language, even though in many of the modern languages they have merged to /s/.

II. *Spelling constancy despite morphophonemic alternation*
In English and Russian, depth is morphophonemic because the orthography does not change when either morphemes or phonemes undergo conditioned alternations: /haws/ ⟨house⟩ becomes /hawz/ when the plural suffix is added, but the spelling does not change: ⟨houses⟩. In Russian, /d/, /t/, and /c/ at the end of a morpheme take on the voicing of a following stop, but the spelling doesn't change: a suffix, водка /vód-ka/ [ˈvotkɐ] 'vodka'; a prefix, отблеск /ót-blʲesk/ [ˈodblʲɛsk] 'reflection, gleam'; or a compound—плацкарта /plac-kárta/ [plɐtsˈkartɐ] 'reserved seat ticket' versus плацдарм /plac-dárm/ [plɐdzˈdarm] 'bridgehead'.

III. *Omission of phonological elements*
In Hebrew and Arabic, most vowels are normally not written: Modern Hebrew orthography writes all the consonants and uses *matres lectionis* for some of the

---

Details *(continued)*

the same sound, some representing different ones—although only capital letters, and not connected texts, were studied: Laurie B. Feldman and Michael T. Turvey, "Word Recognition in Serbo-Croatian Is Phonologically Analytic" (1983).

The first five dimensions of orthographic depth were identified in Peter T. Daniels, "Introduction to Graphonomy" (2012), and another five were contributed by the first author in David L. Share and Peter T. Daniels, "Aksharas, Alphasyllabaries, Abugidas, Alphabets, and Orthographic Depth" (2015), revised in Peter T. Daniels and David L. Share, "Writing System Variation" (2017).

vowels that in Biblical Hebrew were long. Many consonant strings can represent several words: ספר (spr) can be /séfer/ 'book', /safar/ 'count (v.)', /sfar/ 'enumeration', or /sapar/ 'barber'. In English, stress isn't marked: *contráct* (v.) / *cóntract* (n.). The four accent marks that designate the four tones of Mandarin Chinese in *pinyin* (see note * on p. 84) are hardly ever used. Just about every time in all these cases, it is the context that ensures that no problem arises in reading.

IV. *Dual-purpose letters*

The *matres lectionis* of the Aramaic-based writing systems usually retain their consonantal value as well as indicating, or even representing (as with Arabic ا و ِ (ī ū ā)), vowels. The merging of the shapes of Middle Iranian letters does not reflect merging of their sounds (Table 7.2). In English, ⟨h⟩ doubles as a diacritic in the digraphs ⟨ch ph sh th wh⟩ and sometimes ⟨kh⟩, indicating a pronunciation similar to that of the bare consonant, rather than aspiration. Japanese *on* and *kun* readings of *kanji* (§7.1) are a spectacular example.

V. *Diglossia*

Diglossia is the name for the situation in which the language learned by all literate people differs considerably from the language they speak; those languages were referred to as the "High" and "Low" varieties respectively. This isn't a common occurrence; the four original examples were Standard German/Swiss German, Standard Arabic/vernacular Arabics, Standard French/Haitian Creole, and Katharevousa/Dhimotiki in Greece. The spoken language is normally not written, so learning to read is tantamount to learning a foreign language.

VI. *Graphic considerations and allographs*

In an inversion of Dimension I, orthographic depth can result from differentiation for solely graphic reasons. Recall the spelling of English [ʌ] with ⟨o⟩ as in *come, monk, won* because ⟨**come monk won**⟩ were considered easier to read than ⟨**cume munk wun**⟩ (§2.1.1). In Russian, most of the capital and small letters are the same shape, but in English mostly they differ: В в ⟨V v⟩ vs. B b, Д д ⟨D d⟩; here allography carries meaning. Final letters in Hebrew, ץ ף ן ם ך corresponding to צ פ נ מ כ ⟨ṣ p n m k⟩, and Greek, ς corresponding to σ ⟨s⟩, represent a different sort of allography, purely conditioned. The same holds for the remarkable differences between vowel *aksharas* and *matras* in Indic (§5.2) and between independent characters and their component forms in Chinese (Table 6.1).

Details *(continued)*

III The examples of Hebrew ambiguity are entries in E. Ben-Yehuda and D. Weinstein, eds., *Ben-Yehuda's Pocket Hebrew–English English–Hebrew Dictionary* (1961), 225a.

V The concept of diglossia was introduced by Charles Ferguson, "Diglossia" (1959). It is often extended to just about any sort of bidialectal or even bilingual situation, but this is an unfortunate distortion.

VII. *Ligaturing*

Sometimes a coalescence of characters is so trivial that it is never mentioned. In standard typography, ⟨f⟩⟨i⟩ combine into ⟨fi⟩, which, to a novice reader at least, might look very like ⟨h⟩, but the ⟨fi⟩ ligature seems never to be taught, and no resulting confusion is reported. The joining of letters in Arabic might be considered a source of difficulty in learning to read, though this may be more an illusion caused by the way the script is taught (Table 3.4). The considerable variety of techniques for conjunct formation in the Indic scripts (§5.5), on the other hand, may cause considerable difficulty in mastering the orthographies.

VIII. *Visual uniformity or complexity*

The shapes of scripts—their ductus—reflect the esthetic ambiance of the cultures they are used in. Some scripts seem to exhibit far more elaborate shapes than are needed to distinguish 40-odd characters from each other. Among the Indic scripts, compound *aksharas* (§5.5) sometimes bear little resemblance to their unattached components. The Cyrillic alphabet is harder to read than the Roman alphabet because its letters are more similar in shape (Table 2.13); Armenian (Table 2.11) presents even more of the same difficulty—it's been said to be unphotocopiable because the large preponderance of thin strokes tend to disappear in the reproducing—though in contemporary Armenian typography the letters have been considerably assimilated to the Roman ductus: compare traditional ա բ գ դ ե զ է ը թ հ ⟨a b g d e z ē ə tʰ h⟩ with a modern font, ա բ գ դ ե զ է ը թ հ.

IX. *Non-linearity*

Diacritics add a non-linear dimension to many scripts. Among European alphabets they have a number of different functions, sometimes several in a single language (§2.2.1). In Indic scripts, the vowel *matras* can appear on all four sides of a consonant *akshara*; in Chinese characters, the radical usually appears to the left of the phonetic component but can also be to the right, above, below, or surrounding it.

Details *(continued)* —————————————————————————————

VII My re-presentation of Arabic ligaturing, Peter T. Daniels, "Arabic Letters Do Not Have Final Forms" (2013a), has not yet been given written form. Grammars and textbooks for Indian languages rarely include tables of all the possible aksharic combinations in their abugidas. A welcome exception is the pamphlet series typified by K. Srinivasachari, *Learn Sanskrit in 30 Days* (n.d.) (they're called "Learn [Language] Through English" on the spine); there are volumes for Arabic, Bengali, Gujarati, Kannada, Malayalam, Marathi, Oriya, Punjabi, Tamil, Telugu, and Urdu (but not Sinhala, which isn't a language of India). For Devanagari and its two closest relatives, Gujarati and Bengali, see H. M. Lambert, *Introduction to the Devanagari Script* (1953).

IX The effect of non-linearity of Indic vowel *matras* on fluency of reading was investigated by Padmapriya Kandhadai and Richard Sproat, "Impact of Spatial Ordering" (2010).

X. *Inventory size*

A few alphabets have more than fifty signs. Most alphabets have both majuscules and minuscules. If compound *aksharas* are counted individually, they can number in the hundreds. Similarly, the few dozen Korean letters enter into more than a thousand syllable blocks. The several thousand Chinese characters reduce to a few hundred semantic and phonetic components, but there are no such clues to the meaning or sound of the 2000 or so Japanese *kanji*, which must be mastered holistically.

12.3 Creating orthographies

Almost all the adaptations of scripts to new languages we've looked at in this book have been devised by people seeking to record their own language. Oftentimes they've simply used the existing resources as best they can to handle the different sets of consonants and vowels that are found in their language. Sometimes there's a considerable mismatch between those sets—the most obvious example is that Latin had only a single sibilant, /s/ (in later times /z/ came in via Greek loanwords), but just about every European language that took over the Roman alphabet had at least three, adding /ʃ/, and quite a few, notably the Slavic languages, had quite a few more than two. The different languages came up with quite a variety of devices to spell their different sibilants; the prize probably goes to Polish:

[s]	[ɕ]	[ʃ]	[z]	[ʑ]	[ʒ]	[ts]	[tɕ]	[tʃ]	[dz]	[dʑ]	[dʒ]
s	ś	sz	z	ź	ż, rz	c	ć	cz	dz	dź	dż

12.3.1 A curious pattern

But in enough unrelated cases that it seems some sort of pattern might be involved, properties of segments are encoded not in the letters for the segments themselves, but in an adjacent letter. One of these examples figured in the earliest proposal of the term "grapheme": Baudouin de Courtenay's discussion of the vowel letters in Russian (§12.1.4.3), where a palatal segment is signaled by the following vowel letter: а ⟨a⟩ я ⟨ja⟩, э ⟨e⟩ е ⟨je⟩, о ⟨o⟩ ё ⟨jo⟩, у ⟨u⟩ ю ⟨ju⟩; the high non-back vowels и ⟨i⟩ and ы ⟨y⟩ [ɨ] can't be preceded by the glide. Palatalization of consonants or its absence can be signaled by the letters ь and ъ respectively.

The Turkish language has a fairly limited array of consonants but no fewer than eight vowels. The Arabic script used for Ottoman Turkish (until 1928) might seem particularly unsuited, with its 27 consonant letters and provision for just three vowels. But there's a special feature of Turkish, and many other languages of the world, that Ottoman orthography took advantage of: *vowel harmony*. The eight vowels are grouped on three dimensions: four vowels are *front* /i e ü ö/ and four are *back* /ɨ a u o/; four are *high* /i ɨ u ü/ and four are *low* /e a o ö/; and four are *rounded*

/ü ö u o/ and four aren't /i ɨ e a/. The Ottoman solution was to use the letters for "back" consonants for the back vowels, the "regular" consonants for the front vowels: صوص ⟨ṣwṣ⟩ *sus* 'be quiet', سوس ⟨sws⟩ *süs* 'ornamental'; طارلا ⟨ṭārlā⟩ *tarlá* 'field', ترله ⟨trlh⟩ *terlé* 'sweat'.

One word can usually include vowels from only one of those groups, and inflectional endings have to participate in the word's vowel harmony. The plural suffix, for instance, is |lVr|, which becomes -*ler* after front vowels and -*lar* after back vowels. Both allomorphs are spelled لر in Ottoman, but in modern orthography (§12.4) they're different. The five Roman vowels plus two with umlauts are supplemented by an innovation: dotless ⟨ı⟩ spells /ɨ/ and its capital is ⟨I⟩; the capital of ⟨i⟩ /i/ is dotted ⟨İ⟩. Some of the consonants can trip up readers familiar with older applications of the Roman alphabet: ⟨ğ⟩ marks a preceding vowel as long, ⟨c⟩ is /ʤ/, ⟨ş⟩ is /ʃ/, ⟨ç⟩ is /ʧ/.

12.3.2 Missionary scripts

Especially in §§ 2.1.4.2, 2.4, 3.2.3, and 5.6, we've seen examples of the creation of scripts and orthographies in olden times by proselytizers and missionaries for major world religions. The principal exceptions appear in Chapter 8, with missionaries inventing new scripts for their converts. In recent centuries, missionaries and their analogues have been responsible for much, or most, of the creation of new orthographies, and for the most part they've adapted their own alphabet—since most mission activity is Christian, based in Europe and North America, most new orthographies are in the Roman alphabet. During and in the wake of the Age of Exploration, when Europeans set out around the world and discovered people whose souls they believed they needed to save, missionaries were not far behind. The sixteenth century saw the creation of many grammars of indigenous languages, mainly in Latin America, so that clergy could learn to preach and minister to their charges; but there was little or no interest in writing those languages, since only the Latin Scriptures and catechisms were deemed worthy of study.

One of the first languages for which a Roman-alphabet orthography was devised by missionaries was Vietnamese. Portuguese missionaries laid the groundwork, and the French scholar Alexandre de Rhodes (1591–1660) finalized their work. The familiar story of language change and orthographic inertia is responsible for what appear to be some oddities in the use of letters: ⟨đ⟩ is used for [d] and ⟨d⟩ for [z] not out of some desire to confound the Europeans, but because the modern sounds are the result of centuries of changes. Similarly, ⟨ph⟩ is [f] and ⟨kh⟩ is [x], as might be expected—but ⟨th⟩ is [tʰ], not [θ]. The most unusual feature of Vietnamese orthography is the obligatory notation of no fewer than six different tones using five distinct

Details *(continued)* ————————————————————————————————

12.3.1 The Ottoman Turkish examples are from Henry Jehlitschka, *Türkische Konversations-Grammatik* (1895), 16.

Table 12.1 Vietnamese vowels and tones

A. VOWELS				B. TONES			
				Symbol	Description	Phonetics	Meaning
i [i]		ư [ɯ]	u [u]	ma	level	[mā]	'ghost'
				má (acute)	high rising	[má]	'cheek'
ê [e]	â [ə]	ơ [ɤ]	ô [o]	mà (grave)	low (falling)	[mà]	'but'
				mả (hook)	dipping-rising	[mǎ]	'tomb'
				mã (tilde)	high rising glottalized	[máʔ]	'horse'
e [ɛ]	ă [a]	a [ɑ]	o [ɔ]	mạ (dot)	low glottalized	[màʔ]	'rice seedling'

diacritics (Table 12.1B). It is often said that the eleven distinct vowel letters (Table 12.1A) also consist of a base plus a diacritic, but it's better not to consider the differentiations between similar letters to be diacritics because the specific marks used (horns, circumflexes, breve) aren't associated with consistent distinctions between the corresponding vowels, ⟨Cộng hòa Xã hội chủ nghĩa Việt Nam⟩ 'Socialist Republic of Vietnam'.

A different story emerges from missionaries at work on Pacific islands, attending to Polynesian languages. The first Roman alphabets were created in the 1820s, initially for Samoan and Fijian. The Polynesian languages are well known for having very few consonants—Tahitian has /t/ but not /k/, Hawai'ian has /k/ but not /t/, and the early explorers couldn't always decide which letter to use in spelling the names of islands they put on their first maps.

An interesting property of Samoan and Tongan, and Polynesian languages generally, is that they don't have voiced stops /b d g/, which freed up the letter ⟨g⟩ for the third nasal alongside /m n/, namely /ŋ/. The capital of American Samoa

1886	1897	1950
King George I	King George II	Queen Salote

From the author's collection.

Figure 12.3. Stamps of Tonga showing orthographic change

Details *(continued)*

12.3.2 The complicated history of Polynesian orthographies was untangled somewhat for me by Albert J. Schütz (University of Hawai'i).

seems always to have been spelled Pago Pago, and the pronunciation [paŋo paŋo] is familiar. In Tongan, though, at first the phoneme /ŋ/ was spelled ⟨ng⟩ as in English, even though native speakers would have seen no reason to include the ⟨n⟩. When Tonga's first postage stamps were issued (Figure 12.3), imitating a familiar British design, depicting King George Tupou I (1797–1893, r. 1875–93) the name appeared as ⟨Tonga⟩. Shortly after the accession of the new king, his great-grandson George Tupou II (1874–1918, one of the first casualties of the influenza epidemic), the stamps read ⟨Toga⟩ in accordance with local sensibilities. His daughter Salote [i.e., Charlotte] Tupou III (1900–1965) had reigned for more than thirty years before the spelling was again changed for the convenience of foreigners (and perhaps to avoid confusion with Togo, which from 1897 under successive German, Anglo-French, and French administration had stamps of its own).

12.3.3 A politicians' script

When British influence began to expand through India in the eighteenth century, little concern was shown for the consistent spelling of local words taken into English. The ⟨Hindoo⟩ of those days eventually gave way to ⟨Hindu⟩ (it's taken longer for ⟨Moslem⟩ to yield to ⟨Muslim⟩), but ⟨Parsee⟩ has hung on for followers of Zoroastrianism, referring to their Persian origin—it's essentially the same word as "Farsi," the misnomer for the modern Persian language of Iran (as if we called German "Doitch").

A bit more problematic are the words *Punjab* and *pundit*. In Sanskrit and Hindi they're पंजाब ⟨paⁿjāb⟩ and पंडित ⟨paⁿdit⟩. The ⟨a⟩ is pronounced [ʌ], and the most natural spelling for that sound in English is ⟨u⟩. However, when a more "scientific" attempt at pronouncing words borrowed from Hindi set in, a pronunciation ['puwnˌdʒæb] was often heard, even giving rise to the spelling ⟨Poonjab⟩. ⟨Pundit⟩ seems not to have had that problem; instead, ⟨Pandit⟩ was (re)introduced as the spelling for the term when it was used as an honorific, as in *Pandit Nehru*, and it's not surprising that it's likely to be pronounced ['pandɪt] in that context.

The word *juggernaut*—quite aside from the elaborate explanations of how it came into English—represents Sanskrit जगन्नाथः ⟨jagan-nāthaḥ⟩ 'world-lord', with any number of accommodations. The ⟨u⟩ < /a/ we've already met. The doubled ⟨g⟩ is to preserve the sound of the ⟨u⟩, but it may have kept the legitimate double-*n* of the original from being carried over. The ⟨r⟩ is very interesting. In recent British English, ⟨er⟩ represents [ə]. But early in the nineteenth century, dropping post-vocalic [r] was far from fashionable; there's no evidence of it in stressed syllables before 1800, or in unstressed syllables much before the mid eighteenth century—except that it's found in this word in the mid seventeenth! The final ⟨aḥ⟩ had already been dropped in Hindi, the [tʰ] is the usual English sound—but [ɔː] for *ā is a bit odd.

12.3.4 Linguists' scripts

Beginning in the 1930s, important contributions were made by missionary linguists to the development of descriptive linguistics generally, to the description of little-known or unknown languages, and in particular to the creation of writing systems for unwritten languages. Generations of linguists, both missionary and general, between the 1940s and at least the 1960s trained on a series of textbooks by Kenneth L. Pike (1912–2000), the linguist who developed the analytic distinction between *emic* and *etic* (§12.1.4). Particularly significant is the subtitle of *Phonemics: A Technique for <u>Reducing</u> Languages to Writing.* For Pike, a practical orthography was all but equivalent to a phonemic transcription, and his teaching must have played a part in the pervasive view that "one phoneme / one letter" is the only acceptable pattern for a writing system (cf. §2.1.3).

Discussions of creating orthographies frequently point out that on occasion languages have received competing writing systems—because the speakers were arbitrarily divided between (say) French and British colonies, or were proselytized by both Roman Catholic and Protestant missionaries; but beyond lists of spellings of phonemes, they rarely give examples even at the word level. Here, instead, is a pair of orthographies for Kru, a Kwa language of Liberia, that were posited in order to illustrate the problems such conflicts can cause. The "traditional" version reflects a "tradition" going all the way back to 1927, when an "Africa alphabet" for use in all the British colonies was proposed, which in effect intuited the "phonemic principle" that was still somewhat inchoate (cf. §12.1.3). The "Anglicizing" orthography takes advantage of the fact that many Kru-speakers spoke or had studied English and uses conventions taken from that language.

<table>
<tr><td>

Mɔ Pɔɔ. Mɔ Dyipoteh Klasehęh
plesina. Mɔ ke a dedyu
Temɔteh sǫ ǫ tuane. A
ponyneoo Falimɔ, ąą nwene
nyuɛke ąą gbǫmaa nyu.
(*Traditional*)

</td><td>

Maw Paw-aw. Maw dyeepowtayh Klasayh-ayhn
playseena. Maw kay a daydyoo
Taymawtayh sawn-awn tooanay. A
pownynay-ow-ow Faleemaw, an-an nwaynay
nyoo ehkay an-an gbown-maa nyoo.
(*"Anglicizing"*)

</td></tr>
</table>

'Paul, a prisoner of Christ Jesus, and Timothy our brother, To Philemon our dear friend and co-worker ...' (Philemon 1 *NRSV*)

Details *(continued)*

12.3.4 The history of linguists' remarks on the creation of orthographies is outlined by Richard L. Venezky, "Principles for the Design of Practical Writing Systems" (1970a). The *locus classicus* for "one phoneme / one letter" is Kenneth L. Pike, *Phonemics* (1943).

"The Africa alphabet" was set forth in International Institute of African Languages and Cultures, *Practical Orthography of African Languages* (1930); a quixotic proposal to replace all African orthographies with strictly phonemic symbols chosen from a large, uniform set of letters—also under the auspices of the International African Institute, as it had come to be called—is found in Michael Mann and David Dalby, *Thesaurus of African Languages* (1987),

Here for comparison is a different verse from a translation published in 1921, before the introduction of the Africa alphabet, exhibiting a plethora of diacritics.

> Dâke we̱ ū neâ nigba ū dâ Jordan winti, o̱ mū nȯ bo ne o̱ phedo Nyesŏa tae nie
> o̱ pō nyepo ni dibo nie be̱ yeâ kpenê kukui dey ser;

> 'He went into all the region around the Jordan, proclaiming a baptism of repentance for forgiveness of sins, ...' (Luke 3:3 *NRSV*)

William A. Smalley (1923–1997), by contrast, paid close attention to interaction between scripts, orthographies, and their users. When an existing alphabet is adapted, sometimes the community wants its orthography to resemble that of the local authority or of the former colonial power—and sometimes the community wants its orthography to be as distinctive as possible. Smalley urged the adaptation of local scripts for unwritten languages and provided nearly a dozen examples of the use of Thai-based orthographies for local languages in Thailand. In his view, the cooperation of speakers of the language is absolutely essential—a writing system must not be imposed on a community "from above."

Smalley's influence, though never explicit, is pervasive in a recent collection that includes programmatic articles on non-linguistic factors in orthography design and on orthographic depth, as well as case studies of orthography creation for a wide variety of languages, including a Tibetan-script-based orthography for the related Kurtöp language of Bhutan, a nation where the Tibetan script itself is considered too holy for secular use.

12.4 Writing versus language

Now that we've sampled the world's writing systems, we can return to an observation that opened the book: writing is not like language. In this chapter I talked about duality of patterning and emic analyses, which don't work for phenomena organized consciously. There are a few other major differences.

Most importantly, written language differs in significant ways from spoken language, and the study of written language is a whole different discipline from

---

Details *(continued)* ————————————————————————————

206–19. The Kru examples are from Joseph E. Grimes, Augustus B. Marwieh, and Amy Bauernschmidt, "Several Kru Orthographies" (1960), 118, with the comparison verse in E. A. Nida, ed., *The Book of a Thousand Tongues* (1972), 238 #679. Smalley's observations with case studies are set out in *Orthography Studies* (1963); the examples of the application of Thai script to minority languages are in his *Phonemes and Orthography* (1976); and in *Linguistic Diversity and National Unity* (1994) his views are presented in the most detail. The Smalley approach to orthography creation finds exemplary application in M. Cahill and K. Rice, eds., *Developing Orthographies for Unwritten Languages* (2014). The development of a new script in Bhutan is described by Gwendolyn Hyslop, "Kurtöp Orthography Development in Bhutan" (2014).

graphonomy. The way most directly related to the physical existence of writing is the evanescence of speech versus the protracted availability of writing. The ensuing questions of literacy and society, of literacy and the individual have engaged many scholars from many disciplines beyond linguistics and could provide the subject matter for an entirely different exploratory essay.

Returning to graphonomy: language is constantly changing, while writing generally obeys tradition and does not readily respond to changes. Simplification in some areas of language is accompanied by complication in other areas, as a language's overall "efficiency" tends to remain constant; but a script's efficiency—its "goodness of fit" to its language—is maximal when it's devised, and deteriorates thereafter. Writing systems with long histories end up quite "deep" on Dimension I.

Because writing is learned—studied—rather than acquired automatically like native languages, there's no particular pressure on writing systems to be easy to learn. Whether someone is born into a scribal family, as seems to have been the case in Mesopotamia at least, or whether they have to go to school until they're at least 14 years old so that society can attain the elusive goal of "universal literacy," as in most of the developed world, they're required to master their society's writing system no matter how little or much time it might take to do so. Writing systems can thus grow more and more complex, for various reasons, without any counterpressure until some significant change in society prompts a change.

Notably, writing systems can be altered by fiat. Kemal Atatürk could not have ordered the minority peoples of Turkey to stop speaking their languages and use

Details *(continued)* ──────────────────────────────────────

12.4

> Putting words down on paper and having them printed is dangerous because, once printed, they have a kind of immortality that the spoken word does not. The spoken word, no matter how wise, goes up in smoke and is lost forever.
>
> Andrew A. Rooney, *Sweet and Sour* (1992), 1–2* †

I won't recommend a particular work on written language, but a very good portrayal of the place of writing in world history is Nicholas Ostler, *Empires of the Word* (2005).

A fine introduction to the evolution of language is James R. Hurford, *The Origins of Language* (2014).

─────────────

* The quotation reached me as the solution to Michael Ashley, *Giant Book of Acrostics* (New York: Fall River Press, 2013), #126. It appears in the introduction to a collection of recent newspaper columns by the well-known CBS-TV writer and commentator Andy Rooney.

† At this point I might be expected to quote Plato: "[Writing] will introduce forgetfulness into the soul of those who learn it: they will not practice using their memory because they will put their trust in writing" (*Phaedrus* 275a, trans. Alexander Nehamas and Paul Woodruff, p. 551). This is usually taken out of context as a condemnation of writing, but Lane Wilkinson, "Reading, Writing, and What Plato Really Thought" (2010), considering the passages just before and after the anecdote about Thoth's invention of writing, concludes that "To Socrates, the problem with writing is not that it 'creates forgetfulness in the learners' [Jowett's translation] but that people mistakenly hold the written word up as the only path to knowledge, when in reality, books are just information and the real knowledge comes from within the reader."

only Turkish, but he could decree that the Turkish language would be written with a Roman-based writing system rather than an Arabic-based one beginning on November 3, 1928. Noah Webster could not successfully tell Americans to not split infinitives, say, but he could successfully recommend dropping the ⟨u⟩ from words like ⟨colour⟩.

What is the root of these differences between writing and language?

Humans have had language for a very long time indeed, and the brain and the speech and hearing organs long ago evolved to perfect the ability to talk. But writing has been around for only a little over 5000 years—and we have no evidence that people who can read are more successful at making descendants than people who can't—so evolution hasn't provided us with brains that create and process writing automatically. This is why emic sorts of analysis, and other language-derived analytical tools, are not so well suited to writing.

Let's look at Stanislas Dehaene's *Reading in the Brain*, mentioned in n. 22 above. Dehaene integrates hundreds of studies of the brain and of behaviors involved in reading. But what's missing is almost any awareness that writing systems denote any stretch of speech other than the segment or, in a few mentions of Chinese characters, the morpheme; nor does he recognize the existence of the two-character Chinese word. He also doesn't acknowledge that language evolved long before certain brain regions were co-opted for reading. And why did he settle on the segment—the phoneme—as the stretch of speech to be connected with units of writing? Why did Baudouin de Courtenay settle on the segment for what "phoneme" designates?

The answer is the same for both these scholars, and for almost all the others who have been mentioned in this chapter: They were literate in French and English, Russian and Polish and German, Latin and Greek at least. What they read were alphabets. What if their first languages had been written with a syllabary? Then perhaps the most basic division would have been the syllable: are *pa* and *pu* any *more* different from each other than *p* and *t* are?

The following passage is especially valuable because the author is quite innocent of any linguistic or graphonomic theory. Referring to students attempting to learn to read and write Cherokee using the "alphabetic" arrangement of the characters as in Table 1.1, she says,

> ... the syllabary organized in this way vexes learners. They have a difficult time finding the right character because first they have to locate the sound according to alphabetical order and the English sound system. Spelling becomes the arduous task of first relying on English transliterations then locating the correct syllabary character within the alphabetical order.

Details *(continued)* ───

The best account of Atatürk's script reform is the on-the-spot report from Maynard Owen Williams, "Turkey Goes to School" (1929).

The beginnings of neuroscience investigation of writing are presented by Stanislas Dehaene, *Reading in the Brain* (2009).

Half a century earlier, one of the leading American Descriptivist linguists, the Chinese-American Yuen-Ren Chao (1892–1982), had put it this way:

> To one who is used to an alphabetic system of writing, it seems to be the simplest thing to talk about the sound 'o', the sound 'e', the sound 'l' [ɛɫ], the sound 'b' [biː], or even the sound 'w' [ˈdʌbljuː]. But to one used to a logographic system of writing like the Chinese, or a syllabic system of writing like the Japanese, the nature of sound segments in the form of consonants and vowels is not at all obvious and even seems highly abstract. As an intermediate type we may cite Sanskrit or Tibetan writing in which each symbol has what is called an inherent vowel in addition to a consonant, so that it will represent a syllable with a vowel of generally [a]-quality, unless marked otherwise.

"Why segments?" may look like a crazy question. But not long after Baudouin worked out his systematic analysis of linguistic units, Roman Jakobson (1896–1982) began to identify units smaller than segments that he showed were really what made the differences between morphemes. He called them "phonetic features." These are properties like voicing vs. voicelessness, stop vs. continuant, oral vs. nasal—the things that label the rows and columns in Table 2.1. As we saw in the mention of the obsolescence of phoneme theory, Jakobson's disciple and collaborator Morris Halle (b. 1923) used featural analysis to justify his approach. Yet his analyses, and those of all the varieties of phonological theory that have sprung from it, continue to segment speech into precisely the units that are denoted by alphabets—even though phoneticians had meanwhile been demonstrating that there are no physical segments in the speech stream (§12.1.3). A systematization of a phonetic analysis could be done in terms of overlapping articulatory gestures: Voice Onset Time, Advanced Tongue Root, etc., but that has not been attempted: current approaches to phonology are still laden with C-onsonants and V-owels.

Linguists being guided—or misguided—by their scripts is not new. It's my opinion that the notion of consonantal roots arose when Arab grammarians first began to study the Arabic language as it was written in the Qur'ān, when all that appeared on the page were consonant letters. They thought of the vowel sounds as evanescent connections between the consonants, whereas the consonants had real existence because they appeared on the page before them. This is the opposite of what the

---

Details *(continued)*

The quotation about learning Cherokee is from Ellen Cushman, *The Cherokee Syllabary* (2011), 45; the other is from Yuen Ren Chao, "Graphic and Phonetic Aspects of Linguistic and Mathematical Symbols" (1963), 71. Jakobson's clearest presentation of feature theory is in Roman Jakobson and Morris Halle, *Fundamentals of Language* (1956), and Halle's development is found primarily in Morris Halle, *The Sound Pattern of Russian* (1959), with its application to English in Noam Chomsky and Morris Halle, *The Sound Pattern of English* (1968). The post-Hallean, non-phonetic, but segment-bound approach to syllables is encapsulated by San Duanmu, *Syllable Structure* (2009).

etymologies of *our* words tell us: "sonant" is an old term for a sound that has "voice," like *a i u* and *b d g* (matched with "surd" for the corresponding "voiceless" sounds, *p t k*); and a "*con*-sonant" is thus a letter that goes *with* a voiced sound, such as a vowel.

Indian grammarians, on the other hand, were at work before the Indic languages were written; as we have seen (Chapter 5), they did not deem consonants and vowels to require equivalent representation. One of the early commentaries on Pāṇini's grammar, the *Vājasaneyi-Prātiśākhya* i.99–101, states *svaro 'kṣaram: sahādyair vyañja-naiḥ: uttaraiś cāvasitaiḥ* "A syllable is composed of a vowel, together with initial consonant(s) and, *in pausa*, a following consonant."*

Chinese grammarians, on a third hand, saw syllables but heard them in two parts: the initial and everything else, the rhyme (§6.1).

Given all the ways of subdividing the speech stream, why should just one—the "segmental" approach reflecting articulatory activity—have prevailed in the description of language?

Perhaps an insightful way to look at the nature and hence the origins of writing is to recognize that people write what they *hear* rather than what they *say*: alphabetic writing records successive "gestures" of the vocal tract, such as the touching of the tongue to parts of the oral cavity. The activities of the speech organs are not consciously available to a speaker, and they are equally unavailable to a listener. The only thing available to the listener is the sound itself; and as we saw in §12.1.2, the only acoustic unit of divisibility is the syllable. That's why the syllable is so important in the origins and evolution of writing.

Writing is how the writer communicates with the reader.

---

* The word for 'syllable' is *akṣara*, and the question arises whether this description might have been influenced by the writing system. The putative date, third century BCE, of the commentary means that that possibility is not entirely ruled out.

Details *(continued)*

The quotation of the Indian grammarian is from W. S. Allen, *Phonetics in Ancient India* (1953), 80.

The background of the concept of "gesture" of the vocal tract is traced by Catherine F. Browman and Louis M. Goldstein, "Towards an Articulatory Phonology" (1986), and they introduce an approach to phonological analysis based on continuous gestures rather than discrete segments. The approach does not seem to have attracted many followers, but its inversion provided the insight into the nature of writing.

Maps

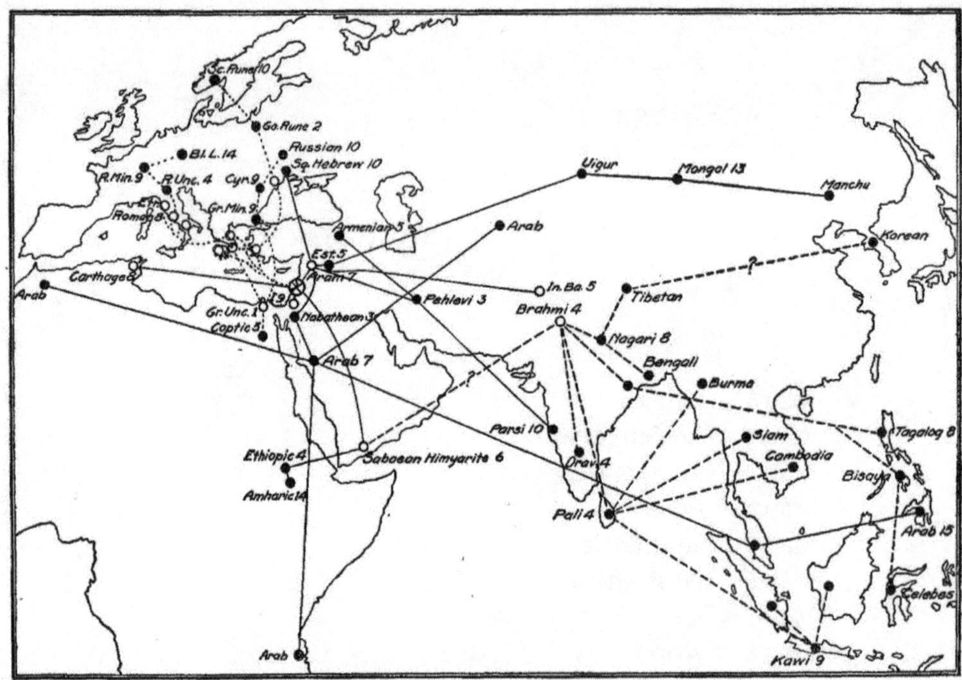

FIG. 30. The spread of alphabetic writing. Course of Occidental alphabets in dotted lines; West Asiatic, continuous lines; Indic, broken lines. The numbers stand for centuries: with hollow circles, before Christ; with solid circles, after Christ. Crossed circle, point of origin, Phœnicia, 11th century B.C. *Abbreviations:* Aram, Aramæan; Bl L, Black Letter (Gothic); Cyr, Cyrillic; Est, Estrangelo; Etr, Etruscan; Go, Gothic (Runes); Gr Min, Unc, Greek Minuscule, Uncial; In Ba, Indo-Bactrian (Kharoshthi); I, Israelite; R Min, Unc, Roman Minuscule, Uncial; Sc, Scandinavian (Rune). The flow was often back and fourth; compare the 2,000 year development from Phœnician to Ionian to Athens to Alexandria (Uncial) to Constantinople (Minuscule) to Russian; or from Phœnician northward to Aramæan, thence south to Nabathean and Arabic, east to Pehlevi and back west to Armenian.

Figure M.1. The finest script map ever created
From Alfred L. Kroeber, *Anthropology* (1923), fig. 30 facing p. 284
It served as the inspiration for the maps included here.

Kroeber's map was lightly revised, but not improved, in the second edition of 1948 (530 fig. 26). Based on the information in Isaac Taylor, *The Alphabet* (1883), it was already outdated when it was published, but no more reliable source was available even in time for the new edition.

The content of the present maps is derived from many of the sources mentioned in the text, and D. C. Sircar, "Introduction to Indian Epigraphy and Palaeography" (1970–71), with invaluable advice received from numerous individuals named in the Acknowledgments. Scripts shown are selective rather than comprehensive.

Geographic data were obtained from many specialty maps found by internet Google searches, as well as Wikipedia articles that include latitude and longitude data for cities and sites. Not to be overlooked are print atlases! Arnold J. Toynbee and Edward D. Myers, *Historical Atlas and Gazetteer* (1959); *National Geographic Atlas of the World* (2011); S. Mumford, ed., *Compact World Atlas* (2015); and Patricia S. Daniels, *Atlas of the Ancient World* (2016), have each provided a different sort of information.

I cannot praise too highly the patience and skill of the cartographer, Don Shewan, who interpreted complicated, sometimes contradictory, and often changing instructions with skill and patience to achieve extraordinary results.

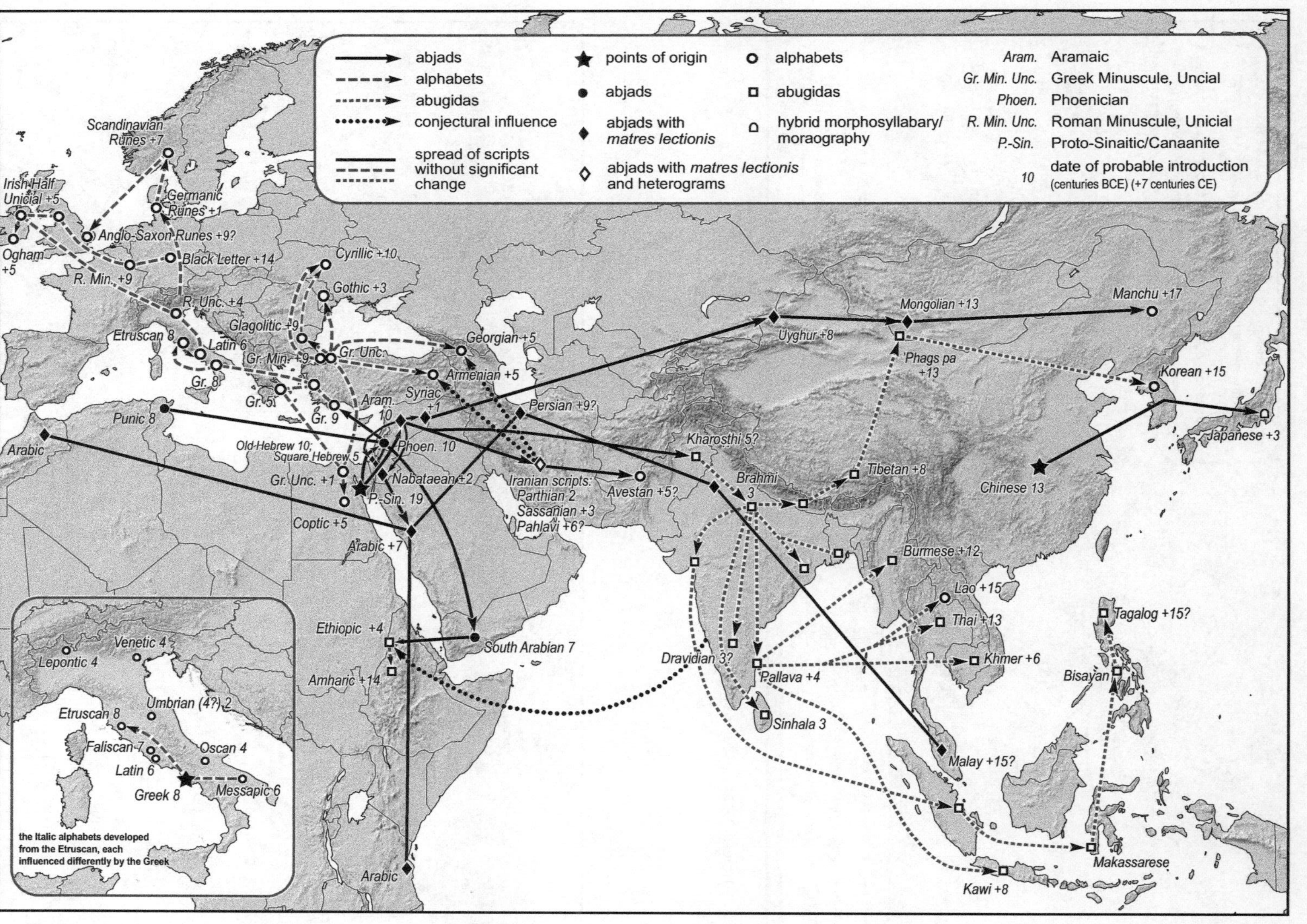

Map 1 The development of modern scripts

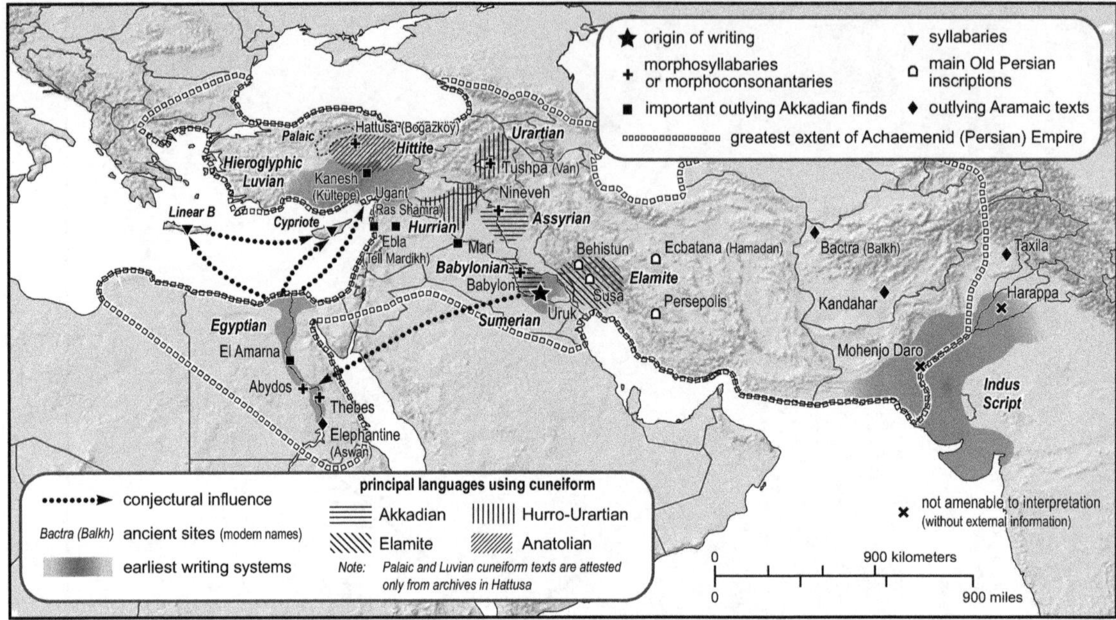

Map 2 Ancient Near Eastern syllabic scripts

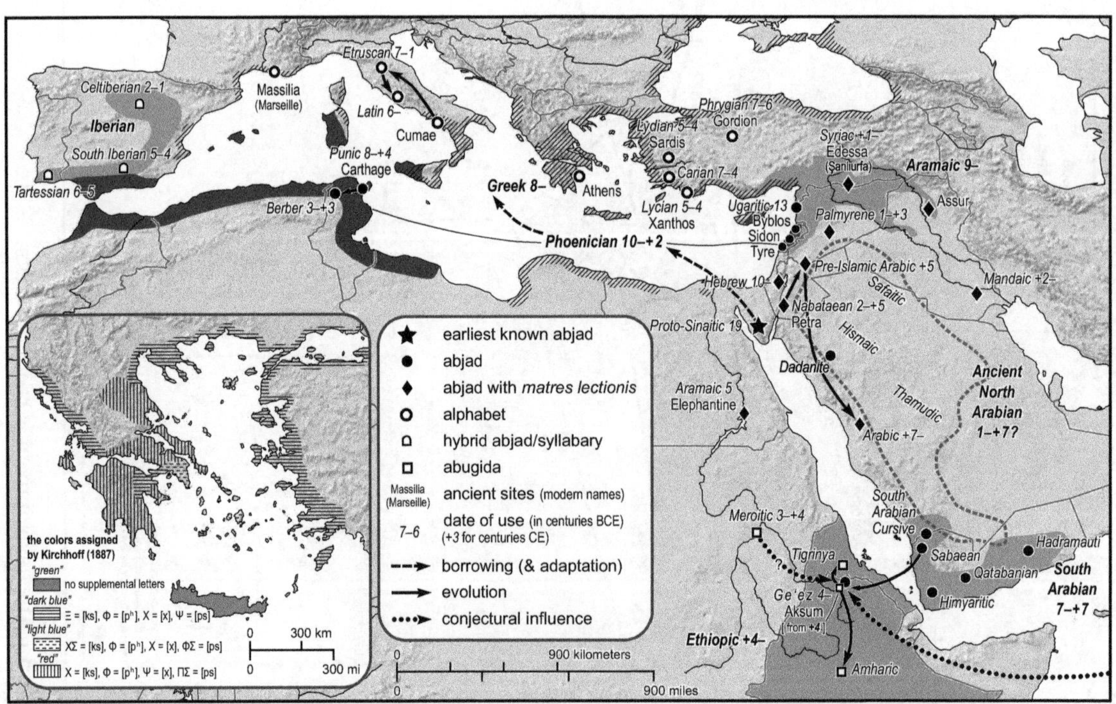

Map 3 Ancient Near Eastern segmental scripts

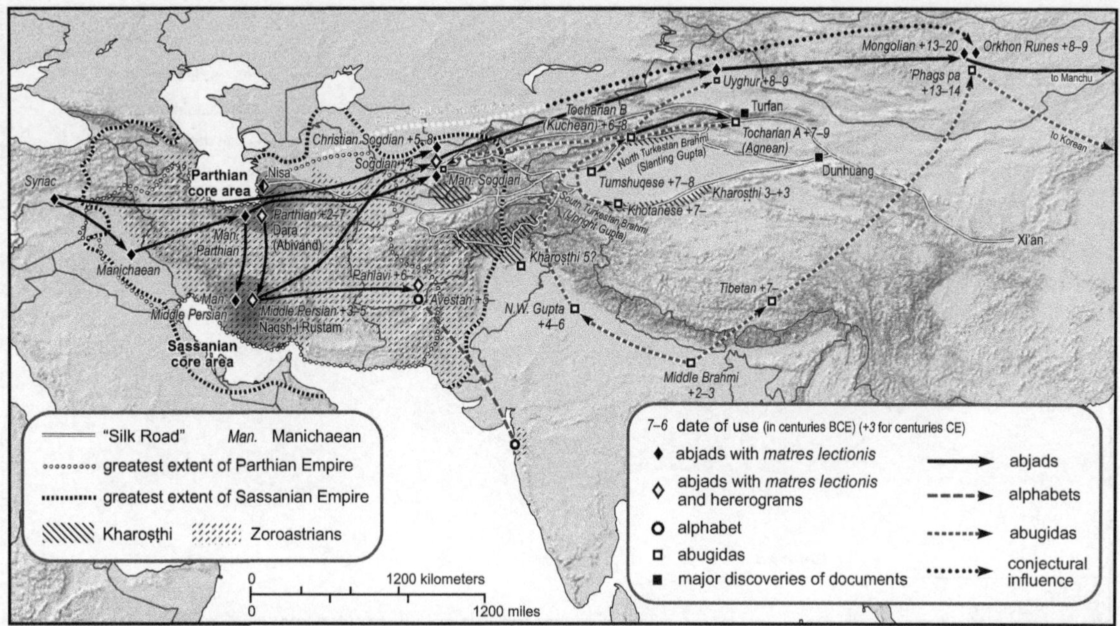

Map 4 Iranian and Indic scripts of Inner Asia

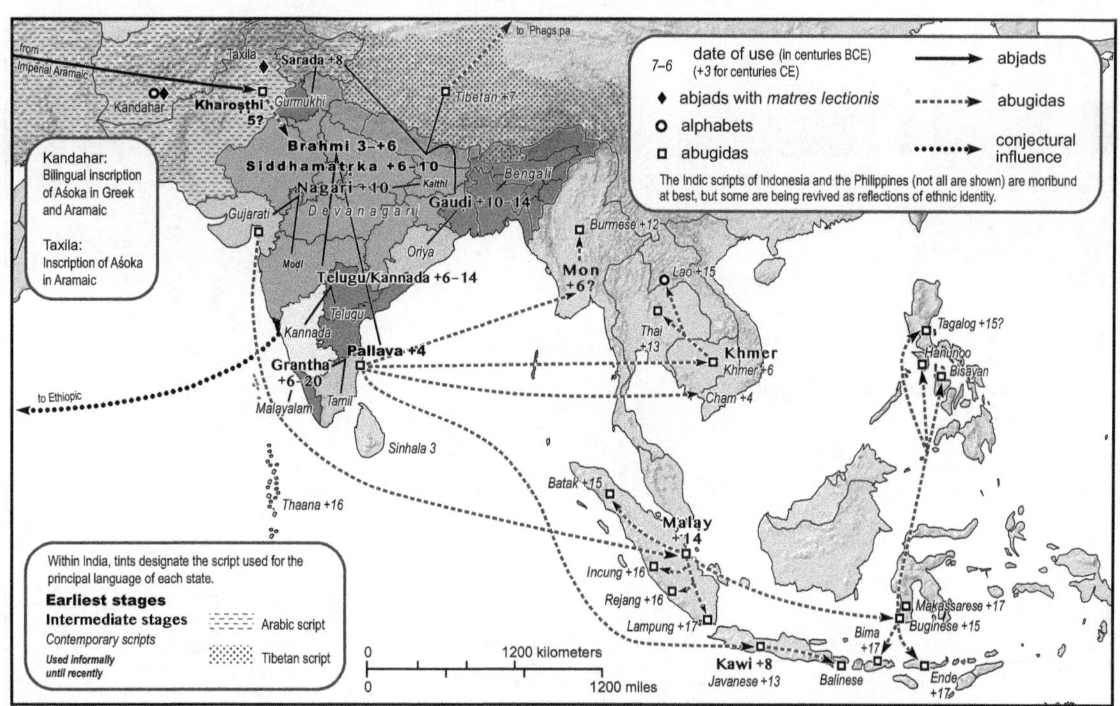

Map 5 Spread and modern-day distribution of South and Southeast Asian scripts

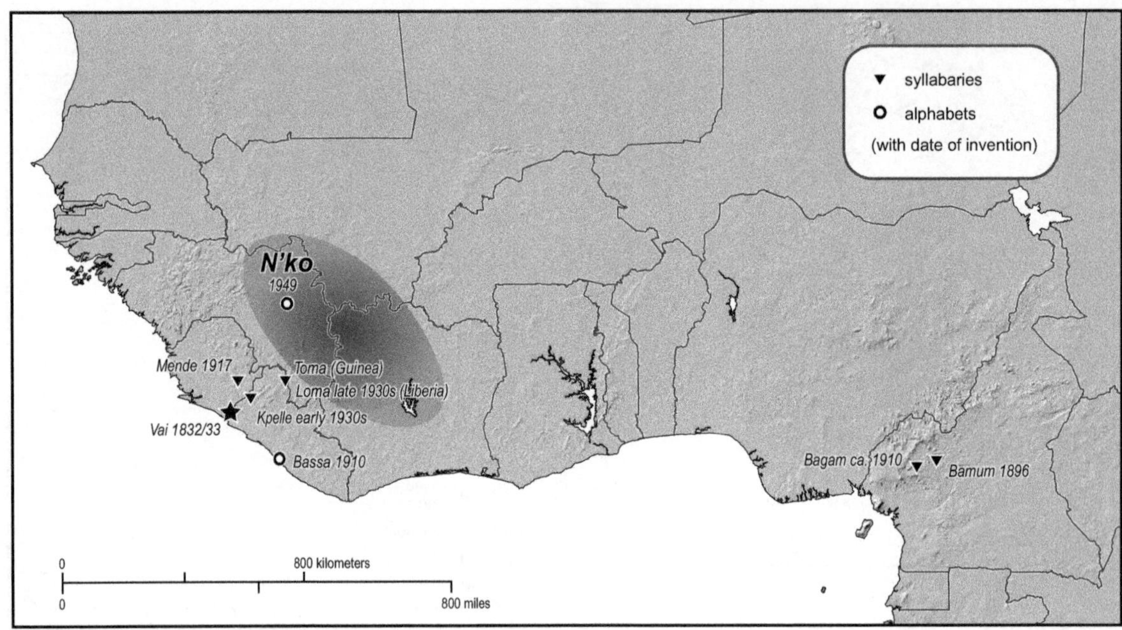

Map 6 Modern scripts of West Africa that found at least some use

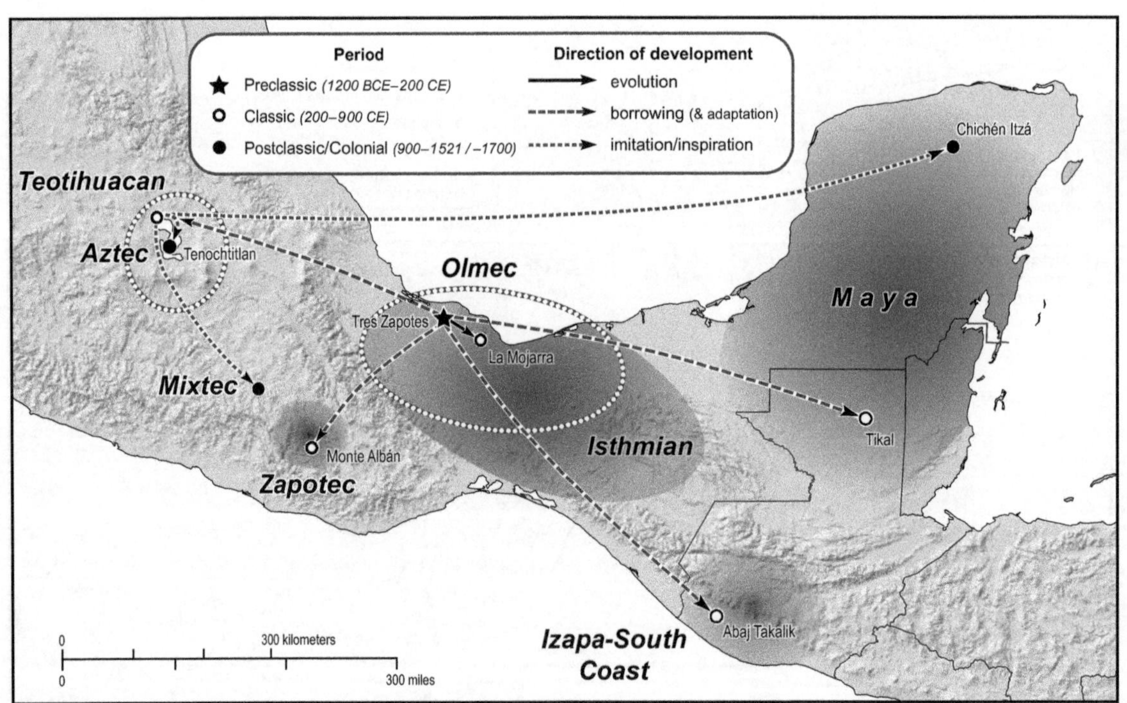

Map 7 Mesoamerican pre-writing and writing systems

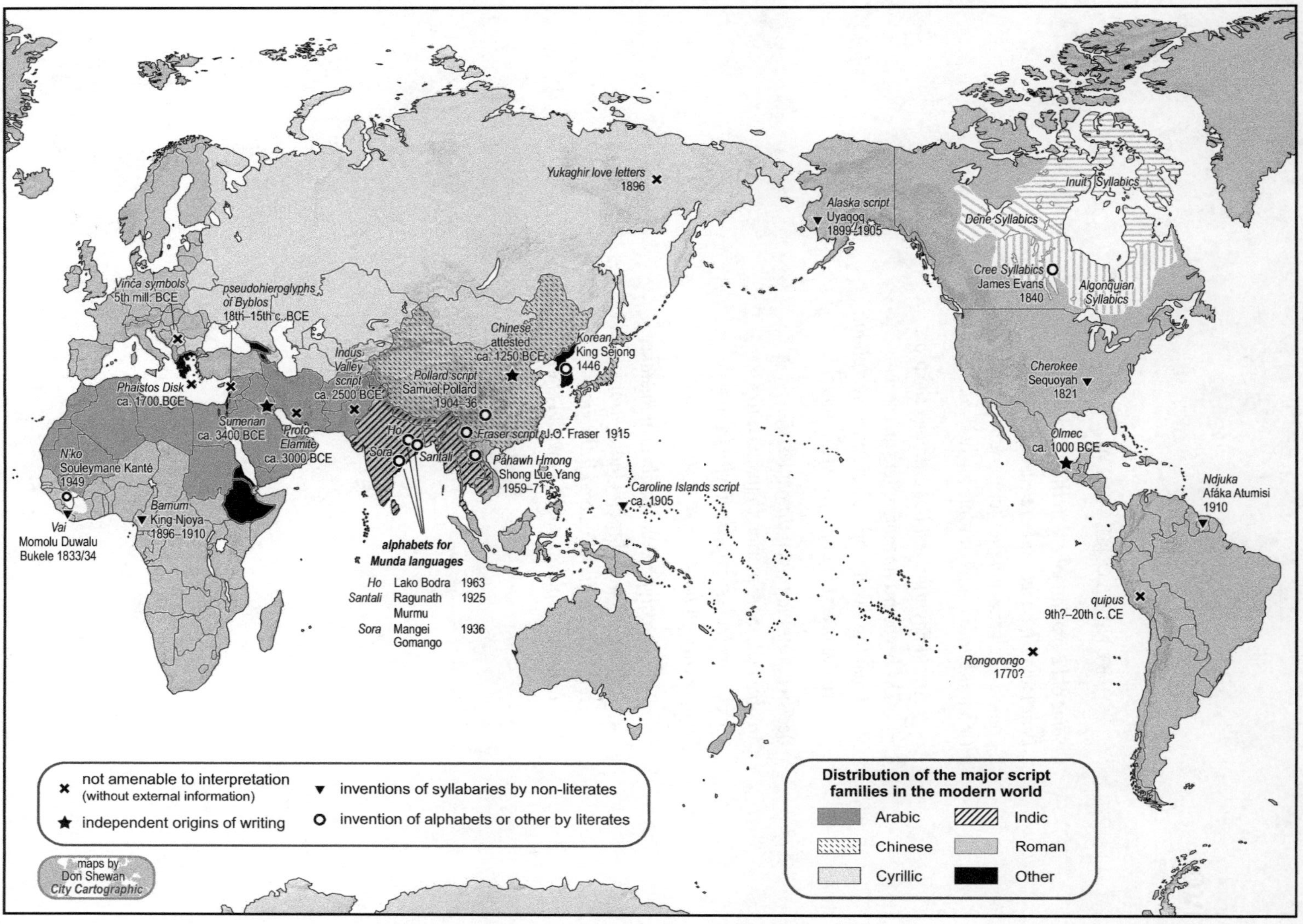

Map 8 Distribution of scripts in the modern world, and ancient and modern inventions of visual communication systems

Envoi

BY NILUS ONCE I KNEW ...

Some old Egyptian joke is in the air,
Dear lady—the poet said—release your hair;
Come, search the marshes for a friendly bed
Or let us bump heads in some lowly shed.

    An old Egyptian jest has cramped the tape.
    The keyboard no more offers an escape
    From the sweet jeopardy of Anthony's plight:
    You've overruled my typewriter tonight.

Decisive grammar given unto queens,—
An able text, more motion than machines
Have levers for,—stampede it with fresh type
From twenty alphabets—we're still unripe!

    This hieroglyph is no dumb, deaf mistake.
    It knows its way through India—tropic shake!
    It's Titicaca till we've trod it through
    And then it pleads again, "I wish I knew."

Hart Crane, 1933

References

Abercrombie, David. 1949. "What Is a 'letter'?" *Lingua* 2: 54–63. (Repr. in his *Studies in Phonetics and Linguistics*, 76–85. Language and Language Learning 10 [London: Oxford University Press, 1965].)

Abercrombie, David, and Peter T. Daniels. 2006. "Spelling Reform Proposals: English." In *Encyclopedia of Language & Linguistics Second Edition*, edited by Keith Brown, 12: 72–75. Oxford: Elsevier.

Adiego, Ignacio-Javier. 1993. "Algunas reflexiones sobre el alfabeto de Espanca y las primitivas escrituras hispanas." In *Studia paleohispanica et indogermanica J. Untermann ab amicis hispanicis oblata*, edited by I.-J. Adiego, J. Siles, and J. Velaza, 11–22. Aurea Saecula 10. Barcelona: Universitat de Barcelona.

Adiego, Ignacio-Javier. 2007. *The Carian Language*. Handbuch der Orientalistik 1.86. Leiden: Brill.

Ainsworth, W. A. 1973. "A System for Converting English Text into Speech." *IEEE Transactions on Audio and Electroacoustics* AU-21 (3): 288–90.

Albright, Eric Scott. 2001. "Design of an Electronic Method for Describing Writing Systems." M.A. thesis, Graduate Institute of Applied Linguistics, Dallas. www.tei-c.org/Activities/Workgroups/CE/Design_of_an_Electronic.pdf (accessed May 18, 2017).

Allan, Keith, ed. 2013. *The Oxford Handbook of the History of Linguistics*. Oxford: Oxford University Press.

Allen, W. S. 1953. *Phonetics in Ancient India*. London Oriental Series 1. London: Oxford University Press.

Anderson, Donald M. 1969. *The Art of Written Forms*. New York: Holt, Rinehart & Winston. (Repr. as *Calligraphy: The Art of Written Forms* [New York: Dover, 1992].)

Anderson, James M. 1988. *Ancient Languages of the Hispanic Peninsula*. Lanham, Md.: University Press of America.

[Anon.]. 1912. "Isaac Taylor (1829–1901)." In *The Dictionary of National Biography, Supplement, January 1901 – December 1911*, edited by Sidney Lee, 3: 485–86. N.p.: Smith, Elder & Co. (Repr. N.p.: Oxford University Press [3 vols. in 1]. Revised by C. E. A. Cheesman, *Oxford Dictionary of National Biography*, 2004. DOI 10.1093/ref:odnb/36433.).

Ascher, Marcia, and Robert Ascher. 1981. *Code of the Quipu: A Study of Media, Mathematics, and Culture*. Ann Arbor: University of Michigan Press.

Asfaha, Yonas Mesfun, Jeanne Kurvers, and Sjaak Kroon. 2009. "Grain Size in Script and Teaching: Literacy Acquisition in Ge'ez and Latin." *Applied Psycholinguistics* 30: 709–24.

Athenaeus. 1930. *The Deipnosophists*, vol. 4: *Books VIII–X*, translated by Charles Burton Gulick. Loeb Classical Library. London: Heinemann; Cambridge: Harvard University Press.

Baines, John. 2004. "The Earliest Egyptian Writing: Development, Context, Purpose." In *The First Writing: Script Invention as History and Process*, edited by Stephen D. Houston, 150–89. Cambridge: Cambridge University Press.

Baines, John, John Bennet, and Stephen D. Houston, eds. 2008. *The Disappearance of Writing Systems: Perspectives on Literacy and Communication*. London: Equinox.

Bar-Asher Siegal, Elitzur. 2013. *Introduction to the Grammar of Jewish Babylonian Aramaic*. Münster: Ugaritica-Verlag.

Baudouin de Courtenay, Jan. 1901. "Wskazówki dla zapisujących materiały gwarowe na obszarze językowym polskim." *Materiały i prace Komisii Językowej Akademii Umiejętności w Krakowie* 1: 115–39.

Baudouin de Courtenay, Jan. 1908. "Zur Frage über die 'Weichheit' und 'Härte' der Sprachlaute im allgemein und im slavischen Sprachgebiete insbesondere." In *Jagić-Festschrift: Zbornik u slavu Vatroslava Jagića*, 583–90. Berlin: Weidmann.

Baudouin de Courtenay, Jan. 1910 [1972]. "Phonetic Laws," translated by Edward Stankiewicz. In *A Baudouin de Courtenay Anthology: The Beginnings of Structural Linguistics*, by Jan Baudouin de Courtenay, edited by Edward Stankiewicz, 260–77. Indiana University Studies in the History and Theory of Linguistics. Bloomington: Indiana University Press. (French original: summary, pp. 57–82, of "O prawach głodowych." *Rocznik Slawistyczny* (Cracow) 3:1–57.)

Baudouin de Courtenay, Jan. 1929 [1972]. "The Influence of Language on World-View and Mood," translated by Edward Stankiewicz. In *A Baudouin de Courtenay Anthology: The Beginnings of Structural Linguistics*, by Jan Baudouin de Courtenay, edited by Edward Stankiewicz, 284–90. Indiana University Studies in the History and Theory of Linguistics. Bloomington: Indiana University Press. (Trans. not from the orig., "Einfluss der Sprache auf Weltanschauung und Stimmung," *Prace Filologiczne* 14:184–255 at 211–21, but from Избранные труды по общему языкознанию, ed. V. P. Grigor'ev & A. A. Leont'ev [Moscow, 1963], 2:331–36.)

Baxter, William H., and Laurent Sagart. 2014. *Old Chinese: A New Reconstruction*. New York: Oxford University Press.

Bazell, C. E. 1966 [1956]. "The Grapheme." In *Readings in Linguistics II*, edited by Eric P. Hamp, Fred Householder, and Robert Austerlitz, 359–61. Chicago: University of Chicago Press. (Repr. from *Litera* (Istanbul) 3 [1956]: 43–46.)

Bell, Alexander Melville. 1867. *Visible Speech*. London: Simpkin, Marshall.

Ben-Yehuda, Ehud, and David Weinstein, eds. 1961. *Ben-Yehuda's Pocket Hebrew-English English-Hebrew Dictionary*. New York: Washington Square Press.

Berg, Kristian, and Mark Aronoff. 2017. "Self-Organization in the Spelling of English Suffixes: The Emergence of Culture out of Anarchy." *Language* 93 (1): 37–64.

Bergsträßer, Gotthelf. 1995. *Introduction to the Semitic Languages: Text Specimens and Grammatical Sketches*, translated by Peter T. Daniels. Winona Lake, Ind.: Eisenbrauns. (1st ed., 1983. German original, 1928.)

Bhaskararao, Peri, ed. 2003. *International Symposium on Indic Scripts Past and Future: Working Papers*. Tokyo: Research Institute for the Languages and Cultures of Asia and Africa.

Blair, Sheila S. 1998. *Islamic Inscriptions*. Edinburgh: Edinburgh University Press.

Blair, Sheila S. 2006. *Islamic Calligraphy*. Edinburgh: Edinburgh University Press.

Bloch, Bernard, and George L. Trager. 1942. *Outline of Linguistic Analysis*. LSA Special Publications, Miscellaneous [3]. Baltimore: Linguistic Society of America.

Bloom, Jonathan M. 2001. *Paper before Print: The History and Impact of Paper in the Islamic World*. New Haven: Yale University Press.

Bloomfield, Leonard. 1926. "A Set of Postulates for the Science of Language." *Language* 2: 153–64. (Repr. in *Readings in Linguistics [I]*, edited by Martin Joos [Washington, D.C.: American Council of Learned Societies, 1957; 4th corr. ed., Chicago: University of Chicago Press, 1966], 19–25, and in *A Leonard Bloomfield Anthology*, edited by C. F. Hockett [Bloomington: Indiana University Press, 1970], 128–38.)

Bloomfield, Leonard. 1933. *Language*. New York: Holt, Rinehart and Winston.

Bolger, Donald J., Charles A. Perfetti, and Walter Schneider. 2005. "Cross-cultural Effect on the Brain Revisited: Universal Structures Plus Writing System Variation." *Human Brain Mapping*

25 (1): 92–104. DOI:10.1002/hbm.20124.

Bolinger, Dwight. 1985. *Intonation and Its Parts: Melody in Spoken English*. Stanford, Calif.: Stanford University Press.

Bolinger, Dwight. 1989. *Intonation and Its Uses: Melody in Grammar and Discourse*. Stanford, Calif.: Stanford University Press.

Boltz, William G. 1994. *The Origin and Early Development of the Chinese Writing System*. American Oriental Series 78. New Haven: American Oriental Society.

Bordreuil, Pierre, and Dennis Pardee. 2009. *A Manual of Ugaritic*. Linguistic Studies in Ancient West Semitic 3. Winona Lake, Ind.: Eisenbrauns.

Branner, David Prager, ed. 2006. *The Chinese Rime Tables: Linguistic Philosophy and Historical-Comparative Phonology*. Current Issues in Linguistic Theory 271. Amsterdam and Philadelphia: John Benjamins.

Brekle, Herbert. 1994. *Die Antiqualinie von ca. –1500 bis ca. +1500: Untersuchungen zur Morphogenese des westlichen Alphabets auf kognitivischer Basis*. Münster: Nodus.

Brengelman, F. H. 1980. "Orthoepists, Printers, and the Rationalization of English Spelling." *Journal of English and Germanic Philology* 79: 332–54.

Bright, William. 2000. "A Matter of Typology: Alphasyllabaries and Abugidas." *Studies in the Linguistic Sciences* (Urbana) 30: 63–71. (Also in *Written Language and Literacy* 2 [1999]: 45–61.)

Browman, Catherine F., and Louis M. Goldstein. 1986. "Towards an Articulatory Phonology." *Phonology Yearbook* 3: 219–52.

Brown, J. Marvin. 1985. *From Ancient Thai to Modern Dialects and Other Writings on Historical Thai Linguistics*. Bangkok: White Lotus. (Original publications, 1965–79.)

Bühler, Georg. 1898. *On the Origin of the Indian Brāhma Alphabet, together with Two Appendices on the Origin of the Kharoṣṭhī Alphabet and the Origin of the So-Called Letter-Numerals of the Brāhmī*. 2nd ed. Strassbourg: Trübner.

Bühler, Georg. 1904. *Indian Paleography*. New Delhi: Oriental Books Reprint Corp.

Burling, Robbins. 2016. *Spellbound: Untangling English Spelling*. Sheffield: Equinox.

Burnaby, Barbara, ed. 1985. *Promoting Native Writing Systems in Canada*. Ontario Institute for Studies in Education Occasional Papers 24. Toronto: OISE Press.

Cahill, Michael, and Keren Rice, eds. 2014. *Developing Orthographies for Unwritten Languages*. SIL International® Publications in Language Use and Education 6. Dallas: SIL International.

Cammarosano, Michele. 2014. "The Cuneiform Stylus." *Mesopotamia* 49: 53–90 and pl. 1.

Carney, Edward. 1994. *A Survey of English Spelling*. London: Routledge.

Caro Baroja, Julio. 1954. "Historia del desciframiento de las escrituras hispánicas prerromanas." In *Historia de España*, pt. 1: *España prerromana*, vol. 3: *Etnología de los pueblos de Hispania*, edited by Ramón Menéndez Pidal, 681–702. Madrid: Espasa-Calpe.

Carroll, Lewis. 2013. *Alice's Adventures in Wonderland: An Edition Printed in the Shaw Alphabet*. Westport, Ireland: Evertype.

Catach, Nina. 1979. "Le graphème." *Pratiques* 25: 21–32.

Catach, Nina. 1986. "The Grapheme: Its Position and Its Degree of Autonomy with Respect to the System of the Language." In *New Trends in Graphemics and Orthography*, edited by Gerhard Augst, 1–10. Berlin: de Gruyter.

Chadwick, John. 1987. *Linear B and Related Scripts*. Reading the Past. London: British Museum.

Chall, Jeanne S. 1967. *Learning to Read: The Great Debate (An Inquiry into the Science, Art, and Ideology of Old and New Methods of Teaching 1910–1965)*. Carnegie Series in American Education. New York: McGraw-Hill.

Changizi, Mark A., and Shinsuke Shimojo. 2005. "Character Complexity and Redundancy in Writing Systems over Human History." *Proceedings of the Royal Society B Biological Sciences*

272: 267–75.

Changizi, Mark A., Qiong Zhang, Hao Ye, and Shinsuke Shimojo. 2006. "The Structures of Letters and Symbols throughout Human History Are Selected to Match Those Found in Objects in Natural Scenes." *American Naturalist* 167 (5): E117–39.

Chao, Yuen Ren. 1940. "A Note on an Early Logographic Theory of Chinese Writing." *Harvard Journal of Asiatic Studies* 5 (2): 189–91.

Chao, Yuen Ren. 1963. "Graphic and Phonetic Aspects of Linguistic and Mathematical Symbols." In *Structure of Language and Its Mathematical Aspects*, edited by Roman Jakobson, 69–82. Proceedings of Symposia in Applied Mathematics 12. Providence, R.I.: American Mathematical Society.

Chao, Yuen Ren. 1968. *Language and Symbolic Systems*. Cambridge: Cambridge University Press.

Chomsky, Noam. 1959. Review of *Verbal Behavior*, by B. F. Skinner. *Language* 35: 26–58.

Chomsky, Noam, and Morris Halle. 1968. *The Sound Pattern of English*. New York: Harper & Row.

Chomsky, William. 1952. *David Kimhi's Hebrew Grammar (Mikhlol) Systematically Presented and Critically Annotated*. Philadelphia: Bloch.

Choy, Rita Mei-Wah. 1990. *Read and Write Chinese: A Simplified Guide to the Chinese Characters*. San Francisco: China West Books.

Civil, Miguel. 2013. "Remarks on AD-GI₄ (a.k.a. 'Archaic Word List C' or 'Tribute')." *Journal of Cuneiform Studies* 65: 13–67.

Coblin, W. South. 2007. *A Handbook of 'Phags-pa Chinese*. Honolulu: University of Hawai'i Press.

Coe, Michael D. 1973. *The Maya Scribe and His World*. New York: Grolier Club.

Coe, Michael D. 2012. *Breaking the Maya Code*. 3rd ed. New York: Thames & Hudson. (1st ed., 1992.)

Cohen, Marcel. 1958. *La grande invention de l'écriture et son évolution*. Paris: Imprimerie Nationale.

Coulmas, Florian. 1989. *The Writing Systems of the World*. The Language Library. Oxford: Blackwell.

Coulmas, Florian. 1996. *The Blackwell Encyclopedia of Writing Systems*. Oxford: Blackwell.

Coulmas, Florian. 2003. *Writing Systems*. Cambridge Textbooks in Linguistics. Cambridge: Cambridge University Press.

Court, Christopher. 1996. "The Spread of Brahmi Script into Southeast Asia." In *The World's Writing Systems*, edited by Peter T. Daniels and William Bright, 445–49. New York: Oxford University Press.

Cross, Frank Moore, and David Noel Freedman. 1952. *Early Hebrew Orthography: A Study of the Epigraphic Evidence*. American Oriental Series 36. New Haven: American Oriental Society.

Cruttenden, Alan. 1997. *Intonation*. 2nd ed. Cambridge Textbooks in Linguistics. Cambridge: Cambridge University Press. (1st ed., 1986.)

Crystal, David. 2008. *Txtng: The Gr8 Db8*. Oxford: Oxford University Press.

Crystal, David. 2012. *Spell It Out: The Curious, Enthralling, and Extraordinary Story of English Spelling*. New York: St. Martin's.

Crystal, David. 2016. *The Oxford Dictionary of Original Shakespearean Pronunciation*. Oxford: Oxford University Press.

Crystal, David, and Ben Crystal, interviewed by Kurt Andersen. 2016. "All Shakespeare All the Time," episode of *Studio 360*. New York: Public Radio International. Broadcast November 24, 2016, WNYC-FM. www.wnyc.org/shows/studio (accessed May 19, 2017).

Cummings, D. W. 1988. *American English Spelling: An Informal Description*. Baltimore: The Johns Hopkins University Press.

Cushman, Ellen. 2011. *The Cherokee Syllabary: Writing the People's Perseverance*. American Indian Literature and Critical Studies series 56. Norman: University of Oklahoma Press.

Dalby, David. 1967. "A Survey of the Indigenous Scripts of Liberia and Sierra Leone: Vai, Mende, Loma, Kpelle and Bassa." *African Language Studies* 8: 1–51.

Dalby, David. 1968. "The Indigenous Scripts of West Africa and Surinam: Their Inspiration and Design." *African Language Studies* 9: 156–97.

Dalby, David. 1969. "Further Indigenous Scripts of West Africa: Manding, Wolof and Fula Alphabets and Yoruba 'Holy Writing'." *African Language Studies* 10: 161–81.

Dani, Ahmad Hasan. 1986. *Indian Palaeography*. 2nd ed. New Delhi: Munshiram Manoharlal. (1st ed., Oxford: Clarendon, 1963.)

Daniels, Patricia S. 2016. *Atlas of the Ancient World: Exploring Great Civilizations*. National Geographic Special Publication. Washington, D.C.: National Geographic.

Daniels, Peter T. 1984. "A Calligraphic Approach to Aramaic Paleography." *Journal of Near Eastern Studies* 43: 55–68.

Daniels, Peter T. 1985. "Toward a Sociolinguistic Prehistory of Aramaic." Paper presented at annual meeting, North American Conference on Afroasiatic Linguistics, Ann Arbor, April 18.

Daniels, Peter T. 1986. "Toward the Linguistic Study of Writing Systems: Aramaic Orthographies." Paper presented at annual meeting, Linguistic Society of America, New York, December 29.

Daniels, Peter T. 1988. "'Shewing of Hard Sentences and Dissolving of Doubts': The First Decipherment." *Journal of the American Oriental Society* 108: 419–36.

Daniels, Peter T. 1989. "'Proto-Euphratic' and the Syllabic Origin of Writing." *Proceedings Eastern Great Lakes and Midwest Biblical Societies* 9: 23–33.

Daniels, Peter T. 1990. "Fundamentals of Grammatology." *Journal of the American Oriental Society* 110: 727–31.

Daniels, Peter T. 1991a. "Ha, La, Ḥa or Hōi, Lawe, Ḥaut? The Ethiopic Letter Names." In *Semitic Studies in Honor of Wolf Leslau on the Occasion of His Eighty-fifth Birthday*, edited by Alan S. Kaye, 1: 275–88. Wiesbaden: Harrassowitz.

Daniels, Peter T. 1991b. "Is a Structural Graphemics Possible?" *18th LACUS Forum* (Ann Arbor) 528–37.

Daniels, Peter T. 1991c. Review of *The Origins of Writing*, by Wayne M. Senner. *Language* 67 (4): 835–42.

Daniels, Peter T. 1992a. "Contacts between Semitic and Indic Scripts." In *Contacts between Cultures: Selected Papers from the 33rd International Congress of Asian and North African Studies, Toronto, August 15–25, 1990*, vol. 1: *West Asia and North Africa*, edited by Amir Harrak, 146–52. Lewiston, N.Y.: Edwin Mellen.

Daniels, Peter T. 1992b. "The Syllabic Origin of Writing and the Segmental Origin of the Alphabet." In *The Linguistics of Literacy*, edited by Pamela Downing, Susan D. Lima, and Michael Noonan, 83–110. Typological Studies in Language 21. Amsterdam and Philadelphia: John Benjamins.

Daniels, Peter T. 1992c. "What Do the 'Paleographic' Tablets Tell Us of Mesopotamian Scribes' Knowledge of the History of Their Script?" *Mār Šipri: Newsletter of the Committee on Mesopotamian Civilization, American Schools of Oriental Research* 5 (1): 1–4. www.academia. edu/10150540/Mar_Shipri_Newsletter_of_the_Committee_on_Mesopotamian_ Civilization_5_1 (accessed May 19, 2017).

Daniels, Peter T. 1994. "Edward Hincks's Decipherment of Mesopotamian Cuneiform." In *The Edward Hincks Bicentenary Lectures*, edited by Kevin J. Cathcart, 30–57. Dublin: University College Dublin, Department of Near Eastern Studies.

Daniels, Peter T. 1995. "The Decipherment of Ancient Near Eastern Scripts." In *Civilizations of the Ancient Near East*, edited by Jack M. Sasson, 1:81–93. New York: Scribner's.

Daniels, Peter T. 1996a. "Methods of Decipherment." In *The World's Writing Systems*, edited by Peter T. Daniels and William Bright, 141–59. New York: Oxford University Press.

Daniels, Peter T. 1996b. "The Study of Writing Systems." In *The World's Writing Systems*, edited by Peter T. Daniels and William Bright, 3–17. New York: Oxford University Press.

Daniels, Peter T. 1997. "The Protean Arabic Abjad." In *Humanism, Culture, and Language in the Near East: Studies in Honor of Georg Krotkoff*, edited by Asma Afsaruddin and A. H. Mathias Zahniser, 83–110. Winona Lake, Ind.: Eisenbrauns.

Daniels, Peter T. 1998. Review of *Ancient Scripts and Phonological Knowledge*, by D. Gary Miller. *Written Language and Literacy* 1 (1): 141–47.

Daniels, Peter T. 1999. "Some Semitic Phonological Considerations on the Sibilants of the Greek Alphabet." *Written Language and Literacy* 2 (1): 57–61.

Daniels, Peter T. 2000a. Review of popular books on writing, by Johanna Drucker, Georges Jean, Marc-Alain Ouaknin, Andrew Robinson, and Leonard Shlain. *Sino-Platonic Papers* 98: 47–57. http://sino-platonic.org/complete/spp098_book_reviews.pdf (accessed May 19, 2017).

Daniels, Peter T. 2000b. "Syllables, Consonants, and Vowels in West Semitic Writing." *Lingua Posnaniensis* 42: 43–55.

Daniels, Peter T. 2001. "Writing Systems." In *The Handbook of Linguistics*, edited by Mark Aronoff and Janie Rees-Miller, 43–80. Oxford: Blackwell.

Daniels, Peter T. 2002. "The Study of Writing in the Twentieth Century: Semitic Studies Interacting with Non-Semitic." *Israel Oriental Studies* 20: 85–117.

Daniels, Peter T. 2006a. "On Beyond Alphabets." *Written Language and Literacy* 9: 7–24.

Daniels, Peter T. 2006b. Review of *Writing Systems*, by Florian Coulmas. *Linguist List* 17: 2534. www.linguistlist.org/issues/17/17-2534.html (accessed May 19, 2017).

Daniels, Peter T. 2006c. "Three Models of Script Transfer." *Word* 57 (pub. 2014): 371–78. (Paper presented at the Annual Meeting of the International Linguistic Association, New York, 2004.)

Daniels, Peter T. 2007. "*Littera ex occidente*: Toward a Functional History of Writing." In *Studies in Semitic and Afroasiatic Linguistics Presented to Gene B. Gragg*, edited by Cynthia L. Miller, 53–68. Studies in Ancient and Oriental Civilization 60. Chicago: Oriental Institute of the University of Chicago. http://oi.uchicago.edu/pdf/saoc60.pdf (accessed May 19, 2017).

Daniels, Peter T. 2008. "Rawlinson, Henry. ii. His Contributions to Assyriology and Iranian Studies." *Encyclopedia Iranica* http://www.iranicaonline.org/articles/rawlinson-ii (accessed May 19, 2017).

Daniels, Peter T. 2009a. "Grammatology." In *The Cambridge Handbook of Literacy*, edited by David R. Olson and Nancy Torrance, 25–45. Cambridge: Cambridge University Press.

Daniels, Peter T. 2009b. "Peter Stephen Du Ponceau and the Typology of Writing Systems: His *Dissertation on the Nature and Character of the Chinese System of Writing*." Paper presented at annual meeting, American Oriental Society, Albuquerque, March.

Daniels, Peter T. 2009c. "Two Notes on Terminology." *Written Language and Literacy* 12 (2): 277–81. DOI:10.1075/wll.12.2.09dan.

Daniels, Peter T. 2010. "Chomsky 1951a and Chomsky 1951b." In *Chomskyan (R)evolutions*, edited by Douglas Kibbee, 169–214. Amsterdam and Philadelphia: John Benjamins.

Daniels, Peter T. 2012. "Introduction to Graphonomy." Paper presented, Workshop on Writing Systems, Haifa University, April.

Daniels, Peter T. 2013a. "Arabic Letters Do Not Have Final Forms." Paper presented at annual meeting, North American Conference on Afroasiatic Linguistics, New Haven, February.

Daniels, Peter T. 2013b. "The Arabic Writing System." In *Oxford Handbook of Arabic Linguistics*, edited by Jonathan Owens, 412–32. Oxford: Oxford University Press.

Daniels, Peter T. 2013c. "The History of Writing as a History of Linguistics." In *Oxford Handbook of the History of Linguistics*, edited by Keith Allan, 53–69. Oxford: Oxford University Press.

Daniels, Peter T. 2014a. "Aramaic Documents from Achaemenid Bactria: Connections to the West—and the East—and the Future." Paper presented, International Society for Arabic Papyrology, Munich, October 7.

Daniels, Peter T. 2014b. "The Type and Spread of Arabic Script." In *The Arabic Script in Africa*, edited by Meikal Mumin and Kees Versteegh, 17–31. Leiden: Brill.

Daniels, Peter T. 2017a. "The Further Quest for Ugaritic." In *"Like ʾIlu Are You Wise": Studies in Northwest Semitic Languages and Literature in Honor of Dennis G. Pardee*, edited by H. H. Hardy II, Joseph Lam, and Eric D. Reymond. Chicago: Oriental Institute Press.

Daniels, Peter T. 2017b. "Writing Systems." In *The Handbook of Linguistics Second Edition*, edited by Mark Aronoff and Janie Rees-Miller, 75–94. Malden, Mass.: Wiley-Blackwell.

Daniels, Peter T. 2017c. "The Writing Systems of Indo-European." In *Handbook of Comparative and Historical Indo-European Linguistics*, edited by Jared Klein, Brian Joseph, and Matthias Fritz, 26–61. Handbücher zur Sprach- und Kommunikationswissenschaft 41.1. Berlin: de Gruyter Mouton.

Daniels, Peter T. in press a. "The Decipherment of Ancient Near Eastern Languages." In *Blackwell Companion to Ancient Near Eastern Languages*, edited by Rebecca Hasselbach. Malden, Mass.: Wiley-Blackwell.

Daniels, Peter T. in press b. "'Look with thine ears': Why Writing Is Syllable-based." In *Signs of Writing*, edited by Christopher Woods and Edward Shaughnessy. Chicago: Oriental Institute.

Daniels, Peter T. in press c. "Moraic Writing Systems versus Syllabic Writing Systems." In *"May You Favor the Work of His Hands": Essays in Memory of M. O'Connor*, edited by Peter T. Daniels, Edward L. Greenstein, John Huehnergard, Mark S. Leson, and Philip C. Schmitz. Winona Lake, Ind.: Eisenbrauns.

Daniels, Peter T. in press d. "Uses of Hebrew Script in Jewish Languages." In *Jewish Languages, Past and Present*, edited by Benjamin Hary and Sarah Benor. Berlin: de Gruyter.

Daniels, Peter T. submitted. "Indic Writing: History Typology Study." In *Handbook of Literacy in Akshara Orthographies*, edited by Catherine McBride and R. Malatesta Joshi. Dordrecht: Springer.

Daniels, Peter T., and William Bright, eds. 1996. *The World's Writing Systems*. New York: Oxford University Press.

Daniels, Peter T., and David L. Share. 2017. "Writing System Variation and Its Consequences for Reading and Dyslexia." *Scientific Studies of Reading* 22 (2018): 101–16. DOI: 10.1080/10888438.2017.1379082.

Darnell, John C., F. W. Dobbs-Allsopp, Marilyn J. Lundberg, P. Kyle McCarter, and Bruce Zuckerman. 2005. "Two Early Alphabetic Inscriptions from the Wadi el-Ḥôl: New Evidence for the Origin of the Alphabet from the Western Desert of Egypt." *Annual of the American Schools of Oriental Research* 59: 63–124.

Davies, Mark, and Dee Gardner. 2010. *A Frequency Dictionary of Contemporary American English: Word Sketches, Collocates, and Thematic Lists*. London: Routledge.

DeFrancis, John. 1984. *The Chinese Language: Fact and Fantasy*. Honolulu: University of Hawaiʻi Press.

DeFrancis, John. 1989. *Visible Speech: The Diverse Oneness of Writing Systems*. Honolulu: University of Hawaii Press.

Dehaene, Stanislas. 2009. *Reading in the Brain: The Science and Evolution of a Human Invention*. New York: Viking.

Dehaene, Stanislas, Laurent Cohen, José Morais, and Régine Kolinsky. 2015. "Illiterate to Literate: Behavioural and Cerebral Changes Induced by Reading Acquisition." *Nature Reviews: Neuroscience* 16 (4): 234–44. DOI:10.1038/nrn3924.

Dennett, Daniel C. 2017. *From Bacteria to Bach and Back: The Evolution of Minds*. New York: W. W. Norton.

Dewey, Godfrey. 1923. *Relativ Frequency of English Speech Sounds*. Harvard Studies in Education 4. Cambridge: Harvard University Press. (Slightly augmented 2nd ed., 1950.)

Dewey, Godfrey. 1970. *Relative Frequency of English Spellings*. New York: Teachers College Press.

Dickerson, Wayne B. 1975. "Decomposition of Orthographic Word Classes." *Linguistics* 163: 19–34.

Dickerson, Wayne B. 1978. "English Orthography: A Guide to Word Stress and Vowel Quality." *International Review of Applied Linguistics in Language Teaching* 16: 127–47.

Dickerson, Wayne B. 1989. *Stress in the Speech Stream: The Rhythm of Spoken English. Student text* (3 vols.); *Teacher's manual* (3 vols.). Urbana: University of Illinois Press. (CD-ROM ed., Savoy, Ill.: Author, 2004.)

Diringer, David. 1968. *The Alphabet: A Key to the History of Mankind*, 3rd ed., edited by Reinhold Regensburger. New York: Funk & Wagnall's. (1st ed., 1948.)

Dobson, E. J. 1957. *English Pronunciation 1500–1700*. 2 vols. Oxford: Oxford University Press. (2nd ed., 1968.)

Dotan, Aron. 2007. "Masorah." In *Encyclopedia Judaica*, edited by Michael Berenbaum and Fred Skolnik, 603–56. 2nd ed. Detroit: Macmillan Reference. (1st ed., 1971–72.)

Downing, John. 1965. *The Initial Teaching Alphabet Explained and Illustrated*. 5th ed. rev. London: Cassell.

Downing, Pamela, Susan D. Lima, and Michael Noonan, eds. 1992. *The Linguistics of Literacy*. Typological Studies in Language 21. Amsterdam and Philadelphia: John Benjamins.

Dreyer, Günter, Ulrich Hartung, and Frauke Pumpenmeier. 1998. *Umm el-Qaab I: das prädynastische Königsgrab U-j und seine frühen Schriftzeugnisse*. Archäologische Veröffentlichungen 86. Mainz: Zabern.

Driver, G. R. 1957. *Aramaic Documents of the Fifth Century B.C.* Abridged and revised edition. Corrected 2nd impression, 1965. Oxford: Clarendon. ("With help from a typescript by E. Mittwoch, H. J. Polotsky, W. B. Henning, F. Rosenthal"; 1st ed., 1954.)

Driver, G. R. 1976. *Semitic Writing*, 3rd ed., edited by S. A. Hopkins. Schweich Lectures, 1944. London: Oxford University Press for the British Academy. (1st ed., 1948.)

Du Ponceau, Peter S. 1838. *A Dissertation on the Nature and Character of the Chinese System of Writing in a letter to John Vaughan, esq.* Transactions of the Historical and Literary Committee of the American Philosophical Society 2. Philadelphia: M'Carty and Davis.

Duanmu, San. 2009. *Syllable Structure: The Limits of Variation*. Oxford: Oxford University Press.

Durkin-Meistererernst, Desmond. 2000. "Erfand Mani die manichäischen Schrift?" In *Studia Manichaica: IV. Internationaler Kongreß zum Manichäismus, Berlin, 14.-18. Juli 1997*, edited by Ronald E. Emmerick, Werner Sundermann, and Peter Zieme, 161–78. Berlin: Akademie Verlag.

Eden, Murray. 1963. "On the Formalization of Handwriting." In *Structure of Language and Its Mathematical Aspects*, edited by Roman Jakobson, 83–88. Proceedings of Symposia in Applied Mathematics 12. Providence: American Mathematical Society.

Eimas, Peter D. 1975. "Speech Perception in Early Infancy." In *Infant Perception: From Sensation to Cognition*, vol. 1: *Perception of Space, Speech, and Sound*, edited by Leslie B. Cohen and Philip Salapatek, 193–213. New York: Academic Press.

Eisenstein, Elizabeth L. 1979. *The Printing Press as Agent of Change: Communications and Cultural Transformations in Early Modern Europe*. 2 vols. Cambridge: Cambridge University Press.

Emerson, Ralph H. 1997. "English Spelling and Its Relation to Sound." *American Speech* 72: 260–88.

Farmer, Steve, Richard Sproat, and Michael Witzel. 2004. "The Collapse of the Indus-Script Thesis: The Myth of a Literate Harappan Civilization." *Electronic Journal of Vedic Studies* www.ejvs.laurasianacademy.com/ejvs1102/ejvs1102article.pdf (accessed May 19, 2017).

Feldman, Laurie B., and Michael T. Turvey. 1983. "Word Recognition in Serbo-Croatian Is Phonologically Analytic." *Journal of Experimental Psychology: Human Perception and Performance* 9 (2): 288–98.

Ferguson, Charles. 1959. "Diglossia." *Word* 15: 325–40.

Février, James-Germain. 1959. *Histoire de l'écriture.* 2nd ed. Paris: Payot. (1st ed., 1948.)

Filliozat, Jean. 1953. "Paléographie." In *L'Inde classique: Manuel des études indiennes,* by Louis Renou and Jean Filliozat, 665–712. Paris: Imprimerie Nationale.

Fimi, Dimitra, and Andrew W. Higgins. 2016. "Coda: The Reception and Legacy of Tolkien's Invented Languages." In *A Secret Vice: Tolkien on Invented Languages,* by J. R. R. Tolkien, edited by Dimitra Fimi and Andrew W. Higgins, 118–33. London: HarperCollins.

Finkel, Irving. 1998. "A Babylonian ABC." *British Museum Magazine* 31 (Summer): 20–22.

Finkel, Irving. 2014. *The Ark before Noah: Decoding the Story of the Flood.* London: Hodder & Stoughton.

Finkel, Irving, and Jonathan Taylor. 2015. *Cuneiform.* Ancient Scripts. London: The British Museum Press.

Firth, J. R. 1953. "Foreword." In *Introduction to the Devanagari Script,* by H. M. Lambert, v–vi. London: Oxford University Press.

Foreman, Grant. 1938. *Sequoyah.* Norman: University of Oklahoma Press.

Frellesvig, Bjarke. 2010. *A History of the Japanese Language.* Cambridge: Cambridge University Press.

Friedrich, Johannes. 1966. *Geschichte der Schrift.* Wiesbaden: Harrassowitz.

Frost, Ram. 2005. "Orthographic Systems and Skilled Word Recognition Processes in Reading." In *The Science of Reading: A Handbook,* edited by Margaret J. Snowling and Charles Hulme, 272–95. Blackwell Handbooks of Developmental Psychology. Oxford: Blackwell.

Frye, Richard N. 2005. "The Sassanians." In *The Cambridge Ancient History,* 2nd ed., vol. 12: *The Crisis of Empire, A.D. 193-337,* edited by Alan K. Bowman, Peter Garnsey, and Averil Cameron, 461–80. Cambridge: Cambridge University Press.

Gamkrelidze, Thomas V. 1994. *Alphabetic Writing and the Old Georgian Script: A Typology and Provenience of Alphabetic Writing Systems.* Delmar, N.Y.: Caravan Books. (Georgian original with Russian summary, which is what is translated here, 1989.)

Gardiner, Alan H. 1957. *Egyptian Grammar.* 3rd ed. Oxford: Griffith Institute.

Gaur, Albertine. 2000. *Literacy and the Politics of Writing.* Portland, Ore.: Intellect Books.

Gelb, I. J. 1931, 1935, 1942. *Hittite Hieroglyphs I-III.* Studies in Ancient Oriental Civilization 2, 14, 21. Chicago: University of Chicago Press.

Gelb, I. J. 1952. *A Study of Writing: The Foundations of Grammatology.* Chicago: University of Chicago Press. (2nd ed., 1963.)

Gelb, I. J. 1969. *Sequential Reconstruction of Proto-Akkadian.* Assyriological Studies 18. Chicago: University of Chicago Press.

Gelb, I. J. 1977. "Thoughts about Ibla: A Preliminary Evaluation, March 1977." *Syro-Mesopotamian Studies* 1 (1): 3–30.

Gelb, I. J., Piotr Steinkeller, and Robert M. Whiting, Jr. 1989–91. *Earliest Land Tenure Systems in the Near East: Ancient Kudurrus.* 2 vols. Oriental Institute Publications 104. Chicago: Oriental Institute.

Geller, M. J. 1997. "The Last Wedge." *Zeitschrift für Assyriologie* 87: 43–95.

Geller, M. J. 1997–2000. "The Aramaic Incantation in Cuneiform Script (AO 6489 = TCL 6,58)." *Jaarbericht "Ex Oriente Lux"* 35–36: 127–46.

Gershevitch, Ilya. 1979. "The Alloglottography of Old Persian." *Transactions of the Philological Society* 77: 114–90.

Gibson, Eleanor J., and Harry Levin, eds. 1963. *A Basic Research Program on Reading.* Cooperative Research Project 639. Ithaca, N.Y.: Cornell University, Department of Psychology, and U.S. Office of Education.

Gimbutas, Marija. 1991. *The Civilization of the Goddess: The World of Old Europe.* San Francisco: HarperCollins.

Gippert, Jost, Wolfgang Schulze, Zaza Aleksidzé, and Jean-Pierre Mahé. 2009–10. *The Caucasian Albanian Palimpsests of Mount Sinai*, vols. 1–2. Monumenta palaeographica Medii Aevi, series Ibero-Caucasica 2. Turnhout: Brepols. (Vol. 3 publishes an additional Armenian undertext on other folios of the Georgian text.)

Glinert, Lewis. 2017. *The Story of Hebrew.* Princeton, N.J.: Princeton University Press.

Gnanadesikan, Amalia E. 2009. *The Writing Revolution: Cuneiform to the Internet.* Malden, Mass.: Wiley-Blackwell.

Gnanadesikan, Amalia E. 2012. "Maldivian Thaana, Japanese Kana, and the Representation of Moras in Writing." *Writing Systems Research* 4 (1): 91–102. DOI: 10.1080/17586801.2012.693459.

Go Ping-gam. 1995. *What Character Is That? An Easy-Access Dictionary of 5,000 Chinese Characters.* San Francisco: Simplex Publications.

Gordon, Arthur E. 1973. *The Letter Names of the Latin Alphabet.* University of California Publications, Classical Studies 9. Berkeley and Los Angeles: University of California Press.

Grimes, Joseph E., Augustus B. Marwieh, and Amy Bauernschmidt. 1960. "Several Kru Orthographies." *The Bible Translator* 11 (3): 111–15. (Repr. in *Orthography Studies*, edited by W. A. Smalley [London: United Bible Societies, 1963]: 114–19.)

Haas, William, ed. 1969. *Alphabets for English.* Mont Follick Series 1. Manchester: Manchester University Press.

Haas, William. 1970. *Phono-Graphic Translation.* Mont Follick Series 2. Manchester: Manchester University Press.

Haas, William. 1976. "Writing: The Basic Options." In *Writing without Letters*, edited by William Haas, 131–208. Mont Follick Series 4. Manchester: Manchester University Press.

Hall, Jeremy. 2005. "The Initial Teaching Alphabet." *Eye* 14 (55). www.eyemagazine.com/feature/article/the-initial-teaching-alphabet (accessed May 19, 2017).

Hall, Robert A., Jr. 1948. *French. Language* Monograph 24, Structural Sketches 1, supp. to vol. 24(3). Baltimore: Linguistic Society of America.

Halle, Morris. 1959. *The Sound Pattern of Russian.* Description and Analysis of Contemporary Standard Russian 1. The Hague: Mouton.

Hamilton, Gordon J. 2006. *The Origins of the West Semitic Alphabet in Egyptian Scripts. Catholic Biblical Quarterly* Monograph Series 40. Washington, D.C.: Catholic Biblical Association of America.

Hanks, William F., and Don S. Rice, eds. 1989. *Word and Image in Maya Culture: Explorations in Language, Writing, and Representation.* Salt Lake City: University of Utah Press.

Haring, Ben. 2015. "*Halaḥam* on an Ostracon of the Early New Kingdom?" *Journal of Near Eastern Studies* 74 (2): 189–96. DOI:10.1086/682330.

Harris, Marvin. 1976. "History and Significance of the Emic/Etic Distinction." *Annual Review of Anthropology* 5: 729–50.

Harrison, Maurice. 1964. *The Story of the Initial Teaching Alphabet.* New York: Pitman. (Published in Great Britain as *Instant Reading*.)

Haug, Martin. 1870. *Essay on the Pahlavi Language (from the Pahlavi-Pazand Glossary edited by Destur Hoshangji and M. Haug).* Stuttgart: Carl Grüninger.

Headland, Thomas M., Kenneth L. Pike, and Marvin Harris, eds. 1990. *Emics and Etics: The Insider/Outsider Debate.* Frontiers of Anthropology 7. Newbury Park, Calif.: Sage.

Heimpl, George. 1899. "The Origin of the Latin Letters *G* and *Z*." *Transactions and Proceedings of the American Philological Association* 30: 24–41.

Henderson, Leslie, ed. 1984. *Orthographies and Reading: Perspectives from Cognitive Psychology, Neuropsychology, and Linguistics*. Hillsdale: Erlbaum.

Henderson, Leslie. 1985. "On the Use of the Term 'grapheme'." *Language and Cognitive Processes* 1 (2): 135–48.

Henning, W. B. 1958. "Mitteliranisch." In *Iranistik*, 20–130. Handbuch der Orientalistik I/4.1. Leiden: Brill.

Herrick, Earl M. 1966. *A Linguistic Description of Roman Alphabets*. Hartford Studies in Linguistics 19. Hartford, Conn.: Hartford Seminary Foundation.

Herrick, Earl M. 1994a. "Of Course a Structural Graphemics Is Possible!" *LACUS Forum* 21 (Vancouver): 413–24.

Herrick, Earl M. 1994b. "Reply to Daniels's Reply." *LACUS Forum* 21 (Vancouver): 432–40.

Higginbottom, Eleanor M. 1962. "A Study of the Representation of English Vowel Phonemes in the Orthography." *Language and Speech* 5: 67–117.

Hockett, Charles F. 1951a. Review of *Nationalism and Language Reform in China*, by John DeFrancis. *Language* 27 (3): 439–45.

Hockett, Charles F. 1951b [2003]. "Two Lectures on Writing." Edited by Peter T. Daniels. *Written Language and Literacy* 6: 131–75.

Hockett, Charles F. 1952. "Speech and Writing." In *Report of the Third Annual Round Table Meeting on Linguistics and Language Teaching*, 67–76. Monograph Series on Language and Linguistics 2. Washington: Georgetown University Press.

Hockett, Charles F. 1958. *A Course in Modern Linguistics*. N.p.: Macmillan.

Hockett, Charles F. 1960 [1977]. "Logical Considerations in the Study of Animal Communication." In *Animal Sounds and Communication*, edited by W. E. Lanyon and W. N. Tavolga, 392–430. Symposium Series 7. Washington, D.C.: American Institute of Biological Sciences. (Expanded repr. in his *The View from Language: Selected Essays 1948-1974* [Athens: University of Georgia Press, 1977], 124–62.)

Hockett, Charles F. 1978. "In Search of Jove's Brow." *American Speech* 53 (4): 243–313.

Hogg, Richard M., ed. 1992–2001. *The Cambridge History of the English Language*. 6 vols. Cambridge: Cambridge University Press.

Holle, K. F. 1999. "Table of Old and New Indic Alphabets: Contribution to the Paleography of the Dutch Indies." Edited by Carol Molony and Henk Pechler. *Written Language and Literacy* 2 (2): 167–246. (Dutch original, 1877–82.)

Hosking, R. F., and G. M. Meredith-Owens, eds. 1966. *A Handbook of Asian Scripts*. London: British Museum.

Houston, Keith. 2016. *The Book: A Cover-to-Cover Exploration of the Most Powerful Object of Our Time*. New York: Norton.

Houston, Stephen D. 1989. *Maya Glyphs*. Reading the Past. London: British Museum.

Houston, Stephen D., ed. 2004. *First Writing: Script Invention as History and Process*. Cambridge: Cambridge University Press.

Houston, Stephen D., ed. 2012. *The Shape of Script: How and Why Writing Systems Change*. Santa Fe, N.M.: School for Advanced Research Press.

Hudson, Richard. 2010. *An Introduction to Word Grammar*. Cambridge Textbooks in Linguistics. Cambridge: Cambridge University Press.

Huehnergard, John. 2004. "Afroasiatic." In *The Cambridge Encyclopedia of the World's Ancient Languages*, edited by Roger D. Woodard, 138–59. Cambridge: Cambridge University Press.

Hurford, James R. 2014. *The Origins of Language: A Slim Guide*. Oxford: Oxford University Press.

Hyslop, Gwendolyn. 2014. "Kurtöp Orthography Development in Bhutan." In *Developing Orthographies for Unwritten Languages*, edited by Michael Cahill and Keren Rice, 211–30. SIL International® Publications in Langage Use and Education 6. Dallas: SIL International.

International Institute of African Languages and Cultures. 1930. *Practical Orthography of African Languages*. Memorandum 1. Rev. ed. London: Oxford University Press for the International Institute of African Languages and Cultures. (1st ed., London: International Institute of African Languages and Cultures, 1927.)

Jakobson, Roman. 1971. "The Kazan' School of Polish Linguistics and Its Place in the International Development of Phonology." In *Selected Writings II: Word and Language*, 394–428. The Hague: Mouton. (Polish original: "Kazańska szkoła polskiej lingwistyki i jej miejsce w światowym rozwoju fonologii," *Biuletyn Polskiego Towarzystwa Językoznawczego* 19 [1960]: 3–34.)

Jakobson, Roman, and Morris Halle. 1956. *Fundamentals of Language*. Janua Linguarum Series Minor 1. The Hague: Mouton.

Jeffery, Lillian H. 1990. *The Local Scripts of Archaic Greece*, edited by A. W. Johnston. 2nd ed. Oxford: Clarendon. (1st ed., 1961.)

Jehlitschka, Henry. 1895. *Türkische Konversations-Grammatik*. Heidelberg: Groos.

Jensen, Hans. 1969. *Sign, Symbol and Script*, translated by George Unwin. New York: Putnam's.

Jochelson, Waldemar. 1926. *The Jesup North Pacific Expedition*, vol. 9: *The Yukaghir and the Yukaghirized Tungus*, edited by Franz Boas. Memoirs of the American Museum of Natural History 13. Leiden: Brill.

Johnson, Samuel. 1755. *A Dictionary of the English Language* .... London.

Johnson, Scott A. J. 2013. *Translating Maya Hieroglyphs*. Norman: University of Oklahoma Press.

Joos, Martin, ed. 1957. *Readings in Linguistics [I]*. Washington, D.C.: American Council of Learned Societies. (4th corrected ed., Chicago: University of Chicago Press, 1966.)

Joos, Martin. 1986. *Notes on the Development of the Linguistic Society of America*. Ithaca, N.Y.: privately printed, J Milton Cowan & C. F. Hockett.

Junker, Heinrich F. J. 1925–26. "Das Awestaalphabet und der Ursprung der armenischen und georgischen Schrift." *Caucasica* 2: 1–82, 3: 82–139.

Justeson, John S. 1976. "Universals of Language and Universals of Writing." In *Linguistic Studies Offered to Joseph Greenberg on the Occasion of His Sixtieth Birthday*, vol. 1: *General Linguistics*, edited by Alphonse Juilland, 57–94. Saratoga, Calif.: Anma Libri.

Justeson, John S. 1989. "The Representational Conventions of Mayan Hieroglyphic Writing." In *Word and Image in Maya Culture: Explorations in Language, Writing, and Representation*, edited by William F. Hanks and Don S. Rice, 23–38. Salt Lake City: University of Utah Press.

Justeson, John S. 2013. "Early Mesoamerican Writing Systems." In *Oxford Handbook of Mesoamerican Archaeology*, edited by Deborah L. Nichols and Christopher A. Pool, 830–44. Oxford: Oxford University Press.

Kahn, Lily, and Aaron D. Rubin, eds. 2015. *Handbook of Jewish Languages*. Brill's Handbooks in Linguistics 2. Leiden: Brill.

Kammerzell, Frank. 2001. "Die Entstehung der Alphabetreihe: Zum ägyptischen Ursprung der semitischen und westlichen Schriften." In *Hieroglyphen Alphabete Schriftreformen: Studien zu Multiliteralismus, Schriftwechsel und Orthographieneuregelungen*, edited by Dörte Borchers, Frank Kammerzell, and Stefan Weninger, 117–58. *Lingua Aegyptia* Studia monographica 3. Göttingen: Seminar für Ägyptologie und Koptologie.

Kandhadai, Padmapriya, and Richard Sproat. 2010. "Impact of Spatial Ordering of Graphemes in Alphasyllabic Scripts on Phonemic Awareness in Indic Languages." *Writing Systems Research* 2: 105–16.

Kara, György. 2005. *Books of the Mongolian Nomads: More than Eight Centuries of Writing Mongolian*, translated by John R. Krueger. 1st English ed., revised and expanded by the author. Indiana University Ural and Altaic Series 171. Bloomington: Indiana University Research Institute for Inner Asian Studies. (Russian original, 1972.)

Karlgren, Bernhard. 1923. *Analytic Dictionary of Chinese and Sino-Japanese.* Paris: Geuthner. (Repr. Mineola, N.Y.: Dover Publications, 1991.)

Karlgren, Bernhard. 1926. *Philology and Ancient China.* Oslo: Aschehoug; Cambridge: Harvard University Press. (Repr. Philadelphia: Porcupine, 1980.)

Katz, Leonard, and Laurie B. Feldman. 1981. "Linguistic Coding in Word Recognition: Comparisons between a Deep and a Shallow Orthography." In *Interactive Processes in Reading,* edited by Alan M. Lesgold and Charles A. Perfetti, 85–106. Hillsdale, N.J.: Erlbaum.

Katz, Leonard, and Laurie B. Feldman. 1983. "Relation between Pronunciation and Recognition of Printed Words in Deep and Shallow Orthographies." *Journal of Experimental Psychology: Learning, Memory, and Cognition* 9 (1): 157–66.

Kaye, Alan S., ed. 1997. *Phonologies of Asia and Africa (including the Caucasus).* Winona Lake, Ind.: Eisenbrauns.

Kendall, Joshua. 2010. *The Forgotten Founding Father: Noah Webster's Obsession and the Creation of an American Culture.* New York: Putnam's.

Kent, Roland G. 1953. *Old Persian Grammar Texts Lexicon.* American Oriental Series 33. New Haven: American Oriental Society.

Kilbury, James. 1976. *The Development of Morphophonemic Theory.* Studies in the History of Linguistics 10. Amsterdam: John Benjamins.

Kim-Renaud, Young-Key, ed. 1997. *The Korean Alphabet.* Honolulu: University of Hawai'i Press.

Kirchhoff, A. 1877. *Studien zur Geschichte des griechischen Alphabets.* 3rd ed. Gütersloh: Bertelsmann. (1st ed., 1867.)

Klima, Edward. 1972. "How Alphabets Might Reflect Language." In *Language by Ear and by Eye,* edited by James F. Kavanagh and Ignatius G. Mattingly, 57–80. Communicating by Language 4. Cambridge: MIT Press.

Kohrt, Manfred. 1986. "The Term 'Grapheme' in the History and Theory of Linguistics." In *New Trends in Graphemics and Orthography,* edited by Gerhard Augst, 80–96. Berlin: de Gruyter.

Kroeber, Alfred L. 1923. *Anthropology.* New York: Harcourt, Brace. (2nd ed., *Anthropology: Race Language Culture Psychology Prehistory.* New York: Harcourt, Brace & World, 1948.)

Kroeber, Alfred L. 1940. "Stimulus Diffusion." *American Anthropologist* N.S. 42: 1–20.

Kuipers, Joel C., and Ray McDermott. 1996. "Insular Southeast Asian Scripts." In *The World's Writing Systems,* edited by Peter T. Daniels and William Bright, 474–84. New York: Oxford University Press.

Lacadena, Alfonso. 2010a. "Historical Implications of the Presence of non-Mayan Linguistic Features in the Maya Script." In *The Maya and Their Neighbours: Internal and External Contacts through Time (Proceedings of the 10th European Maya Conference, Leiden, December 9-10, 2005),* edited by Laura van Broekhoven, Rogelio Valencia Rivera, Benjamin Vis, and Frauke Sachse, 29–39. Acta Mesoamericana 23. Markt Schwaben: Verlag Anton Saurwein.

Lacadena, Alfonso. 2010b. "On the Origins of Maya Script." Paper presented, The Maya Meetings, March 16–19, Early Maya Iconography and Script, Antigua, Guatemala. PowerPoint.

Ladefoged, Peter. 1982. *A Course in Phonetics.* New York: Harcourt, Brace, Jovanovich.

Lambert, H. M. 1953. *Introduction to the Devanagari Script for Students of Sanskrit, Hindi, Marathi Gujarati and Bengali.* London: Oxford University Press.

Ledyard, Gari K. 1966. "The Korean Language Reform of 1446: The Origin, Background and Early History of the Korean Alphabet." Ph.D. dissertation, Oriental Languages, University of California, Berkeley.

Ledyard, Gari K. 1997. "The International Linguistic Background of the Correct Sounds for the Instruction of the People." In *The Korean Alphabet,* edited by Young-Key Kim-Renaud, 31–87. Honolulu: University of Hawai'i Press.

Lewis, Naphtali. 1974. *Papyrus in Classical Antiquity*. Oxford: Clarendon. (*A Supplement*, Brussels: Fondation Égyptologique Reine Élisabeth, 1989. Papyrologica Bruxellensia 23.)

Liberman, Alvin M., Franklin S. Cooper, Donald P. Shankweiler, and Michael Studdert-Kennedy. 1967. "Perception of the Speech Code." *Psychological Review* 74: 431–61. (Repr. in *Human Communication: A Unified View*, edited by Edward E. David, Jr., and Peter B. Denes, 13–50. Inter-University Electronics Series 15. New York: McGraw-Hill, 1973.)

Liberman, Isabelle Y., Donald Shankweiler, F. William Fischer, and Bonnie Carter. 1974. "Explicit Syllable and Phoneme Segmentation in the Young Child." *Journal of Experimental Child Psychology* 18: 201–12.

Lipiński, Edward. 1994. *Studies in Aramaic Inscriptions and Onomastics II*. Orientalia Lovaniensia Analecta 57. Leuven: Peeters.

Lockwood, David G. 2000. "Phoneme and Grapheme: How Parallel Can They Be?" *27th LACUS Forum* 307–16.

Loprieno, Antonio. 1995. *Ancient Egyptian: A Linguistic Introduction*. Cambridge: Cambridge University Press.

Losos, Jonathan B. 2017. *Improbable Destinies: Fate, Chance, and the Future of Evolution*. New York: Riverhead.

Macdonald, M. C. A. 2004. "Ancient North Arabian." In *The Cambridge Encyclopedia of the World's Ancient Languages*, edited by Roger D. Woodard, 488–533. Cambridge: Cambridge Univesity Press.

MacKenzie, D. N. 1967. "Notes on the Transcription of Pahlavi." *Bulletin of the School of Oriental and African Studies* 30: 17–29.

MacKenzie, D. N. 1971. *A Concise Pahlavi Dictionary*. London: Oxford University Press.

Macri, Martha J., and Matthew G. Looper. 2003. "Nahua in Ancient Mesoamerica: Evidence from Maya Inscriptions." *Ancient Mesoamerica* 14 (2): 285–97. DOI:10.1017/S0956536103142046.

Mafundikwa, Saki. 2004. *Afrikan Alphabets: The Story of Writing in Afrika*. West New York, N.J.: Mark Batty.

Mair, Victor H. 1996. "Modern Chinese Writing." In *The World's Writing Systems*, edited by Peter T. Daniels and William Bright, 200–208. New York: Oxford University Press.

Mallory, J. P. 2010. "Bronze Age Languages of the Tarim Basin." *Expedition* 53 (3, November): 44–53. www.penn.museum/sites/expedition/bronze-age-languages-of-the-tarim-basin/ (accessed May 19, 2017).

Mann, Michael, and David Dalby. 1987. *A Thesaurus of African Languages: A Classified and Annotated Inventory of the Spoken Languages of Africa, with an Appendix on Their Written Representation*. London: Zell.

Marcus, Joyce. 2006. "Mesoamerica: Scripts." In *Encyclopedia of Language & Linguistics Second Edition*, edited by Keith Brown, 8:16–27. Oxford: Elsevier.

Marotta, Giovanna. 2000. "The Features of the Roman Alphabet: A Tentative Study." *Rivista di Linguistica* 12 (2): 283–306.

Marotta, Giovanna. in preparation. *The Phonology of Latin*.

Martin, Samuel E. 1972. "Nonalphabetic Writing Systems: Some Observations." In *Language by Ear and by Eye: The Relationships between Speech and Reading*, edited by James F. Kavanagh and Ignatius G. Mattingly, 81–102. Communicating by Language 4. Cambridge: MIT Press.

McCarthy, Suzanne. 1995. "The Cree Syllabary and the Writing System Riddle: A Paradigm in Crisis." In *Scripts and Literacy: Reading and Learning to Read Alphabets, Syllabaries and Characters*, edited by Insup Taylor and David R. Olson, 59–75. Neuropsychology and Cognition 7. Dordrecht: Kluwer.

McCawley, James D. 1968. *The Phonological Component of a Grammar of Japanese*. Janua Linguarum Series Practica 5. The Hague: Mouton.

McIntosh, Angus. 1961. "'Graphology' and Meaning." *Archivum Linguisticum* 13: 107–20. (Repr. in *Patterns of Language: Papers in General, Descriptive and Applied Linguistics*, by A. McIntosh and M. A. K. Halliday [Bloomington: Indiana University Press, 1967], 98–110.)

McLean, John. 1890. *James Evans: Inventor of the Syllabic System of the Cree Language.* Toronto: William Briggs.

McMurtrie, Douglas C. 1943. *The Book: The Story of Printing and Bookmaking.* 3rd ed. New York: Oxford University Press. (1st ed., New York: Covici-Friede, 1937.)

Melchert, H. Craig, ed. 2003. *The Luvians.* Handbuch der Orientalistik 1.68. Leiden: Brill.

Michalowski, Piotr. 2004. "Sumerian." In *Encyclopedia of the World's Ancient Languages*, edited by Roger D. Woodard, 19–59. Cambridge: Cambridge University Press.

Mickelthwait, David. 2000. *Noah Webster and the American Dictionary.* Jefferson, N.C.: McFarland.

Miller, Christopher Ray. 2014. "Devanagari's Descendants in North and South India, Indonesia and the Philippines." *Writing Systems Research* 6 (1): 10–24. DOI:10.1080/17586801.2013.857 288.

Miller, D. Gary. 1994. *Ancient Scripts and Phonological Knowledge.* Current Issues in Linguistic Theory 116. Amsterdam and Philadelphia: John Benjamins.

Miller, Roy Andrew. 1956. *The Tibetan System of Writing.* Washington, D.C.: American Council of Learned Societies.

Mishra, R., and R. Stainthorp. 2007. "The Relationship between Phonological Awareness and Word Reading Accuracy in Oriya and English." *Journal of Research in Reading* 30: 23–37.

Monaghan, Jennifer. 1983. *A Common Heritage: Noah Webster's Blue-Back Speller.* Hamden, Conn.: Archon.

Morag, Shelomo. 1961. *The Vocalization Systems of Arabic, Hebrew, and Aramaic.* Janua Linguarum Series Minor 13. The Hague: Mouton.

Morais, José, Luz Cary, Jésus Alegria, and Paul Bertelson. 1979. "Does Awareness of Speech as a Sequence of Phones Arise Spontaneously?" *Cognition* 7: 323–31.

Morais, José, and Régine Kolinsky. 2005. "Literacy and Cognitive Change." In *The Science of Reading: A Handbook*, edited by Margaret J. Snowling and Charles Hulme, 188–203. Blackwell Handbooks of Developmental Psychology. Malden, Mass.: Blackwell.

Mora-Marín, David. 2003. "The Origin of Mayan Syllabograms and Orthographic Conventions." *Written Language and Literacy* 6: 193–238.

Mora-Marín, David. 2010. "Consonant Deletion, Obligatory Synharmony, Typical Suffixing: An Explanation of Spelling Practices in Mayan Writing." *Written Language and Literacy* 13: 118–79.

Morison, Stanley. 1972. *Politics and Script: Aspects of Authority and Freedom in the Development of Graeco-Latin Script from the Sixth Century B.C. to the Twentieth Century A.D.*, edited by Nicolas Barker. Lyell Lectures, 1957. Oxford: Clarendon.

Mouraviev, Serge. 1980. "Les caractères daniéliens"; "Les caractères mesropiens." *Revue des études arméniennes* 14: 55–85; 87–111.

Mugdan, Joachim. 2011. "On the Origins of the Term *Phoneme*." *Historiographia Linguistica* 38 (1–2): 85–110. DOI:10.1075/hl.38.1/2.03mug.

Mumford, Simon, ed. 2015. *Compact World Atlas.* 6th ed. New York: DK Publishing.

Mumin, Meikal, and Kees Versteegh, eds. 2014. *The Arabic Script in Africa: Studies in the Use of a Writing System.* Studies in Semitic Languages and Linguistics 71. Leiden: Brill.

Nakanishi, Akira. 1980. *Writing Systems of the World: Alphabets, Syllabaries, Pictograms.* Rutland, Vt.: Tuttle.

Nakano, Miyoko. 1971. *A Phonological Study in the 'Phags-pa Script and the Meng-ku Tzu-yün.* Faculty of Asian Studies: Oriental Monograph Series 7. Canberra: Australian National University Press.

National Geographic Atlas of the World. 2011. 9th ed. Washington, D.C.: National Geographic.

Naveh, Joseph. 1987. *Early History of the Alphabet.* 2nd ed. Jerusalem: Magnes.

Naveh, Joseph, and Shaul Shaked. 2012. *Aramaic Documents from Ancient Bactria (Fourth Century BCE) from the Khalili Collections.* London: The Khalili Family Trust.

Nida, Eugene A., ed. 1972. *The Book of a Thousand Tongues.* Rev. ed. London: United Bible Societies. (1st ed., 1939.)

O'Connor, M. 1983. "Writing Systems, Native Speaker Analyses, and the Earliest Stages of Northwest Semitic Orthography." In *The Word of the Lord Shall Go Forth: Essays in Honor of David Noel Freedman in Celebration of His Sixtieth Birthday,* edited by Carol L. Meyers and M. O'Connor, 439–65. Winona Lake, Ind.: Eisenbrauns.

Olson, David R. 1994. *The World on Paper: The Conceptual and Cognitive Implications of Writing and Reading.* Cambridge: Cambridge University Press.

Oppenheim, A. Leo. 1959. "On an Operational Device in Mesopotamian Bureaucracy." *Journal of Near Eastern Studies* 18 (2): 121–28.

Oppenheim, A. Leo. 1977. *Ancient Mesopotamia: Portrait of a Dead Civilization,* 2nd ed., edited by Erica Reiner. Chicago: University of Chicago Press.

Ostler, Nicholas. 2005. *Empires of the Word.* London: HarperCollins.

Oswalt, Robert L. 1973. "English Orthography as a Morphophonemic System: Stressed Vowels." *Linguistics* 102: 5–40.

Packard, Jerome Lee. 2000. *The Morphology of Chinese.* Cambridge: Cambridge University Press.

Parpola, Asko. 1994. *Deciphering the Indus Script.* Cambridge: Cambridge University Press.

Patel, P. G., P. Pandey, and D. Rajgor, eds. 2007. *The Indic Scripts: Palaeographic and Linguistic Perspectives.* New Delhi: D. K. Printworld.

Pedersen, Holger. 1931. *The Discovery of Language: Linguistic Science in the Nineteenth Century,* translated by John Webster Spargo. Cambridge: Harvard University Press. (Danish orig., 1924. Repr. Bloomington: Indiana University Press, 1962 [Indiana University Studies in the History and Theory of Linguistics].)

Peterson, David J. 2015. *The Art of Language Invention: From Horse-Lords to Dark Elves, the Words behind World-Building.* New York: Penguin.

Petrie, W. M. Flinders. 1901. *The Royal Tombs of the Earliest Dynasties, Part II.* Egypt Exploration Fund Memoir 21. London.

Pike, Kenneth L. 1943. *Phonemics: A Technique for Reducing Languages to Writing.* Glendale, Calif.: Summer Institute of Linguistics.

Pike, Kenneth L. 1954–59. *Language in Relation to a Unified Theory of the Structure of Human Behavior.* 3 vols. The Hague: Mouton. (2nd ed., 1967.)

Pitman, James, and John St. John. 1969. *Alphabets and Reading: The Initial Teaching Alphabet.* New York: Pitman.

Plato. 1997. *Complete Works,* edited by John M. Cooper and D. S. Hutchinson. Indianapolis: Hackett.

Pope, Maurice. 1999. *The Story of Decipherment: From Egyptian Hieroglyphs to Maya Script.* 2nd ed. New York: Thames & Hudson. (1st ed., as *The Story of Archaeological Decipherment: From Egyptian Hieroglyphics to Linear B,* 1975.)

Poser, William J. 1992. "The Structural Typology of Phonological Writing." Paper presented at annual meeting, Linguistic Society of America, Philadelphia.

Primus, Beatrice. 2004. "A Featural Analysis of the Modern Roman Alphabet." *Written Language and Literacy* 7: 235–74.

Proceedings … Endangered Scripts of Island Southeast Asia. 2014. *Proceedings of the International Workshop on Endangered Scripts of Island Southeast Asia.* Tokyo: Tokyo University of Foreign Studies, Research Institute for Languages and Cultures of Asia and Africa.

Qiu Xigui. 2000. *Chinese Writing*, translated by Gilbert L. Mattos and Jerry Norman. *Early China* Special Monograph 4. Berkeley: Society for the Study of Early China & Institute of Early Asian Studies, University of California. (Chinese originals, 1988 [Beijing] and 1994 [Taipei].)

Quack, Joachim Friedrich. 2003. "Die spätägyptische Alphabetreihenfolge und das 'südsemitische' Alphabet." *Lingua Aegyptiaca* 11: 163–84.

Ratcliffe, Robert R. 2001. "What Do 'Phonemic' Writing Systems Represent? Arabic Huruuf, Japanese Kana, and the Moraic Principle." *Written Language and Literacy* 4: 1–14.

Read, Charles, Zhang Yun-fei, Nie Hong-yin, and Ding Bao-qing. 1986. "The Ability to Manipulate Speech Sounds Depends on Knowing Alphabetic Writing." *Cognition* 24: 31–44.

Reddick, Allen. 1996. *The Making of Johnson's Dictionary 1746–1773*. Rev. ed. Cambridge: Cambridge University Press.

Rilly, Claude, and Alex de Voogt. 2012. *The Meroitic Language and Writing System*. Cambridge: Cambridge University Press.

Robinson, Andrew. 2002. *Lost Languages*. New York: McGraw Hill.

Rogers, Henry. 1995. "Optimal Orthographies." In *Scripts and Literacy: Reading and Learning to Read Alphabets, Syllabaries and Characters*, edited by Insup Taylor and David R. Olson, 31–43. Neuropsychology and Cognition 7. Dordrecht: Kluwer.

Rogers, Henry. 2005. *Writing Systems: A Linguistic Approach*. Blackwell Textbooks in Linguistics. Malden, Mass.: Blackwell.

Rollston, Christopher A. 2010. *Writing and Literacy in the World of Ancient Israel: Epigraphic Evidence from the Iron Age*. SBL Archaeology and Biblical Studies 11. Atlanta: Society of Biblical Literature.

Rooney, Andrew A. 1992. *Sweet and Sour*. New York: Putnam Adult.

Roth, Martha T. 1997. *Law Collections from Mesopotamia and Asia Minor*. 2nd ed. SBL Writings from the Ancient World 6. Atlanta: Scholars Press.

Ruszkiewicz, Piotr. 1978. "Jan Baudouin de Courtenay's Theory of the Grapheme." *Acta Philologica* (Warsaw) 7: 111–28.

Sáenz-Badillos, Angel. 1993. *A History of the Hebrew Language*, translated by John Elwolde. Cambridge: Cambridge University Press.

Salomon, Frank. 2008. "Late Khipu Use." In *The Disappearance of Writing Systems: Perspectives on Literacy and Communication*, edited by John Baines, John Bennet, and Stephen D. Houston, 285–310. London: Equinox.

Salomon, Richard G. 1998. *Indian Epigraphy*. New York: Oxford University Press.

Salomon, Richard G. 2002. "Gāndhārī and the Other Indo-Aryan Languages in the Light of Newly-discovered Kharoṣṭhī Manuscripts." In *Indo-Iranian Languages and Peoples*, edited by Nicholas Sims-Williams, 119–34. Proceedings of the British Academy 116. Oxford: Oxford University Press.

Salomon, Richard G. 2006. "Kharoṣṭhī Syllables Used as Location Markers in Gandhāran Stūpa Architecture." In *Architetti, capomastri, artigiani: L'organizzazione dei cantieri e della produzione artistica nell'Asia ellenistica, Studi offerti a Domenico Faccenna nel suo ottantesimo compleano*, edited by Pierfrancesco Callieri, 181–224. Serie Orientale Roma 100. Rome: Istituto Italiano per l'Africa e l'Oriente.

Salomon, Richard G. 2007. "Writing Systems of the Indo-Aryan Languages." In *The Indo-Aryan Languages*, edited by George Cardona and Dhanesh Jain, 67–103. Routledge Language Family Series. London: Routledge.

Sampson, Geoffrey. 2015. *Writing Systems*. 2nd ed. Sheffield: Equinox. (1st ed., London: Hutchinson, 1985; corrected pbk. reprint, 1987.)

Sander, Lore. 1986. "Brahmi Scripts on the Eastern Silk Roads." *Studien zur Indologie und Iranistik* 11–12: 159–192.

Sander, Lore. 2005. "Remarks on the Formal Brāhmī Script from the Southern Silk Route." *Bulletin of the Asia Institute* NS 19: 133–144.

Sanders, Seth L. 2009. *The Invention of Hebrew.* Urbana: University of Illinois Press.

Sass, Benjamin. 1988. *The Genesis of the Alphabet and Its Development in the Second Millenium B.C.* Ägypten und Altes Testament 13. Wiesbaden: Harrassowitz.

Sass, Benjamin. 1991. *Studia Alphabetica: On the Origin and Early History of the Northwest Semitic, South Semitic and Greek Alphabets.* Orbis Biblicus et Orientalis 102. Göttingen: Vandenhoeck & Ruprecht.

Sass, Benjamin. 2005. *The Alphabet at the Turn of the Millennium.* Tel Aviv Occasional Publications 4. Tel Aviv: Tel Aviv University.

Saussure, Ferdinand de. 1916. *Cours de linguistique générale*, edited by Charles Bally, Albert Sechehaye, and Albert Riedlinger. Paris: Payot.

Saussure, Ferdinand de. 1959. *Course in General Linguistics*, edited by Charles Bally, Albert Sechehaye, and Albert Riedlinger, translated by Wade Baskin. New York: Philosophical Library. (French original, 1916.)

Saussure, Ferdinand de. 1983. *Course in General Linguistics*, edited by Charles Bally, Albert Sechehaye, and Albert Riedlinger, translated by Roy Harris. London: Duckworth. (French original, 1916.)

Scancarelli, Janine. 1992. "Aspiration and Cherokee Orthographies." In *The Linguistics of Literacy*, edited by Pamela Downing, Susan D. Lima, and Michael Noonan, 135–52. Typological Studies in Language 21. Amsterdam and Philadelphia: John Benjamins.

Schele, Linda, and David Freidel. 1990. *A Forest of Kings: The Untold Story of the Ancient Maya.* New York: Morrow.

Schele, Linda, and Peter Mathews. 1998. *The Code of Kings: The Language of Seven Sacred Maya Temples and Tombs.* New York: Scribner's.

Schele, Linda, and Mary Ellen Miller. 1986. *The Blood of Kings: Dynasty and Ritual in Maya Art.* Fort Worth: Kimbell Art Museum.

Schmandt-Besserat, Denise. 1978. "The Earliest Precursor of Writing." *Scientific American*, June, 50–59.

Schmandt-Besserat, Denise. 1992. *Before Writing.* 2 vols. Austin: University of Texas Press.

Schmandt-Besserat, Denise. 2015. "Writing after Accounting in the Ancient Near East." Paper presented at the conference The Chinese Writing System and Its Dialogue wtih Sumerian, Egyptian, and Mesoamerican Writing Systems, Confucius Institute, Rutgers University, New Brunswick, N.J., May 30.

Schmitt, Alfred. 1980. *Entstehung und Entwicklung von Schriften*, edited by Claus Haeber. Cologne: Böhlau.

Scholes, Robert J. 1995. "Orthography, Vision, and Phonemic Awareness." In *Scripts and Literacy: Reading and Learning to Read Alphabets, Syllabaries and Characters*, edited by Insup Taylor and David R. Olson, 359–73. Neuropsychology and Cognition 7. Dordrecht: Kluwer.

Schroeder, Otto. 1922. "Aus den keilinschriftlichen Sammlungen des Berliner Museums III: V. Gesetzte assyrische Ziegelstempel." *Zeitschrift für Assyriologie* 34:157–61.

Scragg, D. G. 1974. *A History of English Spelling.* Mont Follick Series 3. Manchester: Manchester University Press.

Scribner, Sylvia, and Michael Cole. 1981. *The Psychology of Literacy.* Cambridge: Harvard University Press.

Seeley, Christopher. 1991. *A History of Writing in Japan.* Brill's Japanese Studies Library 3. Leiden: Brill. (Repr. Honolulu: University of Hawai'i Press, 2000.)

Segal, J. B. 1953. *The Diacritical Point and Accents in Syriac.* London Oriental Series 2. London: Oxford University Press.

Seland, Elvind Heldaas. 2014. "Archaeology of Trade in the Western Indian Ocean, 300 BC—AD 700." *Journal of Archaeological Research* 22: 367–402.

Senner, Wayne M., ed. 1989. *The Origins of Writing.* Lincoln: University of Nebraska Press.

Seybolt, Peter J., and Gregory Kuei-ke Chiang, eds. 1979. *Language Reform in China: Documents and Commentary*, translated by Elma Kopetsky and others. White Plains, N.Y.: M. E. Sharpe.

Shapiro, Fred R. 1995. "Notes toward a Sample of a Subject Glossary on Historical Principles: Contributions to the History of Linguistic Terminology." *American Speech* 70: 21–29.

Share, David L. 2008. "On the Anglocentricities of Current Reading Research and Practice: The Perils of Overreliance on an 'Outlier' Orthography." *Psychological Bulletin* 134: 584–615.

Share, David L., and Peter T. Daniels. 2015. "Aksharas, Alphasyllabaries, Abugidas, Alphabets, and Orthographic Depth: Reflections on Rimzhim, Katz, and Fowler (2014)." *Writing Systems Research* 8 (2016): 17–31. DOI:10.1080/17586801.2015.1016395.

Shaw, George Bernard. 1962. *The Shaw Alphabet Edition of Androcles and the Lion.* Harmondsworth: Penguin.

Sims-Williams, Nicholas. 1981. "The Sogdian Sound-system and the Origin of the Uyghur Script." *Journal Asiatique* 269: 347–59.

Sircar, D. C. 1970–71. "Introduction to Indian Epigraphy and Palaeography." *Journal of Ancient Indian History* 4 (1–2): 72–136.

Skinner, David. 2012. *The Story of* Ain't: *America, Its Language, and the Most Controversial Dictionary Ever Published.* New York: Harper.

Smalley, William A., ed. 1963. *Orthography Studies: Articles on New Writing Systems.* Helps for Translators 6. London: United Bible Societies.

Smalley, William A., ed. 1976. *Phonemes and Orthography: Language Planning in Ten Minority Languages of Thailand.* Pacific Linguistics C-43. Canberra: Department of Linguistics, Research School of Pacific Studies, Australian National University.

Smalley, William A. 1994. *Linguistic Diversity and National Unity: Language Ecology in Thailand.* Chicago: University of Chicago Press.

Smith, Arden R. 2014. "Invented Languages and Writing Systems." In *A Companion to J. R. R. Tolkien*, edited by Stuart D. Lee, 202–14. Chichester: Wiley-Blackwell.

Smith, Janet S. (Shibamoto). 1999. Review of *The Blackwell Encyclopedia of Writing Systems*, by Florian Coulmas. *Language in Society* 28 (3): 450–54.

Sprengling, Martin. 1953. *Third Century Iran: Sapor and Kartir.* Chicago: Oriental Institute.

Sproat, Richard. 2014. "A Statistical Comparison of Written Language and Nonlinguistic Symbol Systems." *Language* 90 (2): 457–81.

Srinivasachari, K. n.d. *Learn Sanskrit in 30 Days.* National Integration Language Series. Madras: Balaji Publications.

Stein, Peter. 2010. *Die Altsüdarabischen Minuskelinschriften auf Holzstäbchen aus der Bayerischen Staatsbibliothek in München.* Epigraphische Forschungen auf der Arabischen Halbinsel 5/1. Tübingen: Wasmuth.

Stein, Peter. 2011. "Ancient South Arabian." In *The Semitic Languages: An International Handbook*, edited by Stefan Weninger, Geoffrey Khan, Michael P. Streck, and Janet C. E. Watson, 1042–73. Handbücher zur Sprach- und Kommunikationswissenschaft 36. Berlin: de Gruyter Mouton.

Steinkeller, Piotr. 1995. Review of *Zeichenliste der archaischen Texte aus Uruk*, by Margaret W. Green and Hans J. Nissen. *Bibliotheca Orientalis* 52: 689–713.

Stephens, John Lloyd, and Frederick Catherwood. 1841. *Incidents of Travel in Central America, Chiapas and Yucatan.* London: John Murray. (Several later editions; numerous modern reprints.)

Stephens, John Lloyd, and Frederick Catherwood. 1843. *Incidents of Travel in Yucatan*. New York: Harper. (Several later editions; numerous modern reprints.)

Stetson, R. H. 1928. *Motor Phonetics*. Archives néerlandaises de phonétique expérimentale 3. The Hague: Nijhoff. (2nd ed., 1951; repr. with annotations 1988.)

Stetson, R. H. 1937. "The Phoneme and the Grapheme." In *Mélanges de linguistique et de philologie offerts à Jacques van Ginneken à l'occasion du soixantième anniversaire de sa naissance*, 353–56. Paris: Klincksieck.

Stevens, John. 1988. *Sacred Calligraphy of the East*. Boulder, Colo.: Shambhala.

Sturman, Peter Charles. 1997. *Mi Fu: Style and the Art of Calligraphy in Northern Song China*. New Haven: Yale University Press.

Sundermann, Werner. 1985. "Schriftsysteme und Alphabete im alten Iran." *Altorientalische Forschungen* 12: 101–13.

Svantesson, Jan-Olof, Anna Tsendina, Anastasia Karlsson, and Vivan Franzén. 2005. *The Phonology of Mongolian*. Oxford: Oxford University Press.

Swadesh, Morris. 1971. *The Origin and Diversification of Language*, edited by Joel Sherzer. Chicago: Aldine-Atherton.

Taylor, Insup, and David R. Olson, eds. 1995. *Scripts and Literacy: Reading and Learning to Read Alphabets, Syllabaries and Characters*. Neuropsychology and Cognition 7. Dordrecht: Kluwer.

Taylor, Insup, and M. Martin Taylor. 1995. *Writing and Literacy in Chinese, Korean and Japanese*. Studies in Written Language and Literacy 3. Amsterdam and Philadelphia: John Benjamins.

Taylor, Isaac. 1883. *The Alphabet: An Account of the Origin and Development of Letters*, vol. 1: *Semitic Alphabets*; vol. 2: *Aryan Alphabets*. London: Kegan Paul, Trench. (2nd ed., London: Edward Arnold, 1899; cited from US repr., New York: Charles Scribner's Sons, 1899.)

Thompson, J. Eric S. 1962. *A Catalogue of Maya Hieroglyphs*. Norman: University of Oklahoma Press.

Thompson, J. Eric S. 1971. *Maya Hieroglyphic Writing*. 3rd ed. Norman: University of Oklahoma Press. (1st ed., 1950.)

Toussainte, Auguste. 1966. *History of the Indian Ocean*, translated by June Guicharnaud. Chicago: University of Chicago Press.

Toynbee, Arnold J., and Edward D. Myers. 1959. *Historical Atlas and Gazetteer*. A Study of History 11. London: Oxford University Press.

Tsien Tsuen-hsuin. 2004. *Written on Bamboo and Silk: The Beginnings of Chinese Books and Inscriptions*. 2nd ed. Chicago: University of Chicago Press. (1st ed., 1962.)

Tuchscherer, Konrad. 2007. "Recording, Communicating and Making Visible: A History of Writing and Systems of Graphic Symbolism in Africa." In *Inscribing Meaning: Writing and Graphic Systems in African Art*, edited by Christine Mullen Kreamer, Mary Nooter Roberts, Elizabeth Harney, and Allyson Purpura, 37–53. Washington, D.C.: 5Continents/ Smithsonian/National Museum of African Art.

Tuchscherer, Konrad, and P. E. H. Hair. 2002. "Cherokee and West Africa: Examining the Origins of the West African Script." *History in Africa* 29: 427–86.

Twaddell, W. Freeman. 1935. *On Defining the Phoneme*. *Language* Monograph 16. Baltimore: Linguistic Society of America. (Repr. in Martin Joos, ed., *Readings in Linguistics [I]* [1957, repr. Chicago: University of Chicago Press, 79–55 ,[1966.)

Uhlig, Siegbert. 1990. *Introduction to Ethiopian Palaeography*. Stuttgart: Steiner.

Unger, J. Marshall. 2004. *Ideogram: Chinese Characters and the Myth of Disembodied Meaning*. Honolulu: University of Hawai'i Press.

Unger, J. Marshall, and John DeFrancis. 1995. "Logographic and Semasiographic Writing Systems: A Critique of Sampson's Classification." In *Scripts and Literacy: Reading and Learning to Read Alphabets, Syllabaries and Characters*, edited by Insup Taylor and David R. Olson, 45–58. Neuropsychology and Cognition 7. Dordrecht: Kluwer.

Upward, Christopher, and George Davidson. 2011. *The History of English Spelling*. Malden, Mass.: Wiley-Blackwell.

Vachek, Josef. 1973. *Written Language: General Problems and Problems of English*. Janua Linguarum Series Critica 14. The Hague: Mouton.

van Schaik, Sam. 2011. "A New Look at the Tibetan Invention of Writing." In *New Studies of the Old Tibetan Documents: Philology, History and Religion*, edited by Yoshiro Imaeda, Matthew T. Kapstein, and Tsuguhito Takeushi, 45–96. Old Tibetan Documents Online Monograph Series 3. Tokyo: Tokyo University of Foreign Studies, Research Institute for Languages and Cultures of Asia and Africa. https://otdo.aa.tufs.ac.jp (accessed January 27, 2014).

Vance, Timothy J. 2008. *The Sounds of Japanese*. Cambridge: Cambridge University Press.

Venezky, Richard L. 1966. "The Basis of English Orthography." *Acta Linguistica Hafniensia* 10: 145–59.

Venezky, Richard L. 1967. "English Orthography: Its Graphical Structure and Its Relation to Sound." *Reading Research Quarterly* 2: 75–105.

Venezky, Richard L. 1970a. "Principles for the Design of Practical Writing Systems." *Anthropological Linguistics* 12: 256–70.

Venezky, Richard L. 1970b. *The Structure of English Orthography*. Janua Linguarum Series Minor 82. The Hague: Mouton.

Venezky, Richard L. 1976. "Notes on the History of English Spelling." *Visible Language* 10: 351–65.

Venezky, Richard L. 1995. "How English Is Read: Grapheme–Phoneme Regularity and Orthographic Structure in Word Recognition." In *Scripts and Literacy: Reading and Learning to Read Alphabets, Syllabaries and Characters*, edited by Insup Taylor and David R. Olson, 111–29. Neuropsychology and Cognition 7. Dordrecht: Kluwer.

Versteegh, Kees. 1997. *The Arabic Language*. New York: Columbia University Press.

Walker, C. B. F. 1987. *Cuneiform*. Reading the Past. London: British Museum.

Walker, Willard, and James Sarbaugh. 1993. "The Early History of the Cherokee Syllabary." *Ethnohistory* 40(1): 70–94.

Watson, Wilfred G. E., and Nicolas Wyatt, eds. 1999. *Handbook of Ugaritic Studies*. Handbuch der Orientalistik 1.39. Leiden: Brill.

Waugh, Linda, and Monique Burston, eds. forthcoming. *The Cambridge History of Linguistics*. Cambridge: Cambridge University Press.

Webster, Noah. 1804. *The American Spelling-Book; Containing, the Rudiments of the English Language, for the Use of Schools in the United States*. 90th impression, 1816. Philadelphia: Johnson & Warner. (1st ed., 1783.)

Webster, Noah. 1806. *A Compendious Dictionary of the English Language*. New Haven: Sidney's Press. (Facsimile, ed. by Philip B. Gove, n.p.: Crown Publishers, 1970.)

Webster, Noah. 1828. *An American Dictionary of the English Language ...*. New York: S. Converse. (Facsimile, ed. by Rosalie J. Slater, Anaheim, Calif.: Foundation for American Christian Education, 1967. [American Christian History Series].)

Wells, John C. 1982. *Accents of English*. Cambridge: Cambridge University Press.

Whittaker, Gordon. 2009. "The Principles of Nahuatl Writing." *Göttinger Beiträge zur Sprachwissenschaft* 16: 47–81.

Whorf, Benjamin Lee. 1932 [1956]. "A Central American Inscription Combining Mexican and Maya Day Signs." *American Anthropologist* 34: 296–302. (Repr. in his *Language, Thought, and Reality: Selected Writings*, edited by John B. Carrroll [Cambridge: MIT Press, 1956], 43–50.)

Whorf, Benjamin Lee. 1942 [1956]. "Decipherment of the Linguistic Portion of the Maya Hieroglyphs." In *Smithsonian Report for 1941*, 479–502. Washington, D.C.: Government

Printing Office. (Repr. in his *Language, Thought, and Reality: Selected Writings*, edited by John B. Carrroll [Cambridge: MIT Press, 1956], 173–98.)

Wilder, G. D., and J. H. Ingram. 1934. *Analysis of Chinese Characters*. 2nd ed. N.p.: College of Chinese Studies in China. (1st ed., Peking: North China Language School, 1922; repr. New York: Dover Publications, 1974.)

Wilkinson, Lane. 2010. "Reading, Writing, and What Plato Really Thought." *Sense and Reference* https://senseandreference.wordpress.com/2010/10/27/reading-writing-and-what-plato-really-thought/ (accessed January 22, 2017).

Williams, Maynard Owen. 1929. "Turkey Goes to School." *The National Geographic Magazine*, January, 94–108.

Windfuhr, Gernot, ed. 2009. *The Iranian Languages*. Routledge Language Families. London: Routledge.

Winn, Shan M. M. 1981. *Pre-Writing in Southeast Europe: The Sign System of the Vinča Culture, ca. 4000 B.C.* Calgary: Western Publishers. (Original dissertation, 1973.)

Wolf, Maryanne. 2007. *Proust and the Squid: The Story and Science of the Reading Brain*. New York: HarperCollins.

Woodard, Roger D. 1997. *Greek Writing from Knossos to Homer*. New York: Oxford University Press.

Woods, Christopher. 2010. "The Earliest Mesopotamian Writing." In *Visible Language: Inventions of Writing in the Ancient Middle East and Beyond*, edited by Christopher Woods, Emily Teeter, and Geoff Emberling, 33–50. Oriental Institute Museum Publications 32. Chicago: Oriental Institute of the University of Chicago.

Woods, Christopher, and Edward Shaughnessy, eds. in preparation. *Signs of Writing*. Chicago: Oriental Institute.

Wyrod, Christopher. 2008. "A Social Orthography of Identity: The N'ko Literacy Movement in West Africa." *International Journal of the Sociology of Language* 192: 27–44.

Yarshater, Ehsan. 1983. "Introduction." In *The Cambridge History of Iran*, vol. 3: *The Seleucid, Parthian and Sassanian Periods*, edited by Ehsan Yarshater, xvii–lxxv. Cambridge: Cambridge University Press.

Yip, Moira. 2002. *Tone*. Cambridge Textbooks in Linguistics. Cambridge: Cambridge University Press.

Yu Shaosheng, Sheng Peilin, Yin Peijie, Ding Feng, Yu Rui, and Chen Yijing, eds. 1999. *Quaille's Practical Chinese-English Dictionary*. Hong Kong: Asia 2000 Ltd.

Zimansky, Paul. 1993. Review of *Before Writing*, by Denise Schmandt-Besserat. *Journal of Field Archaeology* 20 (4): 513–17.

Zimmer, Ben. 2010. "On Language: Is This Word Really Pronounced 'fish'?" *New York Times Magazine*, June 27, 14. http://www.nytimes.com/2010/06/27/magazine/27FOB-onlanguage-t.html (accessed May 19, 2017).

Indexes

Index of scripts

page references to tables in italics

Index of names

page references to the main text in italics

Abercrombie, David 3, *165*
Adiego, Ignacio-Javier 122, 123
Aḥirom, King of Byblos *38*
Ainsworth, W. A. 17
Albright, Eric Scott *168*
Alcuin of York *28*
Alegria, Jésus 158
Aleksidzé, Zaza 33, 125
Alexander the Great *56, 65, 108*
Alfred, King of England *20, 165*
Allan, Keith 5
Allen, W. S. 187
Anderson, Donald M. 153
Anderson, James M. 122
Angad, Guru of the Sikhs *75*
Anthony the Great of Egypt, St. (or: Marc
　　Antony) 196
Aronoff, Mark 21
Aronson, Howard I. 32
Ascher, Marcia 129
Ascher, Robert 129
Asfaha, Yonas Mesfun 159
Aśoka, Emperor of India *65, 71*
Atatürk, Kemal *99, 184*

Baines, John 2, 142
Ballthorn, Friedrich 4
Bar Hebraeus, Gregorius abu l-Faruj, called *45*
Bar-Asher Siegal, Elitzur 43
Barthélemy, Jean-Jacques *118–19*
Baskin, Wade 2
Baudouin de Courtenay, Jan *171–73*, 185
Bauernschmidt, Amy 183
Baxter, William H. 85
Bazell, C. E. *166*
Bell, Alexander Melville 156
Bennet, John 2
Ben-Yehuda, Ehud 176
Berg, Kristian 21
Bergsträßer, Gotthelf 47
Berlin, Heinrich *121*
Bertelson, Paul 158
Bhaskararao, Peri 64
Bible
　Genesis 11:7 *23*
　Judges 12:6 *54*
　　Psalms *39*
　　　Ps. 119 *148*

　　Luke 3:3 *183*
　　John *125*
　　Philemon 1 *182*
Blair, Sheila S. 153
Bloch, Bernard 15
Bloom, Jonathan M. 153
Bloomfield, Leonard *x, 2, 158, 162, 163, 170*
Bolger, Donald *xi*
Bolinger, Dwight 20
Boltz, William G. 85
Bordreuil, Pierre 39
Branner, David Prager 86
Brekle, Herbert 151
Brengelman, F. H. 21
Bright, William *xi*, 1, 156
Browman, Catherine F. 187
Brown, J. Marvin *170*
Budge, E. A. Wallis *120*
Bühler, Georg *64, 65, 66, 70, 71*
Bukele, Momolu Duwale *12*
Burling, Robbins 24
Burnaby, Barbara 114
Burston, Monique 5

Cahill, Michael 183
Cammarosano, Michele 92
Carney, Edward 17
Caro Baroja, Julio 122
Carroll, Lewis 25
Carter, Bonnie 158
Carvilius Ruga, Spurius *29*
Cary, Luz 158
Catach, Nina *170–71*
Catherwood, Frederick 121
Caxton, William *16, 22*
Chadwick, John 13
Chall, Jeanne *x*
Champollion, François *112*
Changizi, Mark A. 152
Chao Yuen-Ren 3, 86, *186*
Charlemagne, Holy Roman Emperor *28*
Chen Yijing 86, *168*
Chiang, Gregory Kuei-ke 90
Chomsky, Noam *20, 21, 170*, 174, *186*
Chomsky, William 53
Choy, Rita Mei-Wah 86
Civil, Miguel 94
Clark, Ross *172*

General index

page references to definitions in boldface; *page references in Details in italics*